D0761121

Musica Scientia

MUSICA SCIENTIA

Musical Scholarship in the Italian Renaissance

Ann E. Moyer

Cornell University Press

ITHACA AND LONDON

Copyright © 1992 by Cornell University

All rights reserved. Except for brief quotations in a review, this book, or parts thereof, must not be reproduced in any form without permission in writing from the publisher. For information, address Cornell University Press, 124 Roberts Place, Ithaca, New York 14850.

First published 1992 by Cornell University Press.

Library of Congress Cataloging-in-Publication Data

Moyer, Ann E. (Ann Elizabeth), 1955–
    Musica scientia : musical scholarship in the Italian Renaissance /
Ann E. Moyer.
      p. cm.
    Includes bibliographical references and index.
    ISBN 0-8014-2426-7 (alk. paper)
      1. Music—Italy—15th century—History and criticism.   2. Music—
Italy—16th century—History and criticism.   3. Music—Theory—15th
century.   4. Music—Theory—16th century.   5. Humanism—Italy.
    I. Title.
    ML290.2.M7   1991
    781′.0945′09031—dc20   91-55057

♾ The paper in this book meets the minimum requirements
of the American National Standard for Information Sciences—
Permanence of Paper for Printed Library Materials, ANSI Z39.48-1984.

Contents

Acknowledgments

Research for this project was funded in part by the Gladys K. Delmas Foundation and the Rackham School of Graduate Studies of The University of Michigan. I owe special thanks to the staff of several libraries for their generous and patient assistance: the Biblioteca Nazionale Marciana, Venice; the Biblioteca Nazionale Centrale and the Biblioteca Riccardiana, Florence; the Biblioteca Apostolica Vaticana; the Civico Museo Bibliografico, Bologna.

While several friends and colleagues have offered valuable advice and assistance throughout this project and its revisions, Charles Trinkaus, Thomas Tentler, David Crawford, and Paul Oskar Kristeller were particularly helpful. My greatest thanks go to Marty for his professional advice and personal support throughout this project.

A. E. M.

Musica Scientia

Introduction

The modern reader of Renaissance musical texts might well echo the complaint of the musical scholar Charles Burney, writing in the late eighteenth century: "during the sixteenth century, and a great part of the next, many of the most eminent musical theorists of Italy employed their time in subtle divisions of the scale, and visionary pursuits after the ancient Greek genera; nor was this rage wholly confined to theorists, but extended itself to practical musicians, ambitious of astonishing the world by their deep science and superior penetration, though they might have employed their time more profitably to themselves, and the art they professed. . . . These vain enquiries certainly impeded the progress of modern Music; for hardly a single tract or treatise was presented to the public, that was not crowded with circles, segments of circles, diagrams, divisions, sub-divisions, commas, modes, genera, species, and technical terms drawn from Greek writers, and the now unintelligible and useless jargon of Boethius."[1] The texts themselves are little studied by the nonspecialist; they are difficult to relate to individual Renaissance musical compositions, which are themselves often less than familiar. Attempts to clarify this "unintelligible and useless jargon" collide quickly with larger problems of context. It is not that the sources do not exist; for they are found in abundance. Rather, the rules for reading them seem somehow to have been lost and to have remained lost for a long time.

1. Charles Burney, *A General History of Music* (1789; rpt., New York: Harcourt, Brace, 1935), 2:136.

It would seem natural to look to Renaissance humanism and to the visual arts for similarities and guidance in understanding the development of musical thought and writing. Yet music had not been at the heart of humanistic curricula or study; not only did early humanists frequently ignore the subject, but even those few passages they produced elicited little response from their contemporaries.[2] Nor was music blessed with an equivalent to the art world's Giorgio Vasari, who celebrated and gave narrative shape to the visual arts' "rebirth" and rise to perfection. Neither did the field resemble either art or humanism in the influence of classical models; no examples of ancient musical compositions were discovered until the later sixteenth century. Nevertheless, there is ample evidence that music, especially as an intellectual discipline, interested many thinkers by the early sixteenth century, and continued to do so for some time.[3] For histo-

2. One such case was Coluccio Salutati's *De laboribus Herculis*, ed. B. L. Ullman (Zurich: Artemis, 1951), 1:v–ix, 23–45. On the subsequent neglect of this work, see Ronald G. Witt, *Hercules at the Crossroads: The Life, Works, and Thought of Coluccio Salutati* (Durham, N. C.: Duke University Press, 1983), pp. 218–19.

3. Modern scholarship on Renaissance musical thought dates back some forty years, to survey articles by Paul Oskar Kristeller and D. P. Walker: Kristeller, "Music and Learning in the Early Italian Renaissance," *Journal of Renaissance and Baroque Music* 1 (1946–47): 255–74; Walker, "Musical Humanism in the Sixteenth and Early Seventeenth Centuries," *Music Review* 2 (1941–42): 1–13, 111–21, 220–27, 288–308. Walker returned to the subject several times, concentrating especially on France and Italy during the late sixteenth and seventeenth centuries. These were collected in *Music, Spirit and Language in the Renaissance*, ed. Penelope Gouk (London: Variorum, 1985). His later writings were published as *Studies in Musical Science in the Late Renaissance* (London: Warburg Institute, 1978). Among musicologists who have addressed issues of Renaissance musical thought, Claude V. Palisca's work is of primary importance: *Girolamo Mei: Letters on Ancient and Modern Music to Vincenzo Galilei and Giovanni Bardi, a Study with Annotated Texts*, 2d ed. (Neuhausen-Stuttgart: American Institute of Musicology, 1977); *Humanism in Italian Renaissance Musical Thought* (New Haven: Yale University Press, 1985); *The Florentine Camerata* (New Haven: Yale University Press, 1989). Palisca and Walker have disagreed over several issues, particularly Palisca's characterization of the musical thought of the later sixteenth century as a shift from Platonism to Aristotelianism; Palisca's recent work has qualified but not abandoned this analysis. I have tended toward Walker's side of the debate while retaining some elements of Palisca's description. Palisca's 1985 work in particular complements my own, especially his examination of the translators of ancient sources and their use as seen in detailed, passage-by-passage analyses of Renaissance musical scholars. See also Nino Pirrotta's work, which relates more directly to musical performance: *Music and Culture in Italy from the Middle Ages to the Baroque* (Cambridge: Harvard University Press, 1984). Among historians of science, Stillman Drake had examined the connections between Galileo's work and that of his father; see "Renaissance Music and Experimental Science," *Journal of the History of Ideas* 31 (1970): 483–500; "Vincenzio Galilei and Galileo," in *Galileo Studies: Personality, Tradition, and Revolution* (Ann Arbor: University of Michigan Press, 1970), pp. 43–62. On the importance of musical scholarship to the early connections

rians, the subject has thus remained an attractive puzzle with many missing pieces.

My first goal is to restore some of those missing pieces, so as to study musical thought on its own terms. What irony that the modern difficulty in understanding Renaissance musical writings should have resulted from the very success of these Renaissance scholars. For one of their victories was the complete redefinition of music, from a subject whose theoretical basis rested among the mathematical disciplines of the quadrivium, to one studied in terms of poetics and taste. In the process they divided musical knowledge into two parts, distinguishing the science of sounding bodies (later known as acoustics) from the art of music. Further, they were able to convince later generations of scholars that this new set of definitions was true, natural, and universal. The intellectual implications of music's earlier placement as a branch of mathematics have therefore too often been ignored. Thus the musical thought of the earlier Renaissance and its principal context should be sought first not among the humanists or the artists but, rather, at the university, among the astronomers and mathematicians.[4]

This change in definition and classification helps explain the difficulties of later readers, certainly since the days of Burney, in making sense of these Renaissance musical texts. Instead of focusing on rules for composition or examples of musical pieces for analysis, as did music treatises from the seventeenth century and beyond, many of these Renaissance works seem to consist largely of now-obscure technical terms drawn from the Greek, charts and geometric diagrams, and long discussions of equally technical detail. For the reader who expects a modern treatment of the subject, Burney's reference to "vain enquiries" seems apt indeed. What the change does not explain is why the field of musical thought appealed to so many sixteenth-century writers. At the end of the fifteenth century, it was the search for answers to new questions about music and its study, some of them small

between physical phenomena and mathematical analysis, see Paul Lawrence Rose, *The Italian Renaissance of Mathematics: Studies on Humanists and Mathematicians from Petrarch to Galileo* (Geneva: Droz, 1975).

4. Several studies have begun to examine music's role as an important discipline in medieval intellectual life, e.g., the writings of Michael Masi, esp. "Arithmetic," in *The Seven Liberal Arts in the Middle Ages*, ed. David Wagner (Bloomington: Indiana University Press, 1983): 147–68; *Boethian Number Theory: A Translation of the "De institutione arithmetica"*, trans. Michael Masi (Amsterdam: Rodopi, 1983); Michael Masi, ed. *Boethius and the Liberal Arts: A Collection of Essays* (Bern: Peter Lang, 1981); David Wagner, "The Seven Liberal Arts and Classical Scholarship," in his *Seven Liberal Arts*, pp. 1–31; Umberto Eco, *Art and Beauty in the Middle Ages*, trans. Hugh Bredin (1959 [Italian]; New Haven: Yale University Press, 1986).

and technical and others of greater significance, that spurred music's decisive shift away from quadrivial mathematics. Most of my book concentrates on this debate among scholars from several disciplines, the reasons they posed new questions and disagreed over old ones, and some implications of their conclusions. The outlines of this process merit a brief summary here.

The quadrivial discipline called *musica* comprised much more than the writing of compositions; it was the branch of mathematics devoted to the proportions that describe the behavior of moving or sounding bodies, with direct connections to arithmetic, astronomy, and geometry. Its central text was Boethius's *De institutione musica;* its philosophical orientation was essentially Platonic, specifically Pythagorean. It maintained a relationship with the ecclesiastically based tradition of music composition by referring to the latter as *musica practica,* the scholarly discipline itself taking precedence as *musica theorica.*

The new wave of translations of ancient Greek theorists in the last years of the fifteenth century marked the beginning of change. Music scholars and practicing musicians were attracted to these Greek texts for several reasons. Not only was musical thought already based on ancient texts, but the spread of humanistic education had further strengthened scholarly interest in classical sources generally. In addition, changes in musical practice had begun to conflict with music theory as currently known; many hoped to find the solution in a better understanding of ancient music theory. These attempts to justify current musical practice gradually gave way to an interest in reviving the styles of ancient music as much as possible, with the goal of recapturing its fabled emotional impact on the listener. Yet music scholars found that the task of assimilating these new texts, which they had at first perceived as only a matter of adding more names and information to the list of ancient supporters of Boethian theory, was much more difficult than they had imagined. Further, Renaissance scholars and thinkers from other disciplines became involved in the subject for a variety of reasons, bringing their own intellectual agendas to the debate.

Several humanistic scholars became interested in music while translating these new classical sources, often on commissions from professional musicians or music scholars. Studies in Greek and Roman poetry and drama also began to convince many humanists of the importance of music to these disciplines as understood and practiced in antiquity. Moreover, the Platonic revival at the end of the fifteenth century increased the interest of philosophers in the study of

Pythagorean musical proportions as the source of universal order. This composite of interests and professional education and training assured a complex series of publications and debates. Several of the earliest humanistic scholars to write on music lacked the technical training to address practical issues, ancient or modern; many practicing musicians lacked the linguistic and critical skills for a sophisticated reading of ancient texts. Further, music's common definition as a field between pure mathematics and natural philosophy or physics encouraged many writers to try to apply the investigative rules of Aristotelian natural philosophy to musical studies.[5] Thus music did not simply undergo a transition from scholastic mathematics to humanist art; it also was increasingly studied as a physical, natural phenomenon.

But although much of the initial impetus for change arose from the translations of the late fifteenth century, they are not, by themselves, responsible for the subsequent debates and study. Most obvious is the great lag in time between the introduction of these sources and the transformation of musical thought. Except for a small, though important, infusion of sources at the middle of the sixteenth century (primarily a mediocre translation of the Greek theorist Aristoxenus and the recognition of some Greek musical examples in a manuscript that was itself already known), the body of ancient sources available for study remained much the same after about 1500, with only a few more additions down to the present day. Yet the greatest structural change occurred much later, during the last third

5. The role of this classification, the *scientiae mediae* or "intermediate sciences," in the development of Renaissance scientific thought and classifications of knowledge, and in the debates over relative certainty of knowledge, is too broad a topic to discuss here; it is, in any case, the subject of ongoing research in the history of science. I do, however, refer throughout to some of the more significant opinions of Renaissance musical scholars on this subject. For a discussion of the subject in the Middle Ages (including a discussion of the Renaissance writer Jacopo Zabarella), see Walter Roy Laird, "The *Scientiae Mediae* in Medieval Commentaries on Aristotle's *Posterior Analytics*" (Ph.D. diss., University of Toronto, 1983); James Weisheipl, "Classification of the Sciences in Medieval Thought," *Medieval Studies* 27 (1965): 54–90; Richard D. McMirahan, Jr., "Aristotle's Subordinate Sciences," *British Journal for the History of Science* 11 (1978): 197–220; Martin F. Reidy, "Aristotle's Doctrines concerning Applied Mathematics" (Ph.D. diss., University of Toronto, 1968); M. Mignucci, "Teoria della scienza e mathematica in Aristotele," *Rivista critica di storia della filosofia* 32 (1977): 204–33. For the sixteenth century, see Robert S. Westman, "The Astronomer's Role in the Sixteenth Century: A Preliminary Study," *History of Science* 18 (1980): 105–47; Walter Roy Laird, "The Scope of Renaissance Mechanics," *Osiris*, 2d ser., 2 (1986): 43–68; Paul Lawrence Rose and Stillman Drake, "The Pseudo-Aristotelian *Questions of Mechanics* in Renaissance Culture," *Studies in the Renaissance*, 18 (1971): 65–104.

of the sixteenth century. The translations, then, can be seen as a necessary but not a sufficient cause.

Far more important were the ways in which humanistic methods were adapted to a subject relatively new to humanists. Careful work in philology and exegesis combined with bold new interpretive strategies to alter the ways the ancient texts were individually understood, the interrelationships they were thought to have, and the kinds of authority they commanded. Thus an analysis of Renaissance musical thought does more than illuminate the subject matter itself. It also reveals the vital role later Renaissance humanism played in shaping definitions and classifications of scholarly disciplines which have persisted to the present, relationships among the disciplines, and methods used in their study.

At the same time, no matter how much importance was given to ancient texts, music was not simply a subfield of Renaissance textual criticism. It also had external referents: first in the physical behavior of sounding bodies, but also in musical composition and performance. The changes in the study and interpretation of these phenomena were as significant as, and closely related to, the changes in the interpretation of relevant texts. Many of these changes were in how mathematics was applied to the description and analysis of physical phenomena and had, in turn, a direct effect on the rapid pace of scientific change in the next century. Any Renaissance writer who wished to address the subject of music, then, had to find a way to balance all these sources of authority to develop and sustain an argument.

I, too, have had to establish balance and limits in time, place, and subject matter. I have chosen to examine the writings of a fairly comprehensive selection of the humanists, musicians, scholars, and philosophers working on the Italian peninsula and addressing issues pertinent to music and its study from approximately 1480, the years immediately preceding the new translations, to 1600, when the new definitions of the field were established beyond further serious challenge. Writers from the later sixteenth century shared this sense of chronological boundary, dating the early years of the "modern" discipline as they saw it to the late fifteenth century. Although no single Italian city or region was consistently the center of musical thought, all the writers engaged in the debates, who translated and commented on the ancient treatises, discovered the first known examples of ancient music, and performed the significant observations or experiments, did work in Italy. Writers from north of the Alps may have been influenced by Italian musical thought, but with few exceptions (notably Jacques Lefèvre d'Étaples and Heinrich Glarean) there was little reciprocal influence. The discursive circle, then, centers on later Renaissance Italy.

I have also chosen to limit my focus. The great cosmologists using harmonic models (for example, Francesco Zorzi) worked in traditions distinct enough from musical scholarship to merit separate study. Marsilio Ficino's writings on music have already been examined by D. P. Walker, who noted their lack of direct influence on late fifteenth- and sixteenth-century musical thought; hence I do not treat Ficino separately here. Excluded too are those treatises devoted solely to some aspect of the practical tradition, such as manuals for composition or instruction books for choirboys, unless they in some way address larger issues of the nature of music and its study. Nor are music compositions themselves examined here. The relationship of music as scientia to these practical arts was very much contested during the sixteenth century; writers often disagreed about whether musical theory should begin from contemporary musical practice or whether new theoretical findings should lead to demands for change in composition and performance. In fact, they even disagreed about how closely actual musical performances related to musical theories, especially in terms of intonation; in the absence of modern electronic recording and analytic instruments, their arguments could not (and cannot now) be entirely resolved. Therefore I treat music composition and performance here only as another source of evidence or authority Renaissance writers used along with ancient texts and sounding bodies. For reasons of consistency most translations from these sources are my own, though I acknowledge gratefully a number of modern English editions of the works cited.

In attempting to determine the direct influence of a given writer on his contemporaries, we are aided by a general improvement during this period in the use of citations; luckily for the modern scholar, sixteenth-century writers began to quote sources with greater accuracy and cite them with greater precision. In addition to referring to one another's published works, they also engaged in public or printed debates, carried on collegial correspondence, and occasionally even conducted feuds through their students. Nonetheless, simply establishing one author's use of another's work is an insufficient measure of continuity and change; there are other considerations, particularly the need to separate heat from light in some of the more vituperative debates. Understanding not just how Renaissance musical thought changed but also why can only come from exploring such broader issues as the methods and purposes of studying music, the types of argumentative proofs and authorities that the participants in this discursive circle held to validate an argument, and their explicit and implicit assumptions about the nature of the discipline.

Mathematical and technical aspects of the current theories of tuning and intonation remained burning issues to nearly all the writers discussed, although (especially among the lesser thinkers) many of these arguments can seem pedantic and even futile to the modern reader. Only the last generation of writers substantially rejected this preoccupation with the details of scales, modes, and the precise proportions of small parts of a given musical scale. There are several reasons for their concern. First, the purity of mathematical proportions was essential to Pythagorean musical thought, and Pythagoreanism remained the main philosophical orientation of the discipline. Second, the practice of using groups of mixed instruments in performances of polyphonic music presented everyday problems of ensemble tuning which had to be dealt with, if not solved. Available ancient sources, exemplified by Boethius, also treated these matters of mathematical proportions in more detail than any other subject; to the extent that these ancient sources helped determine the agenda of study and writing, that study would concentrate on issues of pitch and proportion. Third, these masses of detailed, seemingly precise information (always, nonetheless, in conflict) provided lesser scholars with almost endless opportunity to dispute minor points. Thus these arguments over tuning and intonation require analysis not only (or sometimes even primarily) to understand their content but to distinguish the structurally important from the merely incidental or tendentious.

Despite this caveat, the greater impression most of these writers leave is not pedantry but very lively inquiry and scholarship, a growing sophistication, and a high degree of interaction and collegiality among intellectual and professional groups not often thought to have much in common: humanists and mathematicians, philosophers and professional musicians, language scholars and historians of architecture. Because of these interconnections, a better understanding of musical scholarship reveals not only the exercise but also the development of several important features and products of later Renaissance thought. It adds, for example, to our understanding of the enormous appeal of syncretic Platonism and Pythagoreanism in sixteenth-century thought and offers some reasons for their decline. Musical scholarship played an important role in the union of natural science and mathematics, essential not just to the development of the science of sound but other sciences as well. Finally, we see in the later writers the development of a genuine historical and critical sense applied to the study of other disciplines, an ability to distinguish subtleties not only among the varieties of ancient traditions but also among the relationships between ancient music and that of their own day.

Because of the recursive nature of the field, a survey of the classical tradition is necessary in order to establish the contexts of fifteenth-century thought. It should also help define some of the technical discourse, much of which is less than familiar outside the usage of the Boethian tradition. Because no thorough Renaissance treatise is itself complete without a discussion of the ancient origins of musical science, it is only proper to begin where they began, with the Greeks and especially with Pythagoras.

CHAPTER 1

The Discipline of Music
in Antiquity and
the Middle Ages

Authors of musical studies in the late fifteenth century approached their work from a range of professional backgrounds. Some had specialized in musical scholarship since their youth. Others came to the subject as mature scholars trained and educated in other disciplines; motivated by issues and concerns raised in these other disciplines, they were drawn into a new one. In both cases, their writings show they were conscious of working in a long scholarly tradition. They might wish to expand that tradition's boundaries, to recover more of its past, or to take issue with some of its tenets; their knowledge might meet the highest professional standard or fall short of it. Yet musical scholarship's basic outlines—its technical terminology, its essential subject matter, its canon of authorities, its place among other fields of knowledge, and the kinds of knowledge claims it made—were not in question. To study and write on music was certainly not to revive some neglected subject but, rather, to participate in an ongoing intellectual endeavor that could boast its fair share of recent scholarship.

To make sense of the late Renaissance writers on music, it is therefore necessary to understand this scholarly tradition. An outline of the issues and terms of the scholarly study of music is also useful for several reasons beyond establishing the contexts in which the Renaissance writers worked. First, this intellectual landscape is largely unfamiliar to the modern reader, partly because musical studies of any sort have ceased to form part of the standard canon mastered by all educated persons. During the fifteenth and sixteenth centuries, anyone who had mastered the rudiments of Euclidean geometry could be

11

assumed to have mastered the rudiments of music as well. We have kept the first and lost the second; thus technical terms such as *secant* or *isosceles* may cause only minor discomfort, while *tetrachord* or *diapason* are confusing or meaningless. This very unfamiliarity serves to illustrate the success of the later Renaissance writers. Their efforts to redefine music included removing from its study those topics and technical terms they found no longer useful. The lasting impact of their work makes it all the more difficult for the modern reader to trace the shape of the field as it was before they so dramatically altered it.

Second, a major cause of the sixteenth-century redefinition of music was the development of fuller and more sophisticated readings and interpretations of ancient musical traditions. Renaissance scholars first sought to admit for study many classical sources unused or inaccessible in the Middle Ages (often because they had been written in Greek). Expanding the canon of texts forced scholars to examine the sources as a group to try to accommodate them to one another. When accommodation proved impossible, they were forced to reconsider the relationships among sources and to the subject they purported to discuss. This reconsideration altered their understanding of ancient music as well as their theories about antiquity's relation to current musical practice. Thus it is important to trace not only the Renaissance discoveries of factual information about antiquity but also the Renaissance interpretive strategies for making sense of the information and deciding how they should use it. These patterns of intellectual assimilation have long been noted by modern scholars of the period. Modern scholarly knowledge about antiquity, presumably more complete than that in the Renaissance (though still frustratingly imperfect) should not be confused with opinions held on the subject during the fifteenth and sixteenth centuries.

Third, the availability and quality of sources at any given time are, then, matters of some importance. The texts available in 1550 were significantly greater in number, quality, and availability than in 1450 or even 1480. There might at any time be a few scholars with access to a larger body of sources than their contemporaries, owing perhaps to their broader general education, knowledge of Greek, or a translator friend whose translations became public later or not at all. It is true that the availability of a given text is not a rigid determinant of a writer's thoughts, though its unavailability certainly constrains his knowledge. Issues about the precise nature and use of available sources became increasingly contested over the course of the sixteenth century. Fourth, equally important are the kinds of readings and interpretations of the tradition given by an individual writer and his colleagues' understanding of and agreement with those readings.

For example, the Plato of musical scholars circa 1500 is not the same as the Plato of fifty years later, although both generations of writers had access to all of Plato's works. The Plato of 1500 is still mainly the author of the *Timaeus;* the other dialogues are cited only as supporting material. This emphasis is not really so surprising; for the *Timaeus* is the Platonic dialogue most relevant to the subject of music. It also had an established body of scholarship surrounding it that dated from the Middle Ages, and it was one of the few dialogues available when these scholars were educated and began their professional lives. The new Ficino translation of the *Opera omnia*, insofar as they used it at all, altered their working understanding only slightly. Thus their Plato is in many ways the medieval Plato. Later scholars exhibit a much fuller reading; they see the *Timaeus* as one dialogue among many and can base an argument or an allusion on any passage in the corpus.

Fifth, the historical framework an author may use to understand changes in the subject under analysis is also important. Most writers in 1500 understood musical knowledge much as we might casually describe scientific knowledge: as progressively better ways of understanding, through study and research, the changeless natural laws "out there" in the universe. By the later sixteenth century, most wanted to explain music and musical studies as cultural artifacts subject to historical change, like language, dress, or customs. For all these reasons, and because of the broad range of the discipline called "music," explorations of the study of music involved questions about cosmology, the role of mathematics in other fields of knowledge, and the classification and hierarchy of those fields. Thus, to understand the ways these authors asked and answered questions, we must first turn to the tradition itself.

Musical Thought among the Greeks

Greek traditions of musical thought were not one but many, with adherents frequently in strenuous disagreement.[1] But one tradition,

1. Of the many important studies of musical thought and practice in ancient Greece, see esp. Herbert M. Schueller, *The Idea of Music: An Introduction to Musical Aesthetics in Antiquity and the Middle Ages* (Kalamazoo, Mich: Medieval Institute Publications, 1988); Solon Michaelides, *The Music of Ancient Greece: An Encyclopaedia* (London: Faber and Faber, 1978); Edward A. Lippman, *Musical Thought in Ancient*

the Pythagorean, could claim with justice to have predominated over the long term; for all others were compelled to identify themselves in opposition to it. The Pythagorean tradition was able to develop the most detailed and consistent mathematical basis for the study of pitches and to maintain wide appeal with its grand claims to knowledge. This tradition was also the earliest to establish itself, though it was not the only Pre-Socratic philosophy founded on a notion of universal harmony.

The considerable difficulties in separating Pythagoras's teachings from those of his followers, and even from those of his detractors, have engaged scholars since antiquity; Pythagoras himself apparently left no writings, but Pythagorean teachings involving music became and remained significant aspects of his influence.[2] (The tendency of the Neoplatonic and Neopythagorean writers of late antiquity to attribute most major arguments or discoveries to the generations of Pythagoras and Philolaus can cause special problems of anachronism, which, important they are for modern scholarship, involve research generally unavailable to Renaissance writers and hence seldom enter this discussion.) Early Pythagorean thoughts on music received their widest reading audience via Plato's *Timaeus,* and this dialogue became one of the central works of the Pythagorean musical tradition (for which reason I treat it hereafter as part of that tradition, although it was also read as part of more general Platonic thought). Pythagoreans based their interest in music and harmony not on songs or on musical instruments but on cosmology. For them, "music" as a

Greece (1964; rpt., New York: Da Capo, 1975). Collections of source readings that attempt to move beyond the technical tradition discussed here and explore the broader roles of music in ancient Greece are Andrew D. Barker, ed., *Greek Musical Writings,* vol. 1, *The Musician and His Art,* and vol. 2; *Harmonic and Acoustic Theory* (Cambridge: Cambridge University Press, 1984–89); also William Oliver Strunk, *Source Readings in Music History,* vol. 1 (New York: Norton, 1965); Giovanni Comotti, *Music in Greek and Roman Culture,* trans. Rosaria V. Munson (Baltimore: Johns Hopkins University Press, 1989).

2. On Pythagoras's life and work, see J. A. Philip, *Pythagoras and Early Pythagoreanism* (Toronto: University of Toronto Press, 1966); Cornelia de Vogel, *Pythagoras and Early Pythagoreanism: An Interpretation of Neglected Evidence on the Philosopher Pythagoras* (Assen, Netherlands: Gorcum, 1966); Peter Gorman, *Pythagoras: A Life* (London: Routledge & Kegan Paul, 1979). On the Pythagorean tradition in general, see Walter Burkert, *Lore and Science in Ancient Pythagoreanism,* trans. Edwin L. Minar, Jr. (Cambridge: Harvard University Press, 1972). On the Pythagorean musical tradition, see Alan C. Bowen, "The Foundations of Early Pythagorean Harmonic Science: Archytas, Fragment I," *Ancient Philosophy* 2 (1982): 79–104; Richard L. Crocker, "Pythagorean Mathematics and Music," *Journal of Aesthetics and Art Criticism* 22 (1963–64): 189–98, 325–35.

series of ordered sounds was a physical result of the greater "music" that is the source of order in the world. This tradition was instrumental in the development of the quadrivium, with "music" as one of its disciplines.[3]

The Pythagoreans saw creation as order imposed upon formless matter; that order was numerical and was generated from the smallest units, the numbers one through four. These numbers had larger symbolic meanings: the One, or monad, represented both the unity of the cosmos and the all-embracing simplicity of its creator, from whom the rest of creation was generated. Two, or the dyad, signified the multiplicity and hence the imperfection of the created world, a falling away from unity and perfection; three, the first real number (one and two being creators of number and hence not numbers themselves), represented the cosmos in its three dimensions, and so on. Thus the primary elements of the cosmos can be seen as standing in these simple proportions to one another. Plato discusses these numbers and this proportion in his passage on the creation of the World Soul. The World Soul is composed of the first three powers of two and three, in the double series 1:2:4:8 and 1:3:9:27.[4] Hence the frequent statements that the cosmos, the World Soul, or the creator, "is" or "has" number.

To move from mathematical proportions to harmony requires another step in logic, a step provided by the famous story of Pythagoras's discovery of the mathematical basis of musical proportion.[5] The legend in its numerous retellings has many variations, but its core has Pythagoras passing a blacksmith's shop one day and hearing the hammers strike the anvil in harmonious sounds. His examination of the hammers revealed that their weights stood in the proportions 12:9:8:6 to one another. (Some versions mention a fifth—dissonant—hammer whose weight was found incommensurable with others.) Sounding the heaviest and lightest hammers in succession produced the interval called a "diapason" (12:6, or the proportion 2:1), called an "octave" in modern terminology and illustrated by the interval

3. David Wagner, "The Seven Liberal Arts and Classical Scholarship," in *The Seven Liberal Arts in the Middle Ages*, ed. David Wagner (Bloomington: Indiana University Press, 1983), pp. 1—31.

4. Plato, *Timaeus* 34c–36d; see also *Plato's Cosmology; The Timaeus of Plato Translated with a Running Commentary*, F. M. Cornford (1937; rpt., Indianapolis: Bobbs-Merrill, 1957), p. 68.

5. Flora R. Levin has noted that the oldest surviving version of this story, in Nicomachus, appears to reflect a well-established oral tradition; see *The Harmonics of Nicomachus and the Pythagorean Tradition* (University Park, Pa.: American Philological Association, 1975), pp. 67–74.

C–c on a piano.[6] The largest and next largest hammers together produced the "diatessaron" (12:9, or 4:3), or "perfect fourth" in modern terms—the interval C–F. The first and third produced the "diapente" (12:8, or 3:2), or "perfect fifth," which falls between the notes C and G. The major musical consonances, then, are a part of the properties of these proportions, which are the foundation of universal order.

Further, "harmony" was defined not only from these consonances standing in proportional pairs but also in the establishment of a mean between them. Pythagoreans distinguished three types of mean: an arithmetic mean (defined as [a + b]/2); a geometric mean a/m = m/b); and a harmonic, or subcontrary, mean (m = 2ab/[a + b]).[7] From the proportions of Pythagoras's hammers and these three types of mean, the basic Pythagorean divisions of the diapason are formed. In modern terms, this division produces the principal notes of the one-octave scale. The diapason, diatessaron, and diapente (octave, fourth, and fifth) are called the consonant intervals of harmony. In a modern scale, they are still the notes with the greatest structural importance (as, for example, C, F, G, c). The tone (9:8), or whole step, while not a consonant interval, was used melodically.

It is in fact not true that such differences in the weight of the hammers could cause these differences in pitch.[8] Many versions of the tale therefore add a second and even a third experiment, by stretching and plucking strings in ways that involved these same proportions. Iamblichus claims, for example, that Pythagoras suspended equal strings with the weights of the hammers; this is also incorrect because pitch varies with the square root of the tension, so that the proportion of weights needed to produce an octave would actually be 4:1.[9]

These traditional "Pythagoreans" proportions are indeed valid, however, for describing the changes in pitch caused by the variation in

6. I refer to the piano keyboard as an aid to readers unfamiliar with musical terminology. Use of this example ignores the differences in tuning caused by the modern use of equal temperament as well as the technicalities of keyboard tuning. On tuning systems in general, see J. Murray Barbour, *Tuning and Temperament: A Historical Survey* (1951; rpt., East Lansing: Michigan State University Press, 1972).

7. See, inter alia, D. H. Fowler, *The Mathematics of Plato's Academy: A New Reconstruction* (Oxford: Clarendon, 1987); Jamie Croy Kassler, "Music as a Model in Early Science," *History of Science* 20 (1982): 105.

8. For an introduction to the physical behavior of musical instruments, see Arthur H. Benade, *Horns, Strings, and Harmony* (Garden City, N.Y.: Doubleday, Anchor, 1960), esp. chap. 6. See also Alexander Wood, *The Physical Basis of Music* (Cambridge: Cambridge University Press, 1913). A more technical discussion can be found in Benade, *Fundamentals of Musical Acoustics* (New York: Oxford University Press, 1975).

9. *Iamblichus' Life of Pythagoras*, trans. Thomas Taylor (1818; rpt., London: Watkins, 1965), pp. 61–65; cf. Benade, *Horns, Strings, and Harmony*, pp. 110–11.

length of strings of equal material and thickness, stretched under equal tension, or of a single string divided into proportional sections by means of bridges. All treatises that discuss the subject in any detail move immediately to these more correct illustrations. The example of the single divided string was developed as a specialized instrument for establishing tuning systems, called a monochord. Various systems for tuning an octave scale could then be expressed as varying methods of dividing the single string of this instrument, divisions that are described in terms of mathematical proportions.[10]

Even so, it may seem surprising that classical sources did not question the legend itself or attempt to retell it in a manner more consistent with the known behavior of sounding bodies. This apparent incongruity serves to illustrate the dual nature of authority in the Pythagorean musical tradition. On the one hand, this tradition claims that the truth of its interpretation can be seen in the behavior of physical objects in the world, behavior that can be measured and expressed in precise mathematical terms. The lack of challenge to the legend may be due in part to the ready availability of equipment that verifies the theory but not that which would contradict it. A monochord proves the validity of the Pythagorean proportions for its own set of conditions. Unless someone were bent on experimental verification, however, a set of trials to duplicate the legend of the hammers would demand equipment and skills beyond the range or interest of the average musical scholar.[11] Inasmuch as the behavior could be seen to work on a daily basis with the instruments actually used as sounding bodies, there were no questions to raise.

On the other hand, Pythagorean theory has as its basis not the "empirical" world of physical objects and their behavior but, rather, a set of supposedly universal principles that also happen to explain physical phenomena. The theory is founded on rational order, not sense perception; the physical objects that produce sound may reproduce the divine order with greater or lesser precision, but they are definitely secondary in status. Some behaviors of these objects are thus considered regular and quantifiable, whereas others are seen as erratic and qualitative, symptomatic of the mutable and imperfect

10. Cecil Adkins, "Monochord," *New Grove Dictionary of Music and Musicians* (hereafter cited as *New Grove*); Adkins, "The Technique of the Monochord," *Acta Musicologica* 39 (1967): 324. The standard ancient source on the monochord is Euclid [?], *Sectio canonis;* for an English translation, see Thomas J. Mathiesen, "An annotated Translation of Euclid's *Division of the Monochord," Journal of Music Theory* 19 (1975): 236–58.

11. For references to such experiments in antiquity, see Levin, *Harmonics of Nicomachus,* pp. 71–73.

nature of the physical world. The versions of the legend that include strings stretched by weights could, for example, have been corrected with reference to known phenomena; virtually all stringed instruments use tuning pegs to adjust pitch, so it was common knowledge that string tension affects pitch. Yet this type of physical behavior was classed as qualitative, based on variable features of the individual string (a classification strengthened by Aristotelian logic), and hence not subject to the same explanatory model. This distinction between quality and quantity would be challenged by several sixteenth-century scholars.

Once the Pythagoreans established this notion of consonant musical proportion to their own satisfaction, the matter of human response to these intervals had to be addressed. Plato's *Timaeus* does so by arguing that the human soul is patterned on the World Soul and is therefore ordered in these same proportions.[12] Similarly, the three parts of the soul, and even the physical proportions of the human body itself, all participate in these ratios. The consonant intervals, then are pleasant to the ear because of their similarity to these same proportions within the listener. This argument accounts for the effects of music on the soul or on the emotions: by a sort of sympathetic vibration, the sounds resonate with and therefore emphasize similar aspects of the soul. Appreciation of beauty or ugliness in music may therefore be seen as a physiological response as well as a conscious judgment by the intellect.

The universe of planets and stars is composed in the same manner. Through diligent study and contemplation, humans can perceive this order by means of their intellect and reason, just as they are affected by audible music. Theoretically, the motion of the planets would produce harmony, though this is generally assumed to be inaudible to humans. Plato describes such music in the myth of Er (*Republic* 10.614b). Pythagoras himself was widely credited with the ability to hear this celestial music.[13]

Just how these theories related to practicing mathematics or science is not entirely clear. Modern assessments vary, from classifying Pythagorean theories as a "musical model" of scientific explanation, to hailing them as the origin of classical mathematics, to denying their "scientific" nature in favor of viewing them as a religious poetic. It

12. Plato, *Timaeus* 42e–44e; 47c–e; see also Alfred E. Taylor, *A Commentary on Plato's Timaeus* (Oxford: Clarendon, 1928), pp. 268–71 and 493–516.
13. See, inter alia, *Iamblichus' Life of Pythagoras*, chap. 15, pp. 31–35.

appears, in fact, that there may have been no unity of ancient opinion either.[14]

The Pythagorean approach to musical studies did not win universal acceptance among the Greeks. Aristotle rejected it explicitly, along with so much else of Plato's teachings. Because he defined music not as a universal principle but simply as one human activity among many, he never took the trouble to address the subject in a coherent and detailed manner, though he did devote some fairly long passages to the subject in several treatises, such as the *Politics.* Thus there was no great Aristotelian treatment to serve as a textual counterweight to the Pythagorean tradition. Nonetheless, since his passages on music were frequently cited by later scholars, his views deserve a brief survey.

Aristotle rejected entirely the notion of cosmic harmony, or of harmonic number as the basis of creation. He makes these arguments several times in the *Metaphysics,* in rejecting both Plato's forms (Book Alpha 985b ff.) and the notion that mathematical proportion might have any greater metaphysical (or ontological) status than mere analytic category. In *De caelo* (290b) he attacks the concept of music of the spheres as well. He accepts the mathematical proportions of the musical consonances but restricts them to mere descriptions of those particular phenomena.

Aristotle must therefore account for music's effects on the listener in a different way. He notes in the *Ethics* that music should not be classified as a virtue, simply as a skill. The role of this skill in education, as well as its capacity to cause emotional changes in the listener he

14. On music as scientific model see Kassler, "Music as a Model," pp. 103–39; although the Pythagorean conception of cosmic harmony became the most widespread and best developed, it was not the only one. Kassler discusses two others, those of Heraclitus of Ephesus and Empedocles of Acragas. The former saw the world as a constantly balanced tension of opposites, arisen from fire, and with its elements in a constant state of flux. Its tension he compares to a bow or a lyre: for either string to produce its desired result, it must be under tension. The Stoics adopted this notion. Empedocles, whose system developed from those of both Pythagoras and Heraclitus, posited four elements held together by an attractive power called "love." This notion became part of the thinking of scholars of the various natural philosophies based on elements and humors. These theories had no direct relevance to music itself among the Greeks; they are noteworthy because their similarities to the Pythagorean system (even if superficial) caused later readers, notably those of the Renaissance, to equate them all as manifestations of a single truth about the nature of harmony and a single system of thought. For other points of view on the Pythagorean tradition, see Dominic J. O'Meara, *Pythagoras Revived: Mathematics and Philosophy in Late Antiquity* (Oxford: Clarendon, 1989); Fowler, *Mathematics of Plato's Academy.*

takes up in Book 8 of the *Politics*. Music, he says, is naturally pleasurable and therefore intrinsically useful in educating children, so as to make lessons more palatable. He even notes that this natural pleasure in music causes some to claim the soul "is" or "has" harmony (8.5), but he does not pursue the matter.

Restricting his comments to the playing or hearing of musical pieces, Aristotle argues that the adult listener values music either as a pleasant recreation or as a cultured pastime. He encourages neither virtuosity nor public performances, again because music is a mere manual skill. Its emotional effects come from its similarity to the emotions in compositional style and from the song text, he argues, using the example of theater music. Habituation, caused by repeated listening, accounts for long-term change in the listener's character; a preference for well-constructed musical pieces can be taught in the same way. Even the pseudo-Aristotelian *Problems* reflect this orientation toward the practical elements of performance and the enjoyment of listening.[15] The work makes only the most rudimentary statements about proportion, focusing instead on the physical processes involved in singing and similar subjects. Brief remarks about music's influence on morality are not developed in any detail.

Even when Plato's passages on music and education in the *Republic* and *Laws* are added to the mathematical cosmology of the *Timaeus*, the differences between Plato and Aristotle are considerable. Plato and the Pythagoreans all make much greater knowledge claims about the subject of music than does Aristotle. Their aesthetics are changeless and absolute; Aristotle seems to leave open the possibility of more variation. The Pythagoreans focus on the numerically determined relations between pitches as a key to the cosmos and spiritual enlightenment; Aristotle, upon the personal enjoyment of listening to musical compositions. Though classical opinions on the nature and goals of music had undoubtedly differed before Aristotle, there was definitely more than one tradition of thought and writing after him.

Influential as these texts were in the musical theory of the next two millennia, none of them were devoted strictly to the subject of music. The first such writer whose works are extant was a student of Aristotle, Aristoxenus of Tarentum.[16] Sections of at least two of his works

15. Aristotle [pseudo], *Problems*, trans. W. S. Hett (Cambridge: Harvard University Press, 1936), 1.19: 378–415.
16. *The Harmonics of Aristoxenus*, ed. and trans. Henry S. Macran (Oxford: Clarendon, 1902); see also R.P. Winnington-Ingram, "Aristoxenus" and "Greece," pt. 1, "Ancient," *New Grove*.

on harmonics survived through antiquity to the modern era, grouped under the title *Harmonic Elements*.[17] Given its obvious composition as fragmentary (though substantial) portions of larger works, the *Harmonic Elements* contributed to the development of the music treatise as a genre but could not serve as a model. This influential work codified the system of strings and modes from an explicitly non-Pythagorean orientation. Aristoxenus's system of pitches, modes, and harmonic genera formed the core of classical teachings throughout antiquity and was adopted even by those later writers who rejected the arguments about the nature of music that came to be known as "Aristoxenian" in favor of a Pythagorean interpretation. How far his system reflected contemporary practice is much debated,[18] but it certainly affected subsequent eras.

To make sense of Aristoxenus's pitch system, it is perhaps easiest to recall Pythagoras's proportions for the division of the diapason, or octave. This division formed the basic unit of melodic structures: 12:9:8:6. There are two perfect fourths (12:9 and 8:6, both of which reduce to 4:3, the proportion of the diatessaron, or fourth) separated by the interval 9:8, which became one standard proportion for the "tone," or whole melodic step. The Aristoxenian note system is built out of chains of perfect fourths, either conjunct (the last note of one being the first note of the next) or disjunct (separated by a tone, as in the initial example of the Pythagorean octave). These fourths are subdivided by two more notes, placed according to the type of "scale"; the resulting four-note group is called a "tetrachord."

These tetrachords, joined together in ascending and descending order, form a collection of notes referred to as the Greater Perfect System, frequently illustrated as a sixteen-stringed lyre. Its pitches run for two octaves, roughly similar to the white keys A–a′ on a piano. Each string has its own name. After imposing a given type of tetrachord division upon all the tetrachords in the system, one can see that there are seven different patterns of various-sized steps composing the tetrachords; again using the modern piano as a model, by playing octave scales that begin on each of the seven white keys a–g, one finds a different pattern of whole and half steps. These seven patterns are termed the *species* of the octave and given the names of ethnic groups in the Greek world (Mixolydian, Lydian, Phrygian,

17. *Harmonics of Aristoxenus*, pp. 89–93.
18. "Aristoxenus," *New Grove;* see also Wagner, *Seven Liberal Arts*, p. 12. Wagner estimates that this "Aristoxenian" school had "little subsequent influence." A roughly contemporary discussion of the Greater Perfect System can be found in Euclid [?], *Sectio canonis:* see Mathiesen, "Annotated Translation."

Dorian, Hypoldian, Hypophrygian, and Hypodorian for those beginning on the notes B—a). The entire system, when linked to a specific
range of pitches, is referred to as a "*tonos*". Thirteen in all, these *tonoi*
also bear the names of ethnic groups; they later were assimilated into
the octave species. The exact order and range of these species or *tonoi*
were not consistent in antiquity; they varied among writers and eras.

This portion of the Aristoxenian system resembles modern modes
or scales, as played on a piano's white keys. There is more, however, to
the division of the tetrachord. The most common division, the diatonic, did indeed use the keyboardlike pattern of a semitone and two
tones, the only pattern normally used in Western music. The Greeks
had, however, two more methods of dividing the tetrachord. These
three types of division are known together as the "genera" of the tetrachord and called "diatonic," "chromatic," and "enharmonic." If the
tone is taken as the unit, approximate intervals for these genera are
as follows: diatonic, 1/2–1–1; chromatic, 1/2–1/2–1 1/2; enharmonic,
1/4–1/4–2.[19] These genera also have subtypes, with slight variations
in the pitch of the variable notes in each case.[20]

The ideas that came to be known as "Aristoxenian" do not, however, involve these elements of the harmonic system; for those were
adopted by all writers. Rather, they are ways of thinking about pitch.[21]
Aristoxenus took as his starting point the aural experience of the educated ear, its ability to find the consonant intervals pleasing and to
distinguish small differences of pitch. In this he is reminiscent of his
teacher, Aristotle. Proceeding from these principles as categories of
experience, he deduced the pitches of the "varying" internal notes of
the tetrachord without reference to such external means as mathematics. He regarded sound not as a series of static, numbered pitches,
as did the Pythagoreans, but as a single continuum. Like a line, intervals could thus be subdivided into fractional parts without regard
either for the precise string length needed to produce them[22] or for

19. "Greece," pt. 6, "Intonation," *New Grove;* see also Martin Vogel, *De Enharmonik
der Griechen*, 2 vols. (Düsseldorf: Verlag für systematische Musikwissenschaft, 1963).
20. For the relationship of this system to stringed instruments and an extended
discussion of the instruments themselves, see Martha Maas and Jane McIntosh
Snyder, *Stringed Instruments of Ancient Greece* (New Haven: Yale University Press,
1989); Comotti, *Music in Greek and Roman Culture.*
21. Richard L. Crocker, "Aristoxenus and Greek Mathematics," in *Aspects of
Medieval and Renaissance Music: A Birthday Offering to Gustave Reese*, ed. Jan La Rue,
2d ed. (New York: Pendragon, 1978), pp. 96–110; see also Andrew D. Barker,
"Music and Perception: A Study in Aristoxenus," *Journal of Hellenic Studies* 98 (1978):
9–16.
22. Kassler, "Music as a Model," p. 114.

whether a measured division would turn out to be an irrational number, which the Pythagoreans condemned. The length of a string is only one of its qualities among many, such as thickness or material; according to Aristoxenus, length has no claim to absolute truth in explaining why pitches differ or why some intervals sound good or bad. Imprecise intervals, those too small for the ear to define clearly, he designated as shadings of other notes.

Aristoxenian theory, then, almost totally eliminated mathematics, except a few basic fractions based on the primary intervals. Aesthetic response is a function of training, although Aristoxenus did not address the subject in great detail. His system is coherent and organized and solves the problems it chooses to address. It thus provided a continuing challenge (though at some periods in antiquity it seems to have been a minority opinion) to the very different orientation of the Pythagorean system.[23] In contrast, his general system of pitches elaborated in greater detail by many subsequent writers remained the standard analysis of the note systems used in ancient music. The system naturally underwent changes over time but retained its general form throughout antiquity. What Greek musical composition based on this system survives (approximately forty fragments[24]) is monophonic, that is, it relies on a single melodic line. Hence ancient musical thought of whichever school includes no theoretical discussion of chords, counterpoint, or other such elements so important to modern Western music.

In general, ancient sources were much more interested in harmonics than they were in rhythmics. Aristoxenus apparently did write a separate work on rhythm, but it did not survive. Further, though the Greeks used several rather rudimentary systems for notating pitch, they developed none for recording precise rhythms. The *tonoi,* their tuning systems, and the larger philosophical issues of music's place among fields of knowledge became the standard material for music treatises.

These technical features came to be shared by all musical scholars, while followers of the two main ancient schools of thought continued to differ on the use of mathematics as a standard for analyzing pitch and, more important, the level of knowledge music represented. To the Aristoxenians, music as a discipline was based on performance. They did not address questions about music's role in society or in the spiritual development of the individual. For the Pythagoreans, music

23. Ibid., p. 115.
24. Thomas J. Mathiesen, "New Fragments of Ancient Greek Music," *Acta Musicologica* 53 (1981): 14–32.

was the fundamental model for understanding the cosmos, had a direct and significant effect on the human soul, and served as the key to many other disciplines. Their school of thought was transmitted to the medieval West through the work of Boethius, whereas Aristoxenus's works were inaccessible to the West from late antiquity until the sixteenth century. Part of the task of Renaissance scholars will be to identify and separate these two competing traditions and confront the very different positions these schools gave music among fields of knowledge.

Later Antiquity

Although the major schools of ancient musical thought were established in the era of Plato and Aristoxenus, the vast majority of ancient music treatises date from later antiquity. The dominant philosophical influence on these writers is Pythagorean, however much they might rely on the technical descriptions of the pitch system developed by Aristoxenus. As a group, their distinction lies in their codification of mathematical categories in order to account, in Pythagorean terms, for Aristoxenus's pitch system. Several of these writers, whether their works focused on music or more generally on philosophy, merit individual notice because of their importance to Renaissance writers. Most of them wrote in Greek, making them inaccessible to the medieval West.

Several late sixteenth-century writers considered Ptolemy's treatise on harmonics so successful in establishing a middle ground between the Pythagoreans and the Aristoxenians that he could rightly be called the founder of a third school of theorists.[25] Ptolemy criticized the Aristoxenian position for its imprecise and, he thought, incorrect measurements of intervals and intonation. He also attacked the Pythagoreans for arbitrarily assigning many intervals to the category of dissonance for reasons purely mathematical, having nothing to do with the way the listener perceives the interval. One example is the octave plus a fourth (described by the proportion 8:3). The Pythagoreans classified it as a dissonant interval because of its interval type; they accepted only multiple proportions (x:1) and superparticulars ($x+1$:x) as possible consonant melodic intervals. Ptolemy argues

25. For a translation of Ptolemy into modern German, see *Ptolemaios und Porphyrios über die Musik*, ed. and trans. Ingemar Düring (1934; rpt., New York: Garland, 1980), pp. 3–12; see also Lukas Richter, "Ptolemy, Claudius," *New Grove*.

(*Harmonics* 1.6) that, since the pitch system repeats itself at the octave, and since the ear treats the octave almost as if it were a unison, the addition of an octave to the fourth should not alter its status as a consonant interval. Further, he claims, the octave plus a fifth (3:1) was accepted as a consonance; it was therefore illogical to reject the octave plus a fourth. Ptolemy goes on to develop a slightly more sophisticated set of terms for classifying these intervals. *Homophones* are the multiple proportions constituting octaves (2:1 and 4:1)); *symphones* are the superparticulars using the other primary Pythagorean numbers two, three, and four (3:2 and 4:3) and their octave extensions; *emmeles* (also written "ecmeles") are those other superparticulars useful in melodic composition. Ptolemy also systematizes the use of the monochord for establishing tuning systems, though he does use multistringed examples on occasion.

Despite Ptolemy's single concession to "experience"—allowing the octave to be factored out of musical proportions that exceed an octave, as with his octave-plus-fourth—his work remains fundamentally Pythagorean. In fact, he is able to justify even this apparent exception in Pythagorean terms. He simply claims that the octave, the proportion 2:1, is such a strong consonance that it behaves almost as if it were unison. This Pythagorean orientation is most obvious in Book 3, which is devoted to relating the harmonic ratios and the pitch system to the virtues, the human soul, and planetary motion.

The later writer Aristides Quintilianus (fl. ca. third century A.D.) takes a different approach to the Pythagorean tradition.[26] His *De musica* survives intact, permitting us to observe the development of characteristic elements in the writing of a music treatise. The work is in three books, an organization seen also in Ptolemy, though probably by accident (since he may have died before completing the work), and Aristoxenus, where it was probably imposed retrospectively by later copyists, as the books do not correspond exactly with the endpoints of the fragments.[27] Book 1 begins with a praise of music that outlines the subjects to be discussed in the treatise; Aristides Quintilianus repeats this outline before commencing the body of the work. Then (1.6–12) he discusses the technical aspects of musical pitches, genera, *tonoi*, and so on, as outlined by Aristoxenus. The next sections are

26. Aristides Quintilianus, *On Music, in Three Books*, trans. Thomas J. Mathiesen (New Haven: Yale University Press, 1983); see also Schueller, *Idea of Music*, pp. 151–69.

27. Aristides Quintilianus, *On Music*, p. 14; *Harmonics of Aristoxenus*, pp. 89–90; "Aristoxenus," *New Grove*.

new, though probably based on Aristoxenian fragments;[28] they are devoted to rhythmics and metrics. He sets a unit called a *"chronos protos"* to determine, in its combinations, the various metric feet.

In Book 2 he discusses the role of music in education and its effects on the soul. The first part (2:1–6), dealing directly with education, is based especially on both Aristotle (*Politics* 8) and Plato (*Timaeus, Republic, Laws,* and parts of the *Phaedrus*). He also includes contemporary Roman examples and some criticism of Cicero, then deals more directly with the nature of the soul and the development of virtue, concluding by relating these ideas to the technical discussions in Book 1.

In Book 3 he presents the mathematical basis of the preceding topics. Here his sources are more in the Platonic tradition; he relies on Plutarch's *On the Generation of the Soul in the Timaeus,* Ptolemy's *Harmonics,* and Theon of Smyrna's *Mathematics Useful for Understanding Plato.*[29] He goes into considerable detail, linking consonances with geometry and the categories spirit and matter, among many others (3.11). He also associates the strings of the Greater Perfect System with the senses, elements, and virtues; other systems, such as the planets, he treats in the same way.

This tendency of Aristides Quintilianus to assimilate and organize a wide range of sources of varying philosophical persuasions into a single Pythagorean system is one frequently seen in the works of other late–antique writers. Aristides Quintilianus's work itself serves as a major source for many of these writers; the section on music in Martianus Capella's *The Marriage of Philology and Mercury,* for example, is taken from his Book 1.[30]

A few Latin writers not normally known as musical scholars happened nonetheless to address the subject in one or another of their works. The general reputation of such figures as Cicero or Quintilian would suffice to call attention to these passages, which in a few cases were referred to separately as if they really did constitute regular works on music.[31] The most noteworthy is Book 6 of Cicero's *Republic,*

28. Aristides Quintilianus, *On Music,* p. 24.
29. Ibid., pp. 38–39.
30. Ibid., p. 5; *Martianus Capella and the Seven Liberal Arts,* trans. Will Harris Stahl and R. Johnson, with E.L. Burge (New York: Columbia University Press, 1977), 2:345–82; see also Wagner, *Seven Liberal Arts,* p. 19. Much of Capella's work is based on Marcus Terentius Varro's lost work, *Nine Books of Disciplines.*
31. The range of evidence examined by modern scholars of musical practice in Roman culture is not examined here; see Günther Wille, *Musica Romana: Die Bedeutung der Musik im Leben der Römer* (Amsterdam: P Schippers, 1967); Comotti, *Music in Greek and Roman Culture.*

preserved despite the loss of much of the rest of the work because of the later commentary by Macrobius.[32] Known as the "Dream of Scipio," it was written as a parallel to the "Dream of Er" in Plato's *Republic*. It is reminiscent also of the *Timaeus* (as is Macrobius's commentary) in its focus on Pythagorean cosmology rather than on the technical matters of musical performance, such as scales or modes. Whatever Cicero's intent, this fragment passed into the tradition of Pythagorean works on harmony. He also left a few other remarks about music, notably throughout the *Tusculan Disputations*, which received more attention in the sixteenth century.

Quintilian's writings on music were focused differently. They occur as part of his discussion of the general education of the orator (*Institutio oratoria* 1.10), music belonging with geometry and astronomy. He begins with a long passage in praise of music; the contents of this *laus musice* were by this time fairly well established.[33] Music, he begins, was valued highly by the ancients, who held that the world itself was harmonic. It was considered essential to the educated person. It is useful in lightening labors and can also cure madness. He then returns to his principal subject of oratory by stressing the relationship between music and grammar, which he does by claiming that Archytas and Aristoxenus both held that grammar was part of musical study. To the orator, music is directly relevant both in the sounds of one's voice and in the motions of one's body (1.10.22). But it is also essential for understanding poetry, as poetry was written to be sung. Music affects the character and certainly causes changes in the emotions sufficient to affect behavior. At this point Quintilian abandons the subject, without a conclusion, and goes on to discuss the utility of geometry.

The importance of Quintilian's discussion lies, first, in its concern for connecting music with grammar and poetry, a concern that is not surprising given the nature and subject of the work itself. Yet, as a result, his approach to understanding and explaining music's effects on the listener is novel. He moves the emphasis away from the mathematics of proportion and toward the social uses of music, especially in accompanying poetry, as the means for understanding music's emotional effects. Second, despite this focus on poetics and culture,

32. Ambrosius Aurelius Theodosius Macrobius, *Commentary on the Dream of Scipio*, trans. Will Harris Stahl (New York: Columbia University Press, 1952); Marcus Tullio Cicero, *On the Commonwealth*, trans. G. H. Sabine and S. B. Smith (Columbus: Ohio State University Press, 1929).

33. *Quintilian's Institutes of Oratory*, trans. J. S. Watson (London: Bell, 1903) 1:77–85. On the *laus musice*, see James Hutton, "Some English Poems in Praise of Music," in *Essays on Renaissance Poetry*, ed. Rita Guerlac (Ithaca, N.Y.: Cornell University Press, 1980), pp. 17–73; he discusses Quintilian in some detail.

Quintilian nevertheless seems ultimately to base his explanation of music's effects on Pythagorean theory. His discussion of celestial music and the lyre's imitation of it precedes the rest of his remarks on the subject (1.10.9–13). His vagueness on this point, taken together with his constant association of music with grammar, left these passages open to various interpretations by future writers.

Augustine's six-book *De musica* received varying degrees of attention from later readers, though modern scholars have found it relatively uninteresting.[34] This mixed influence is due in part to its idiosyncratic form and subject matter. Augustine had intended to write on the related subjects of harmonics, metrics, and rhythmics, but he apparently completed only the portion on metrics.[35] This combination of topics had certainly not been part of the older Greek Pythagorean tradition; it is more reminiscent of Quintilian. Yet Augustine interprets rhythm in the light of Neoplatonic and Pythagorean thought, discussing it not only in terms of proportion but also in ascending levels of participation in bodily or spiritual natures. The extent of Augustine's influence on medieval rhythmics merits further study.[36] Later readers saw the treatise, like the writings of Cicero or Quintilian, as a work that discussed a part of the tradition of musical scholarship but whose subject matter was not the core of it.

Despite their late date of composition (late seventh century), Isidore of Seville's writings on music (*Etymologies* 3.15–23) are probably best approached as the last example of the late antique encyclopedia, because they refer solely to classical sources and not to the emerging medieval tradition.[37] Although they are able to stand more independently than the passages of Quintilian on music, they occupy a similar sort of middle ground between an explicitly Pythagorean approach

34. For a summary of scholarship, see William G. Waite, "Augustine of Hippo," *New Grove;* Karl F. Morrison, "Incentives for Studying the Liberal Arts," in Wagner, *Seven Liberal Arts,* pp. 32–57, esp. 38–45; William Roy Bowen, "St. Augustine in Medieval and Renaissance Musical Science," in *Augustine on Music: An Interdisciplinary Collection of Essays,* ed. Richard R. La Croix (Lewiston, N.Y.: Mellen, 1988), pp. 29–51. For modern translations, see Augustine, *On Music: De musica,* ed. and trans. R.C. Taliaferro (Annapolis: St. John's Bookstore, 1939), pp. 153–79. See also W. F. Jackson Knight, *St. Augustine's De musica: A Synopsis* (London: Orthological Institute, 1949).

35. Knight, *St. Augustine's De musica,* pp. 6–7. For a sensitive discussion of Augustine's treatise, see Schueller, *Idea of Music,* pp. 239–56.

36. See William Waite, *The Rhythm of Twelfth-Century Polyphony* (New Haven: Yale University Press, 1954), pp. 35–39; see also W. R. Bowen's assessment of Waite, in "St. Augustine," pp. 39, 44 n. 2.

37. Isidore, *Etymologiarum sive originum libri XX,* ed. W. M. Lindsey, 2 vols (Oxford: Oxford University Press, 1911).

and an Aristoxenian one. Isidore adds biblical references to the range of ancient authorities. For example, to illustrate music's curative power, his *laus musice*, uses the story of David singing for Saul rather than the classical anecdotes about the youth of Taormina or Alexander the Great (3.17).

After his prefatory remarks about the harmonic order of the cosmos, Isidore divides music into the very non-Pythagorean categories of harmonics, rythmics, and metrics. This would again seem, as with Augustine, to link music with grammar and poetry and is very much in keeping with Isidore's general emphasis on grammar. Most of his classical references are to Virgil's *Aeneid*, rather than to any real music treatises (though the work itself is clearly a digest based on several sources). Much of the work is devoted to brief statements about individual types of musical instruments, consisting of remarks about the instruments' putative origin, the etymology of its name, or a brief classical reference to the instrument.

Although Isidore's treatise was certainly influential throughout the Middle Ages, its does not seem to have posed a serious challenge to the discursive categories of Boethius. This may be because it is so much more rudimentary. Thus later scholars would perhaps have been more likely to try to fit information from Isidore's more general treatise into the more rigorously organized framework of Boethius.

Boethius on Music

Most ancient writers on music found a medieval audience only through the works of Boethius. When knowledge of Greek declined in the West, so, naturally, did access to the Greek treatises. Chalcidius's commentary and partial translation of Plato's *Timaeus* saved it for the medieval West and might have been sufficient in itself to assure the preeminence of the Pythagorean tradition. It was, however, Boethius's direct contribution to the organization of a general curriculum and to the writing of textbooks that made his version of ancient scholarship dominant for the next millennium. Boethius's advocacy of musical mathematics as a path to knowledge and virtue is not unique to the *De institutione musica;* it permeates not only his treatise on arithmetic but also his influential *Consolation of Philosophy.*[38]

38. *Boethian Number Theory: A Translation of the "De institutione arithmetica,"* trans. Michael Masi (Amsterdam: Rodopi, 1983), esp. pp. 11–12, 39–41. On Boethius's biography and work, see Henry Chadwick, *Boethius: The Consolations of Music, Logic,*

The music and arithmetic treatises are sufficiently closely related that their respective introductory chapters overlap in subject matter and argumentation. That of the *De institutione arithmetica* discusses music's place in the quadrivium, the nature of mathematical quantity, and finally, why arithmetic must be studied before the other subjects can be mastered. The proem to the *De institutione musica* presents an extended discussion of human and animal perception, stressing the importance of hearing for its influence on the soul and concluding with a passage in praise of music. Taken together, the two introductions offer a clear and consistent definition and classification of music as a quadrivial discipline in the Pythagorean tradition.

Boethius's five books on music focus almost entirely on the science of proportionate pitches.[39] After the first book's exordium and *laus musice*, he defines the types of proportion; only the first two of five types (multiple and superparticular) can compose consonant intervals, though he notes that Ptolemy occasionally accepted the third type $(x+2:x)$, called superpartiens (1.4). Before he begins his discussion of the proportions of specific intervals, Boethius pauses to address the relationship between sense perception and reason in musical analysis. Here he follows Ptolemy, noting that the perception of all musical principles derives from sense. Yet sense alone is fallible, perhaps defective in some cases, and has no certainty unless it is ruled by reason (1.9). This is a moderate Pythagorean position, moderate in that it acknowledges sense perception as the point of departure. Boethius makes much throughout the treatise of his achieving a middle ground among ancient theories; since his champion is generally Ptolemy, it follows that his idea of a middle ground would lie more in the direction of Pythagoras than of anyone else.

In addition to recounting the familiar story of Pythagoras and the hammers (1.10), Boethius discusses the nature of sound as wave mo-

---

Theology, and Philosophy (Oxford: Clarendon, 1981); John Matthews, "Anicius Manlius Severinus Boethius," in *Boethius: His Life, Thought and Influence*, ed. John Matthews (Oxford: Blackwell, 1981), pp. 15–43.

39. Anicius Manlius Torquatus Severinus Boethius, *De institutione arithmetica libri duo; De institutione musica libri quinque*, ed. Gottfried Friedlein (1867; Frankfurt a.M.: Minerva, 1966). The English translation, used for subsequent references, is Boethius, *Fundamentals of Music*, trans. Calvin M. Bower, ed. Claude V. Palisca (New Haven: Yale University Press, 1989). On Boethius and music, see, in addition to Bower's introduction, Leo Schrade, "Music in the Philosophy of Boethius," *Musical Quarterly* 33 (1947): 188–200; David S. Chamberlain, "Philosophy of Music in the *Consolatio* of Boethius," *Speculum* 45 (1970): 80–97; John Caldwell, "The *De institutione arithmetica* and the *De institutione musica*," in Matthews, *Boethius*, pp. 135–54. In the same volume, see also Alison White, "Boethius in the Medieval Quadrivium," pp. 162–205, and Anthony Grafton, "Epilogue: Boethius in the Renaissance," pp. 410–15.

tion (1.14) and theories about the perception of consonances. Here he refers both to Plato (*Timaeus* 80a–b) and to Nicomachus, siding with the latter (1.31). He concludes the first book with a very Pythagorean passage on the definition of a *musicus*. He acknowledges the relationship between music and poetry, so dear to other Latin writers, by placing the poet in the middle of a three-part classification, above the instrumentalist and below the *musicus*. Yet he also emphasizes the poet's secondary status in that hierarchy. The poet composes "not so much by thought and reason as by a certain natural instinct" (1.34, p. 51). A true musician (*musicus*) is the one who indeed makes his judgments by reason. Later readers might therefore find enough grounds for the further accommodation of poetry into the Boethian tradition, but only with recourse to additional sources from antiquity.

In the remainder of the work, Boethius discusses in more detail much of the material he introduced in the first book. Book 2 focuses on proportions and means, their use in determining intervals, and the addition of proportions to one another. In Book 3 he discusses the intervals smaller than a tone. Book 4 presents various divisions of scales and genera, using the intervallic proportions discussed in Books 2 and 3. The last book, Book 5, either remained unfinished or failed to survive in full; Chapters 20–30 exist only as titles. The surviving portion was, however, extremely influential. In it, Boethius addresses the points of difference among the major ancient scholars. Because of the language barrier, scholars of the medieval West had to rely on Boethius for their evaluations and assessments of classical scholarship that remained in Greek. His interpretation became, by default, the standard; his elevation of Ptolemy was taken as an indication of universal agreement of late classical opinion on music and the value of Ptolemaic arguments.

Boethius repeatedly attacks any Aristoxenian position in favor of his "moderate" Pythagorean stance, following Ptolemy. He sets up a dichotomy between the two schools which he bases on the roles of sense and reason; then he claims, as always, to find a middle ground supported by references to Ptolemy. His more explicit rejection of anything that might be considered Aristoxenian is significant, however, for the distinctions it forces between the supposed deficiencies of sense perception and the role of mathematical analysis.

Boethius claims that sense and reason need not conflict; for they are mixed in the perception of harmony (5.3). The senses inform, and reason determines the proportions between the sounds. While the sense of hearing may be deficient or untrained, its main problem is its inability to maintain a precise standard (5.2). Small misjudgments can accumulate into a large miscalculation in the absence of an external standard. Further, the ear may be able to perceive and recognize a simple ratio, such as 2:1, but it is incapable, on its own, of determining a more complex proportion and identifying it with precision.

This latter argument assumes that the Pythagorean proportions do exist and are not simply a convenient description; their prior existence is essential to his argument. Boethius does acknowledge that these proportions of string length are not the only determinants of pitch, noting that increased tension or thinness of a string would raise its pitch, but he declines to pursue the discussion (5.4) very far. Moreover, he appears to have claimed all along (1.3) that it is the speed of vibration that varies with pitch no matter how that speed is caused, a position that might lead to a serious contradiction with the role of proportions. Boethius avoids any such problem by arguing that a change in a string's tension affects both that string's thickness and the timbre of the resulting sound, thus putting tension in a different category altogether and leaving quantitative description connected solely with the length of the strings.

Boethius's treatise remained the standard textbook on music throughout the Middle Ages, until the end of the fifteenth century; it was still widely used in the sixteenth. The subjects covered in musical studies, the mathematical orientation, the concern for pitch nearly to the exclusion of rhythm, and the Pythagorean foundation all remained essentially unchallenged for a millennium. Boethius's interpretation of the Greek sources also had no competitor, and his work provided the only, if indirect, link with the early Greek sources for the musical scholars of the Latin Middle Ages.

The Medieval Tradition

For several centuries after Boethius, there were few new works written on music, or at least few of which any record remains. When such writings began to appear again by the late ninth century, an entirely new tradition had begun to develop.[40] Treatises such as the anonymous *Musica enchiriadis* (ca. 850–900) or Hucbald's *De harmonica institutione* (ca. 900) are devoted not to discussions of proportions

---

40. On the transition from classical and patristic to medieval aesthetics, see Schueller, *Idea of Music*, pp. 203–434.

but to the singing of ecclesiastical chant.[41] They discuss a version of the Greater Perfect System, but with modifications based on plainchant practice. Hucbald recommends a simplified Greek form of pitch notation, based on the Lydian mode, and a system of syllables assigned to the notes of the tetrachord, intended to serve as a memory aid in learning notes and pieces.

These treatises are well known to students of music history for their mention of organum, a means of embellishing plainchant and the precursor of polyphony.[42] A second singer accompanies the singer of the main chant melody, duplicating the shape of the original chant tune with greater or lesser exactness at an interval of a fourth, fifth, or octave from the original. There is no evidence for such a practice in antiquity; no theoretical writings even implied its existence. No ancient works had, for that matter, discussed the practical aspects of singing or composition (in any style) in the detail these early medieval treatises do.

The eleventh-century writings of Guido Aretinus further distinguished this new tradition from that of antiquity.[43] Guido abandons the Greek string names of the Greater Perfect System in favor of the Latin letter names still in use today. The innovations attributed to him are designed for the ease of learning and transmitting plainchant: a pitch notation system based on a lined staff marked with a clef, a solmization system based not on tetrachords but on a six-note pattern of tones and semitones called a hexachord (ut-re-mi-fa-sol-la), and a method for teaching plainchant without notation that assigns these syllables and pitches to parts of the human hand to which the choirmaster can then point, a technique referred to as the Guidonian hand. This new medieval tradition, then, differs in four fundamental ways: It is practical, involving very little mathematics. Because it is designed for the singing of ecclesiastical chant, it labels and organizes pitches in a way that is different from, yet similar to, the Greek diatonic genus. It uses Guido's new and effective methods for notating pitch, which suited the new principles of church modes. It can account for polyphony, the presence of more than one melodic

41. Hucbald, *De harmonica institutione*, in *Hucbald, Guido, and John on Music: Three Medieval Treatises*, trans. Warren Babb, ed. Claude V. Palisca (New Haven: Yale University Press, 1978); Claude V. Palisca, "Guido of Arezzo," *New Grove;* Anonymous, *Musica enchiriadis*, trans. Leonie Rosenstiel (Colorado Springs: Colorado College Music Press, 1967).

42. Fritz Reckow and Rudolf Flotzinger, "Organum," *New Grove;* Norman E. Smith, "Organum and Discant; Bibliography," *New Grove.*

43. Guido Aretinus, *Micrologus*, in *Hucbald, Guido, and John on Music;* "Guido of Arezzo," *New Grove.*

line sounding at the same time in a single piece, as well as the single melodic line retained by Gregorian chant. These very different goals and practices would naturally give rise to a different scholarly tradition.

Guido's innovations (genuine and attributed) spread through European ecclesiastical schools as part of a more general curricular reform, reform in which the works of Boethius played an important role. Quadrivial education had both theoretical and practical aspects; manuals on music notation, the Guidonian hand, and the church modes seen in the divisions of the monochord became associated not only with their theoretical counterpart Boethius, but also with other practical components of quadrivial education such as abacus and computus. Later university scholarship maintained this distinction, while adding to it Aristotelian disciplinary classifications.[44]

The two traditions of theory and practice were linked by several similarities. The medieval practical tradition unquestionably had some of its roots in late antique practice, though the records are too poor for us to trace its evolution in detail. A two-octave range of diatonic pitches, the use of a monochord to establish those pitches, and the same classification of consonant and dissonant intervals serve as landmarks for both theory and practice. Each half of the field complements the other; Boethian theory (referred to as *musica theorica* or *speculativa*) did not emphasize notation and used no musical compositions as examples, and the ecclesiastical tradition (*musica practica*) had no intellectual justification for its use of pitches or consonances except in the Boethian tradition.

The regular ecclesiastical obligations of quadrivially educated clerics kept the theoretical and practical traditions from complete separation into different specialties. Yet the differences between the two were too great for full integration. Practical manuals entirely devoted to the rudiments of singing, especially for the training of choirboys, continued to be written throughout the Middle Ages and Renais-

44. On music in the liberal arts tradition, see—both in Wagner, *Seven Liberal Arts*—Theodore C. Karp, "Music," pp. 169–95; and Karl F. Morrison, "Incentives for Studying the Liberal Arts," pp. 32–57. See also Umberto Eco, *Art and Beauty in the Middle Ages*, trans. Hugh Bredin (1959 [Italian]; New Haven: Yale University Press, 1986); Marilynn Smiley, "Eleventh Century Music Theorists," in *The Eleventh Century*, ed. Stanley Ferber and Sandro Sticca, Acta 1:61–90 (Binghamton, N.Y.: Center for Medieval and Early Renaissance Studies, 1974); Guy Beaujouan, "L'enseignement du 'quadrivium,' " in *La scuola nell'occidente latino dell'alto medioevo*. Settimane di studio, Centro italiano di studi sull'alto medioevo 19.2:639–67 (Spoleto: Centro, 1972); Pearl Kibre, "The *Quadrivium* in the Thirteenth Century Universities (with Special Reference to Paris)," in *Studies in Medieval Science: Alchemy, Astrology, Mathematics, and Medicine* (London: Hambledon Press, 1984), I.

sance. Yet the major scholarly music treatises from the thirteenth through the fifteenth centuries combined both traditions with varying degrees of emphasis on one or the other, treating the whole as a single unity divided into two weakly interated sections. This continuing coexistence was supported by three circumstances. First was the expansion of interest after Guido in counterpoint and polyphony, which drew attention away from melodic proportion per se. Second was the new focus of medieval theorists on developing systems of rhythmic notation to match the efficiency and accuracy of pitch notation. (Both of these developments have received detailed scholarly attention.) Third, the dominance of harmonic proportion as a general æsthetic standard assured its continued importance to musical composition and performance and to the arts in general.[45]

By the later Middle Ages, then, the Boethian and ecclesiastical traditions had settled into their roles as complementary parts of a single field. Both were the subjects of scholarly investigation and writing; both were treated essentially as a branch of "scientific" inquiry, based on logical and mathematical analysis and a progressive accumulation of knowledge. The composite musical tradition passed on to Renaissance scholars is thus both complex and contradictory. Its classical foundation was primarily Boethius's *De institutione musica,* which served as a single filter for the works of the Greek scholars. Other major sources were the *Timaeus* with Chalcidius's commentary, Cicero's *Dream of Scipio* with Macrobius's commentary, Martianus Capella, Isidore, a few biblical passages, and numerous supporting references from the *Aeneid* (both of the latter sources having been introduced, in turn, by Isidore). The ecclesiastical portion based its authority on Gregory the Great (legendary originator of the ecclesiastical chant commonly named after him), Guido, and the various scholarly medieval theorists working in a continuous tradition into the fifteenth century. The scholars of the late fifteenth century thus had the task of reinterpreting this multifaceted tradition in the light of new sources, new musical practices, and the era's new interpretive methods.

45. On medieval aesthetics and the importance of proportion, see Eco, *Art and Beauty,* pp. 41–42, 124; Michael Masi, "Arithmetic," in Wagner, *Seven Liberal Arts,* pp. 157–60; Masi, "Boethian Number Theory and Music," in *Boethian Number Theory,* pp. 23–30.

CHAPTER 2

Expansion of the
Medieval Tradition

In many respects the music scholarship of the later
fifteenth century proceeded in an unbroken line from that of the previous generation. Writers cited their predecessors with great frequency, sometimes using the earlier work as models for portions of
their own. Their list of "modern" authorities extended back into the
previous century in a continuous chain of thought and writing:
Ugolino of Orvieto, Marchetto of Padua, Prosdocimo de Beldoman-
dis, Giorgio Anselmi, and the northerners Philippe de Vitry and Jehan de Muris. The standard genres remained constant, primarily the
scholarly treatise based on Boethius, along with practical manuals of
singing or counterpoint. The scholarly treatise itself had been standardized in content and organization, allowing for a range of variations. Its use of proofs and demonstrations, concise and functional
prose, and a technical vocabulary all identified its authors as ongoing
participants in a scholastic tradition.

Yet these late fifteenth-century writers also changed their field; in
fact the major scholars a century later would consistently date the beginning of their own discursive tradition to Nicolaus Burtius, Bartolomeo Ramos, and especially Franchino Gaffurio and Giorgio Valla.
Some changes were subtle, such as the increasing signs of humanistic
influence in their writing styles, their use of quotations, and their inclusion of introductory verse. Others were more dramatic, such as
their expansion of the canon of ancient authorities to include both
previously unknown Greek sources and ancient literary works. Still
other innovations, notably the new interest in poetics and metrics, remained tentative in their hands and only revealed their importance in

37

the works of later writers. Of course, every generation of scholars might hope to make an impact; musical scholars were no exception, and musical studies had been anything but stagnant. That these particular writers should raise new issues or seek better answers to old problems was not itself revolutionary but rather the expected result of active study. The real difference lies in the degree of innovation and the influence of these innovations during the next century.

These writers formed a relatively small and close circle distinct from that of their elders of the early fifteenth century (with a few minor transitional figures, such as John Hothby, falling in between). In their careers and training, though, they differed little from those working earlier in the century. Nicolaus Burtius was trained in canon law, Giorgio Valla in humanities as well as mathematics, and the rest in the practice of music. Most were at some point connected with universities. Burtius and Bartolomeo Ramos taught in Bologna at the same time. Franchino Gaffurio and Giorgia Valla worked contemporaneously at Genoa, Pavia, and Milan. Gaffurio carried on an extended criticism of Ramos with Ramos's student, Giovanni Spataro, and worked with Johannes Tinctoris in Naples. All these scholars viewed the ancients who had written on music as the great discoverers of universal laws and the originators of the systems of pitch and tuning, who had produced a peak of achievement before the valley of the Middle Ages.

Despite their frequent disagreements, the late fifteenth-century writers worked similar changes on their field. Individually and collectively they sought to increase musical knowledge by expanding the classical sources, a goal they pursued in two major ways. First, they discovered more music treatises from antiquity, primarily those written in Greek. By translating them into Latin and then, later, into Italian (or by having them translated), they brought these works into the musical canon. Second, they began to study the references to music in ancient works other than music treatises, most notably the literary works the humanists were studying. Although these literary references provided little new technical information, they did address (either directly, as the subject matter, or in casual asides) the roles music played in ancient life, something the ancient music treatises did not do. Even those writers most oriented toward practical music were forced to reexamine the core of the tradition, as changes in musical composition and performance raised questions about the relationship between theory and practice, and they needed the scholarly tools the other writers provided. The practical musicians, in turn, contributed an interest in comparing ancient and modern musical practice.

This generation, then, marks the transition between the active medieval scholarship of the fourteenth and fifteenth centuries and the fundamental questioning of the sixteenth-century writers. We turn first to Nicolaus Burtius not because his work was the earliest of the group (though it is nearly so) but because of his self-defined role as a conservative. His *Musices opusculum* serves as a good starting point for understanding the genre of the technical treatise and some sources of innovation. Franchino Gaffurio serves as the other chronological boundary; later scholars would identify him as the greatest and most influential scholar of these years.

Nicolaus Burtius of Parma

Nicolaus Burtius wrote his treatise, *Musices opusculum* (1487) in response to another treatise, the *Musica practica* of Bartolomeo Ramos de Pareja, published five years earlier. Rejecting the latter's work as an ill-conceived attempt at innovation, Burtius not only attacks Ramos and his treatise but also presents a comprehensive discussion of music as he claims it is traditionally and properly studied.[1]

Burtius's professional life seems to correlate with this scholarly role; for there is little to distinguish it from the careers of similar scholars from earlier years. Born about 1450 in Parma, Burtius studied music there with Joannes Gallicus of Namur.[2] Sometime after becoming a subdeacon in 1472 he moved to Bologna, where he began the study of canon law, became a reader in music at the university, and enjoyed the partonage of the Bentivoglio family. When the Bentivoglio were forced from power in 1506 he returned to Parma, where he became rector of the oratorio of S. Pietro in Vincoli, then was made

1. For biographical information on Burtius, see Giuseppe Massera, ed., *Nicolai Burtii Parmensis: Florum libellus* (Florence: Olschki, 1975), pp. 1–18; see also Clement A. Miller "Burtius, Nicolaus," *New Grove;* G. Ballistreri, "Burzio, Nicholao," *Dizionario biografico degli italiani* (hereafter cited as *DBI*). On his reputation among later Renaissance writers, see *Nicolaus Burtius: Musices opusculum*, intro., trans. Clement A. Miller (N.p.: American Institute of Musicology, 1983), pp. 19–20. The degree of interaction between humanists and writers on music before this generation deserves further study, although the contacts appear to be few. Roy Martin Ellefson has demonstrated the weakness of connections between musical scholars and humanism before 1450; see his "Music and Humanism in the Early Renaissance: Their Relationship and Its Roots in the Rhetorical and Philosophical Traditions" (Ph.D. diss., Florida State University, 1981). Nonetheless, not all his assertions are borne out by the sources.

2. On Joannes Gallicus (also know by his family name, Legrense), see Albert Seay, ed., *Johannes Gallicus: Ritus canendi* (Colorado Springs: Colorado College Music Press, 1981), 1:iii–iv.

choirmaster (*guardacoro*) at the cathedral (1518); though there is no official record of his death, his vacancy at the cathedral was filled in 1528.

Most of Burtius's written production dates from his years at Bologna and reveals more contact with humanistic issues than would have been typical of earlier musical scholars. His best-known work was not the music treatise but *Bononia illustrata* (1494), a guidebook to the city. He left some Latin lyrics, including a poem for the wedding of Annibale Bentivoglio and Lucrezia d'Este (1486), two manuscripts on singing and notation, a short Bolognese chronicle, and an (attributed) arithmetic treatise.[3]

Some aspects of Burtius's biography resemble those of his contemporaries and predecessors; there are also signs of change and some features simply unique to him. His career path resembles that of many other fifteenth-century musical scholars: university training and appointments, some private patronage (the extent of Bentivoglio support is unknown), and ecclesiastical positions as a performer and a teacher of choirboys. University appointments in another subject, such as mathematics or law, were also not uncommon.[4] But Burtius's written works show more interest in humanistic study and less in mathematics or astronomy than would have been likely earlier in the century. By comparison, his close contemporary Gaffurio, though noted for his erudition, had an intellectual background much more like that of earlier scholars. Burtius's own teacher Joannes Gallicus, despite his studies with Vittorino da Feltre,[5] had shown in his own writings little interest in or influence from the humanists.

Burtius's *Musices opusculum* (also called *Florum libellus* in his introduction) begins with an attack on Ramos and his work, stemming from Ramos's supposed innovations. The body of the treatise he devotes to the presentation of a more "correct" version of the theory

3. Burtius's writings include *Musices opusculum* (Bologna, 1487); *Fax Maroniana, id est observationes eruditae in Vergilium* (Bologna, 1490); *Bononia illustrata* (Bologna, 1494); *Musarum nympharumque ac summorum deorum epitomata* (Bologna, n.d. frequently reprinted). Probable works: "De prolatione sesquialtera perfecto minore antecedente," London, British Library, Add. 22315; a lost poem, "Chronichetti di Bologna"; and an arithmetic treatise, Parma, Biblioteca Palatina 922.

4. Marie Boas Hall has examined the trends of scientific education and employment in the fifteenth and sixteenth centuries. Though she does not specifically discuss musical scholars, their careers fall within the fairly broad range of professional life she describes. See Hall, "Renaissance Science and Professionalisation," *Annali dell'istituto e museo di storia della scienza di Firenze* 7 (1982): 53–64.

5. Massera, *Nicolai Burtii*, pp. 26–40; "Burtius," *New Grove*; "Burzio," *DBI*; Seay, *Johannes Gallicus* 1:78.

and practice of music, following Boethius and Guido Aretinus as taught by his teacher Gallicus. This conservative goal combines with Burtius's broader humanistic interests to make his treatise a good baseline for establishing the subject matter, issues, and directions of innovation for the discipline in the last decades of the century.

The attack on Ramos is nearly as much ad hominem as it is substantial. Ramos, he claims, has both contradicted and misunderstood Boethius and Guido and ignored Gallicus. These "errors" are largely technical; they consist mainly of Ramos's division of the monochord and his replacement of Guido's old six-syllable system of solmization with a new eight-syllable system, matters that might appear to be related mainly to the medieval tradition of musical practice. Yet to Burtius they constitiute an assault on musical tradition dating back to late antiquity, the days of saints Ambrose and Gregory. Burtius then offers a valuable outline of his own book and the topics he wishes to treat:

> Our compendium, which is composed of three treatises, is called *Florum libellus* . . . . In this treatise will be shown: First, what music is and its praise. Second, how many divisions in [the subject of] music, who is a musician, and the difference between musician and singer. Third, what is sound and a definition of sound in general, what is voice and how it is formed, what is a consonance and what a dissonance. Fourth, I will explain what harmony is, who was the first man to sing, and the three genera of melody . . . . Fifth and finally, what are musical structures or compositions and which are more necessary; further, what are tropes or modes and by whom invented . . . . In the second treatise: that which is concerned with combined song, commonly called counterpoint . . . . The third treatise, which completes our book, concludes briefly with what is figured song, the notation of time and value, what is number, what is proportion, and the measurement of the monochord. These things extracted from the books of famous authors and collected with our immense and painstaking labor will be introductory to those dear readers who wish to progress further in the subject.[6]

6. Burtius, *Musices opusculum*, fol. 3r (pages are unnumbered, so I follow Massera in assigning fols. with text beginning on 1r): "Compendium igitur nostrum quod tribus tractatibus fulcitur: florum libellus nuncupatur. . . . Primo siquidem quid sit musica: ac eius laudes in hoc nostro tractatu ostendam. Secundo quotplex sit musica: quidve musicus: et differentia inter musicum et cantorem. Tertio vero quid sit sonus et diffinitio soni generalis. Quid vox et qualiter formetur. Quid consonantia: quidve disonantia. Quarto vero quid sit armonia: quis hominum primo cecinerit. Atque de tribus melorum generibus explicabo. . . . Quinto et ultimo quid sint constitutiones vel coniunctiones musicales: et que plus necessarie: qui sint preterea tropi sive modi: et a quo inventi. . . . In secundo vero tractatu quid sit cantus commixtus qui vulgariter contrapunctus nuncupatur: quomodo componatur reiectis quorundam cantorum opinionibus tractabimus ac facili via enodabimus. Tertius vero tractatus: qui et libelli

The first of Burtius's "three treatises" seems to be the one of most importance to him. Not only is it the longest, but he also gives it the longest and most detailed description in this outline. Most of his colleagues and predecessors would approve; for the theoretical section was the prerequisite for understanding any discussion of practice. The work's second treatise, the *musica practica* (in this case counterpoint) is much shorter, consisting largely of rules for composition and the presentation of a musical example. Other authors might have included a section here on musical notation; Burtius has instead moved that discussion into the third treatise so that he can address as a unit several areas of disagreement with Ramos, thereby placing most of his mathematical discussions together. The work's form, then, varies, though not radically, the standard structure of scholarly music treatises in order to serve a partucular argumentative purpose.

That standard was still principally Boethius's treatise *De musica*. Given Burtius's heated defense of the Boethian tradition, it is hardly surprising that his first treatise in particular should closely follow Boethius's Book 1. After all, even Ramos's treatise, despite its explicit and controversial attempt at modernity, had followed Boethius's general outline. This format remained the norm until well into the sixteenth century. Burtius also makes use of his teacher Gallicus's treatise, *Ritus canendi*, itself modeled on Boethius but more loosely.[7] His definition of music comes directly from Gallicus but nonetheless is reminiscent of Boethius's definition of the musician: "Music is that art, pleasing to God and man, of discerning and judging anything sung, and inquiring into the true cause [ratio] of all things made through arsis and thesis, that is by intension and remission of tones."[8]

Burtius offers a brief discussion of etymology based on Isidore and Gallicus, then summarizes Boethius's discussion from the proem to *De arithmetica* on the elements of music and its place in the quadrivium: "The elements of this discipline are consonances, proportions,

nostri finem comprehendit: quid sit cantus figuratus. tempus. ac valor notularum. quid numerus: quid proportio cum dimensione monocordi: sub brevitate concludet. Hec etenim amantissimi immenso labore ex clarorum auctorum extracta codicibus ac nostra industria vobis cumulata introductorium erunt unicuique ad maiora huiusmodi velle transcendere."

7. The most recent edition of this treatise is that of Seay (see n. 2 above), based on two manuscripts at the British Library. The older edition of E. de Coussemaker in *Scriptorum de musica medii aevii* (Paris, 1869), 4:298–396 (hereafter cited as *CSM*), is based on the same two manuscripts.

8. Burtius 1.1, fols. 3v–4r: "Musica igitur ars est deo placens: ac hominibus; omne quod canitur discernens et diiudicans: ac de cunctis que fiunt per arsim et tesim id est per vocularum intensionem et remissionem: veram inquirere rationem."

and parts of proportions, the tone, semitone, ditone, and the like, which are reduced to consonances, as will be most plainly shown below. Arithmetic is the ratio of numbers; geometry of magnitudes; astrology of the motions, magnitudes, and distances of stars; and music of the motions of sounds."9

Thus Burtius has clearly defined the subject according to the Boethian tradition: not as a set of rules for musical composition or stylistic analysis, as a modern reader might expect, but as the mathematical study of the proportions between the sounds of different pitches, related to the other subjects of the quadrivium. He continues along this path by stressing the importance of consonance, defined by the nature of the proportions between the sounds. Music's elements are not just measurable quantities but ordered quantities; that is, music is the study not of all sounds that can be measured but of those that form consonances or can be resolved into consonances. Burtius's one innovation in this part of the treatise is his reference to Cicero on the importance of beginning with a clear definition of first principles.10 Modest as this sounds in comparison with any work in a humanistic field, Burtius's book is one of the earliest works on music to include such a source.

This first chapter of the first treatise is typical of Burtius's approach. He tries to bring new life to the traditional subject by introducing these "things extracted from the books of famous authors" into his writing, where they serve a triple function: They make his subject more accessible and interesting to an audience with a humanistic education; as his own biography shows, this could include many readers who were not professional humanists. He can exploit these classical literary sources, new to the field of music but well known to the humanistically educated reader, for their information on music. And he can argue that these books support the study of music as defined by Boethius.

Burtius next turns to his chapter in praise of music. The *laus musice* had remained a standard feature of music treatises throughout the

---

9. Burtius, fol. 4r: "Elementa enim huiusmodi discipline sunt consonantie et proportiones: membraque proportionum. Ut tonus: semitonum: dytonus. et huiusmodi: que ad consonantiam rediguntur: ut luculentissime infra patebit. Quemadmodum igitur arithmetica de numeris est ratio. de magnitudinibus geometria. de syderum motibus magnitudinibusque: ac distantiis astrologia: ita de sonorum motibus est musica." Boethius' proem is based in turn on Nicomachus's *Eisagoge arithmetica*, but this was unknown to Burtius.

10. Burtius, fol. 3v.

Middle Ages.[11] Yet Burtius does not make use of these very brief medieval models; instead he composes an original piece based on classical authors, citing Valerius Maximus, the pseudo-Aristotelian *Problems*, Celsus, Cicero, and Pliny, as well as the biblical King David. From Boethius he takes the names of several additional Greek writers whose works were not translated until the next century and hence unavailable to the (apparently) Greekless Burtius: Nicomachus of Gerasa and Aristoxenus. These authors serve to support standard arguments in praise of music: the study of music trains youthful souls to regular, moderate, and harmonious discipline; people of all ages take a natural delight in it; even the birds and the dolphins exercise the art, as Orpheus and Amphion charmed the stones and forests; David with his singing calmed the troubled mind of Saul, and Asclepiades restored the insane to health; music can calm the turbulent or excite a calm person to fury. All these arguments pertain to the effects of music on the soul, both the transient ones and the more permanent ones, caused by repeated listening. Burtius also offers a few illustrations of the social importance of music to the ancients: all guests at a banquet were expected to take their turn at the lyre or cythara; noted scholars such as the arithmetician Nicomachus and the geometers Archytas and Aristoxenus wrote on music; and "Plato theologus" was able to hear the music of the spheres (1.2, fol. 5r). Any medieval treatise would have included a brief summary of any or all of these remarks, yet Burtius's *laus musice* stands out. First, he gives it its own chapter with the genre's explicit heading, "de laudibus musice." Second, he takes the trouble to compose it himself rather than simply copy it from an earlier model, as he does with so much of the technical material in the treatise. Third, to support and illustrate the otherwise traditional list of powers he ascribes to music, he uses sources not previously considered in works on music.

Next Burtius discusses the "music of the spheres." In this chapter he returns to the structure of Boethius's treatise to distinguish the three types of music: *mundana, humana,* and *instrumentalis. Musica mundana* involves the relations between the heavenly bodies, as reflected in the definition of music as "the study of proportion in motion." Certainly the proportions between the heavenly bodies cannot be perceived by the senses; they are known solely through reason. This highest form of music thus demonstrates the superiority of reason over sense perception in mastering the subject. Burtius gives

11. James Hutton, "Some English Poems in Praise of Music," in *Essays on Renaissance Poetry,* ed. Rita Guerlac (Ithaca, N.Y.: Cornell University Press, 1980), pp. 18–41.

the distances and proportions between the planets, beginning with the earth and the moon (126,000 stades, the proportion of a tone, 9:8) and proceeding through the fixed stars (a full octave, 2:1, with the earth). Relevant passages from Macrobius and Pliny support these figures,[12] which allow the reader to calculate the distance in stades between any and all parts of the universe. He takes from Cicero (*The Dream of Scipio*) the argument explaining why humans do not hear this music: having heard it since birth, we have become deaf to it. Cicero is also the source for a brief discussion of the musical proportions among the four elements. For this assistance, Cicero merits a paragraph's digression in praise of his writings (1.3, fol. 7r) until Burtius brings him back (in his *Tusculan Disputations* this time), along with Lactantius, Macrobius, and Hierophilus, as authorities for the brief discussion of *musica humana*. This branch of music deals with the proportions among the four humors, the parts of the soul, and the relations between soul and body. Burtius moves quickly over the subject and on to a brief discussion of instrumental music and musical instruments.

Much of this discussion involves categories and classifications. Instruments may be of two types, natural (the voice) and artificial, the latter divided in turn between those that incite delight and are used especially in divine service (such as the organ, lyre, and cythara) and those that incite fury and are used to rouse an army's courage and to strike fear in the breast of the enemy (horn, trumpet, or drums). The study of instrumental music has three parts: sound, word, and number, the last including poetic meter. Burtius cites Guido's famous verse distinguishing between *musicus* and cantor,[13] based on whether the actor understands musical principles or simply performs; the verse, in turn, is a simplified version of Boethius's argument in *De musica* 1.34. Instrumental music's speculative principles depend on both sense and reason. Burtius argues against attempts to proceed solely from the former, echoing Boethius on the virtue of Ptolemy's

12. Ambrosius Aurelius Theodosius Macrobius, *Commentary on the Dream of Scipio*, trans. Will Harris Stahl (New York: Columbia University Press, 1952), 2.3, pp. 196–97; Pliny, *Naturalis historia*, ed. Carl Mayhoff (Stuttgart: Teubner, 1967), 2:19–20.

13. Burtius, 1.6, fol. 9v: "Musicorum et cantorum magna est distantia; Isti dicunt, illi sciunt quae componit musica. Nam qui facit quod non sapit diffinitur bestia." (Great is the distance between musicians and singers; the latter claim, the former know how to compose music; he who acts without knowledge is a mere beast.) From Guido Aretinus, *Musicae regulae rhythmicae*, in *Scriptores ecclesiastici de musica sacra*, ed. M. Gerbert (1784; Rochester, N.Y.: Rochester University Press, 1955) 2:25 (hereafter cited as *GS*).

insistence on using both reason and sense. Once again, little of this section is new; it follows Boethius more or less chapter by chapter.

These opening chapters of the first treatise, then, describe a subject clearly based on Boethius and the Pythagorean tradition. The mathematical priciples at its core are also the first principles of Pythagorean universal order. That this cosmic order is musical places music in a very important position among the other disciplines. Instrumental music, the lowest of the three classes of musical study, proceeds from the highest class and follows the same precepts, though in a manner accessible to the senses. Thus in instrumental music these fundamental laws may be understood and practiced more or less well but are not subject to change. Burtius accounts for change in terms of the acquisition (or loss) of knowledge about universal principles, not in terms of cultural diversity or some other variable. Burtius uses the ancient "extracts" as classical confirmations of Boethius's statements; their purpose is to clarify the argument and convince the reader by their cumulative weight. Burtius does not use them to provide new information, nor do they alter either the topics discussed or the order of discussion.

Burtius continues this treatise by following Book 1 of Boethius in offering a further series of definitions and classifications. Sound he defines as a physical phenomenon: "a percussion of the air undissolved until it is heard."[14] Sounds are pitched and unpitched. Unpitched sound is of three types: *sonitus* (noise), *tinnitus* (clanging, as by a bell), and echo. Pitched sound may be constant in pitch, as in singing a given note, or variable, as in declaiming poetry. Sound may also vary in quality, depending on the quality of the sounding body, which is a function of the proportions of the four elements composing the body and explains why a body of gold, silver, or copper is more sonorous than one of lead.

After a brief discussion of the voice, Burtius addresses in Chapter 9 the subject of consonance and dissonance, and here he first departs significantly from Boethius, employing several means to slip these departures past the reader. He lists as consonant intervals the fifth, the octave plus a fifth, and the double octave, "as will be seen when we examine mixed chant."[15] After another flurry of definitions, he moves on to dissonance and its types. Nowhere does he discuss the fourth, which Boethius considered a consonance. This is apparently

14. Burtius 1.7, fols. 9v–10r: "Percussio aeris indissoluta: usque ad auditum." Albertus Magnus, he notes, concurs in his second book, *De anima.*
15. Burtius 1.9, fol. 11v: "Et proprie consonantia est diapente: dispason cum diapente: et bisdiapason. ut infra constabit cum de cantu commixto pertractabimus."

not an error; for he returns to consonance as promised in his section on "mixed chant" and omits the fourth once again. Nor does he list it among the dissonances; in fact, he offers no list of dissonances at all.

Ramos had demoted the fourth to the status of a dissonance, because composers no longer used it as a consonant interval. Burtius may be reluctant to agree with his rival, but neither is he willing to contradict him where contemporary musical practice is so obviously on Ramos's side. He simply skirts the issue and does not treat the fourth, thus avoiding any obvious conflict with the ancients while remaining true to contemporary musical practice. He could not treat the fourth as a consonance in his section on counterpoint because music was not written that way. But neither could he label it a dissonance without departing blatantly from Boethius on proportions and classification of intervals, one of the few points truly held in common between classical theory and European practice. Later authors will try to argue their way through this apparent contradiction; Burtius hides his disagreement, as his retelling of the story about Pythagoras and the hammers further illustrates. Both Boethius and Macrobius, Burtius's main sources, use the story to begin a discussion of the consonances;[16] Burtius simply notes Pythagoras's discovery that "all things consist in measure, number, and weight."[17] He also locates the story among the lives and discoveries of the first musicians, away from discussions of consonance and dissonance.

The remainder of the first treatise covers such technical subjects as modes, psalm tones, Guidonian syllables, and Greek string names. Here Burtius mostly follows Gallicus rather than Boethius; for he has moved his treatment of number and quantity to his third treatise and needs to prepare the reader to understand counterpoint, the subject

16. Macrobius, following the narration: "Of the infinite store of numerical combinations those that would unite to produce harmony were found to be few and simple. They are six: sesquitertian, sesquialter, double, triple, quadruple, and superoctave....[The latter are then identified as 4:3, 3:2, 2:1, 3:1, 4:1, and 9:8.] And so the consonant chords are five in number, the fourth, the fifth, the octave, the octave and fifth, and the double octave." *Commentary*, pp. 188–89. Boethius reverses the logical order of the passage and begins with a shorter list of consonances: "Although some musical consonances were called 'diapason,' some 'diapente,' and some 'diatessaron' (which is the smallest consonance) before Pythagoras, Pythagoras was the first to ascertain through this means by what ratio the concord of sounds was joined together. So that what has been said might be clearer, for sake of illustration, let the weights of the four hammers be contained in the numbers written below: 12:9:8:6." Boethius, *Fundamentals of Music*, trans. Calvin M. Bower, ed. Claude V. Palisca (New Haven: Yale University Press, 1989), 1.10, pp. 18–19.

17. "Omnia siquidem ut inquit sapiens: in mensura: et numero: ac pondere consistunt." The phrase itself comes from Wisdom 11:20.

of the second treatise. He does, however, keep two subjects closely based on Boethius: the Greek melodic genera and the Greek string names. But he does not integrate them well with the surrounding material, nor does his discussion of them contribute to the course or context of his arguments. Although these technical subjects will hold a great fascination for later authors, who will use them to support arguments about intonation, chromaticism, and ancient musical practice, just as they will return to the problem of the fourth, Burtius simply walks through them, apparently mentioning them simply because they are in Boethius.

The second treatise opens with a quotation from Lactantius: "There is no sweeter food for the soul than knowledge of the truth."[18] Brief and compact, it is the shortest of the three. The writing style also changes, becoming terse and compact, much less literary. The Lactantius line is the only classical reference, not surprising for a subject with no roots in antiquity. This lack of pedigree nonetheless presents a problem of continuity, which Burtius attempts to resolve by using literary devices, as he did in the first treatise. He intersperses the discussions of practice with passages of theory, without trying to relate or integrate the differing lines of argument, and the result lacks topical or narrative consistency. He also continues his strategy of playing up points of agreement with ancient authorities while ignoring points of conflict.

Burtius begins the body of this treatise by listing again the types of consonances (now shifting mainly to the vernacular terms such as third, sixth, and octave). Then he moves on to such familiar topics as resolutions, suspensions, and the parallel motion of voices. While describing the order in which voices should be composed (2.5), he digresses to mention the eight church modes or tones, citing Guido as his authority. Rather than give the reader a general or technical description of the modes, however, he wishes only to list the emotions each induces:

> For the first tone induces delight, as is reported in the teachings of musicians; it is variable and capable of producing every emotion. The second is heavy and doleful and fit for lamentations. The *deuterus*, the mode that is third in order and the second authentic, is capable of producing rage, for which reason, according to Aretinus, it was depicted in antiquity as fiery in color. Boethius mentions a certain Taorminian so violently in-

18. Burtius 2.0, fol. 34r: "Cogitanti mihi viri disertissimi quod nullus est suavior aiunt cibus teste Lactantio. quam veritatis cognitio." From Lactantius, *Divinae institutiones* 1.1.20.

cited that he sought to break down the doors of a prostitute's house until the cytharist changed his mode. Its plagal, which is the fourth, elicits pleasure; it is fit for inciting pleasure and tempering rage. The *tritus*, which is called the fifth and is the third authentic, according to Guido is called delightful, modest, and jovial, gladdening the sad and anxious. The plagal, which in order is sixth, is sad and mournful and befits those who are easily moved to tears. The *tetrardus*, the seventh in order and fourth authentic, is part playful and cheerful, part impetuous, that is, passing between or holding a mean between both. Its plagal, eighth in order, induces happiness and excites great jollity.[19]

The logical support for this passage must come from the Pythagorean arguments about macrocosm and microcosm which Burtius presented in the first treatise, especially since he cites Boethius; yet Burtius does not clarify how or why the slight change of tessitura or in the placement of the semitone, the distinctions between one mode and another, should cause these great changes in emotional content. Nor do these statements relate to his specific rules for composition. Later writers will pursue these subjects more aggressively; Burtius seems content simply to identify the connections he wishes to make and then to abandon them.

In the third treatise, Burtius continues his attempt to connect ancient and modern by the simple device of placing passages based on each tradition side by side and using similar terminology for both. He begins with several chapters on musical notation, then follows Boethius's Book 2 on numbers and their properties and Book 4 on the monochord. He concludes with a chapter on the emotional effects of the planets and the zodiac, which he takes from Sacrobosco, Cicero, and Persius. Here he returns to the argument about the fourfold division of mathematics: "Though the mathematical art is divided into

19. Burtius 2.5, fols, 37v–38r: "Primus namque tonus inducit letitiam ut musicorum repertum est documentis: et mobilis ac habilis est ad omnes affectus producendos. Secundus vero est gravis: et flebilis in lamentationibusque habilis. Deuterus qui modo est tertius in ordine et secundus autenticus: habilis est ad iracundiam provocandam. Unde teste Aretino antiquitus igneo colore depingebatur. Reffert quoque Boetius quendam tauronomitanum hoc vehementer incitatum: ita quod scorti fores frangere cepisset: nisi cytharedus illico tonum mutasset. Eius vero plagalis: qui nunc est quartus: voluptatem eligit id est aptus est ad voluptatem incitandam et temperandam iracundiam. Tritus vero qui nunc est quintus nominatus: et tertius autenticus: teste Guidone: dicitur delectabilis: modestus: et hyllaris: tristes et anxietate detentos letificans. Plagalis vero eius: qui in ordine est sextus. est pius: lachrymabilis: et illis conveniens: qui de facili provocantur ad lachrimas. Tetrardus namque qui est septimus in ordine: et quartus autenticus: partem habet lascivie et jucunditatis partemque incitationis: atque varios habens saltus. hoc est medium inter utrumque tenens. Eius vero plagalis magis letificat qui in ordine est octavus. et jucunditatem excitat."

parts—arithmetic embracing number; geometry, dimension; music, sounds; and astrology, the heaven and the stars—nonetheless the latter has not consisted purely of mathematics but is a mean between the mathematical and the natural since, as they say, it applies mathematical principles to natural things. On this see the very eminent treatises *De sphaera* and the Philosopher's work *De caelo et mundo*"[20] This interesting paragraph is reminiscent of Ptolemy by way of Boethius. Yet the reader wishes in vain for more development of the arguments about mathematics and nature; Burtius simply moves on to describe the cosmos, the types of heavenly motion, and the zodiac.

This passage, like the other examples of Burtius's argumentation, implies lines of argument it fails to make at all explicit. First is the connection between the mathematical nature of astronomy and the theory of planetary effects. It seems clear from the order of topics that Burtius wishes to invoke the proportions between the planets to explain why, for example, Jupiter is "the planet of wisdom, intelligence, and skill."[21] Yet he does not even suggest how the connection works and how (or whether) it affects styles of musical composition or performance. Second is the way this passage echoes a claim about music's nature that we come across in many authors: that music occupies a middle ground between pure mathematics and the study of nature, which makes it relevant to the study of morality.[22] Burtius seems to want to relate music, astronomy, and morality, but he never makes the connection distinctly. Third is his avoidance of the question

20. Burtius 3.22, fols. 64r–v: "Quamquam ars mathematica quattuor in partes sit divisa. arithmeticam videlicet que numeros. geometriam que dimensiones. musicam que sonos. astrologiam que celum et stellas complectitur: nihilominus hanc non pure mathematicam nonnulli conscripsere: sed inter mathematicam et naturalem mediam esse. quum haec ut dicunt principia mathematicalia applicat ad res naturales. de qua vide tratatum de spera quam plurimum egregium: et apud philosophum in libro de celo et mundo."

21. Burtius 3.22, fol. 65r: "Jupiter enim est planeta sapientie et intellectus et usus."

22. Boethius's passage on the subject, at least, would have been known to Burtius: "Further, when someone sees a triangle or a square, he recognizes easily that which is observed with the eyes. But what is the nature of a triangle or a square? For this you must ask a mathematician.

"Now the same can be said with respect to other sensible objects, especially concerning the witness of the ears: the sense of hearing is capable of apprehending sounds in such a way that it not only exercises judgment and identifies their differences, but very often actually finds pleasure if the modes are pleasing and ordered, whereas it is vexed if they are disordered and incoherent.

"From this it follows that, since there happen to be four mathematical disciplines, the other three share with music the task of searching for truth; but music is associated not only with speculation but with morality as well." Boethius, *Fundamentals of Music* 1.1, pp. 1–2.

of how far the celestial matter should be considered "natural"; for to claim it so would not be entirely consistent with Aristotle, whom Burtius immediately cites.

Burtius's work reveals several traits characteristic of the study of music in the late fifteenth century: the primacy of the Boethian tradition; the inclusion of the "modern" practical tradition of church modes, solmization, and rules for notation; and most noteworthy, the uneasy alliance between these two traditions. Both the alliance and its unease merit brief attention.

Burtius's attempt to promote this alliance is hardly original with him (it is a standard feature of postclassical musical scholarship), but he emphasizes the alliance by repeating the points of similarity throughout his work, though he could easily have restricted his effort to the first treatise. He even introduces connections when they interrupt the flow of the topic at hand. One might attribute this thoroughness of purpose to Burtius's argumentative goal: to discredit Ramos by claiming that modern music can and does follow the Boethian tradition. Yet the work of his contemporaries (for example, Gaffurio) displays this same strenuous effort to unite the two traditions.

Burtius's treatment of the diatessaron, or fourth, best illustrates the weakness of the alliance: forced to suppress this portion of Boethius's theory of consonance, he therefore cannot present a truly systematic analysis or even a summary of Boethius's work. Often, the best Burtius can do is simply to place similar subjects side by side and imply a relationship. It is not entirely clear why he is content with such an incomplete and imprecise argumentative method. Certainly he lacks a critical perspective on the ancient tradition, since he has no access to many of Boethius's own sources. Perhaps he therefore lacks the technical apparatus to dissect the ancient and modern traditions and fix their precise relationship at a given point. Or he may just be an unsystematic thinker content to imply chains of thought rather than construct solid arguments.

Finally, Burtius's book exhibits an early concern with adding to the body of classical sources available, especially works commonly associated with humanists. He sometimes plumbs these works only for a phrase or a literary or rhetorical device but more often for anecdotes. At times (e.g., Cicero's *Dream of Scipio*) they support structural parts of his argument. Yet Burtius never uses these sources to develop an argument independent of Boethius. Nor do these new sources themselves deal systematically with the subject of music.

Burtius himself does not write about issues in the use of different types of sources, so we cannot determine precisely how aware of them he is. He certainly has not considered the possibility that the classical sources might contribute to more than one tradition of ancient musical scholarship. But once in the repertoire of available and relevant sources for musical scholarship, these "new" works provide information and raise issues that increase in importance through the next century.

Ramos de Pareja, Hothby, and Tinctoris: A Range of Opinion

Despite the controversy over his one extant treatise, Musica practica (Bologna, 1482), we know relatively little about Bartolomeo Ramos de Pareja. Born around 1440, he lectured on Boethius at the University of Salamanca before coming to Italy about 1472, possibly first to Florence, but certainly settling in Bologna, where, he tells us, he again "lectured publicly."[23] Apparently disappointed at not receiving the university position he sought (or having his position terminated),[24] he moved to Rome, where he lived at least until 1491.

Very little of his work survives; of his compositions, only a canon remains, though he is known to have written masses and motets.

23. See Musica Practica Bartolomei Rami de Pareia Bononiae, ed. Johannes Wolf (Leipzig: Breitkopf und Härtel, 1901), pp. xi–xvi (hereafter cited as Wolf); Massera, Nicolai Burtii Parmensis, pp. 19–25; Albert Seay, "Ramos de Pareja, Bartolomeo," New Grove. Pages are unnumbered, so I follow the pagination of Wolf's edition. Ramos mentions that he composed a mass in Salamanca and read Boethius's De musica there; he also states that he "read publicly" at Bologna (Ramos 3.1.4, in Wolf, p. 91). His student Spataro and contemporary Gaffurio confirm this in their own writings, using nearly the same words; no specific post is mentioned (Wolf, p. xiii).

24. Spataro adds, "In quanto a lopera del mio preceptore, la quale desiderati di haver tuta et complecta, Ve dico certamente che lui ma non dete complemento a tale opera, et quella che si trova non e complecta, perche lui fece stampare a Bologna tale particole, perche el se credeva de legerla con stipendio in publico. Ma in quello tempo acade che per certe cause lui non hebe la lectura publica, et lui quasi sdegnato ando a Roma et porto con lui tute quelle particule impresse con intentione de fornirle a Roma. Ma lui non la fornite mai, ma lui attendeva a certo suo modo de vivere lascivo, el quale fu causa della sua morte." (In regard to the work of my preceptor, which you had wanted to have whole and complete: I tell you truly that he never offered the complement to that work, and that which is available is not complete; for he had those portions published in Bologna, because he thought he would read them with a public stipend. But at that time it happened for certain reasons that he did not get the public lectureship, and quite indignant he went to Rome, taking with him those published sections with the intention of finishing them at Rome. But he never finished them, taking up his loose manner of living that was the cause of his death.) Spataro to Aron, 13 March 1532, Vatican City, BAV, Vat. Lat. 5318; copy, Bologna, Civ. Mus. 1.6. See also Wolf, p. xiv. This passage provides much of the known biographical information on Ramos. The circumstances of his departure from Bologna are not clear, nor is his employment in Rome.

Other writers have referred to an introductory study of musical practice, and his student Spataro later mentioned that Ramos had taken a
portion of a *musica theorica* with him to Rome, intending to complete
and publish it there, but had not yet done so;[25] no manuscript is extant. From this fragmentary written corpus we cannot determine
with finality either Ramos's assessment of musical scholarship as a
whole or whether his later thinking was affected by the controversy
surrounding the *Musica practica*.

Yet a careful reading of the treatise does reveal a consistent approach to its subject that goes beyond its innovative exposition of
rules for singing. If Burtius wants to prove the necessity of the Boethian tradition to the modern world, Ramos's purpose is surprisingly
similar: to present the modern world with a Boethius simplified to
make him acceptable to singer and theoretician alike. This means, as
it did for Burtius, selective development or suppression of elements
of the *De musica*.

"Boethius simplified" is the argument Ramos chooses to attract the
reader in a *prologus* written with the hyperbole of a sales pitch.
Through his labors, he promises novice and expert alike an easy as-
cent of a musical Parnassus:

> Since Boethius's *Discipline of Music* rests upon the deepest foundations of
> arithmetic and philosophy, it cannot be easily understood by everyone;
> generally it seems obscure and sterile to the half-taught singers of our
> day, and subtle, yet firm and credible to the learned and better educated.
> So it is that just as it is and always has been neglected by the ignorant,
> among the more knowledgeable it has always been greatly prized. Thus
> we, who study to benefit all and to confer something upon the common
> good, have composed this work as a brief compendium of three books; it
> reduces the verbose to brevity, the difficult to simplicity, the obscure to
> clarity, and omits nothing of art and skill, for use both by practical sing-
> ers and for those scholars we call by Greek name theoreticians I
> have been able to collect over a long time, with many a late night's work
> as if from some abundant and universal fountain, something from the
> best authors and the teaching of the most famous instructors. Hence by
> extremely rapid study one will be able to take it in and most easily attain
> the highest summit of music.[26]

25. See Spataro's letter, n. 24 above. Since the *Musica practica* is certainly the "tale
particole" referred to, it is clear that Spataro did not consider the work to be
complete on its own.

26. Ramos, Prologus; Wolf, p. 1: "Boetii musices disciplina quinque voluminibus
comprehensa quoniam profundissimis arithmeticae philosophiaeque fundamentis
innititur nec passim ab omnibus intelligi potest, solet a semidoctis nostri temporis
cantoribus quo obscurior est eo sterilior, doctis vero et altius intuentibus quo

One might argue that such a glib introduction serves to mask an attack on the Boethian tradition; it may be the source of the frequent musicological stereotype of Ramos as an enemy of Boethius.[27] But this stereotype does not stand up to a continued analysis of the treatise, or even of the *prologus* itself. Ramos returns to Boethius's work immediately, first with a brief introductory quotation on astronomy, then with a summary treatment of the *laus musice* from *De musica* 1.1. He continues (in Chap. 1) by dividing music into the Boethian categories *mundana, humana,* and *instrumentalis,* then states that he will treat the last first. He classifies *musica instrumentalis* into natural (voices) or artificial instruments, again after Boethius 1.2. Ramos relies on Boethius at such structural points throughout the treatise and criticizes other authors for failing to understand Boethius's work. Thus Ramos's statement of purpose does seem to be an honest assessment of his intent.

Ramos divides his treatise into three parts: practice, theory, and "musica semimathematica, semiphysica" (which turns out primarily to be notation).[28] The first part treats his innovations in tuning and solmization, the source both of his fame and of controversy, and he loses no time in their presentation. These innovations bear a brief summary, despite their technical nature. His new scale has tuned fifths and thirds (5:4 and 6:5 for the major and minor third). The scale of Boethius tuned the fifth, fourth, and tone, as we have seen; thirds were established by addition and subtraction of the main intervals. Thus Ramos's scale sounds better than that of Boethius in musical styles that favor thirds over fourths.

---

subtilior probabiliorque est eo firmior meliorque videri, quo fit, ut, sicut ab indoctis neglecta semper fuerit et sit, ita apud peritiores in magno pretio semper habita sit et habeatur. Unde nos, qui omnibus prodesse et aliquid in communem utilitatem conferre studemus, hoc brevi compendio tribus libellis distincto prolixitatem eius in angustum, asperitatem in planum, obscuritatem in lucem reducentes nihilque quod ad artem usumque faciat praetermittentes et cantoribus quos practicos et speculantibus quos theoricos graece dicimus. . . . Hinc quasi ex quodam redundanti publicoque fonte quicquid ego longo tempore multis vigilis et assiduis lucubrationibus ex probatissimorum auctorum lectione et clarissimorum praeceptorum disciplina colligere potui, perquam celerrimo facillimoque studio licebit haurire et ad summum musicae culmen placidissimo gressu pervenire."

27. See "Ramos," *New Grove*; also *Johannis Octobi: Tres tractatuli contra Bartoholomeum Ramum,* ed. Albert Seay (Rome: American Institute of Musicology, 1964), pp. 8–12. Seay notes (on p. 11), however, that many of Ramos's passages quoted in Hothby's *Excitatio* support Boethius.

28. Ramos, Prologus; Wolf, p. 3: "Operis igitur sit ista partitio. In primo libro subtilem practicam ponemus, in secundo theoricam accurate discutiemus, in tertio musicam semimathematicam, semiphysicam congrua ratione probabimus."

But this is not the feature emphasized when Ramos introduces his scale. Rather, he extols only its simplicity: "Boethius divided the monochord very precisely in number and measure. But though it is useful and agreeable to theoreticians, to singers it is laborious and difficult to understand. Since we have promised to satisfy both, we offer a very easy division of the monochord which anyone may understand with moderate effort."[29] He acknowledges that his procedures produce some tones that are slightly imperfect but states that for practical purposes the imperfections are too small to worry about.[30]

This discussion leads directly to his new system of solmization. This new eight-note system, using the syllables "psal-li-tur per vo-ces is-tas," was designed to allow for accidental semitones more easily than the Guidonian system. It is also simpler, since one would avoid the complicated shifts (mutations) from one hexachord to another necessary under the Guidonian system. But his line of argument here is very different from his presentation of the "simplified" Boethian tuning. He begins by summarizing the Greek system of string names, emphasizing that they are organized into two distinct groups of four notes (the tetrachords) which comprise an octave. After quoting Virgil in agreement, Ramos moves on to Gregory and the Christian tradition, which assigned seven letter names (A through G) to the notes, repeating at the octave.[31] Thus he portrays Gregory's system as an extension of the classical tradition, not as a separate development.

After establishing this continuity, Ramos moves on to attack Guido as "perhaps a better monk than a musician" ("monachus fortasse melior quam musicus") who settled on a six-note plan simply because six is a "perfect" number (its factors 1, 2, 3 also produce the number in sum). Guido's hexachord mutations arose from his desire to imitate Boethian tetrachords,[32] but he erred in not identifying the conjunct and disjunct tetrachords, putting the mutations in the wrong places as a result, and thus making a mess of the whole subject. Ramos concludes with some sarcasm on the fate of Guido's pious, if ignorant soul: "Certainly, he might have been saved by many other means; in any event, I have no doubt that he is saved; for Christ on the cross

29. Ramos 1.1.2; Wolf, pp. 4–5: "Regulare monochordum numeris et mensura subtiliter a Boetio dividitur. Sed illud, sicut theoricis utile iocundumque est, ita cantoribus laboriosum intellectuque difficile. Verum quia utrisque satisfacere polliciti sumus, facillimam regularis monochordi divisionem reddemus. . . . Et eam quilibet vix dum etiam medorcriter eruditus facile intelligere poterit."
30. Ramos 1.1.3; Wolf, p. 6.
31. Ramos 1.1.3; Wolf, p. 8.
32. Ramos 1.1.4; Wolf, p. 11.

prayed for those who know not what they do."[33] By this reasoning, Ramos makes himself the true heir to the tradition of Boethius and Gregory, while Guido is dismissed as an ignorant aberration. Along with continued general criticism of Guido's incompetence, Ramos sustains this type of attack on Guido throughout the rest of the work.[34]

Ramos relies on simple arguments and proofs based on Boethian mathematics both to defend his innovations and to clarify problems in musical notation. For example, his choice of eight solmization syllables over Guido's six or even Gregory's seven is supported not only by the above-mentioned historical argument but also by the two proofs of the superiority of the number eight. First he remarks that although six is claimed to be a perfect number and seven the number of the planets, the number eight adds the sphere of the fixed stars, following Cicero's description in the *Dream of Scipio*.[35] Further, he adds, we can argue from mathematical bodies. Beginning with a point, we add another to determine a line, and another line to determine a plane. By duplicating this in turn, we get a solid body, a cube, which contains eight angles.[36] Or as Macrobius says, by the third multiple of the first number (two) we arrive at eight, the plenitude or the first solid.[37]

Similar tenets of Pythagorean mathematics provide the basis for other terms, definitions, and categories. To demonstrate that the terms *perfect* and *imperfect* in rhythmic notation (divisions into groups of three and of two notes, respectively) are appropriate, he resorts to Pythagorean claims about the nature and symbolism of the first numbers: three is a perfect number as the sum of all preceding numbers, whereas two is a step removed from unity in perfection.[38]

At such isolated points he appears slightly more concerned than Burtius about relating the Boethian tradition to the Guidonian (or as he would have it, Gregorian), especially regarding musical notation. In addition to the examples seen above, he uses the discussion from Boethius 1.1–2 on sound and types of sound to introduce his section on musical notation.[39] The human voice, he states, is a type of sound

33. Ramos 1.1.5; Wolf, p. 14: "Multis etiam aliis modis posset salvari; ego equidem illum salvum esse non dubito, quoniam Christus in cruce pro his oravit, qui nesciunt, quid faciunt."
34. See, for example, Ramos 1.1.7, 1.2.7; Wolf, pp. 19, 44–45.
35. Ramos 1.1.8; Wolf, p. 22.
36. Ramos 1.1.8; Wolf, p. 23.
37. Ramos 1.1.8; Wolf, p. 24.
38. Ramos 3.1.1; Wolf, pp. 80–81.
39. Ramos 1.2.1; Wolf, pp. 25–26.

that, like all sound, may be continuous (as in speaking, where pitch changes constantly) or discrete, as in singing, where each change in pitch is distinct. Although the voice itself cannot be depicted as a line or a plane because it radiates outward like a sphere from its source, he continues, the discrete pitches of a voice can be denoted as a series of points on a plane, assisted by a system of lines to indicate degree of difference in highness or lowness. Thus Ramos is consistently concerned to show that musical notation is not arbitrary but a logical extension of musical mathematics.

He is less successful at integrating the more substantial issues of the two traditions. For example, he discusses *musica humana* and *mundana* very much as Burtius does, relating each of the eight church modes to an emotional effect in the listener.[40] From here he continues by relating *mundana* and *instrumentalis* through the association of planets not only with strings but also with modes, emotional effects, and the muses, based on Macrobius, Cicero, and Martianus Capella.[41] He also follows Boethius (1.1) in assigning ethnic names to the modes: "Boethius gives these distinct modes their own name. Whence he says: the race which takes delight in it gives its name to it; in this way the Dorian mode was named, which the Dorians enjoyed, made of the first species of diapente and the first species of intense diatessaron above the diapente."[42] Elsewhere he implies that the rules for counterpoint will produce such effects as a logical consequence of these principles:

By this means, harmony generates in the souls of listeners a certain natural charm which cannot be explained in words. Truly our singers hardly consider this, but believe that those things which please their imagination or fancy happen by accident. And so it is that the common person is not moved spontaneously to music, or to be more precise, to the new harmony, as was the case in antiquity. We will discuss this most clearly in the second book. But we have said that we will draw those singers away from such erroneous opinions and lead the way back to true musical knowledge.[43]

40. Ramos 1.3.3; Wolf, pp. 56–57.
41. Ramos 1.3.3; Wolf, pp. 57–60.
42. Ramos 1.3.2; Wolf, p. 54: "Apellat enim Boetius hos modos nomine proprio distinctos. Unde dicit ipse: quo enim unaquaeque gens gaudet, eodem nomine nuncupatus est, ut dorius, quia Dorici eo gaudebant, sic appellatus est et ex prima specie diapente et prima specie diatessaron intensa supra diapente constat."
43. Ramos 2.1.2; Wolf, p. 71: "Hoc enim modo harmonia generat in animos audientium quandam insitam dulcedinem, quae non potest explicari sermone. Verum nostri cantores haec minime considerant, sed illud tantum, quod imaginationi seu fantasiae suae placet, secundum accidentem dispositionem credunt

Apparently Ramos and his "true musical knowledge" will return the "natural charm" and appeal to music that was common among the ancients. Since he never completed his second book we cannot know how or whether he planned to detail such a program to relate modern counterpoint and Boethian theory. But we can see in this work many of the same problems that plagued Burtius in revising or reforming Boethian practice.

Most obvious is the problem of tuning and the fourth. Where Burtius was able to avoid the issue, Ramos makes his new tuning system the centerpiece of his treatise, and it treats the fourth as dissonant. Use of this system would conflict directly with Boethian or any other Pythagorean theories of the effects of music on the soul, and this is one of the major charges directed against him by his critics. Some later scholars will indeed confront this issue and attempt to accommodate the third into the system. Ramos, however, is left with the same problem of interpretation that confronted Burtius; because of this conflict he can neither develop a rigorous, systematic theory nor attempt a thorough understanding of Boethius.

Ramos's work received immediate criticism from one John Hothby (Johannes Octobus, d. 1487), an English Carmelite resident at Lucca since 1467. He had received several passing references in the *Musica practica,* and he responded to its publication with three short refutations of various asspects of the work. In and of themselves, the little works are not noteworthy. They introduce no new sources, nor do they offer new interpretations of the old ones. Yet they give us a chance to observe not only the type of disagreements but also the forms of argument used against Ramos by his contemporaries.

The *Epistola* (intended recipient unknown), written in Italian, is the simplest of the three. Here Hothby takes up Ramos's abandonment of the hexachord system. He measures Ramos against two standards: current practice and Boethius's treatise. Ramos's eight-syllable system falls to the first standard;[44] his tuning system with its imperfect fourths, tones, and semitones succumbs to the second. Of the two innovations, the matter of tuning receives most of Hothby's attention. He is concerned to point out throughout the *Epistola* that a "simpli-

---

omnibus advenire. Et inde est, quod vulgus ad musicam vel, ut verius loquar, ad harmoniam novam non ita sponte convertitur, sicut solebant antiquitus. Verum de his rationibus in secundo libro evidentissime dicemus. Haec autem diximus, ut quosdam cantores ab opinionibus erroneis abstraheremus et ad veram musices agnitionem reduceremus."

44. Johannes Octobus, "Epistola," in *Octobi: Tres tractatuli,* p. 81.

fication" of Boethius cannot be the same as Boethius and that, further, Guido's methods have stood the test of time.

Hothby uses similar types of arguments in his *Dialogus,* the second attack on Ramos. He begins by retelling the story of Pythagoras and the hammers; then he relates his complaints about Ramos's tuning and the hexachords back to Boethius, Pythagoras, and mathematical proportion.[45] The remainder of the work discusses problems in notation; he attempts to establish correct practice by naming numerous contemporary composers and demonstrating their agreement with one another. Although Hothby's attempt to set a standard based on the actual habits of contemporary composers, rather than on theory, is itself interesting, it does not refute Ramos's claim that contemporary composers are in error.

The *Excitatio* is the most scholarly of the three. Here Hothby quotes passages from Ramos's work (both from the *Practica musica* and from other writings that are otherwise lost) and refutes the arguments they contain. He follows the same type of argumentation as in the other works but is clearer and significantly more detailed in this set of disputations.

After repeating his usual complaints about Ramos's tuning system, Hothby develops a more interesting attack on his solmization system. Ramos had discussed a major drawback, as he saw it, of Guido's system: its frequent mutations to allow for accidental semitones caused numerous "qualitative" changes of pitch (that is, shifts between hard, natural, and soft) when differences in pitch should properly be considered "quantitative," as a ratio. Thus confusion arose because notes classified as equal in "quantity" might actually differ in pitch. Ramos complains, "Difference in music is constituted in arsis and thesis and not in the magnitude, strength, or weakness of a voice. Since according to Guido three properties of voice are given to differ among themselves, it is necessary to distinguish among equal voices."[46] Ramos then gives some examples of the problems involved and mentions Hothby among others who try to defend Guido even in such absurd cases.

While it is not surprising that Hothby would have taken offense at the remark, his response is more complex than might be expected: he

45. Octobus, "Dialogus Johannis Octobi Anglici in arte musica," in: ibid. pp. 61–71.

46. Ramos 1.2.6; Wolf, pp. 40–41: "Est enim differentia musicae in quantitate arsis vel thesis constituta, non autem in magnitudine sive fortitudine aut vocis debilitate collata. Cum enim in arte Guidonis tres vocum proprietates inter se differentes ponantur, necesse est, inter voces aequales differentiam ponat."

attacks Ramos over his use of the terms *quantitative* and *qualitative*. Hothby then goes on to develop an interesting argument about quantity, quality, and sound. Although it is barely relevant to Ramos and involves some idiosyncratic readings of Boethius, it is worth developing here as an early instance of debate on the subject, and one to which later writers will refer. Its importance, when developed by these later writers, will lie in Hothby's implication that sound can be examined and analyzed in more ways than the traditions of Boethius or Pythagoras had ever accounted for.

After quoting the above passage and much of the rest of Ramos's chapter, Hothby begins by clarifying the definitions (mainly literary, not musical) of *arsis* and *thesis* according to Isidore. This leads him to the conclusion that such distinctions are indeed qualitative: "Thesis, then, is accepted by grammarians as a point of punctuation, as are the comma, colon, and period. Next, an intension of consonances or dissonances is called arsis, and a remission, thesis. Finally, arsis is taken as 'higher,' thesis as 'lower.' Thus according to all these things, arsis as well as thesis are shown to be qualities, whether perceived by a discrete quantity or as continuous, as they are examples of the same qualities in any subject."[47] An object's position or its elevation, he continues, are certainly qualities. He adds an analogy: just as the quality of bread depends upon the flour, so also consonance or dissonance must depend upon the material of which the voice is made, since they are affects of the voice.

Although he will return to arguments about the relationship between sound and the sounding body, he interrupts them in order to refer to Boethius, who had based his discussion on the perception of sound:

> So when a musician thinks about modes he certainly considers their qualities and the qualities of the voices by which they are constituted, that is their properties. Boethius teaches in 5.4, following Aristoxenus's authority, that the differences between higher and lower sounds consist in quality. Again, in the second chapter of the same book: Harmonic virtue is the faculty that evaluates the difference between high and low sounds ac-

47. Octobus, "Excitatio quaedam musicae artis per refutationem," in *Octobi: Tres tractatuli*, pp. 28–29: "Accipitur etiam thesis a grammaticis pro ipsa punctorum positura, cuiusmodi sunt coma, colon et periodus. Dicitur praeterea consonantiarum sive dissonantiarum intensio arsis, et secundum earum remissionem sic thesis quoque. Postremo, arsis pro acuto, thesis vero pro gravi sumitur. Secundum autem horum omnium rationem tam arsis quam thesis qualitates esse ostenduntur, quamvis per quantitatem modo discretam, modo continuam discernantur, ut sunt earundem qualitatum in aliquo subiecto subiecta."

cording to sense and reason. It is almost as if sense and reason are the tools of the harmonic faculty; for as individual arts have tools by which they may give shape to things partly confused, as an adze [the analogy is from Boethius], so indeed harmonic virtue's judgement has two parts: one of them which by sense comprehends the difference between voices or objects, the other by which it considers the true quantity and measure of the same differences.[48]

Thus, insofar as sense perception plays a part in the "musical faculty," the latter depends upon quality. In this passage, based as it is on a chapter of Boethius that is in turn based on Ptolemy, Hothby is arguing for the integration of quality and quantity in the study of music, not the superiority of one over the other.

Finally, he returns to the nature of the sounding body. Boethius, he notes, knew that change of pitch came not only from changes in ratio but also from changes in the body's quality, such as the tension of a string or its thickness. If a string is stretched, it vibrates faster and produces a higher sound; if loosened, it slows and sounds lower. It follows that this string is equivalent to two strings of different lengths, producing the same pitches as the first string had done first in its tense state, then loosened. He continues:

Therefore, who would deny for this reason that musical differences be set in magnitude? And from its contrary, in precision of smallness and brevity? Boethius wrote in the same volume [5], Chapter 13: He [Aristoxenus] thought, very imprudently, that he could distinguish between sounds to which he fixed neither magnitude nor measure. You affirm this, not knowing what you are saying, in Chapter 6: "There are indeed strings different in both length and thickness, as in the cythara, lyre, polichord, clavichord, clavicembalo, psaltery, and many other instruments [Wolf, p. 15]." For which reason, it should be said that musical difference is not seen only in magnitude even if it is the first of the differences, its contrary being thinness; that is, first arose the principle and the beginnings of differences, from which two causes are derived. One lies in experience or practice, in which you say all your work is

48. Octobus, p. 30: "Quare oportet si musicus modos consideret etiam earum qualitates confiteatur et qualitates vocum, id est, proprietates, a quibus ipsi constituuntur, sic enim Boetius, libro quinto, capite quarto, auctoritate Aristoxeni docet: Sonorum differentias secundum gravem atque acutem in qualitate consistere. Item, capite secundo eiusdem libri: Vis armonica est facultas differentias acutorum et gravium sonorum sensu ac ratione perpendens. Sensus vero ac ratio quasi quaedam facultas armonicae instrumenta sunt, nam ut singulae artes habent instrumenta quaedam quibus partim confuse aliquid informent, ut asciculum ita etiam harmonica vis habet duas iudicii partes, unam quidem huiusmodi per quam sensus comprehendit subiectorum differentias vocum, alia vero per quam ipsarum differentiarum integrum modum mensuramque consideret."

closely based, since its goal is action. The other pertains to study and reason, as Boethius (the author I follow) reminds us of Pythagoras in 1.2 [really 1.11], saying: thus led, he began to examine the length and thickness of strings. And so he discovered the rule through which magnitudes of strings and sounds are measured.[49]

This argument is not entirely successful but can be clarified by a brief examination of Boethius. In 1.3, Boethius gives a brief introduction to sound: it is produced by repeated motion that is perceived as a single sound because of the speed of vibration. Changes in tension affect the speed of vibration and hence the pitch. In the early chapters of Book 5, Boethius first discusses the "harmonic virtue," which relies on both sense and reason to determine the differences between notes. Boethius makes it clear that he favors Ptolemy, on whose work this book is based, as a middle ground between Aristoxenus and the Pythagoreans on the relationship between sense and reason; after a few examples he returns to an exposition of Ptolemy's *Harmonics* as far as the latter text survives.

On the basis of these passages, Hothby wishes to argue that some distinctions in pitch are due to quantity but others to qualities. "Quantitative" differences are those dependent upon proportion, as seen in strings of equal thickness and tension but differing in measured length. "Qualitative" differences are those resulting from changes in string thickness, tension, or material, which can be considered qualities of the body. These are not known by means of quantity.

All this, of course, is entirely beside the point of Ramos's argument. He had intended his own comments simply to introduce one more reason why Guido's system was unworkable; he had not planned to

49. Octobus, pp. 32–33: "Quis igitur hac ratione musicae differentiae in magnitudine positam esse denegaret? Et ex eius contrario tenuitatis et brevitatis in subtilitate? Scribit idem Boetius auctor eodem volumine, capitulo tertio decimo: Collocet nimis imiprovide, qui differentiam se scire arbitretur, earum vocum quarum nullam magnitudinem mensuramve constituat. Quod tu quoque quod dicis non respiciens affirmas, capitulo sexto: 'Sunt etiam cordae diversae et in longitudine et in grossitie, ut in cithara et lyra, policordo, clavicordo, clavicembalo, psalterio et in aliis pluribus instrumentis.' Qua ratione non solum magnitudo musicae differentia dicenda est, si omnium differentiarum utique prima, cum ex ea eiusque contrario tenuitate, videlicet, prima orta fuit eius probatio et differentiarum principia, ex quibus duae sumantur rationes, una ad experientiam spectans sive praxim, in quibus totum opus fere tuum versari dicis, cum eius utique finis sit actio. Altera vero ad inspectionem rationemque pertinens, sic enim Boetius, quem auctorem praecipue sequor, libro primo, capitulo secundo, meminit de Pythagora loquens: Hinc etiam ductus longitudinem crassitudinemque cordarum ut examinaret aggressus est. Itaque invenit regulam per quam magnitudines cordarum sonumque metiuntur."

discuss in detail the nature of pitch. Hothby surely is tendentiously misreading Ramos here; and even if his arguments hold, they do not refute Ramos's central thesis. His arguments look to be more bluster than substance.

But in his attempt to attack Ramos at all costs, Hothby exposes a part of Boethian theory that will become increasingly important in the debates of the following century: the nature of quantity and the kinds of physical behavior that can be studied by quantitative means. Although Hothby is not entirely consistent, he has presented some important points based on Boethius and clarified them with recourse to Aristotle. "Quantity" is a matter of mathematics and not of physics. When we speak of "proportion" in instrumental music, we refer to those parts of physical objects (strings of equal thickness, material, and tension) that stand in mathematical relation to one another. Other features about the body such as color, tension, or thickness are qualities of that body. They may or may not cause a change in pitch but in any case do not participate in those mathematical proportions that comprise the study of music.

Hothby wants to retain these qualitative factors as part of musical practice. Unfortunately, he fails to articulate just what role they should play or how they should relate to the study of quantity. Later writers will return to these issues as they attempt to deal more systematically with the written sources as well as the behavior of sounding bodies. Hothby may not be entirely successful in his attack or consistent in his presentation; still, he is one of the first scholars to introduce these very important questions into scholarly discourse.

The work of Johannes Tinctoris, also a foreigner working in Italy, occupies another endpoint in the range of musical thought in the 1470s and 1480s. His numerous extant works are oriented more toward musical practice than toward theories of consonance or number. At several points he reveals that this emphasis is not just due to a lack of interest or training in the scholarly tradition; rather, he wishes to reject the general framework of Boethian theory in favor of an Aristotelian approach based on the *Politics*. Many of his specific injunctions are reminiscent of Ramos (such as the use of the fourth) but are supported by different reasoning.

Tinctoris was born near Nivelles and matriculated in 1463 at the University of Orleans,[50] where he apparently studied law as well as

50. For biographical information on Tinctoris, see Heinrich Hueschen, "Tinctoris, Johannes," *New Grove*.

mathematics; he describes himself in his treatises several times as a lawyer ("in legibus licentiatus")[51] or among those who practice both law and mathematics ("inter eos qui iura scientiasque mathematicas profitentur").[52] He was hired by Ferdinand I of Naples about 1472 as tutor for his daughter Beatrice and apparently remained in Ferdinand's service throughout the 1470s, probably for the rest of the century. His writings seem to date mainly from the 1470s, with the exception of his *Liber de inventione et usu musicae*, composed sometime during the 1480s; most of them circulated only in manuscript.

Although one cannot date his individual works with complete certainty, Tinctoris seems to have maintained fairly consistent opinions about the nature of music. Both an early and a late work, the *Terminorum musicae diffinitorium* and the *Complexus effectus musices* are based on the *laus musice*, combining Christian and classical sources to list and discuss briefly the benefits of music. Similarly, in both his first work (the *Terminorum*) and his last, the *De inventione*, he abandons the Boethian threefold distinction of music (*mundana, humana*, and *instrumentalis*) for that of Isidore: harmonics, organics, and rhythmics.[53] He acknowledges this as a departure from Boethius in a third treatise, *De arte contrapuncti*. In its introduction he digresses briefly in order to explain why he rejects Boethius's arguments about *musica mundana*:

> Before I explain this, I cannot pass over in silence the many philosophers such as Plato, Pythagoras, and their successors, Cicero, Macrobius, Boethius, and our own Isidore, who believe that the spheres of the stars revolve under the rules of harmonic modulation, that is, by the concord of different consonances. But although, as Boethius says, some assert that Saturn is moved with the deepest sound and, taking the remaining planets in proper order, the moon with the highest, while others, however, conversely attribute the deepest sound to the moon and the highest to the stars in their movement. I adhere to neither position. On the contrary, I unshakeably agree with Aristotle and his commentator, together with our more recent philosophers, who most clearly prove that there is neither real nor potential sound in the heavens. For this reason I can never be persuaded that musical consonances, which cannot be produced without sound, are made by the motion of heavenly bodies.[54]

51. Johannes Tinctoris, *Complexus effectuum musices*, in Tinctoris, *Opera theoretica*, ed. Albert Seay (N.p.: American Institute of Musicology, 1975) 1:165.
52. Johannes Tinctoris, *Liber de natura et proprietate tonorum*, in Tinctoris, *Opera theoretica* 1:65.
53. Isidore, *Etymologia* 3.18.
54. Johannes Tinctoris, *The Art of Counterpoint*, ed., trans. Albert Seay (N.p.: American Institute of Musicology, 1961), p. 13.

There are two types of argument here. The first dismisses ancient authority as support for celestial music, by revealing the disagreements to be found among the ancients. Those ancients who did believe in the music of the spheres, he states, disagreed fundamentally among themselves about the pitches produced by any given body, while Aristotle denied that such music exists at all. The second dismisses the possibility of the planets' actually producing sound; without a physical sound, Tinctoris will not accept that there is music. This latter argument marks a distinct break with Pythagorean theory. For Pythagoreans, the presence of the ratios is sufficient to admit the phenomenon to musical analysis. Physical sound would proceed from the higher principles of musical forms. By refusing to allow into discussion anything but the physical sounds themselves, Tinctoris rejects this entire philosophical position.

Yet Tinctoris does not dwell on these issues. He moves on to discuss musical compositions themselves, the focus of his interest. The musical compositions by the learned ancients, he continues, however great they may have been, have not survived. The "old" songs that he has seen are inept and ugly. Only in the last forty years has musical knowledge flourished, with composers on whom he himself has relied as Virgil relied on Homer. This brief historical summary of music composition employs a typical Renaissance historical narrative: ancient achievement, followed by decline, and then a recent renewal. In this case, however, he notes that one element is missing from the usual description of rebirth: the ancient compositions the moderns might use as models.

Tinctoris leaves this historical sense in a fairly rudimentary and unexamined state. Yet it still gives him rather more critical distance from the ancient theorists than most of his contemporaries display. When discussing the consonances, for example, he is able to account for Boethius's omission of thirds and sixths by claiming that Boethius had no knowledge of them.[55] He offers no reasons for this ignorance but clearly is willing to admit not only that musical truths might change over time but also that discoveries might be made that would improve upon ancient knowledge. Tinctoris brings all these ideas to bear in his brief discussion of the modes (or tones) in *De natura tonorum*. First he establishes that, contrary to common assumptions, the church modes are not the same as the Boethian ones, since the two types of modes are formed differently.[56] Then he offers the Boethian

55. Ibid., p. 19.
56. Tinctoris, *Liber de natura*, p. 67.

argument about the naming of the modes after the races that "take delight in them" (Boethius 1.1). Tinctoris notes that Aristotle uses these same names for modes, but he decides on the basis of musical experience that Aristotle has different modes in mind:

> Additionally, it is not useless to know that Aristotle has spoken extensively and elegantly in his *Politics*, of four melodies, that is Mixolydian, Lydian, Phrygian, and Dorian [*Politics*, 8, passim]. He distinguishes these melodies, not from the types of diapason, but from their individual qualities, for he calls the Mixolydian plaintive, the Lydian cheerful, the Phrygian stern and the Dorian neutral. These melodies of the Boethian tones understandably can be named with equal reason by words of the races delighting in them. These former [the Aristotelian tones] are completely different from the latter. Since these latter tones are distinguished according to their types of diapason, and since one type cannot be many, it is impossible for one and the same type of diapason to include many tones. In any one and the same type of diapason any of the Aristotelian melodies can be constructed. To be sure, it will be possible for a song in one and the same tone to be plaintive and cheerful and stern and neutral, not only in regard to composers and singers, but instruments and sound-makers as well. For what person skilled in this art does not know how to compose, to sing and to perform some [melodies] plaintively, others cheerfully, some sternly and others neutrally, although their composition, singing, and performance are carried out in the same tone?[57]

It would seem here that Tinctoris is on his way toward developing a genuinely new Aristotelian theory of modes and effects. He clearly rejects the idea that a given pattern of pitches ("mode" in the Boethian sense) will induce a particular mood, claiming that the emotional power of music lies in other elements controlled by the skill of the composer or performer. After this passage, however, he immediately returns to a much more Pythagorean statement about mode and human personality and emotion: "Certain of these particular harmonies agree, are fitting, and are useful for various ages and customs. There is not the same delight or a similar judgment to all people. A cheerful soul is delighted by cheerful harmonies, and conversely, stern ones are accepted by a stern soul. This, Augustine is seen to believe in a book of his *Confessions,* saying: 'All the affections of our spirit in their diversity have their own modes in the voice and song, by whose secret association they are aroused.' "[58] This passage modifies

57. Johannes Tinctoris, *Concerning the Nature and Propriety of Tones,* ed., trans. Albert Seay (Colorado Springs: Colorado College Music Press, 1976), p. 4.
58. Tinctoris, *Concerning the Nature,* pp. 4–5.

the usual Boethian statements about music's effects on the soul, by emphasizing that the form of the individual soul is a product of various factors; this variety of form makes for a variety of effects of music on human souls. Nonetheless, the basic position of the passage comes out of the Pythagorean tradition rather than anything Aristotelian. Further, at various points in many treatises, Tinctoris makes it clear that he intends to follow Boethius, and he does so.[59]

In sum, then, it appears that Tinctoris was never truly interested in working out a systematic or consistent replacement for Boethian theories of the source of musical order. Given that he viewed music as an Aristotelian "cultured leisure," this is perhaps not surprising; Aristotelian leisure, however cultured, lacks a status sufficiently elevated to require the serious analysis undertaken for the sciences. Further, Aristotle wrote no music treatise himself. Thus, however appealing one may find his general discussions and scattered remarks, they cannot replace Boethius's treatise as a technical base for the subject; nor does Tinctoris's use of them appear to have had direct influence on later writers.

Further, while historical sense is more prominent in Tinctoris's argumentation than in that of his contemporaries, he does not develop it sufficiently for it to achieve a genuine explanatory value that can substitute for Pythagorean theory. He can refer to the previous generation of composers as playing Homer to his Virgil, but he has no way to explain how these figures came by their own knowledge. Yet taken together, Tinctoris's works do represent an innovative use of available sources to understand and interpret ancient and modern music. He attempts to offer an alternative to the standard Boethian grounding of the field; this alternative, based on the "humanistic" Aristotle of the *Politics* and *Poetics,* will eventually offer scholars a genuinely new approach to the subject.

Franchino Gaffurio

Franchino Gaffurio (1451–1522) and his work exemplify the changes in musical scholarship at the end of the fifteenth century; in turn, they are a cause of further change. Gaffurio's first writings were largely compendiums of earlier treatises. His later ones combined traditional organization with new analyses inspired by the new translations of Greek sources, many of which he commissioned. These later

59. See, for example, *Art of Counterpoint,* pp. 39, 47–48, 87–88.

treatises became the standard textbooks on music for most of the six-teenth century.[60] The translations were added to the canon of ancient musical scholarship, and the issues they raised were debated through-out the next century. Gaffurio's friends and colleagues included not only music theorists and composers but also mathematicians such as Luca Pacioli (who wrote extensively on proportion) and Fazio Car-dano (father of Girolamo; see Chap. 4), humanists, and poets, several of whom composed poems for inclusion in his treatises.

Born in Lodi, the son of a soldier and a minor noblewoman, Gaf-furio was ordained a priest in 1474.[61] He then moved to Mantua, where his father was employed by the Gonzaga; there he continued his musical studies. After lecturing in Verona he moved to Genoa, working for the doge Prospero Adorno, with whom he fled to Naples after a revolt. There he became friends with Tinctoris. He returned north, working at Lodi and Bergamo until 1484, when he became maestro di cappella at Milan's cathedral. There he remained until his death, lecturing at the gymnasium founded by Ludovico Sforza in 1492. He was named a professor of music at the University of Pavia between 1494 and 1499. He wrote both musical compositions and treatises on musical theory and practice; several early manuscript treatises have not survived.

Gaffurio's first treatise was probably the *Extractus parvus musice*, written either while he was still at Lodi or shortly after his arrival at Mantua, about 1474.[62] Its title is accurate; the work is a series of ex-tracts, either as quotations or as paraphrases, from the works of ear-lier music theorists. It marks a point of transition from earlier scholarship to Gaffurio's own mature contributions to the field.

60. Irwin Young, "Franchinus Gafurius, Renaissance Theorist and Composer (1451–1522)" (Ph.D. diss., University of Southern California, 1954), pp. 25–26, 35. The works of these translators and Gaffurio's use of them in his work have received detailed study by Claude V. Palisca, *Humanism in Italian Renaissance Musical Thought* (New Haven: Yale University Press, 1985); on the translators and the rediscovery of ancient sources, pp. 23–50, 111–32; on Gaffurio, pp. 166–78, 191–225.

61. For biographical information on Gaffurio, see Alessandro Caretta, Luigi Cremascoli, and Luigi Salamina, *Franchino Gaffurio* (Lodi: Archivio Storico Logidiano, 1951); see also Clement A. Miller, "Gaffurius," *New Grove*. The best contemporary source is the brief biography by Pantaleon Meleguli of Lodi, appended to Gaffurio's *De harmonia musicorum instrumentorum opus* (Milan: Pontano, 1518). It is available in Caretta, Cremascoli, and Salamina, *Franchino Gaffurio*, pp. 20–25, and in English in the translation by Clement A. Miller, *Franchini Gaffurii De harmonia musicorum instrumentorum opus* (N.p.: American Institute of Musicology, 1977), pp. 212–14.

62. *Franchini Gaffurii Extractus parvus musice*, ed. F. Alberto Gallo (Bologna: Forni, 1969), pp. 7–9.

About half the work comes from the writings of Ugolino of Orvieto;[63] the rest is taken from Marchetto of Padua,[64] Philippe de Vitry,[65] and several other treatises of the same era, some anonymous.[66]

The outline of the *Extractus* resembles the order of topics Burtius will use more than a decade later. Gaffurio divides the treatise into twelve books. The first five are based almost entirely on Ugolino; they treat music as a field of learning, the Greek string names, the gamut and Guidonian hand, and the mutations of the hexachords. Books 6 and 7 discuss pitch and the consonances; they are based not only on Ugolino but also on Marchetto of Padua and Jehan de Muris. Book 8 covers plainchant, after Marchetto. In Books 9 and 10 he discusses counterpoint and discant, based on Muris and Anonymous 2 and 3. He concludes with rhythmic notation in Books 11 and 12, taken from Anonymous 3 and 4, Ugolino, and Marchetto.

Despite its formal similarity to Burtius's *Opusculum*, the *Extractus* differs greatly in its overall tone. While the *Opusculum* abounds in classical allusions and literary examples, Gaffurio's writing style in the *Extractus* can best be described as scholastic. Burtius lavishes attention on his *laus musice;* Gaffurio, on the other hand, works systematically from one logical proof to the next, establishing music as a speculative science and defining the elements in its study. He devotes all of Book 1 to this exercise, noting in Chapter 1 that "the common school of philosophers numbers music among the speculative sciences, as will be sufficiently shown in the following chapters."[67] The few classical references in this first book come straight from Ugolino, even a brief reference to the *Tusculan Disputations.* Not surprisingly, most of these classical references came from the "old" Aristotle or Boethius, though a few are drawn from Augustine's *De musica* or from Isidore. Even these disappear once he turns his attention to the practical discussions of counterpoint and notation.

63. Ugolinus Urbevetanus, *Declaratio musicae disciplinae,* ed. A. Seay (N.p: American Institute of Musicology, 1962).

64. *The Lucidarium of Marchettus of Padua,* ed., trans. Jan W. Herlinger (Chicago: University of Chicago Press, 1985).

65. Phillippi de Vitraiaco, *Ars nova,* ed. G. Reaney, A. Gilles, and J. Maillard (N.p: American Institute of Musicology, 1964).

66. Most of these have been edited in *CSM*; see 1:303–19; see also Anonymous 3, *Compendiolum artis veteris ac novae,* in *CSM* 3:370–75; Anonymous 4, *Compendium artis mensurabilis tam veteris quam novae,* in *CSM* 3:376–79; and Philippus de Caserta, *Tractatus de diversis figuris,* in *CSM* 3:118–24. Gallo's edition of the *Extractus* indicates the use of these sources as they appear throughout the work.

67. *Gaffurii Extractus,* p. 17: "Comunis schola philosophorum eam musicam inter speculativas scientias connumerat, quod satis patebit in capitulis sequentibus."

It might therefore be easy to conclude that Gaffurio's intellectual development moved linearly from this early scholastic analysis imitating earlier scholars to the more original and humanistic understanding in his later works. Gaffurio's exordium to the *Extractus* demonstrates, however, that humanistic training and interests date even from this early period. This introduction, dedicated to his fellow musician Philippus Trexenus of Lodi, cleric and professor of music, is very different from the treatise itself. In addition to "traditional" authorities such as Isidore and Rabanus Maurus, Gaffurio quotes Virgil's *Georgics* and cites Lucan, Cicero, and Jerome as part of a brief but original *laus musice*. His flowery prose style here is far removed from the concise, dry, technical Latin of the treatise itself. This literary tone is balanced at the work's end by an epigram in hexameters, referring to Gaffurio and his comrades at Lodi. The body of the *Extractus* takes its style from the prose of the authors of the extracts; thus one cannot infer much from it about Gaffurio's own outlook.

Yet it does serve in several ways as a useful benchmark for the education of a musical scholar. The selection of authors studied and held up as examples, the topics they covered as perceived and chosen by Gaffurio, and the way those topics were organized can all be clearly seen. The contrast between the parts of the work reveals Gaffurio as a scholar willing and able to adopt distinct and different stylistic voices when approaching the same subject at the same time.

Gaffurio's best-known works are the three treatises published in Milan: the *Theorica musice* (1492), the *Practica musicae* (1496), and the *De harmonia musicorum instrumentorum opus* (1518). Numerous crossreferences among these texts suggest that he saw them as related works and developed them (at least in part) at the same time, despite their differing publication dates. Most of his other manuscript and published treatises are condensations, vernacular translations, or partial early drafts of these volumes. Of the three, the *Theorica* was probably begun first. His earliest published work, the *Theoricum opus* (Naples, 1480) is an early draft of part of the 1492 version.[68] It is not an especially original treatise in either draft, but by providing a detailed presentation of general music theory, it gives Gaffurio a clear starting point for his other works.

The *Theorica* consists of five books; though much of the content is based on Boethius, it does not follow him book by book. Book 1 is most like Boethius in subjects covered: a praise of music, its threefold division, the distinction between *musicus* and cantor, and the discovery

---

68. Irwin Young, "Franchinus Gafurius," p. 30.

of the consonances. Book 2 discusses the nature of sound and of number and the formation of consonances in general. In Book 3, Gaffurio covers quantity and proportion in more detail, and he uses Book 4 to discuss individual intervals such as the tone, diapente, and diapason. In the last book, he describes the formation of tetrachords and modes, the division of the monochord, and the species of intervals as they are used to form the various modes. The work resembles that of Boethius in many ways but has less emphasis on the study of proportion per se.

Gaffurio's introductory chapter in praise of music (1.1, comprising thirteen pages) serves both to set the body of the treatise in its proper context and to exemplify Gaffurio's approach to the written sources. He begins by discussing the origins of music (Fig. 1), acknowledging that different sources name different figures as the first musician:

> As is understood through extensive study and reading, according to the bards the discipline of music was held in very high honor in ancient times among the most learned men, as indeed in Josephus. And they say in the Holy Writ that Jubal of the house of Cain first established the study in the cythara and organ by measuring sounding hammers. Some consider that others first discovered it by various and diverse modes and instruments. Indeed, Heraclides Ponticus, whom Plato on sailing to Sicily made head of the Academy, recorded that Amphion, son of Jove and Antiope, taught by his father Jove, was the first author of song for the cythara and cytharists. Others gave the honor to Linus Euboeus of Chalcis, son of Apollinus and Terpsichore; or according to others, born of Amphimarus or Mercurius as father and Urania as mother, first discovered the lyre.[69]

Although Gaffurio's citations of sources are generally more precise than he is able to make them here, his overall use of the sources is similar throughout the work. He presents the arguments from each source on a given subject clearly and accurately and then discusses where sources differ from one another. He attempts to build from these pieces a reasonably coherent narrative of the discovery of

69. Gaffurio, *Theorica musice* (Milan: Castanum, 1492), 1.1, unpaged: "Diuturni studii lectione depraehendi musices disciplinam antiquis temporibus apud vates maximo doctissimorum honore complecti quippe quam Iosephus. ac sacre littere Iubalem de stirpe chaym cythara et organo primum instituisse ferunt ex numeraro maleorum sonitu exquisitam. Nonnulli tamen alios existimant variis atque diversis modis instrumentisque primitus claruisse. Heraclides nanque ponticus quem Plato in Siciliam navigans Academie praefecit Amphionem Iovis et Antiope filium cythare cytharisticique cantus primum auctorem a patre Iove instructum rettulit. Alii Linum euboeum ex chalcide insignem habuerunt Apolinis et Terpsicore filium vel secundum alios Amphimaro Mercurio ve patre uraniaque matre natus liram primus reperit."

Figure 1 The discovery of consonant proportion. From Franchino Gaffurio, *Theorica musice (Milan, 1492),* 1.8.

musical truths and then to discuss the contents of those truths. Some facts, as in this example of the "first musician" myths, he acknowledges are impossible to establish with certainty. In such cases, he presents the entire range of opinion without rendering a final judgment.

After a brief discussion of music's effects on animals, Gaffurio moves to its use in healing the sick and insane, its use in raising the spirits of soldiers before battle, and then its role in divine service. This allows him to list not only the association of tones with the planets but also their connections with the celestial hierarchy (taken from Giorgio Anselmi, ultimately from Pseudo-Dionysius). Further, by identifying the church modes with the Greek ones and by combining classical and biblical references, Gaffurio links both traditions in a more substantial way than the usual brief connections between *tonoi* and the church modes. His apparent assumption that the Byzantine scholar Manuel Bryennius was an ancient writer aids his attempt.[70]

Much of the remainder of the *laus musice* covers the expected subjects in the expected ways. Music's role in educating the young, especially with gymnastics, comes largely from the *Republic,* as does its importance for instilling love and concern for one's state. He notes that many writers have emphasized the importance of music to the fields of grammar and oratory, others to the rest of the quadrivium.

The bulk of the *Theorica* is less an original composition than a set of detailed expositions of the major points raised by Boethius. Other authorities serve mainly to corroborate this main source or to provide more detail, In Book 2.1, ("On the definition of music and on the accidental properties of sounds"), for example, Gaffurio has drawn the substance of the discussion from several chapters of Boethius Books 2, 4, and 5. After his Boethian definition of *music* as the numeric ratios between sounds, dependent on sense and reason, and a list of the usual etymologies of the term, he appends a brief reference to Bacchius: according to the latter, the elements consist in highness and lowness, that is, interval.[71] Boethius provides the substance, while Bacchius adds an interesting bit of additional information. Gaffurio's definition of motion, necessary for the production of sound, comes from Aristotle's *Physics* 5.[72] The detailed description of the motion of

70. Ibid.
71. Ibid., 2.1.
72. Ibid., 2.1: "Pulsus vero atque percussio nullo modo potest esse nisi precesserit motus: nam si cuncta fuerint immobilia non poterit alterum alteri concurrere ut unum impellatur ab altero: sed cunctis stantibus motuque carentibus nullum fieri necesse est sonum: quo circa quinto phisicorum motus dicitur transmutatio successiva que fit in tempore. Tempus nanque sequitur motum. nam quarto phisicorum Tempus est numerus motus." (Pulse and percussion cannot exist unless

sound waves through air (that is, that the air set in motion by the sounding body moves other air, which in turn strikes the ear) comes from Themistius's *De anima* as commented on by Ermolao Barbaro. Since this chapter is not modeled after any single passage of Boethius, Gaffurio might seem free to use these other sources in more structurally important ways if he chose. Yet he restricts them to this sort of passing reference, relying on Boethius for the main portion of the argument.

Such a pattern in earlier writers generally stemmed from problems of accessibility: these "other" writers had to remain mere names or brief references because the author had no access to their works and had simply gleaned the name and reference from a third source. There are some cases where this is clearly Gaffurio's situation. All references to Aristoxenus and Nicomachus, for example, can be found in Boethius or Bryennius, and no known translations of these Greek writers were available at this period. In contrast, references to Aristides Quintilianus, the "Anonymous Bellarmannianus," and Bacchius are apparently genuine but of recent vintage. Gaffurio is known to have commissioned these translations in Milan, and the first complete manuscript copies date from 1494, two years after the *Theorica* was published.[73] He must have had access to drafts of the translations in order to cite them here, but he certainly was not able to study them thoroughly. These references have the appearance of last-minute addenda; they corroborate the main text but do not provide the basis or principal evidence for the argument.

Gaffurio's *Practica musica* was apparently composed in several sections over a long period.[74] Its organization cannot therefore be ascribed with certainty to a single period or a single conceptual plan. Yet its final form dates from 1492 to 1496, so that at least some pas-

---

preceded by motion. For if all were immobile, they could not come together so that one would be struck by another, but by lacking all resting and motion, no sound would of necessity be made. In *Physics* 5, motion is called successive transposition in time. For time follows motion; as in *Physics* 4, time is mobile number.)

73. In addition to Palisca's discussion of these translations (*Humanism,* see n. 60 above), see F. Alberto Gallo, "Musici scriptores graeci," *Catalogus translationum et commentariorum: Medieval and Renaissance Translations and Commentaries,* ed. F. Edward Cranz and Paul Oskar Kristeller (Washington: Catholic University of America Press, 1976), 3:63–73.

74. Clement Miller, "Gaffurius's *Practica Musicae:* Origin and Contents," *Musica Disciplina* 22 (1968):105–28; see also Miller's introduction to Gaffurio, *Practica musicae,* trans. Miller (N.p: American Institute of Musicology, 1968), p. 10. Another early manuscript of Book 2 dates from 1482; the *Tractato vulgare del canto figurato* (Milan, 1492), published under the name of a student, Francesco Caza, is a vernacular condensation of Book 2 much nearer the final version. See Miller, "Gaffurius' *Practica musica,*" p. 108.

sages and the finished draft postdate the *Theorica*. It was an immensely popular treatise, issued in five editions and an Italian translation during Gaffurio's lifetime.

Given its piecemeal composition and its nonclassical subject matter, the work might be expected to demonstrate an approach to classical sources little different from the *Theorica*. Indeed, most of the important references throughout the work come from Marchetto of Padua, Giorgio Anselmi, Guido, and Tinctoris. The exceptions are found mainly in the introductions to each of the four books and in a few other passages. Apparently written last, these introductions serve to unify both the parts of the treatise and the classical tradition with the modern. Burtius had set similar tasks for himself a decade earlier but had accepted much more rudimentary solutions than those Gaffurio attempts. Of particular interest is Gaffurio's writing on rhythmics.

An example resembling the *Theorica* is seen in *Practica* 1.4; the subject matter is hexachord mutations. Gaffurio introduces the discussion with a set of references to numerous classical authors:

> Ecclesiastics attest to many mutations of sounds. According to Bacchius, mutation is an exchange of subjects or a transposition of something similar to a different place. Gregory says in his *Moralia* that to mutate is to go from one place to another and not to be stable in itself; for any one thing tends toward another to the degree that it is subject to the motion of its own mutability. Yet Martianus calls such a mutation a transition, which he explains as a "change of one sort of sound to another." Bryennius said that mutation is a change in the system of a subject and the character of a tone.[75]

The order in which the authorities appear here is determined solely by the narrative needs of the passage itself, without regard to chronology of authorship or to the philosophical differences among the writers. The references serve to show simply that "authorities agree" about the nature of modulation, in substance if not always in detail; Gaffurio implies that they would also agree about the matters discussed in the rest of the chapter (based on Marchetto of Padua).

75. Gaffurio, *Practica musicae* (Milan, 1496), 1.4, unpaged: "Multimodas insuper sonorum mutationes clerici protestantur. Est enim Mutatio apud Baccheum Alteratio subiectorum sue Alicuius similis in dissimilem locum transpositio. Hinc in moralibus Mutari Gregorius inquit est ex alio in aliud ire et in semetipsum stabilem non esse: unaquaeque enim res quasi tot passibus ad aliam tendit: quot mutabilitatis suae motibus subiacet. Verum huiusmodi mutationem Martianus transitum appellat: quem vocis variationem in alteram soni figuram interpretatur. Briennius autem mutationem dixit esse subiecti systematis ac vocis characteris alienationem."

Similar uses of ancient sources can be seen in 3.1 as well as briefer
references scattered throughout the work.

Genuine innovations appear, however, in his introductions to Books
2 and 4. Book 2 covers rhythmic notation, based primarily on
Anselmi and Jehan de Muris; this notation had developed during the
fourteenth and fifteenth centuries. It is based on mathematical proportion (especially duples and triples). In Book 4, Gaffurio examines
an application of the principles of mathematical proportion in the
notation of rhythm in polyphonic or contrapuntal composition. He
pushes these two related topics in opposite directions, one toward
mathematics and the other toward poetics. In this way, he expands
musica practica to touch on the broadest possible range of scholarship.

Practica 4.1, "Definition and Division of Proportion," begins with a
Euclidean definition of the term: "the relation of any two quantities
of the same kind to each other. It may be rational or irrational."[76] Rational and irrational are distinguished by the presence or absence of
a common measure between them; Gaffurio notes that such a distinction does not occur in arithmetic proportions, since all integers have
at least the number one in common. Musical proportions are linear,
he continues, creating sound through numerical ratios on a vibrating
string. None of this is especially new, though it is a clear summary of
these mathematical definitions. The originality lies in Gaffurio's extension of these rules, traditionally limited to discussions about proportions of pitch, to proportions in time: "Thus we propose a twofold
consideration of musical proportion: first, in the disposition of
sounds through consonant intervals (which is theory), and the other
refers to a temporal quantity of those same sounds by the numbers of
notation, which is an active or practical consideration."[77]

Although rhythmic notation had developed from the general
mathematical study of proportion, Gaffurio has finally established a
systematic association between these two subjects. He also gives the
study of rhythm and rhythmic notation two scholarly contexts; he
does not simply describe its rules as an arbitrary system of conventions. The first of these contexts is the Pythagorean tradition, previously discussed only in terms of pitch. The second is the world of

76. Ibid., 4.1: "Proportio apud Euclidem est duarum quantaecunque sint eiusdem
generis quantitatum certa alterius ad alteram habitudo. Verum Alia rationalis: Alia
irrationalis."
77. Ibid., 4.1: "Inde duplicem proponimus musicae proportionis effectum:
primum in sonorum dispositione per consona intervalla (quod theorici est) alterum
in ipsorum temporali quantitate sonorum per notularum numeros: qui activae seu
practicae ascribitur consyderationi."

contemporary mathematical scholarship. He cites Alberti and Marliani; only a little earlier he had mentioned Campano. Thus he argues that the rhythm of a musical piece is subject to the same laws, and bears nearly the same importance, as the proportions among the pitches involved. Gaffurio devotes the rest of the book to a detailed, original exposition of Boethian proportion as applied to rhythm.[78]

This book expanded the range of musical scholarship explicitly open to mathematical analysis; in Book 2, Gaffurio extends the study of musical rhythm to the literary realm of metrics. He begins by defining short and long syllables, citing Diomedes' grammar. These meters, he states, are the equivalent of musical rhythmic notation: "Musicians themselves in fact have assigned figures to the quantities of voices just like proper and fitting names, by which they compose every song in diverse measures of time (just as poetry in many meters)."[79] He then summarizes a few rules of poetics and returns to technical aspects of the study (2.2) by connecting the preceding discussion to Pythagoras:

Musicians have promulgated the measurement of sounds by the use and arrangement of various figures. This is twofold: one kind consists of a continuous quantity of sound which they reckon in time; this was assigned to each figure by these authorities as much by reason as by their judgment; for it was customary for Pythagoreans that reason in teaching was the equal of authority in learning. The other kind consists of distances or intervals of sounds arranged according to proportional dimensions by reason alone, as in musical instruments. Therefore, measurement of time is the quantitative arrangement of each figure (which must be considered in two ways).[80]

78. See *Practica Musicae*, ed., trans. Miller, pp. 124–28, for a discussion of these chapters. Don Harrán also discusses Gaffurio's treatment of the related issues of pitch and text in *Word-Tone Relations in Musical Thought from Antiquity to the Seventeenth Century* (Neuhausen-Stuttgart: Hänssler, 1986). Harrán's text follows this issue through the works of several other writers included in this book (such as Rossetti, Vicentino, Zarlino), focusing especially on the practical tradition.

79. Gaffurio, *Practica* 2.1: "Verum figuras quasdam veluti propria et congrua nomina: quibus concepta inde mensuratorum temporum diversitate omnem conficerent cantilenam (nec secus quam omne pluribus pedibus carmen) musici ipsi vocum quantitatibus ascripserunt."

80. Ibid., 2.2: "Sonorum mensuram diversis figuris pronunciatione et divisione musici promulgarunt: est enim duplex una quae in ipsius soni continuata quantitate consistit quam tempori ascribunt: hanc unicuique figurae ab ipsis auctoribus constat esse institutam: tum ratione: tum instituentis arbitrio: quod et ipsis Pythagoricis rationi ipsi docentis auctoritatem aeque ducentibus: mos fuit. Altera quae in sonorum intervallis distantiisve: secundum proportionabilem dimensionem sola ratione disponitur ut in musicis instrumentis. Est igitur mensura temporis dispositio quantitatis uniuscuiusque figurae (duobus quidem modis consyderanda)."

The inclusion of metrics as part of musical studies was not new with Gaffurio; it was known in the medieval tradition and occasionally referred to via Isidore. Gaffurio, however, has done more than simply mention this connection; he has also developed it, in both *musica practica* and *theorica*. He does so under the influence of two classical authors, Aristides Quintilianus and Augustine.

Augustine's *De musica* had been known but seldom used by medieval writers on music, since it deals almost exclusively with metrics. Through Aristides Quintilianus's treatise, Gaffurio is able to find a place for Augustine's work among classical authorities. In the process, he introduces the analytic tools of metrics and poetics to a field previously studied systematically only by means of mathematics. Still, the introduction is by no means thorough or complete. Gaffurio returns to his fourteenth- and fifteenth-century sources for the rest of the work, with only scattered references back to metrics as such. He also remains vague about the precise relationships among these parts of the subject: whether rhythmic notation developed out of metrics or only serves a similar function, and just how these rhythmic proportions would fit into Pythagorean theories of the effects of music on the soul. Despite these problems, the work marks the beginning of a genuine change in the field. Its wide circulation assured these innovations a large audience and helped establish a place for these "new" classical sources in the canon of musical authority.

Gaffurio's third major treatise, the *De harmonia musicorum instrumentorum opus,* was also composed and revised over a long time. The earliest known manuscript dates from 1500.[81] Gaffurio had already referred to the work in the *Practica,* so it was at least in the planning stages at the time the latter was prepared for publication. Nonetheless, the work's final version reflects a more mature consideration of the new classical sources; some had been accessible for two decades by the time it was published. Their influence can be seen in all aspects of the treatise, in contrast to Gaffurio's earlier works. Since the *De harmonia* was meant to complement, not replace, the earlier works, it should not be taken as the complete statement of Gaffurio's final thoughts on musical scholarship. Yet for later scholars, this work set the standard for discussion of the topic.

Gaffurio divides the treatise into four books. By defining its subject not as "music" in its entirety but more narrowly as "the harmony of musical instruments," he is free from the Boethian organizational

81. It underwent numerous changes, most notably the addition of references to modern sources, before its final publication. See Clement Miller's introduction to *Gafurii De harmonia*, pp. 11–15.

model and can order the work as he sees fit. Accordingly, Book 1 summarizes the work's major topics, which are then treated in detail in the subsequent books. In Book 1 he defines sound and its types, then moves immediately to a description of the intervals, the Greek fifteen-string system, the harmonic genera, and proportions. Book 2 discusses the harmonic genera; 3, proportionality; and 4, modes, their properties, and their place in Pythagorean theory.

Noteworthy in this plan is the focus on the pitch system; it, not theories of ratio and proportion (as in Boethius), forms the center of the work. Factors other than pitch—for example, rhythm— are excluded from this treatise; hence there is no place for developing the discussions of metrics begun in the *Practica*. The subjects treated and the sources used in their study are all directed toward strengthening and expanding the Pythagorean basis of the field. These sources serve to corroborate, not to challenge, the tenets of the discipline.

As Gaffurio introduces each new subject, he stops to discuss its history. These little histories follow a narrative structure that resembles the one used in his earlier works. An early era of discovery, usually beginning with Apollo or Mercury (whom he treats as historical figures and not as deities), progresses gradually to the great achievements of Pythagoras. Later figures, such as Plato and Aristotle, Ptolemy, and Aristides Quintilianus, then added discoveries of their own. The majority of the population in antiquity, however, had, according to Gaffurio, little understanding of music or its importance, and the discipline was always in danger of succumbing to ignorance.[82] Boethius, Gregory, and then Guido were lights in otherwise dark ages, until the dawn of modern scholarship. Gaffurio's narrative assumes, as had that of Burtius, that "music" is a single system of truths which can be understood well or badly by a given scholar or historical epoch, which may be either cultivated or neglected, and which is subject to progressive advancement by means of further research and discovery; the principles themselves, however, are not subject to historical change.

This historical sense is evident at an early point in the work, in Gaffurio's discussion of the Greek string system. The historical origin of each string (the strings were presumably added individually over time) is considered important to an understanding of its place and function in the pitch system; thus Gaffurio goes into each one at great length, including mention of its discoverer:

82. Gaffurio, *De harmonia* (Milan, 1518), 1.1, unpaged.

After the first tetrachord of Mercury, others added more strings, up to seven. Orpheus, instructed in this seven-stringed lyre by Mercury, added nothing to it himself. So this ancient seven-stringed lyre would have remained down to our own times, had not Pythagoras, learned in these matters as in others, come to its aid. For he added an eighth string for the special perfection of the octave system, in place of the conjunct tetrachords of the seven strings. For while others, as I mentioned in 1.5 of *Theorica,* superimposed more strings up to the fifteenth, Pythagoras himself arranged the science of harmony with skill.[83]

Pythagoras, then, becomes for Gaffurio the pivotal figure in the development of music as a science. Through him, musical study acquired a knowledge of its true fundamental principles, the mathematical study of proportion:

Pythagoras was the first to give rational consideration to the art of music, which could be esteemed as so useful and proper as it attained nobler employment. He linked the fifteen strings in quadruple proportion; any exceeding them he considered unsuitable and useless. But the musical faculty assigned to itself numbers from arithmetic and quantities from geometry. Their use is known to be proper for the conjoining of sounds; for one knows that struck strings sounding with different vibrations, when proportionally arranged, produce harmonic concord. Pythagoras himself altered the strings on a musical instrument very carefully by various extensions according to the division of the three genera, first according to the diatonic genus.[84]

83. Ibid., 1.4, fol. 5r–v: "Post primum illud Mercurii tetracordum nonnulli reliquas chordas ad eptachordum usque texuerunt: cuiusquidem septem chordarum lyrae edoctus ab ipso Mercurio Orpheus nullum studio se memorandum facinus apposuit: Inde antiqua illa septem chordarum lyra ni Pythagoras in ipsa (ut in reliquis) studiosus operam navasset ad nostra forte usque tempora pervenisset. Is enim octavam adiecit chordam ad specialem diapason systematis perfectionem tetrachorda in eptachordo invicem coniuncta disgregans. Verum cum nonnulli ut primo quinti theoricae memoravi reliquas ad quintam decimam usque superposuerint chordas: Pythagoras ipse harmonicam scientiam artificio utrinque disponens ac quousque cantus melodicus in acutius intendi."
84. Ibid. 1.5, fol. 7v: "Musicam artem quam tanto utilem et digniorem aestimari licet quanto pervenerit usui nobiliori Pythagoras primus rationis consyderatione notavit quindecim ipsis chordis quadrupla proportione connexam: quarum excessum in sonis importunum et infructuosum esse censebat. Verum quoniam Musica facultas proprium sibi delegit: ab Arythmetica numeros: a Geometris mutuari quantitates: quarum medio noscitur non abuti ad sonorum coaptationem: nanque chordarum intervallis proportionaliter dispositis sonoras chordas variis pulsibus percussas harmonicum concentum promere percepit. Pythagoras ipse chordas secundum trium generum distributionem accurratissime variis extensionibus permutavit. Ac primum quidem in sonoro instrumento ipsas ita secundum diatonicum genus."

Gaffurio returns to Pythagoras's accomplishments when he discusses the origins of the modes.

This discussion of Pythagoras's development of the lyre and its string and pitch systems exemplifies one narrative type about the discovery of ancient music. In this type the origin of each significant feature or practice can be identified with the career of a notable individual of antiquity. Pythagoras figures large in such narratives; more recent names like Gregory or Guido may also appear.

Boethius had invoked another type of story in discussing, albeit briefly, the origin of the modes (*De musica* 1.1). He states that the modes acquired the names of peoples according to the groups who found a given mode especially pleasing, as befitted the level of their character. Such a story tends to associate musical practice with ethnic or regional habits or customs rather than with the higher and more abstract realm of scientific truths.

Gaffurio wavers between these two types of explanation or narrative, as is especially apparent in his discussion of the modes, the subject of *De harmonia*'s fourth and last book. He begins in his usual manner, by citing several ancient authorities, and then shifts to the Boethian argument about the origin of modes:

Peter of Abano testifies that according to the thirtieth *Problem*, in the opinion of Aristotle the ancients used three modes: Dorian, Phrygian, and Lydian. Lucius Apuleius, who notes in *Florida* 1 that after the contest between Apollo and Marsyas the piper Antigenidas played a charming piece, describes five modes, asserting that the player is the regulator of all modes, whether you want a simple Aeolian, a varied Iastian, a plaintive Lydian, a bellicose Phrygian, or a religious Dorian. According to Martianus, five authentic and principal modes and ten borderline or collateral modes are known in the Aristoxenian tradition. Polymnestor and the Argive Sacadas assert that the three most ancient types were the Dorian, Phrygian, and Lydian. They took their names from those peoples who enjoyed their constant use.[85]

85. Ibid. 4.1, fol. 83r: "Modos apud veteres de mente Aristotelis trigesimi luciditate Problematis Petrus Apponensis tris tantum fuisse testatur Dorium. Phrygium: et Lydium. Lucius autem Apulaeus primo Floridorum post Apollonis et Marsiae luctam Antigenidam tibicinem voculae omnis melleum modulatorem commemorans; quinque modos describit: asserens ipsum omnimodis peritum modificatorem: seu tu velles aeolium simplicem: seu hyastium varium: seu lydium querulum. seu phrygium bellicosum: seu dorium religiosum. A Martiano vero quinque autentici et principales ac decem collimititii seu collaterales iuxta traditionem Aristoxeni: sunt annotati. Apud Polymnestrem tamen et Sacadam argivum tres ipsos Dorium: Phrygium: et Lydium genere fuisse antiquissimos constat: quos agentibus quas ipsorum modulationes assidua professione delectabant appellatos asseverant."

In the several chapters that follow, Gaffurio uses both types of narrative explanation. At one point he states that these modes (with their ethnic names) were indeed invented by individuals: "There are some who believe that this mode was created by Melampis; others ascribe the use of the Lydian harmony to Chorebus, as Dionysius (surnamed Iambus) reports. So indeed Pindar, in reciting his paeans on the wedding of Niobe, said that the Lydian mode was the first taught in musical studies."[86] Not far from this passage, however, he suggests a correspondence between the Dorian mode and other customs of the Dorians. Gaffurio's usual procedure for dealing with divergent sources seems to be partly at work here: he sets out a given point clearly as discussed by each author, notes where they differ from one another, and passes no judgment.

This lack of concern with trying to assess these sources or to reconcile them with one another implies that for Gaffurio the precise origin of the modes, or of many other elements of the subject, is not of primary importance. More significant to him is the simple fact of their discovery and the field's subsequent organization by the great philosophers. When he states that "different kinds of melodies . . . have been composed in an elegant way according to the affections and customs of men,"[87] it is unclear exactly how he thinks those differing customs are grounded. They might stem from some physiological reality of ethnic difference, resulting in a difference in the soul's response, as Tinctoris implies. Or perhaps they are simply contingent variations in human behavior, subject to historical change or even arbitrary variation. The latter explanation, closer to the claims of some later writers, would of course contradict the rest of Gaffurio's Pythagorean, Boethius-based theory. Perhaps he has simply included the information because it was present in his sources and has not thought through the implications and potential contradictions. Nonetheless, his inclusion of these descriptions of "mode as ethnic custom" will render them accessible to a later generation of scholars in search of explanations of musical practice based on cultural habit or custom, not on physics or mathematics.

Despite these flirtations with cultural explanations, the *De harmonia*'s general orientation is strongly Pythagorean, perhaps even more

86. Ibid. 4.2, fol. 84r: "Sunt tamen qui hunc modum a Melampide coeptum credant. Alii Chorebum perhibent lydii harmonia usum esse: ut Dionysius cognomento Iambus refert. Verum Pindarus in paenibus quum de Niobes nuptiis loquitur Lydii moduli harmoniam: primam fuisse in musicis doctrinam dicit."
87. Ibid. 1.1, fol. 2v: "Cum sensibus item et moribus hominum caeteras melodiae species (quod posterius dicendum est) non inconcinne componebant."

so than his earlier treatises. Most of his newly translated classical authorities had worked in this tradition themselves. They had provided
him not only with corroboration of Boethian arguments but also with
examples of Pythagorean principles at work in various aspects of music. This allows him to integrate more of the treatise itself along these
Platonic or Pythagorean lines, rather than simply inserting a passage
on music of the spheres or the soul as microcosm into the middle of
a given chapter on another subject, as earlier authors had done.

Frequently his use of these "new" authorities goes no further than
metaphor. In 1.1, Gaffurio takes from Aristides Quintilianus the connection between the tetrachords and the elements,[88] which he describes only as a simple sort of similarity:

> It should be said first that the four elements, from whose combination is
> produced all things of the lower regions, have the properties and oppos-
> ing powers of the first tetrachord, said to be invented by Mercury. Some
> contend the relation is this: hypate, the first string and lowest sound,
> conforms in quality to earth; parhypate, the second string, produces a
> weak and less low sound and is similar to water. They believed the third
> string, paranete, having a higher sound, matched air; nete, the last
> string, with the highest sound, fire.[89]

He also compares the three types of mean—arithmetic, geometric,
and harmonic—to three types of government. Here the metaphor is
more elaborate but scarcely more substantial:

> Pythagoras and Plato compared the three above-mentioned means to
> public magistrates; so they ascribed the arithmetic mean to the republic
> governed by a few; for that mean imparts greater authority and propor-
> tion with smaller numbers. That republic which is governed by all (that

88. Aristides Quintilianus, *On Music, in Three Books*, trans. Thomas J. Mathiesen
(New Haven: Yale University Press, 1983), p. 182.

89. Gaffurio, *de harmonia* 1.1, fol. 2r: "Atque ideo praefari libuit: quod quattuor
horum elementorum quorum permistione gignuntur in inferioribus his omnia:
proprietates et contrarias potentias primo tetrachordo: cuius ferunt Mercurium
inventorum: Antiqui nonnulli ratione adesse contendunt: Hypaten siquidem
primam chordam graviorem sonumque habeat: cum terrae conformen qualitate:
Secundam vero parhypaten: quoniam obtusum seu minus gravem sonum a prima
reddat: cum aquis non absimilem. Tertiam paraneten soni acutioris cum aere: et
ultimam Neten cum Igne acutissimo sono convenire putabant." Michael Masi has
referred to this metaphoric usage of number as "mystical number theory," as
opposed to "philosophical theory," or theory having to do with actual mathematical
properties of numbers. While both types are clearly held to be important by
Renaissance writers such as Gaffurio, Masi's distinction is a useful heuristic device;
see his "Arithmetic," in *The Seven Liberal Arts in the Middle Ages*, ed. David Wagner
(Bloomington: Indiana University Press, 1983), pp. 149–50.

is, by the people) they signified as the geometric mean, which is formed by different terms in equal proportions; for a certain parity is maintained between larger and smaller, the mean distinguishing an equal proportion, as if derived from the equality of the citizens. And the harmonic mean marks a greater proportion in its larger numbers; to it is ascribed the republic that is ruled in its arrangement by the best men, whose greater authority the citizens heed.[90]

Such passages serve only as anecdotal references; the metaphors are not pursued further, nor do they play a direct role in the topic under discussion. They appear to serve two functions. First, they mark the text as Pythagorean. They do so primarily by repeating Pythagorean associations throughout the work, thus keeping them in the reader's mind. This literary device is itself a typical stylistic feature of works in the Pythagorean tradition, so their presence helps to identify this treatise as a participant in that tradition. Second, the metaphoric associations are assumed to have genuine truth value, even if the logical connections are not made clear. Thus the magistrates really do serve as an example of the arithmetic mean in the realm of politics; they show that the mean really does exist as an organizing principle, not only in sounding bodies but also in other genuine, physical objects, although the passage itself might not convince the skeptical reader.

In other cases, Gaffurio seems simply to allow the classical sources to determine the course of his arguments, as in his discussion of intonation and pitch systems. This technical subject is heavily based on Boethius, whose diatonic genus he follows; it features pure fourths and fifths and dissonant thirds and sixths. The latter intervals are held to be unstable ("vagantes et instabiles ac variabiles," 3.37, fol. 64r) because the pitch of the upper note varies with the type of tetrachord in use, and so the interval may vary greatly in size while bearing the same name. He refers readers back to *Practica* 3.2 for a more extended discussion.

90. Gaffurio, *De harmonia* 3.8, fol. 76v: "Sed praedictas tres medietates Pythagoras et Plato ita rerum publicarum magistratibus compararunt: ut ei rei publicae quae a paucis regitur Arythmeticam ascriberent mediocretatem: quippe quae maiorem paucioribus numeris auctoritatem tribuit et proportionem. Eam vero rem publicam quae a cunctis (etiam popularibus) gubernatur: quoniam in maioribus et minoribus paritas quaedam servatur mediocritatis aequum in proportione distribuentis: quasi quodammodo ex civitatis aequalitate deductam: geometrica: quae aequalibus terminorum ac differentiarum proportionibus contexitur: proportionalitate notarunt. Medietas autem harmonica quae maioribus numeris maiorem notet proportionem: ei ascribitur rei publicae: quae optimatum quos maiore cives observant auctoritate regitur dispositione."

This position brings Gaffurio into the ongoing argument about tuning systems. He disagrees with Ramos (specifically, by reference to Ramos's student Spataro, see infra) that the proportion 5:4 forms a major third, 6:5 a minor third, and so on. He argues in 3.8 that the ratio 3:5:6 neither forms a harmonic mean (the correct answer would be 3:4:6, an octave divided into a perfect fourth and fifth) nor can be truly called an octave divided by a "major sixth" and a "minor third." That is, Gaffurio will not even acknowledge Ramos's proportions to be out-of-tune thirds and sixths; the only proportions that qualify for the terms are those of the Pythagorean tradition as described by Boethius. By committing himself to follow Boethius so closely, Gaffurio seems, then, not only to disagree with Ramos on technical matters of tuning but also to disallow the use of thirds and sixths as consonances.

Yet when Gaffurio confronts the musical practice of his day, he cannot be so strict. He is a practicing composer, after all, as well as a scholar. Musical styles of the early sixteenth century used thirds and sixths as consonances; that is, notes sounding together in these intervals as part of the work's main modes constituted structural elements of that composition. The interval of the fourth no longer served this function and was treated as a dissonance. Burtius had been able to deal with the problem by ignoring it. The thirty years separating Burtius's work and the *De harmonia*, however, had seen musical styles move even further away from use of the consonant fourth toward use of consonant thirds and sixths. The issue had also been raised numerous times in print and could no longer be avoided entirely by a serious writer. Gaffurio attempts a piecemeal solution to the problem: he devises a third category of interval, neither consonant or dissonant. He acknowledges that thirds and sixths are "elegant" if not truly harmonious, a note "shared" between a fit proportion and the interval, and offers an example:

In his elegant connection of the ditone and semiditone, Ptolemy (as mentioned above) adjusted the intervals in superparticulars by making the smaller proportion larger and the larger smaller, as we have demonstrated in 2.8 on close genera. With such a ditone, a conjunct diatessaron above will establish a mean in a major sixth elegantly (but not harmonically), since a smaller proportion is formed from larger numbers and longer strings. With a semiditone, he also produces an elegant mean in a minor sixth, almost like the harmonic mean from which they are drawn, partners and kindred (although they differ through smallness). But if you place over the consonance of the diatessaron a complete or smaller ditone or also an exact or enlarged semiditone, the sixth will have a discordant mean; for in this case the middle term has no essential agreement with a harmonic mean.[91]

By carefully manipulating the notions of proportion, harmonic genus, and the necessary compromise of practice, Gaffurio is able to resolve his problem and find a place for these intervals that are so necessary to practice but such a problem in Pythagorean thought. Needless to say, this compromise leaves gaping holes in Pythagorean theory. It ignores the issue of how an interval can be perceived as elegant if it is not harmonious, and it muddies the discussions of the harmonic mean. Such a position, however useful in practice, could not sustain systematic criticism; later authors, in fact, will abandon it in favor of other approaches to the problem more consistent with the rest of Pythagorean harmonics.

In Book 4, Gaffurio returns to the concerns of Pythagorean cosmology. The music of the spheres and its association of planets with both the muses and the celestial hierarchy had, as has been seen, long been an essential part of Pythagorean musical scholarship. Most medieval writers on music had mentioned the subject, though in a perfunctory manner; Tinctoris had felt obliged to argue with it. Gaffurio elevates his own discussion above the merely formulaic in two ways. First, he makes references to the subject throughout the treatise; second, he presents the subject itself twice (Fig. 2). In his first presentation he summarizes the association between modes and planets, then declines further explanation on the grounds of ignorance:

Many other things could be said in general about the proportions of the planets, but since others are capable, and the mathematicians Marcus Manilius, Ptolemy, and Haly discuss them fully, and especially John of Saxony in particular has cited them carefully in his commentaries on Al-cabitius in his second distinction of the natures of the seven planets, I

91. Ibid., fol. 78r: "Ipsarum vero concinnitatum ditoni scilicet et Semiditoni intervalla Superparticularibus hůiusmodi applicata maius minuendo: augendo minus Ptholomaeus (quod supradiximus) adaptavit: ut decimo octavo secundi In generibus spissis monstratum est. At Ditono huiusmodi coniuncta Diatessaron in acutum Sextam ipsam maiorem mediabit et concinnam (non tamen harmonice) cum in maioribus numeris ac longioribus chordis minor proportio deducta sit: semiditono pariter Sextae minoris medietam producet concinnitatem quasi affines harmonicae Medietatis a qua trahuntur et participes atque cognatas (quanquam ipsa diminutione diversas). Verum quum Diatessaron consonantiae superduxeris in acutum integrum seu diminutum ditonum sive etiam rectum vel adauctam Semiditonum sexta ipsa discorditer mediata manebit: quia nullam habet huismodi Mediocritas cum Harmonica medietate essentialem convenientiam."

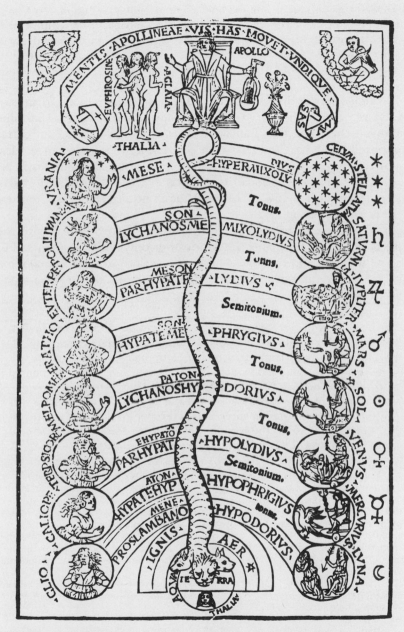

Figure 2 Musica mundana. From Franchino Gaffurio, *De harmonia musicorum instrumentorum opus* (Milan, 1518), 4.12, fol. 94v.

decided they should be omitted and no more said about them, lest I be
accused of error. Those who exert themselves in fields foreign to them
show themselves off at great cost and are rejected by learned men; for
when they try to interpret astronomy accurately they pervert it
shamelessly.[92]

Taken alone, this disclaimer might seem to be just a tactful dismissal
of an irrelevant subject. But Gaffurio follows it with a lengthy Sapphic
poem on the subject by Lancinus Curtius, for which Gaffurio has
composed a two-part setting in the Dorian and Hypodorian modes.
Unfortunately, it is not clear whether the use of these modes is intended to provoke emotions in the listener (he notes that "they will
flatter the ear agreeably"),[93] or whether, as he also remarks, their use
here is simply customary.[94]

In addition to inserting this composition, Gaffurio returns to the
subject itself. He associates the modes not only with the planets but
also with colors and humors. These associations are occasionally explained by the intervallic characteristics of the mode, or the mode's
relative pitch:

Nature has compared various human constitutions to the four modes.
For the bards considered the Dorian, most appropriate for serious affects of the soul and bodily motion, to be the mover of phlegm. In the
same way, it was connected to men of great talent, and it was represented
by painters as nearly crystalline in color . . . . They depict the Phrygian
with a fiery color (as it provokes a greater movement of bile); for it is
considered appropriate for harsh and severe men, exciting them to an-
ger. The cause of this is the very high whole tone placed above two conjunct tetrachords; it has a forcible sharpness in velocity.[95]

92. Ibid. 4.9, fol. 88v: "Complura quoque ad ipsorum planetarum rationem
in medium afferri possent: sed quoniam aliorum sua sit facultas: et uberrime
a Mathematicis Marco Mannillio: et Ptholomeo: atque Haly disputata sunt: et
quos presertim in commentariis super Alchibitio secunda differentia in naturis
septem planetarum Joannes Saxon studiose citavit: supersedendum duxi: ne cuius
complures arguuntur: aliquando vitio corripiar: qui dum in alienis professionibus
ostendandi ingenii gratia impendio elaborant: ab hominibus doctis explosi fuerunt:
namque dum Astronomiam interpretari exacte conantur: ipsam impudenter
invertunt."
93. Ibid. 4.10, fol. 90r: "Quod si duo Lyrici invicem modulentur: alter scilicet
Doricam ipsam constitutionem: alter Hypodoricam: concentus ipse quam iucun-
dissime ipsa delectatione auditum demulcebit."
94. Ibid., fol. 89v.
95. Ibid. 4.4, fol. 84v; 4.5, fol. 85v: "Sed quattuor ipsis modis varias hominum
complexiones Natura comparavit. Namque Dorium ad graviores animi affectus et
motus corporis aptissimum Vates phleugmatis motorem existimarunt perinde viris
ingenio praeclaris facile convenire: cuius figuram cristallino colori persimilem

He extends these Pythagorean characteristics and associations to other fields of knowledge as well, summarizing parts of Aristides Quintilianus's *De musica* 3. Here he is much more vague, as when he comments on the visual arts:

> Once again its utility is easily seen when considering the other arts, just how much proceeds from these numbers. For when you look at a picture, you find nothing in it that is without the proportion of numbers. You see the measure of the bodies and mixture of the colors in numbers and proportions, and so too the ornament of the picture. Again, it is through numbers themselves that this first art imitates nature. This proportion made such beauty in natural bodies and accordingly in their proportion of their measure and color, that it caused painters to want to explain life and customs in colors, form, and figure.[96]

He also discusses medicine, friendship, politics, and the military. They seem to be included for suggestive value, not for substantial analysis, since he develops the arguments no farther nor with greater specificity.

Similarly metaphoric are his comparisons of intervals to the parts of the mind. Citing Ptolemy, he begins with one philosophical manner of division:

> Many ancients thought that the human mind should be considered by means of consonant numbers, which the Pythagorean Philolaus called

---

pictoribus concessere.... Igneo autem colore (que bilem incitatioribus motibus provocet) phrygium modulum pingunt: quippe qui asperiores et severos viros quibus congruit ad iracundiam lacessere creditur: huius rei causa est acutissimus tonus duobus eius coniunctis tetrachordis superductus: ipsa acuminis velocitate vehementior." Much of this section is drawn from Aristides Quintilianus, *On Music* 3.9–28; for a discussion of Aristides Quintilianus's sources in turn, see pp. 42–57. On the humors, editor Mathiesen notes (p. 47), "Aristides Quintilianus may have developed this section from traditional Pythagorean lore (which associated 6, 8, 9, and 12, respectively, with the four humors: lacteus, sanguineus, caro, and corpus), drawing on the work of Censorinus, Varro, and others. But in view of his apparent widespread use of Plutarch's *On the Generation of the Soul in the Timaeus*, it seems likely that he may once again have turned to this treatise (1017e–1018d) as well as Aristotle's *History of Animals* 7.3–4, and Plato's *Republic* 3.12."

96. Gaffurio, *De harmonia* 4.16, fol. 96v: "Rursus exhibita in alias artes consyderatione quanta ex ipsis numeris prodierit utilitas facile percipi potest: Namque dum picturam animadvertis: nihil absque numerorum proportionibus in ea factum comperies: sed et corporum mensuras: colorumque mixtiones per numeros et symetrias: atque ita picturae ornamenta conspicies esse disposita: rursus per numeros ipsam artem primam imitari naturam. Qualis namque proportio in naturalibus corporibus fecerit pulchritudinem talis et in figurarum mensuris et colorum comparationibus est subsecuta: ob quam causam coloribus forma atque figura Pictores ipsi mores atque vitam intelligi voluerunt."

harmony. In 3.5 of the *Harmonics*, Ptolemy compared the three simple consonances to the first three parts of the soul, that is, intellectual, sensitive, and habitual: the diapason for the intellectual, the diapente for the sensitive, and the diatessaron for the habitual. For the diapente is closer to the equisonant octave than is the diatessaron and is more consonant. It departs less from equality, as the sensitive is closer to the intellectual than to the habitual; thus it participates in the apprehension of the others.[97]

He goes on to list other ways of distinguishing the powers of the mind, and similar types of proportions between those powers. The succeeding chapters cover the numeric proportions in human conception (taken largely from Macrobius), the senses, the ages of man, the virtues, and the seasons. None is covered in sufficient depth to include details that would support or justify such an association, although at several points he notes that a fuller discussion of these topics can be found in his sources.

At two points, however, he does make it clear that he takes seriously these symbolic associations and the role of music in intellectual and spiritual growth. The first is his very Platonic description of the imprisonment of the soul in the body and its subsequent struggle to recall its former, divine nature:

Aristides asserted in Book 3 of his *Musica* that the first divine furor and natural origin was represented by melodic proportion. For the soul, cast down into the terrestrial orb, falling (as Plato believes) from wisdom to ignorance, by its corporeal weight, is filled with turbulent thought and action, constituting everything unsuitable, so to speak, at the time of its generation. For this reason, it is said in this case to lead a life according to a greater or lesser cycle. For owing to great ignorance and forgetfulness it is brought to senselessness; they believed that melody should mitigate it. For melody is an ornament of the soul and intellect.[98]

97. Ibid. 4.17, fol. 97r–v: "Animam autem ipsam humanam per consonantes numeros complurimi antiquorum considerandam esse voluerunt: quam Phylolaus Pythagoricus harmoniam dixit. Tribus autem primis Animae partibus Intellectuali scilicet Sensitivae et Habituali Ptholomeus quinto tertii harmonices tres simplices symphonias comparavit: ac Diapason quidem Intellectuali: Diapenten Sensitivae: Diatessaron Habituali: quoniam dispason aequisonantae Diapente proximior est quam distessaron: tanquam magis consonans: quia habet excessum viciniorem aequalitati: et Intellectuali proximius est sensitivum quam habituale: quoniam et ipsius alicuius apphraehensionis est particeps."

98. Ibid., fol. 98r: "Ex Melodiae itaque proportione naturalissimum principium ac primus ille divinus furor demonstratur ut tertio suae musicae asserit Aristides. Namque Anima in hunc terrarum orbem abiecta prudentia (ut putat Plato) in ignorantiam decidens ob corpoream gravitatem turbulenta consyderatione et actione repletur: incongruum quippiam tanquam in ipso generationis tempore constituens:

Gaffurio's second, later passage on the subject begins by discussing the audibility of the music of the spheres. Gaffurio takes from Plato his description of the soul's struggle for the sublime as it purifies itself of vice:

> We consider it not inconsistent to agree with the consensus of Plato and the Pythagoreans, who asserted that celestial sounds are produced according to the order of instrumental sounds. Yet they are inaudible to us because we have ears that can scarcely hear due to the very great distance and the body's confused mixture. There are those who by chance have a weaker sense of hearing and who hear little or nothing of a human voice. But those who are endowed with virtue and excellent habits and are removed from baser men (who live like beasts) can hear with hardly any difficulty the celestial sounds with the uncorrupted senses of their nature.[99]

Certainly Gaffurio's interest in the Platonic and Pythagorean traditions can be seen to extend beyond the background needed to study a field based on Boethius. He is actively concerned with music's influence on the soul and its fundamental role in the structures of the universe. As a musician, he will not venture too far into the details that do not relate directly to instrumental music, but he leaves no doubt that he believes genuine musical learning is based in this branch of philosophy and study.

Nonetheless, Gaffurio did not himself develop a fully coherent or consistent system of thought about music. His attempted solutions to problems posed by discrepancies between theory and practice, such as the use of thirds and sixths, could not stand up to continued scrutiny; in fact, if examined closely, they would further damage the Pythagorean tradition he wished to advance. Such solutions can be seen only as attempts to smooth over problems in the

---

qua re in presenti vita secundum quosdam circuitus eam plus minusve uti ferunt. Quam quidem ob multam ignorantiam et oblivionem insania refertam: melodia mitigandam esse censuerunt. Est enim Melodia ornamentum animae et intelectus."

99. Ibid. 4.14, fol. 95v: "Non igitur incongruum existimamus Pythagoricis ipsis atque Platoni preberi consensum: qui sonos ipsos aethereos secundum subiectum instrumentalium sonorum ordinem productos esse asserunt: nobis tamen inaudibiles: quod aures haud aptas habemus ob maximam distantiam et turbidiorem corporis commixtionem. Sunt namque et qui accidentaliter debiliorem retinent auditum: humanam vocem parum aut nihil audientes. Verum virtute praediti et praeclaris moribus ornati: a vilioribus virsi (qui ut belvae degunt) distincti: sonos ipsos caelestes incorruptis naturae sensibus: auribus precipere haud difficile possunt."

simplest way possible, not as a carefully developed intellectual undertaking. He is also better at reciting the names of newly available classical sources and their authors than he is at placing them in any sort
of context.

Yet his emphasis on strengthening the ancient Pythagorean tradition as the basis for understanding and interpreting the study of music sets Gaffurio apart from earlier scholars; he began and inspired
more innovations in musical thought than he actually completed himself. This, as much as his technical rules for counterpoint or tuning,
is his legacy to his successors.

Giorgio Valla

Giorgio Valla's writings on music differ in several ways from
those of his contemporaries. First, they are not contained in independent treatises; instead, they form a five-book section of the encyclopedic *De expetendis et fugiendis rebus opus* (1501). Second, as the
first non-musician of his era to produce a major treatment of the
subject, Valla is not compelled to address any contemporary technical issues of composition or performance, so his writings deal
solely with ancient tradition. As a result, they contain the most
complete and systematic discussion of that tradition possible to the
scholars of his generation and to those of succeeding decades. In
these five books on music, Valla presents a compendium, based on
the most recent research and designed for the learned reader, of
ancient musical learning and its role in defining and uniting other
fields of knowledge. He seems to have succeeded; writers on the
subject during the first half of the sixteenth century, musicians
and nonmusicians alike, will make frequent references to the
work. His writings on music thus mark a major change in approach
to classical sources as well as in the possible focuses of musical
scholarship.

Valla's choice of genre, whether it is referred to as an "encyclopedia" or a "summa," allows him to include a general book introducing
the work as a whole. In it he offers a general discussion of fields of
knowledge and the nature of mathematics. One result of this discussion is an explicit and relatively detailed account of music's place as
one of the mathematical sciences, attributing to it the same certainty
of knowledge as the other quadrivial fields and doing so with authority and considerable reflection.

Recent scholarly attention to Valla, notably by Paul Lawrence Rose, has made his biography relatively familiar.[100] Born in Piacenza in 1447, he went to Milan in 1462 to study Greek with Constantin Lascaris. Three years later he moved to Pavia to continue his studies at the university (Lascaris having left Milan), adding mathematics and sciences with Giovanni Marliani to his continuing Greek studies. He taught at Pavia, as well as in Genoa and Milan, until 1485, when he was called to replace Giorgio Merula at the school of S. Marco in Venice. He remained there until his death in 1500.

Most of his publications are either translations or editions with commentary of classical works on a variety of subjects. Scientific and mathematical works include a translation of Galen, the *Astronomici veteres*, Pliny's *Natural History*, Cleonides' *Harmonicum introductorium*, and translations and editions of numerous shorter works. Among his humanistic projects are commentaries on various works of Cicero, of Juvenal, and on Aristotle's *Magna moralia* and *Poetics*. It was on this substantial body of work, his teaching, and his large personal library, that his fame rested during his lifetime,[101] rather than on his own literary productions as such.

To the modern scholar he is better known for his huge *De expetendis et fugiendis rebus*. Published posthumously by his adopted son Giovanni Pietro da Cademosto, it was apparently composed piece by piece throughout his stay in Venice; Valla probably finished the first draft in 1498.[102] Since the work was brought into publishable form by his son, it certainly lacks the consistent style of a final draft, and perhaps the form as well.[103] It is organized around the framework of the liberal arts, with humanistic and scientific subjects added. Valla first discusses the quadrivium (in the order arithmetic, music, geometry, and astronomy); then physics, metaphysics, and medicine; the trivium, with the additions of poetics and moral philosophy; then economics and politics (including law and military science); the human body; and ends with a section on miscellaneous subjects. The total

100. Paul Lawrence Rose, "Bartholomeo Zamberti's Funeral Oration for the Humanist Encyclopaedist Giorgio Valla," in *Cultural Aspects of the Italian Renaissance: Essays in Honor of Paul Oskar Kristeller*, ed. Cecil H. Clough (Manchester: Manchester University Press, 1976), pp. 299–310; Gianna Cardenal, "Cronologia della vita e delle opere di Giorgio Valla," in *Giorgio Valla: tra scienza e sapienza: studi di Gianna Cardenal, Patrizia Landucci Ruffo, Cesare Vasoli*, ed. Vittore Branca (Florence: Olschki, 1981), pp. 93–97; J. L. Heiberg, Beiträge zur Geschichte Georg Vallas und seiner Bibliothek," in *Beihefte zum Centralblatt für Bibliothekwesen* (Leipzig, 1896), 16:3–44. Heiberg reproduces many relevant documents.
101. Rose, "Zamberti's Funeral Oration."
102. Cardenal, "Cronologia," p. 96.
103. Rose, "Zamberti's Funeral Oration."

number of books (seven times seven, noted in the chapter headings as seven "hebdomads") would seem to be significant for a work showing other Platonic influences yet appears in practice to be almost coincidental; there is no pattern in the number of chapters per subject or per curricular group.

Valla treats each grouping of subjects as a self-contained unit, except for the connective tissue of transitional passages; each can thus be studied individually without a serious misreading of the whole. In fact, references to the work by later writers seem to indicate that they used the book in this way, as a reference work or encyclopedia rather than as a single, coherent treatise. It is not certain whether this was Valla's intent or whether it is a function of his son's assembling pieces of drafts for which a greater unity had been originally planned but not completed. Still, each section serves as a compendium of classical learning rather than an original treatise, and the sources for each section are unique, contributing to the independence of each one.

The music section's five-book form resembles that used by Gaffurio in the De harmonia (though Gaffurio, unlike Valla, saves his major discussion of musica mundana for the work's end). It is difficult, given the works' composition dates, to tell which author copied the format of the other; their long years of professional proximity help account for the similarity. This form is more utilitarian than literary, designed to organize a general discussion based on all the sources. That is, Valla organizes topics as he feels they work best in moving from general introductory material to more complex matters. Valla does not "privilege" a single classical source by using it as the model for organization and argumentation, as an earlier author might have used Boethius's De musica.

But Valla does privilege one classical tradition over others: the Pythagorean. This preference testifies to the tradition's continued strength, since Valla had certainly read such non-Pythagorean writers as Aristoxenus (he owned a Greek copy).[104] Yet despite this extensive study, he interprets all classical writers as contributors to this single intellectual tradition. Thus his narrative framework, like that of Gaffurio, is the "discovery of universal truths." Even as his own career marks the beginning of a new generation of scholarship by his making accessible a whole new range of classical sources, the tools he uses for

104. Claude V. Palisca, "The Impact of the Revival of Ancient Learning on Music Theory," in International Musicological Society: Report of the Twelfth Congress, Berkeley 1977, ed. Daniel Heartz and Bonnie Wade (Kassel: Bärenreiter, 1981), p. 871. Palisca discusses in some detail the specific passages of ancient writers upon which Valla bases his various books on music in Humanism, pp. 67–87.

organizing and understanding those sources are still very much part of the fifteenth-century tradition.

Music's mathematical orientation is established by its very location in the *De expetendis,* among the quadrivial subjects. Valla introduces it by relating music to his preceding discussion of arithmetic: "Just as the knowledge of numbers, which we call by the Greek name 'arithmetic,' can become known well enough by the inexperienced, as I think we show in the preceding books, and since we have treated it first of the mathematical subjects, it is also right that after it we consider music. Not only is it also one of the mathematical subjects, as we have demonstrated, but it is also perceived in discrete parts, as arithmetical quantity."[105] He mentions the importance of musical studies for understanding the cosmos, as seen in the *Timaeus;* this passage forms the bridge to his long praise of music, based as usual on classical literary authors (Aristophanes, Cicero, Plautus, Lucretius, and Aeschylus as well as the more usual Aristoxenus, Aristides Quintilianus, Porphyry, and Ptolemy). Some of its passages rely directly upon Bryennius or Boethius. Of the rest, Valla's only real innovation is the addition of more Greek authors to the usual list of references in a *laus musice.*

Much of the rest of the first book is based on Ptolemy and especially on Bryennius, with brief references to such figures as Aristotle and Aristides Quintilianus. Like Gaffurio, he does not identify Bryennius as a recent writer but treats him as if he were another classical scholar. Valla uses almost all of Bryennius's treatise, in fact, in various parts of the work: the fourth and fifth books are fairly close renditions of Bryennius's Books 2 and 3, and Book 1 is presented in large pieces throughout the rest of Valla's treatise (see, e.g. Chaps. 7 and 8 of his second book or Chaps. 1–4 of his third). Valla cites the author by name in some, but not all, of these passages; he is more likely to name the relevant author if he makes a brief reference than if an entire chapter, or series of chapters, is a translation of a single source. In such cases Valla has little or no narrative space into which he can inject his own voice with the citation.

Valla's second and third books (on the string system and intervals) are more of a pastiche of several authors. The main source in this case

105. Giorgio Valla, *De expetendis et fugiendis rebus opus* (Venice: Aldus Romanus, 1501), 5.1, unpaged: "Quemadmodum numerorum cognitio, quam voce graeca arithmeticem appellamus rudibus possit innotescere satis ut opinor suprioribus libris ostendimus, et quoniam mathematicarum primam tractavimus, par quoque est, ut post illam, musicam consideremus, tum quod ipsa quoque mathematicarum una, ut demonstravimus est, tum quod in discreta deprehenditur, ut arithmetica quantitate."

is Aristides Quintilianus, but Valla also uses Ptolemy with Porphyry's commentary and makes brief references to other treatises, including those of Bryennius. Valla provides the transitions and the narratives that connect them all together.

In this section and elsewhere in the *De expetendis*, modern scholars have noted problems in the accuracy of Valla's translations, flaws in his manuscript sources, and errors ascribed to his son or the typesetter.[106] Further, an uncritical mixing of authors from such diverse epochs as Plato, Aristides Quintilianus, and Bryennius, along with the dissident philosophical positions of Aristotle, Aristoxenus, and Bacchius, cannot produce an accurate presentation of the arguments of any of these figures. These problems may overshadow an appreciation of the very real benefits Valla's work offered to his sixteenth-century readers.

Perhaps its most obvious and unique feature, as compared with contemporary works, is its attempt to deal with the classical tradition on its own terms without the need constantly to seek analogies in the modern practical tradition. Thus the discussion of the *tonoi*, for example, is not interrupted and confused by comparisons with the church modes, and a discussion of intervals is not marred by the hidden agenda of an author who wishes to use the results in his rules for counterpoint. Given his education and his contacts with Gaffurio, it is likely that Valla had a good general knowledge of the modern tradition. But he was not a composer and thus had no vested interest in preferring one reading of the sources over another as it might apply to modern practice. This freedom allows him a new focus on the classical tradition itself as an appropriate object of interest and study.

Further, many aspects of the classical tradition were indeed shared, to some degree, among the ancient sources; thus Valla's attempt at a composite was not entirely without cause. The fifteen-string system, the *tonoi*, the tuning systems, melodic genera, and consonance are all shared concepts, though the ancients might not agree on all issues within a given subject. Valla hopes to give the reader a general treatment of these common points in a form that makes sense for the educated nonmusician, providing at the same time a reference work for those already learned in the subject. He also presents the main points of difference among classical authors, notably in regard to the definitions of terms. For these purposes, the chosen format makes sense.

---

106. Palisca, "Impact," p. 871; Thomas J. Mathiesen, "Humanism and Music: Response," *International Musicological Society: Report of the Twelfth Congress*, pp. 879–80.

An attempt to follow the argumentation of a single author might well simply have perpetuated the idiosyncrasies of that particular writer.

Thus at certain points, especially when defining terms, Valla lists successively the definitions of one author after another. A fairly typical case is his discussion of the *phthongus* in Chapter 7 of his second book on music, a chapter otherwise taken from Bryennius: "Thus a *phthongus*, as Porphyry says, is a sound produced on one steady note. As likewise Aristoxenus: a *phthongus* is an occurrence of the musical voice coming to a steady note or a melodic voice coming to a single tone; so indeed Bacchius: *phthongus* is the minimum of intervals. So Aristides: *phthongus* is the smallest unit of voice taken per se, as unity in number, and the point in a line. Thus *phthongus* is the smallest part of melodic voice, as Bryennius: *phthongus* is a sound."[107]

This approach to sources is reminiscent of Gaffurio: a careful listing of each author's opinion with no final conclusions drawn. In this case, the authorities more or less agree, although differences in the wording suggest the larger differences among them. But it is easy to grasp Valla's main point, which is after all quite valid: the ancients all use the term *phthongus* and mean by it approximately the same thing. Though this part of the work is based on Bryennius, the reader may feel assured that the subject itself is in no way peculiar to that single author.

Book 1 of *De expetendis* uses classical authorities somewhat differently. The book is designed to introduce the entire work briefly and the field of mathematics in more detail. Here Valla uses, not surprisingly, a different set of sources: mainly Plato and Aristotle, but also Stoics, Neoplatonists, and various other ancient mathematicians. While the term *music* appears here only occasionally, the chapter merits a brief examination because its treatment of the quadrivium defines the major context for the subject of music in subsequent decades, as well as the knowledge claims made about it. Several later writers will refer back to this portion of Valla's work.

Valla first discusses several general topics relative to knowledge and learning, such as the active and passive intellect, and speaks briefly about cognition. He turns then to a paraphrase of Aristotle's *Metaphysics* (Book Epsilon, 1025b–1026b) for the distinction among the

107. Valla, *De expetendis* 6.7 ("De musica" 2.7), sig gii: "Phthongus igitur ut inquit Porphyrius, est sonus per unum tenorem eductus. Ut autem Aristoxenii phthongus est vocis casus sub modulatum veniens ad tenorem unum, aut vocis casus modulatilis ad tonum unum, ut vero Bacchius, phthongus est intervallorum minimum, ut Aristides phthongus est minimum vocis per se electum, ut unitas in numero, et punctum in linea, et hoc modo, phthongus est vocis modulatilis pars minima, ut Bryennius phthongus est sonus."

sciences based on their relationship to material things as objects of study: "Therefore theology is entirely outside of all matter, likewise metaphysics; physiology, medicine, and the like are immersed in the material; and mathematics, in turn, is both within and without."[108] Of all disciplines, he continues, mathematics is the most certain, and learned men agree that it is the most beautiful part of philosophy. Thus, he concludes, after defining philosophy in general, he will begin his work with the study of mathematics.

He continues his analysis of mathematics as a "middle ground" in other respects as well, as between that which is finite and indivisible, and that which is finite and divisible:

> The whole mathematical genus is to be attributed neither to the first of those [things] which are among the genera, nor indeed the last. Rather it must occupy that middle place between those which are indivisible and simple of substance, which are neither composite nor distributed, and those which are found to be composite, liable to being divisible, various, and multiple sections . . . . In the same manner the midpoint of the mathematical genera and forms is understood, as it utterly embraces the mean between indivisible essences and those things which are divisible in matter. Therefore it explains, to those which are penetrating the principles of all, whence emanates the origin of each thing, finite and infinite.[109]

Mathematics, then, deals with both the changing and the changeless, the finite and the infinite. Valla has shifted gears here, away from the *Metaphysics* and into a Platonic argument, an orientation he maintains throughout the rest of Book 1. Mathematics can be divided, he continues, by the nature of the referent, that is by how far it deals with material objects. The goal of its study is the perfection of the scholar's soul, by drawing it toward the perfect.

Valla maintains this definition of mathematics throughout the work; it reappears especially when he wishes to contrast mathematics

---

108. Valla, *De expetendis* 1.6, sig. aiiii: "Extra omnem igitur materiam theologia, ipsaque metaphysica. Immersa materiae physiologia, medicina, et quiquid est huiusmodi. In materia porro, et extra materiam mathematica."

109. Ibid. 1.14: "Mathematicum genus universum, neque primis eorum quae sunt generibus, neque postremis prorsus attribuendum, sed medium quendam locum obtinere necesse est inter ea, quae substantiarum indivisibilium simpliciumque sunt, quae nec componuntur, nec distribuuntur, et ea quae composita inveniuntur, quae divisibilia, variae mulitplicique sectioni sunt obnoxia. . . . Proinde medietas generum mathematicorum, formarumque talis intelligatur, ut medium complectatur indivisibilium prorsus essentiarum, et eorum quae circa materiam sunt divisibilium. Universae igitur mathematices essentiae principia coniectantibus expedit ad ipsa eorum quae sunt omnium penetrare principia, unde rerum cunctarum ortus emanat, finitum inquam et infinitum."

with other disciplines. After he completes his discussions of the mathematical sciences, for example, Valla moves to his books on the humanistic disciplines. He introduces them at the beginning of his first book on grammar; here he repeats the distinction among the sciences as in matter, outside of matter, or either within or without. For his definition of the arts, in contrast, he returns to Aristotle, aided by Cleanthes. An art is knowledge related to use, custom, or practice and may be classified as liberal or mechanical. Medicine, he notes, is considered a science by some, an art by others.

Valla reiterates in his private letters the importance he accords to mathematics in *De expetendis*. Among the several scholars who corresponded with Valla on musical issues was the humanist Jacobus Antiquarius. In one letter Valla praises the certainty of mathematical knowledge and explains that he feels obliged by its nature to treat the various branches of mathematics together as he composes *De expetendis;* each one contributes to the whole, so that he cannot simply separate one and examine it in isolation. In another letter (dated December *1491*) he emphasizes the importance of harmonics in understanding the mathematical unity of the cosmos:

> We have introduced nothing into this world, in which nonetheless we discover very many good things, by which we are reminded to consider that all things look toward one end, form which they drew their beginning. But you number these good things among your own; if you seek their origins in your mathematical books, you find them not in the monad, nor in the triad, nor finally in the decad; not in a point, nor in a line, nor in any figure; not in a moving body, not in motion; not in these things that follow from them, but in all of them, just as some concord, you will show plainly, as if all assert the glory of the creator, from which anything that is dissonant falls outside the octave, and contains no harmony.[110]

To Valla, then, music's classification as a branch of mathematics is unquestioned, and it plays a major role in philosophic study.

110. Rome, BAV, Vat. Lat. 3537, fols. 156r–157v: "Nihil intulimus in hunc mundum: In quo bona tamen multa invenimus a quibus admonemur in unum finem cuncta respicere: a quo principium contraxerunt. Sed tu quae bonae in te numeras. si mathematicis in tuis libris fontes derivas: neque in monade: neque in triade: neque demum in decade compraehendes. Non in punto: non in linea; non in figura aliqua: non in corpore mobili, non in moto: non in his quae inseguuntur: sed in quadam veluti symphonia cuncta manifestius demonstrabis quasi ad conditoris gloriam contendant universa: a quo quicunque dissonat citra diapason est: et nulla continet harmonia." Jacobus Antiquarius composed one of the several dedicatory poems in Gaffurio's *Angelicum ac divinum opus musice* (Milan: Gotardo, 1508), a revised Italian translation of the *Practica musicae*.

Mathematical knowledge can be seen and studied in physical objects, but it also has a superior and independent existence. It also has a moral task. Music is clearly distinguished from the liberal arts of grammar, poetry, rhetoric, and dialectic and of course from the mechanical arts. The significance of his writings to later thinkers lies especially in the attention he devotes to a schema that provides a classification of disciplines based on their proximity to universal truth, with music among the disciplines ranking just below theology in their certainty.

Beyond Boethius

Despite the differences and disagreements among them, the musical scholars of this generation share several major assumptions about the field of music and its study, assumptions that identify these scholars as a loosely knit intellectual group. They are distinct not only from later sixteenth-century writers on music but also from their predecessors in the early fifteenth century. They define the field itself in similar ways, agree on the canon of classical authorities and the kinds of readings given them, and try to expand that canon through very similar means. Their main genre for the organization and presentation of their thought, the treatise, follows a reasonably standard format with a range of expected topics, though an author might choose to write only on a part of the subject and title the work accordingly. These writers also identify a similar group of subjects about which they disagree with one another, largely the specifics of tuning systems and intervals. Thus it is not difficult to describe the general shape of musical scholarship at the end of the fifteenth century.

Most striking to the modern reader is music's unchallenged definition as a functioning part of the quadrivium. Of this group of writers, Giorgio Valla devotes the greatest attention to the nature of mathematical knowledge, music's place among its subjects, and the distinction between mathematics and the arts. The other scholars are more summary in their treatment of the relationship of music to other knowledge but no less straightforward about defining the subject as the study of consonances expressed by numerical ratios of the superparticular type. Music's aesthetic and emotional appeal is determined by the purity of the intervals used; music that moves the soul is thus subject to a mathematical analysis of the pitches involved in order to explain that effect.

Further, these authors see the field as essentially Pythagorean, which affects their analysis in several ways. The Pythagorean system is absolute in its claims; one of its fundamental tenets is the ontological reality of consonant proportion. Thus it leaves no room for alternative approaches to the study of music. Since these writers are themselves part of this tradition (as opposed to simply studying it), they have no way to develop an analysis that accepts competing analyses as ever having been valid. They cannot argue, for example, that even though many, or perhaps most, ancient musical scholars were part of the Pythagorean tradition, other ancient scholars might have dissented (as did Aristoxenus) and formed another, equally valid tradition of thought. To do so would require an admission that musical standards are not absolute but are somehow contingent on other standards, which themselves might be subject to change. Instead, their standards more closely resemble later notions of scientific laws. Musical knowledge might advance, but it cannot change its principles; that is, musical scholarship is furthered by discovery but not invention. Musical principles, in fact, constitute the most fundamental order of the cosmos, an all-pervasive formal reality.

This Pythagorean orientation also provides a clear standard for evaluating and understanding the classical authorities: the author's ability to understand and to further Pythagorean theory. Thus Ramos can condemn Guido for having failed to understand musical truth, exemplified for him in Boethius. Burtius can assume that remarks by Cicero or Pliny must be compatible with the views expressed in Plato's *Timaeus*. Valla can compose a textbook on ancient musical theory in which the ancients are made to speak with a single voice. Such an approach naturally forces certain readings of some sources and forbids others. It allows Gaffurio to mine his "new" sources for comments without dealing with their substance; it also limits any analysis that includes historical change, excepting of course the linear plots of progress and discovery or of loss and ignorance.

Despite such limitations, these scholars share a dedication to expanding the number of sources available to musical studies. To make use either of previously inaccessible ancient treatises or of the scattered references to music in classical literary sources would certainly require the "many late nights of study" to which the authors frequently allude. Just how to interpret these new sources and how to integrate them with the established body of knowledge was a task more difficult still; their attempts share some characteristic features.

First, they assume that the new sources will contribute to, and not conflict with, the Pythagorean tradition as exemplified in Boethius. In many cases, as with Bryennius or Nicomachus, the assumption is valid; in others, such as Pliny or Cicero, it is more of a problem.

Second, they often restrict use of the new sources to anecdotal or metaphorical references, while relying on Boethius or another familiar authority for the structure of the argument. This approach is common in Burtius's treatise but is also seen frequently in the works of the others. Third, they may expand those portions of a treatise to which these sources make a substantial contribution; thus Burtius, Tinctoris, and Gaffurio composed extensive *laudes musice*, which profit by the addition of literary references. Finally, they mine sources for definitions or other small pieces of information they can collect like beads on a string.

None of these approaches, of course, singly or in combination, was entirely successful, nor could they possibly be expected to bear up under the scrutiny of later scholars. One might conclude with some fairness, in fact, that these new sources raised more questions than they answered, at least initially. The new questions, however, help to set the agenda for the musical scholars of the sixteenth century; it is hardly fair to fault Gaffurio or Valla for failing to resolve matters so large they were still occupying scholars some sixty years later.

Even those writers who expressed little interest in the "new" sources shared a concern for returning to the roots of the musical tradition, notably to Boethius. Ramos and Hothby differ strenuously on the means of accomplishing this task, but they do so because they both consider it such an important undertaking. Yet just as the attempt to integrate the new sources founders on the limits imposed by the old, so the attempt to revive Boethius himself is limited by attitudes born in fifteenth-century musical practice. That Boethius may not have written his treatise to allow for polyphonic composition, for example, is not even considered. Thus some possible, if radical, solutions for resolving the conflicts between Boethian theory and contemporary practice (such as a revival of ancient musical styles and a rejection of polyphony, for example, which some later composers will attempt) are impossible for them to contemplate.

Tinctoris stands out as an exception. He rejects the notion of celestial music and, implicitly, the metaphysical and cosmological roles of musical consonance. He seems to favor a general classification of music as a "learned pastime" after Aristotle's *Politics*, thus defining it solely in terms of performance. He is also willing to notice and to acknowledge that such terms as *mode* or *tone* might differ in meaning, and hence define a different musical practice, in the works of different authorities. Tinctoris's work thus shows that it was certainly possible to dissent from the prevailing intellectual tradition in many ways, to support that dissent with recourse to logic and authority, and to maintain a well-respected career and reputation.

Having decided that musical practice was more important than theory, however, he quite sensibly devoted himself to composition and the writing of treatises about composition. Thus he never developed his general ideas about music in any detailed or systematic way and did not train a succeeding generation of scholars to continue along the same path. Further, because he frequently reverted to Pythagorean arguments when discussing matters such as the emotional effects of music, it is difficult to assess his influence on those sixteenth-century writers who expressed similar ideas. Certainly his works brought these arguments into general circulation. Just as later authors had easy access to classical arguments about musical styles as the product of different cultures because Gaffurio included them in his books, so too did Tinctoris introduce musical scholarship to the "new" Aristotle.

The general issues that inspired debate among the scholars of this generation are fairly straightforward. The growing conflict between theory and practice regarding consonance and proportion had become obvious and pressing, but the solutions proposed were all discrete and piecemeal, not systematic or even consistent. Whether thirds and fourths were consonant or dissonant and the exact proportions involved in producing them, and whether or not the Boethian tuning system could be altered, were the issues receiving the most attention. Not only were these issues left unresolved; they proved ever less tractable until well into the next century.

In all these ways, then, the scholars of the late fifteenth century set the agenda for those of the sixteenth. The new sources opened up possibilities for an expanded Pythagorean tradition but also brought to light authorities who seemed to depart from that tradition. Others offered new evidence about the place of music in ancient society. At the same time, the old connections between the theoretical and practical traditions began to look more and more frayed. These problems, singly or together, became the major issues facing later scholars. Thus, when these sixteenth-century writers look back to their distinguished predecessors, it is not the scholars of the early fifteenth century they remember, but Gaffurio, Valla, and the others of their era.

CHAPTER 3

Humanists, Mathematicians, and Composers

By the early years of the sixteenth century a wider range of writers began to turn their attention to the subject of music, often focusing on one of its aspects rather than attempting to compose comprehensive guides like those of Burtius or Gaffurio. The particular topics of study—mathematics, poetics, music composition and performance—had been touched upon by late fifteenth-century scholars, and these younger writers made frequent reference to their work. Some even devoted substantial energy to carrying on the earlier debates about these topics, often in order to defend a teacher or an elder friend and colleague.

Perhaps this interest in specifics and detail helps account for the lack of cohesiveness among these writers. They did not constitute a single intellectual circle or network, as had their predecessors, nor did they all acknowledge one another's scholarship. Yet a wider perspective reveals their links with the generations both preceding and following them, creating a broad but related range of interests. Though they did not all read one another's work, later scholars did so, as they tried to grasp the subject as a whole. Thus the fragmentation of approaches and results in the early sixteenth century was only temporary.

Much of this early sixteenth-century writing, then, gives the initial impression simply of carrying on the agenda set before 1500, either by focusing on specific issues or detail or by pursuing the implications of a general argument made by an earlier author. Giovanni Spataro's publishing career, for example, was largely dedicated to defending the ideas of his teacher, Ramos, against the criticism of Burtius and

Gaffurio. Bartolomeo Zamberti was a friend and colleague of Giorgio Valla and continued Valla's Pythagorean approach to the study of mathematics. Only Raffaele Brandolini came to the subject independently of the others (though he was almost surely acquainted with Tinctoris and perhaps Gaffurio at Naples); as a result, his work seems the most innovative but generated less immediate or obvious response.

Yet this initial impression of fragmented, often derivative work is only partially accurate. Though they could offer few long-term solutions to the problems their predecessors posed, these writers did provide valuable information about how music as a discipline was classified and related to other disciplines. They did not challenge music's place in the quadrivium, organized by Pythagorean principles (in fact, there is clear evidence that writers on other quadrivial disciplines, such as geometry, took these writers seriously when attempting to define and interrelate the fields of knowledge). In addition, they gradually broadened the range of approaches, sources, and issues addressed in the study of music. An author's professional training and choice of genre are less easy to predict; nor can a reader necessarily predict a course of argument, once based so simply on a single authority such as Boethius. Thus this generation's lack of collective professional or intellectual coherence is compensated for by the variety they introduce into the discursive tradition.

Perhaps the most important new development is the serious attention they began to devote to the study of music together with poetry. Gaffurio had taken tentative steps in this direction, but it remained for the humanist Brandolini to devote a measure of his full attention to the subject. That emphasis not only shifts the focus from pitch alone to include metrics but also alters the manner of study. Brandolini, despite his apparent reputation as a performer of his own poetry, lacked the technical background to make detailed connections between his own work and the musical profession at large; nonetheless, his study of music as a vehicle for the declaiming of text marks a major change.

Many sixteenth-century mathematicians, followers of Valla, continued to be interested in a Pythagorean approach to their subject, maintaining an active interest in Pythagorean theory and contributing to its continued strength. Their published works would have circulated among a somewhat different audience than the typical music treatise, thus reaching a broader public than those readers or scholars purely interested in music. Practicing musicians seem to have had less contact than their predecessors with their fellow humanists and mathematicians and to have been concerned more exclusively with the application of theoretical principles to musical practice, both in composition and in performance. Still, they display a wide range of opinion about the role of ancient musical scholars in modern practice, the value of the study of theory, and the nature of the field itself. Further, by publishing not in Latin but in the vernacular, they vastly increased the circulation of their ideas.

Raffaele Brandolini

Not many years earlier, a man like Raffaele Brandolini would have seemed an unlikely author for a work about music. He was a humanist both by training and by profession. In this he differed from Burtius or Gaffurio, whose education had included humanistic studies but not focused upon them, as well as from Giorgio Valla, whose mathematical education had provided the technical basis for his musical scholarship. In fact, there is no evidence that the formal intellectual study of music had been part of Brandolini's education. His interest thus indicates a new interest in music among scholars in other disciplines. It also represents a major shift in the field's focus: Brandolini's *De musica et poetica* is the first independent work to examine music not in the context of mathematical consonance but in the context of the poetry that music accompanies and music's roles in society.

Raffaele, younger brother of the humanist Aurelio Brandolini, was born in Florence about 1465.[1] His family moved to Naples while he was a child. There he began his education with Giovanni Pontano, who mentions him in his *De fortitudine* as an example of courage in the face of his impending blindness;[2] Aurelio suffered the same affliction, which earned for both the appellation "Lippus." Raffaele's early adult years were spent in Florence, Venice, and Rome. He became an Augustinian hermit and priest and studied and taught theology. Returning to Naples in 1493 as tutor to Alfonso II's illegitimate son, Brandolini survived the French invasion of Naples and won a stipend from Charles VIII for an extemporaneous oration delivered in his

1. For biographical information on Brandolini, see G. Ballistreri, "Brandolini, Raffaele," *DBI*; see also John F. D'Amico, *Renaissance Humanism in Papal Rome: Humanists and Churchmen on the Eve of the Reformation* (Baltimore: Johns Hopkins University Press, 1983); John O'Malley, *Praise and Blame in Renaissance Rome: Rhetoric, Doctrine, and Reform in the Sacred Orators of the Papal Court, ca. 1450–1521* (Durham, N.C.: Duke University Press, 1979), pp. 74, 171.
2. Giovanni Pontano, *De fortitudine* (Naples, 1490), 1:1.2.8.

praise. With the return of the Aragonese he moved permanently to Rome, where he first worked as a tutor and composer of orations (his students included the future Julius III), then enjoyed the close patronage of both Julius II and Leo X, including household residence and a professorship of rhetoric at the university. He composed a number of orations, letters, dialogues, and poems.[3]

Brandolini wrote *De musica et poetica* late in life, shortly before Leo X's election in 1513. It is apparently a reworked and expanded version of an earlier piece, *De laudibus musicae et poesos,* which has not survived. Written as a long oration, it serves as an example of the rhetoric common in the Rome of Brandolini's era; the popularity and versatility of the forms of epideictic rhetoric had in fact been furthered by his brother Aurelio.[4] By choosing a rhetorical style of praise and defense rather than the expository form of the treatise that was the norm for musical discussions, Brandolini has given himself a relatively open-ended genre. He is free to develop the content as he sees fit, as it contributes to an argument in favor of the study and practice of music and poetry.

An oration assumes an audience, which Brandolini can choose at will to render his own arguments most persuasive. He chooses an audience of one, an apostolic protonotary named Corradolo Stanga, who had served as host and patron in Rome.[5] Brandolini begins by acknowledging his great debt to Stanga for the learning he received through associating with Stanga and his colleagues. This very learning, he argues, has made possible the skill that he now turns against one of Stanga's own injunctions, Stanga's condemnation of his frequent extemporaneous performances of Latin verse with musical accompaniment. Brandolini defends the practice as part of his ultimate goal: to prove that both music and poetry form parts of true eloquence.

3. See Vatican City, BAV, Vat. Lat. 3590, "Quae in Raphaelis Lippi B. scriptis continentur" (given by Baldovino del Monte to Julius III); Vat. Lat. 3460; Vat. Lat. 7852; a single letter in Rome, Bib. Angelica, ms. 1001.c.5r. For numerous funeral orations in manuscript and in print, see "Brandolini, Raffaele," *DBI.*
4. O'Malley, *Praise and Blame,* Chaps. 2–3.
5. Stanga was from a Cremonese landowning family; he had supposedly corresponded with Brandolini while a Milanese legate, some time before becoming an apostolic protonotary; those letters have apparently not survived. See Vatican City, BAV, Vat. Lat. 3590, fols. 6v, 16v. Stanga's interests in and support of musical scholarship extended beyond this disagreement with Brandolini. Franchino Gaffurio had dedicated an early treatise to Stanga (ca. 1481–83, later incorporated into his *Practica musicae*) while Gaffurio was working in Lodi and Bergamo. See Alessandro Caretta, Luigi Cremascoli, and Luigi Salamina, *Franchino Gaffurio* (Lodi: Archivio Storico Logidiano, 1951), p. 67.

This is not a genre one would choose in order to impart vast amounts of new research or the thought of previously unknown authors; for such information would be better suited to an expository form. Rather, the work's goal is to present known authorities and information in a new light, in order to highlight the importance of music and poetry, both separately and (especially) together. Thus Brandolini employs elements of familiar genres and topoi to construct the body of the text; yet he does so in order to make points not previously considered by his audience. He also includes abundant references to his contemporaries in Rome and elsewhere, information he assumes is familiar to his immediate audience but much of which is new to the modern reader.

It is hardly surprising that he begins the body of the work with a now-familiar theme, the *laus musice*. Brandolini includes nearly all the standard topics of the genre: music's status as one of the first elements of the cosmos, its ability to ease the task of laborers, its use in festivals and divine service, and its importance to civil society.[6] To the usual list of famous ancients skilled at music, he has added modern political leaders such as Ferdinand, king of Naples, and Hieronymus Donatus of Venice.

Yet as Brandolini continues to develop his *laus musice*, it becomes clear that his use of the genre differs significantly from earlier writers. To Burtius or Gaffurio, the *laus musice* was a discrete chapter in a larger treatise, not necessarily related, narratively or thematically, to the rest of the work. Its central point was fairly simple: music was important, even central, in ancient learning and in ancient society. These two facets of the argument were attested to largely by the sheer number of examples mustered in support of each, rather than by any coherently developed thesis.

Brandolini reinvigorates the genre by restoring its argumentative nature. More important than the resurrection of a genre, of course, is its use in developing his case for the study of music. After repeating the familiar passages, his writing begins to take on more direction. His first treatment of the Pythagoreans' claims about music's power is a brief introductory summary; he then returns to the subject as he warms to its topic. The invention of the lyre by Mercury and the establishment of its additional strings, he states, was a discovery of preeminent importance, the discovery of the ratios of physics and

6. James Hutton, "Some English Poems in Praise of Music," in *Essays on Renaissance Poetry*, ed. Rita Guerlac (Ithaca, N.Y.: Cornell University Press, 1980), pp. 23–25.

metaphysics.[7] It was essential to acquiring an understanding of the motions of heavenly bodies, of whirlwinds, and of earthquakes. The obvious importance of this knowledge, he continues, should cause one to value, that much more, the thought and scholarship of the ancients, "whose acuteness of mind discerned so openly and clearly that which to our minds and souls seemed hidden and obscure."[8]

Brandolini then notes that when the ancients discussed music performance, they did not mean solely instrumental music, but rather, instruments as an accompaniment for song. Earlier writers had also noticed this; yet they had simply repeated the fact without comment, focusing on the lyre and its strings rather than the singing. Brandolini returns frequently to this connection, using it to pair music and poetry as coequal in importance:

> Did Terpander (of whom we spoke above) add the seventh string to the lyre's concord and join song to it so fittingly for any other reason than to show the lyre to be the proper task for poets? Either for lamenting loves, as shown so agreeably by Callimachus and Phyletas among the Greeks and by Tibullus, Propertius, and Catullus among the Romans; or for recounting the praises of the gods, the prizes of victory, the witticisms of banquets, and finally, for relating moral precepts and habits.[9]

He rejects the possibility of these singers being at banquets for reasons of bawdy entertainment, as implied by such detractors as Stanga; he supports his own claims about the importance and elevated status of song in antiquity with references to the *Aeneid* and to a number of

7. Raffaele Brandolini, "De musica et poetica opusculum," Rome, Bib. Cas. 805, fols. 20v–21r: "Mercurius (de quo paulo ante) cum rebus plurimis a se praeclarissime inventis, tum praecipue lyra, Jovis hoc est dei maximi et filius, et nuncius habitus; non aliam prorsus nervorum quam physicam ac metaphysicam habuisse rationem videtur. Idem ferme Apollo Terpanderve in septicorde consilii habuere. An non hi docuere lyram esse praeclarissimum musices instrumentum? Cuius concentus humani corporis qualitatibus, mundi primordiis, caelestibus denique corporibus maxime conveniret." [Mercury (of whom we spoke above), who very admirably invented many things, especially the lyre, was son of Jove (that is, of the Great God) and retained as a messenger. He seems to have believed that the ratio of the strings was truly physical and metaphysical. Apollo or Terpander believed the same about the lyre with seven strings. For did they not teach that the lyre was the most eminent musical instrument? Its concord unites the qualities of the human body, the origins of the world, and the celestial bodies.]

8. Ibid., fol. 21v.

9. Ibid., fols. 23v–24r: "An aliam ob causam Terpander (de quo paulo ante) lyrico concentui et septimam adiunxit cordam, et carmen illi aptissime copulavit, nisi ut lyram proprium esse poetarum munus doceret? Sive deplorentur amores, quod apud Graecos Challimacus et Phyletas, apud Romanos Tibullus, Propertius, et Catullus lepidissime praestitere. Sive deorum laudes, victorum praemia, conviviorum sales atque facetiae, morum denique praecepta institutaque enarrentur."

general statements about the habits of Greeks such as the Spartans. By enumerating the various ways music was used among the ancients, he provides grounds for comparing its use among the moderns. Although the modern world has retained the use of martial music, he claims that it has sorely neglected the lyric tradition.

Brandolini then turns to poetry, reiterating that such poetry was originally presented in song. Following the model of his praise of music, he turns immediately to the field's role in increasing human awareness of cosmic order. In this case, however, his arguments come primarily not from the Pythagorean tradition but from that of Renaissance Platonism. Poets touched by furor are brought into contact with the divine and so can move others, just as a magnet not only can move an iron object but is also able to transmit its power through that object to a third one. So too, poetry can impart divinely inspired truths to those who might not otherwise comprehend them. The ancient poets taught about the origins of the world just as the philosophers had, but in a form more easily accessible to the rude musing of their early listeners. To understand this process, he continues, we must interpret classical myths and legends allegorically.

In support of this claim, he offers extended allegorical interpretations of numerous legends, mythical figures, and aspects of classical cosmology, which together form an analysis of the origin and function of ancient mythology like that in some works of his humanist contemporaries and predecessors. The story of Pluto and Proserpine, he states, discusses the changing of the seasons and the phases of the moon. The planets epitomize virtues. The figures and symbols of the elements (such as Juno and her peacocks, associated with air) aid the memory in recalling the elements' attributes. It is the manner in which the material is presented, argues Brandolini, not the subject matter itself, which distinguishes poetry from other disciplines. Further, poetry's moral force means that, just like the disciplines of theology, astrology, and natural and political philosophy, it also deals with universals and not simply mundane particulars.

Returning explicitly to poetry's connection with music, Brandolini discusses the importance of hymns not only to the "gentile" religions but also to Christianity. Here he employs a series of arguments, also typical of many other humanists. Just as the ancient Hebrews prefigured Christianity in their hymns, he writes, so the Greeks were able to capture parts of the truth, though seen from a greater distance, in their own hymns and songs. Brandolini returns to such poets as Homer and Virgil, noting how the earliest poets had a civilizing influence and also remarking on the effectiveness of them all at presenting the rewards of virtue and the errors of vice. These same features apply to elegies and extemporaneous verse, since both require similar study on the part of the poet. The choice between Latin or the vernacular, he continues, should thus depend on the audience, in order that the content be presented most effectively. This leads him to praise modern poets, from Dante and Petrarch to Bernardo Accolti and others.

Brandolini then moves to a discussion of elegiac, or extemporaneous, verse. Here his personal stake in the subject, mentioned briefly several times previously, comes out clearly: he has built part of his career and reputation on the performance of such verse, improvised in text and song, and believes that the practice has played a genuine and significant moral role in the experience of his listeners. Thus Brandolini's arguments are those of an active performer, not simply the armchair observations of a listener or even merely of a poet. The information he offers about the substance of such performance is frustratingly meager. Still, his oration demonstrates that humanistic interest in linking music with poetry has extended to active involvement.

The *De musica et poetica* differs strikingly from earlier writings on music, most notably in its almost total lack of mathematics and technical information. There is no extended discussion of proportion and no mention at all of types of scales or modes, both of which were staples of the music treatise. Brandolini refers to cosmology and mathematics often enough to demonstrate that he accepts music's Pythagorean basis as a given; he does not develop his own argument as a threat or an alternative to its analytic system. Yet an analysis of music's principles is not his intention. He has expanded the range of topics eligible for inclusion in a work about music by developing a genre distinct from the older scholarly tradition, one with its own goals and concerns.

To be sure, he does so by making use of a classical genre already well known to earlier scholars, the *laus musice* (in addition, of course, to a parallel treatment of poetry). Yet he turns the genre to a new end. He establishes that the importance of music and poetry lies in their combination as song or hymn, thus shifting attention away from scales and intervals and toward the rhetorical goals of the singer-poet. Therefore matters such as the nature of the audience, the religious or secular message to be conveyed, and the social setting of the performance become the main objects of investigation. Since ancient song, both pagan and Christian, is so important as a model, Brandolini's approach increases the incentive for careful study of ancient practice in its various cultural contexts. Further impetus would also come from the publications of Carlo Valgulio, an elder contemporary in Rome and translator of the pseudo-Plutarch *De musica* (1507).[10]

This approach to the study of music and poetics is still based in the Pythagorean tradition but has added some of the interests and concerns of Renaissance Platonism. Brandolini's arguments about music's power are based on its Pythagorean status as part of the cosmological order. Poetry's effects depend on transmission of the divine spark received by the poet in his mystical furor, a notion propounded by Ficino. Without such a foundation to his argument, Brandolini would have only anecdotal evidence, not a logical or analytic basis, with which to explain the power of song. He thereby expands the older tradition and enhances the range of sources and approaches to musical scholarship but does not attempt to break away and start anew. Although Brandolini neither states nor implies any antagonism toward the mathematical study of music, his arguments do tend, however, to assert the superiority of a humanistic approach. While the tools for its proper practice lie in the realm of proportion, music's use and effectiveness are connected to the words of the text, its rhetorical goals, and the type of audience. Brandolini does not try to resolve this tension; resolution will have to wait for later scholars, once developments in both mathematics and humanistic studies make that tension impossible to ignore.

Spataro and Aron

The professional musicians whose writings on music followed those of Gaffurio did not exhibit a breadth of scholarly interests, education, or intellectual contacts to equal his. Their major concerns lay in the realm of practical music; they entered the more general discourse about the discipline as a result of practical questions and debates that served both to direct and to limit their investigations.

10. Claude Palisca has devoted considerable attention to the writing and translation of Carlo Valgulio, whose work resembles Brandolini's in its effort to incorporate classical sources on ancient music's social roles within the larger framework of Pythagorean theory. Valgulio is also noteworthy for offering (despite this position) a sympathetic reading of Aristoxenus. His influence seems to have increased gradually over the first half of the sixteenth century. See Palisca, *Humanism in Renaissance Italian Musical thought* (New Haven: Yale University Press, 1985) pp. 88–110. On Valgulio's proem to the Plutarch translation, with an edition and translation of the text, see Palisca, *The Florentine Camerata* (New Haven: Yale University Press, 1989), pp. 13–44.

They exhibited no knowledge of Valla's work and did not refer to that of Brandolini. In fact, their use of the vernacular in their published works stemmed not entirely from choice but from necessity; Giovanni Spataro in particular was explicit about his limited Latin, though Pietro Aron claimed that he published in Italian simply to broaden his readership.

Their extensive publications apparently stemmed from their involvement in the published debates of earlier musicians (Burtius, Ramos, and Gaffurio), owing to their professional contacts with these older figures; they continued to debate similar issues, often in similar terms. Because these musicians so dominated the publishing field with their treatises during the first decades of the century, the issues they chose to address influenced numerous later writers. Thus they merit attention even though some of their work might seem to slow the momentum of the previous generation's innovations.

Giovanni Spataro (ca. 1458–1539 or 1541) was the eldest of these musician-scholars. His training and career were so much based on those of his predecessors at Bologna that the group has been referred to as a Bolognese "school" of musical composition and thought.[11] Not many details of Spataro's life are known. He was born and buried in Bologna, his entire known career being spent at S. Petronio, where he held the post of *maestro di canto* after 1512.

As a student of Ramos, Spataro composed three of his early publications in defense of his master, first against Burtius and especially against Gaffurio: *Bartolomei Ramis Honesta defensio in Nicolai Burtii Parmensis opusculum* (1491); *Dilucide et probatissime demonstratione . . . contra . . . Franchino Gafurio* (1521); and *Errori di Franchino Gafurio da Lodi . . .* (1521). In addition to these three polemical works, he wrote a brief treatise on composition (*Utile e breve regole di canto,* 1510) and a large treatise on rhythmics (*Tractato di musica,* 1531). Many of his letters have also survived; Spataro corresponded regularly with Pietro Aron and Giovanni del Lago on professional matters, largely during the 1520s and 1530s.[12] Most of his written work dates from the later years of his life.

11. For biographical information on Spataro, see Frank Tirro, "Spataro, Giovanni," *New Grove*; see also Giuseppe Vecchi, "Premessa," in Giovanni Spataro, *Tractato di musica* (1531; facsimile, Bologna: Forni, 1970).

12. Spataro's letters are found in the following collections: Vatican City, BAV, Vat. Lat. 5318 and 1543; Bologna, Civ. Mus., "Lettere di Spataro"; Vienna, Oest. Nationalbib., Musiksammlung S.m. 4380; Paris, Bib. Nat., it. 1110. Most are copies, partial or complete, of the originals in Vat. Lat. 5318. See R. Casimiri, "Il Codice

Spataro's earliest treatise, the brief *Honesta defensio,* because it is directed against Burtius in favor of Ramos, addresses arguments about modes and pitches of much the same type as those debated earlier, using two main arguments. The first is an attack more or less ad hominem against Burtius, coupled with a brief description and praise of Ramos as a teacher. The second and more important is Spataro's questioning of the utility of ancient learning to modern practice, in favor of the medieval church tradition.

Most of the personal attacks on Burtius center on his alleged incompetence when a student; at one point, in fact, Spataro lists three witnesses to attest to Burtius's lack of ability, all of them fellow singers at S. Petronio.[13] Spataro takes issue several times with Burtius's apparent errors and lack of learning. Thus he notes that Burtius's proportions are based neither on Boethius nor Aristoxenus and that he uses vernacular terms rather than the proper Latin ones;[14] he also claims that Burtius is in error on such matters of astronomy as the houses under the sign of Venus, so that his discussions of music and the cosmos are inaccurate.[15]

The reference to their student days gives Spataro the opportunity to point with pride to Ramos's teaching curriculum and hence to his own educational background: two of Guido's books, Franco of Cologne, Egidio di Marino, Odo's *Enchiridion,* several treatises "without titles," and Boethius on music and arithmetic.[16] All are part and parcel of the ecclesiastical tradition, relying on Boethius for their theoretical basis. All of them are also Latin treatises, presumably untranslated into the vernacular; thus it would seem that Spataro was taught in Latin. Certainly he needed the language to function as a church musician, yet he never felt able to write it with confidence. This deficiency was clearly a sore point with him, and he returns to it in his later works against Gaffurio.

More substantial than Spataro's assertions about his rival's ignorance are his claims that Burtius overrates the importance and usefulness of the ancients to modern musicians. Spataro expresses

---

Vaticano 5318, Carteggio musicale autografo tra theorici e musici del sec. XVI, dall'anno 1517 al 1543," *Note d'archivio* 16 (1939): 109; Knud Jeppeson, "Eine musiktheoretische Korrespondenz des früheren Cinquecento," *Acta Musicologica* 13 (1941): 3–39.

13. Giovanni Spataro, *Bartolomei Ramis honesta defensio in Nicolai Burtii Parmensis opusculum* (Bologna, 1491), fols. 2v–3r.

14. Ibid., fol. 5r.

15. Ibid., fol. 9r.

16. Ibid., fol. 6r.

serious doubts about their value to working composers. He turns one such passage into another personal attack on Burtius, as he continues to talk about his teacher, Ramos:

> And he [Ramos] does not speak against Boethius but says that which Odo says in his *Enchiridion*, that the whole work is useful only to theoreticians; whereas it clouds the thoughts of practical musicians. Therefore his first book, which he wrote for practical musicians, uses vernacular terms. So there is no need for the practical musician to know arithmetic and other sciences in order to know music, since one can do without it. But you, who have not taken this path, which was most appropriate to your ability, will find yourself without science and without music.[17]

He continues by attacking the ancients themselves, notably the Pythagoreans, for not practicing what they preached. Far from relying on rational thought, he states, they blindly followed the authority of Pythagoras. Despite his aversion to the ancients, this reference to the familiar "ipse dixit" of the Pythagoreans comes from the "theoretician" Boethius, whom he cites (Book 1).[18] Spataro later argues that for music in the diatonic genus, which comprises all of modern music, one need not learn everything discovered by the ancient masters; the works of ecclesiastical writers (such as Benedict and Guido) are sufficient.[19] In fact, when Spataro refers to "antiqui" in any of his writings, he generally means the medieval scholars Franco of Cologne and Marchetto of Padua, not the Greeks or Romans.

Much of the *Honesta defensio* deals with the technical matters of note names and syllables, with Spataro supporting Ramos's ideas. His later works extend this concern with terminology to the realm of rhythmic notation as well. The *Errori di Franchino Gafurio* raises these issues in a point-by-point discussion of errors committed to print by Gaffurio, both in his writings and in his compositions. This often simply provides Spataro with another arena for airing the same general complaints and arguments about musical studies. Nonetheless, his attacks on Gaffurio's would-be Pythagoreanism are substantial enough that the work merits brief attention.

17. Ibid., fol. 6v: "E non parla contra Boetio: ma dice quello che Odo dice nel suo Enchiridion di tutta lopera che solo alli theorici e utile: ma alli pratici offusca lingegno. E perche quello suo primo libro lui lo fa per li pratici usa termini vulgari: acio non sia bisogno al pratico sapere arythmetica et altre scientie per sapere musica poi che senza quelle si po fare: Ma tu che questa via non hai preso: laquale era piu apto al tuo ingegno senza scientia ti troverai et senza musica."
18. Ibid., fol. 10r–v.
19. Ibid., fol. 12v.

The *Errori* begins with another personal attack. Responding to Gaffurio's criticism in the *De harmonia musicorum instrumentorum opus,* he accuses Gaffurio of ignorance in musical practice. Further, Spataro defends his own ability to become learned in the field without Latin letters, arguing that Gaffurio has taken false pride in his own learning. He refers to their long-running private correspondence in which these same issues had been debated, claiming that these letters had been written in Italian not because of Spataro's ignorance but rather because of Gaffurio's embarrassment at the grammatical mistakes in his own Latin.[20]

Even allowing for the often vitriolic nature of Renaissance invective, this introduction does not set a high tone for the work either rhetorically or intellectually. Like his teacher Ramos, Spataro gives the impression of a critic both stubborn and quarrelsome, unwilling to distinguish between matters of substance and those of mere detail. In Book *1*, for example (on Gaffurio's errors in practical music), he seizes on some mistakes that may simply have been printer's errors; in Book *2* he discusses some "errors" of terminology or proportion found only in Gaffurio's Neapolitan publications, which Gaffurio himself had corrected in his later Milanese writings.

Despite the genuine differences in both tuning proportions and terminology between the two figures, the debate itself seems to generate (and to be generated from) more heat than light. Spataro's arguments about the irrelevance of classical learning to musical practice seem to arise more as a defense of his own training than as a considered, scholarly argument. Given that in his later *Tractato* he cites Gaffurio fairly frequently without criticism, those of his attacks that seem petty and technical should probably be taken at that level and no further.

Yet he does raise a few substantial issues, centering on Gaffurio's claim to be a follower of Pythagoras. At one point, for example, Spataro takes issue with the scale Gaffurio had identified as the diatonic scale celebrated by Pythagoras (the *diatonon diatonicum*). Ramos's objections have to do with the precise formation of the scale; he insists (quite accurately) that such a scale must be constructed by forming and then assembling the Pythagorean consonances, not generated from a step-by-step series of tones.[21]

20. Spataro, *Errori de Franchino Gafurio da Lodi* . . . (Bologna: Faelli, 1521), fols. 2v–3r.
21. Ibid., fol. 19v.

This demonstration does more than display Spataro's knowledge of the technical minutia of tuning systems. It establishes an argumentative basis for Spataro's attack on Pythagorean tunings and theory in general. Gaffurio's need to alter some intervals slightly to produce his working "Pythagorean" scale proves to Spataro that, whatever the followers of Pythagoras claim to do in words and writing, they in practice are obliged to depart from actual Pythagorean tunings.[22] He continues with an attack that eventually will become a defense of Ptolemy (a defense that itself echoes Boethius):

> At this point you have composed a great discourse very much contrary to Pythagoras, and to you yourself. For if (excepting the equisone distance on the monochord) all the other consonant distances vary by a certain very small quantity, as you say, it follows that all the Pythagorean doctrine (and indeed your own) will not be suitable for the practice of harmony. For if Pythagorean doctrine (followed by you) has need of help in ascending and descending, such a doctrine cannot in itself be suitable for musical practice . . . . I say that from you one concludes (tacitly) that the Pythagorean doctrine (however it is used) is absolutely useless, fallacious, and vain.[23]

Spataro returns again and again to this point, claiming that it is not he who damns Pythagoras but rather Ptolemy and even Gaffurio himself, the latter for acknowledging that his scales profited from a doctoring of the intervals. Gaffurio, he claims, has tried to cover with the names of ancient authors his own lack of perception in distinguishing actual practice, ancient or modern, from the misguided theories of Pythagoras.[24]

These attacks on Gaffurio continue in Spataro's treatise on rhythm, the *Tractato di musica,* though less strenuously. Here Spataro occasionally cites Gaffurio with approval, mainly when Gaffurio happens to agree with Pietro Aron; Spataro had maintained a long correspondence with Aron and dedicated this treatise to him. The *Tractato* is

22. Ibid.; see also Palisca, *Humanism,* pp. 234–35.
23. Spataro, *Errori,* fol. 23r: "In questo loco hai facto uno grande discurso multo contrario a Pythagora: et a te medesimo: imperoche se (remota la equisona distantia dal monochordo) tute le altre distantie consone variano per certa minime quantita come tu dici: el sequitara/ che tuta la pythagorica doctrina (et etiam la tua) non serano conveniente a lo exercito harmonico: perche se la pythagorica institutione (da te sequitata) ha bisogno de aiuto per intensione: et remisione/ tale institutione non potra/ convenire per se al Musico exercitio. . . . Dico che da te (tacite) e concluso/ che la pythagorica doctrina (in quanto ala exercitatione) essere omnino inutile: frustratoria: et vana."
24. Ibid., fol. 30v.

devoted entirely to rhythmic notation and its accurate analysis and division, using Marchetto of Padua and Franco of Cologne (referred to once again as "antiqui") as authorities. It does not build on Gaffurio's attention to metrics but on the medieval tradition of rhythmic notation; many of Spataro's references to classical writers are, in fact, derived from these medieval scholars and not from the sources themselves. He refers to specific musical pieces by established composers (rather old-fashioned ones at that) such as Dufay and Ockeghem to illustrate the correct application of the rules of rhythmic proportion. Here he reveals himself not only as a careful master of a technical subject but also as a conservator of tradition in the face of an assault by the "new" ancient sources.

Spataro's treatises are significant for several reasons. First, he returns the attention of practical musicians to the proportions of rhythm as well as those of pitch, encouraging later writers to treat the two subjects in a more coordinated way. Second, his more substantial attacks on Gaffurio reveal important weaknesses in the claims of his contemporaries to being followers of Pythagoras. Finally, Spataro contests the value of Greco-Roman sources for modern musicians, a matter on which earlier writers had disagreed but one they had not discussed explicitly. Later writers will therefore need to be more articulate about justifying the use of the "ancients" in their own work.

Pietro Aron's writings were less polemical and apparently more widely read than those of Spataro. His professional career was also more varied; a native Florentine (ca. 1480–ca. 1550), he worked in Venice (for Sebastian Michiel, grand prior of the Crociferi), Padua, Rome (under Leo X), and Bergamo, where he retired as one of the Crociferi himself.[25] Like Spataro, he corresponded regularly with other practicing musicians and composers. Also like Spataro, his written works treat larger theoretical issues only insofar as they relate to the practical tradition that was his main interest. His attempts to expand the practical treatise to incorporate, at least in part, the new sources and new ways of studying them merit particular attention.

Aron's earliest treatise, the *Libri tres de institutione harmonica* (1516) makes use of a translator to this end. The treatise itself discusses the practical tradition, covering such topics as intervals, tones or modes, the Guidonian hand, hexachords, the writing of plainchant

25. For biographical information on Aron (whose surname is frequently spelled "Aaron"), see Peter Bergquist, "Aaron, Pietro," *New Grove*; A. Bonaccorsi, "Aaron, Pietro," *DBI*.

and counterpoint, and related issues. His references to the authority of other writers are sparing; he cites Boethius, Martianus Capella, Aristoxenus, Cleonides, and Guido, though only in passing. Very technical matters such as intonation are not discussed in depth. Had Aron not written other works, this one would mark him simply as another producer of the next generation of vaguely Boethian treatises.

Yet the literary presence of a translator, the Latin poet Giannantonio Flaminio, is something of a novelty. He states in a preface that his friend Aron had discussed the work's composition with him. Flaminio had offered to translate it into Latin for publication, so that it would be a more impressive monument to Aron's efforts. In fact, Flaminio serves not just as translator but also as commentator, with remarks running throughout the treatise. These comments provide such information as references to Greek etymologies of terms, citations of classical sources, and scholarly explanations of the material covered in the main body of the text. This device, almost a joint authorship, makes it difficult to distinguish the contributions of each figure. It would seem to imply that although such material was considered a necessary part of a music treatise, Aron's training did not allow him to compose it himself. The commentator's presence also serves, however, as a convenient rhetorical device for distinguishing technical arguments from the rest of the text and may represent this function more than an actual demarcation of skills between the two writers.[26]

Aron's *De institutione harmonica* is reminiscent in some ways of Burtius's treatise. Both works try to connect the ancient and medieval traditions in ways that work better on the level of style than of logic or substance. Burtius had his extracts from the works of famous authors; Aron has Flaminio's learned commentary. Both give the appearance of following Boethius while discussing numerous topics that are part and parcel of the medieval tradition. Both use references to classical writers simply in anecdotal manners or in order to lend weight to a preexisting argument, not as part of the structure of their analysis.

Aron's more widely circulating works reveal greater innovation. His next treatise, the *Thoscanello de la musica* (Venice, 1523) went through numerous editions (1529, rev. ed. 1539, 1562). The reasons for its popularity are clear enough: Aron had produced a complete practical

26. Franchino Gaffurio assumed that the musical arguments expressed in the work were those of Aron, while the language was Flaminio's. Flaminio sent Gaffurio a copy of the work in 1517, inviting a response. Gaffurio praised the elegance of the Latin but suggested that the argumentation was lacking. Flaminio responded that while he valued their friendship, he must respectfully disagree with Gaffurio's low assessment of Aron's work. See Bologna, Bib. Univ. 1998, pp. 538–43. Flaminio's son Marcantonio, also a poet and humanist, was a student of Raffaele Brandolini.

music treatise, similar in its overall model to the works of Burtius or Gaffurio, including an introductory *laus musice* and a closing discussion of Boethian proportion, all in Italian rather than Latin. Aron explains his goal near the end of the work:

> These are precepts which I have judged, not without tolerable reason, to be fit and sufficient for those who lack Latin letters to enter into the most praiseworthy league of musicians. Of these precepts, written in such style as has been conceded to me by my weak and rough intellect, I have avoided those questions and disputations that are too elevated and obscure and have left out nothing that seemed to me to be necessary of those things pertaining to the practice of singing, such as how to compose songs. Thus it is balanced so that (if my judgment does not deceive me) neither does brevity breed obscurity, nor length superfluity.[27]

Apparently his readers believed he had achieved his aim; both the number of editions and later citations of the work indicate a wide audience.

Aron justifies writing in the vernacular without the defensiveness that had marked Spataro's work. He notes in the first chapter that more readers are literate in their mother tongue, so this book is addressed especially to them. Further, he points out (1.4) that the work's subject is the practical tradition of *musica instrumentalis* rather than scholarship. Yet the use of vernacular seems to be the only concession to audience or theme. He does not water down the style of his prose in more literary passages, nor does he decrease the range or frequency of classical references. The contents of the practical tradition may form the bulk of the work, but that tradition is also discussed in some detail in its Boethian context with *musica mundana* and *humana*. He seeks to make the subject better known to a wide range of readers rather than to attack the tradition itself.

The *Thoscanello* also shows a slight change in emphasis among the parts of the traditional genre; half the treatise is devoted to rhythm and its notation, comparatively more than many earlier practical treatises. Discussions of pitch form a very secondary part of the work and

27. Pietro Aron, *Thoscanello de la musica di Messer Pietro Aaron Fiorentino Canonico da Rimini* (Venice: Bernardino, 1523), unpaged, final page: "Questi sono precetti i quali io non senza tollerabile ragione ho giodicati esser commodi et bastanti a quegli che di lettere lattine mancano, per intrar nel lodatissimo collegio de gli musici, liquali precetti con quello stile che mi ha concesso il mio debile et rozzo ingegno ho servato, et dale questioni et disputationi troppo alte et oscure, mi sono astenuto, et de le cose pertinenti a la pratica si di cantare come di comporre canti, niente ho lasciato che necessario mi sia paruto, con tal temperamento che (sel parer non m'inganna) ne le brevita partorisca oscurita, ne la longhezza superfluita."

are not very technical. Aron's introductory praise of music is nearly as long as Gaffurio's, the result of far more serious attention than Spataro had offered to the subject.

This *laus musice,* based as it is on that of Quintilian, is less noteworthy for its development of new or sophisticated ideas than for its occasional insertions of new forms of argumentation or evidence into its vernacular version of the form. Later readers will explore these points more thoroughly. Aron's use of sources resembles Gaffurio's (and is probably derived from his, though he is not cited); like Gaffurio, Aron frequently strings together names or references without attempting to assess their relative value. The similarity extends to Aron's attempt to connect various types of ancient praises of music by means of Pythagorean theory, though with an emphasis on music and poetry rather than on the mathematics of pitch.

Some of these insertions are individually very brief. Aron compiles a few of them to provide fuller detail about the social uses of music among the ancients, indicating the importance of musical performance both as entertainment and as an integral part of worship.[28] In another case, he extends the traditional arguments about the inborn nature of human response to music, by using not only the evidence of classical authors but also that of everyday observation, connecting the Pythagorean *musica humana* to Aristotelian treatments of music's value as recreation. Here he notes the supposed tabula rasa of an infant's mind: even though the child cannot talk, its mind still a clean slate, a soothing voice will calm its cries while a harsh one disturbs it; therefore the inclination to musical sound is innate.[29]

In a longer passage, Aron notes that Quintilian has stated that grammar connot be mastered without music, since one must know how to sing verses in their proper measure. Thus music is necessary for poets and orators. He continues with a brief history of poetry, based on the logic of this claim rather than on specific sources: "Ancient meters having been badly composed and almost rustic, poetry (says Censorinus) became more emotive and more inflected, almost a genuine music. With metric modulation it polished the harshness and made it all beautiful; but poets most of all embraced rhythms and musical meters and feet, so that they came to be called lyric poets, since they sang their verses to the lyre. They became so abundant, of so

28. Ibid., pp. 2, 4–5 of chap. 1. He repeats this argument in *Trattato della natura et cognitione di tutti gli tuoni di canto figurato* . . . (Venice: Vitali, 1525), unpaged, chap. 25.
29. Aron, *Thoscanello,* p. 3 of chap. 1; he is expanding on a brief remark in Boethius, *De musica* 1.1.

great a number, that Cicero denied there would be time to read all the
lyric poets."[30] Thus musical knowledge was a necessary factor in the
rise of classical poetry. Aron returns to Quintilian to reaffirm music's
importance to oratory, and to learning in general, and concludes with
a reference to Isidore confirming that no one (nor any thing) can
truly exist without music.

Aron's last major treatise, the *Lucidario in musica* (1545), treats some
similar issues with increasing sophistication. It is, he states, intended
to clarify "some ancient and modern opinions, with their oppositions
and resolutions,"[31] along with other questions. This work was also
published in Italian, and once again Aron has taken the high ground
on the language question, this time in a preface to his readers. He
compares their current linguistic situation to that of the Romans, who
had a formal language, Greek, and an everyday mother tongue,
Latin. But Cicero, literate in both, had chosen nonetheless to enrich
his native language. So too Boccaccio, Dante, Petrarch, and others
had improved the *volgare* by their use of it. Therefore he has chosen
it as a vehicle for addressing the learned and unlearned equally, so
that the arguments might be equally well understood by all.

This position sidesteps many questions about the use of technical
terms originating in one tradition or the other in favor of the vernacular vocabulary, while allowing Aron to argue that the language was
a considered and deliberate choice. He has moved beyond merely
claiming that the vernacular reaches a broader audience; he has
defined himself as a scholar who thinks seriously about the use of
language in his work. However much this can be attributed to fash-
ionable conceit, it also affects his general argumentation. Although
Aron does not address linguistic issues or undertake close textual criticism in the *Lucidario,* these matters influence his approach to the distinctions between ancient and modern opinions.

The work itself is divided into four books: the first deals with
plainchant, the second and third mainly with rhythmic notation,
the last with modes. While many of these issues involve no direct

30. Ibid., p. 5 of chap. 1: "Essendo li numeri antichi mal composti et quasi
rustichi: la poetica (dice Censorino) usci fuora piu affettata, et piu modulata, quasi
una legittima musica: la quale cno metrica modulatione pulisse lasprezza, et il tutto
facessi bello: ma sopra tutti quelli poeti abbracciaro li rhythmi, et numeri musichi, et
piedi, che lyrici furo cognominati, perche li loro versi attamente si cantavano alla
lyra: de quali tanta fu la copia, tanto fu il numero appresso li antichi, che Cicerone
niega dovergli bastare il tempo a leggere tutti li poeti lyrici."
31. Aron, *Lucidario in musica di alcune oppenioni antiche, et moderne* . . . (Venice:
Scotto, 1545.)

reference to ancient practices, several do; in these cases, Aron is able clearly to distinguish among possible uses of classical references. For example, in discussing ancient and modern modes, he carefully limits the use of the former to explain the latter:

> Some learned or average musician might argue that it is out of the question to treat that which is no longer seen in use, that is, the understanding and cognition of the modes among the ancients, as intended and practiced. They would judge our task to be one of vanity or worse, that I might want to renew ancient practice. We would respond that we do not want to remove anything from modern practice by introducing something of the antique; rather we intend to demonstrate how some notations of figured song had their birth and origin among those of the ancient musicians.[32]

Aron has no intention here of writing a history of the modes; he contents himself with a brief summary. Nonetheless, he has made several important historical distinctions: ancient musical practice, the modern tradition, a revival of ancient music by modern musicians, and the attempts to seek in the ancients the origins of the modern. Many later writers will fail to keep them so clear.

Perhaps Aron's most interesting argument is his analysis of musical creativity, appearing as part of a disagreement with Spataro over "whether musical composition exists solely in practice" (2.15). Spataro, states Aron, has claimed that, on the one hand, there exist good composers who had never really studied proportions but only "simple sonority"; despite this lack of education, they produce works that delight the listener. On the other hand, some persons with great knowledge of ancient theory have produced only harmonic proportions, not harmonious compositions. The almost supernatural quality of producing the good works, states Aron, proves that composers are born and not made: "whence one can believe that the good composers are born, not made through study, nor from much practice, but indeed thanks to celestial influence and inclination, and truly, that

32. Ibid., fol. 25v: "Se alcun dotto, o mediocre musico facesse discorso essere fuor di proposito trattar di quello, che piu in uso non si vede, cioè intorno alla intelligenza, et cognitione de modi da gli antichi intesi, et essercitati opponendoci tal nostra fatica essere di soverchio, et di piu forse, che io voglia rinovare la consuetudine antica, et riprovata si risponde, che noi non vogliamo altramente removere cosa alcuna dalla consuetudine moderna per introducere alcune di quelle della antica, ma bene intendiamo dimostrare, come alcune segni di canto figurato hanno havuto principio, et nascimento da quegli de gli antichi Musici."

few are so destined."[33] Thus it seems to many, he continues, that music consists solely in practice; whereas for theoreticians, it seems to consist of making manifest the result of their study:

> And so, as we see that if different sculptors in marble or some other material produce the same figure or form, nonetheless one of them will be much more perfect than another, by as much as one's artifice is better than the other, I say that it happens likewise with our harmonic faculty, in which we may observe many composers, each of whom would know the material or musical intervals of harmonic form. Yet it is present in greater excellence by one of them than another, and with greater sweetness according to which one has more understanding and grace in such faculty than the other. And through such arguments and demonstrations one concludes that the art of composing harmony consists of more than just practice.[34]

This argument about composers and the origin of their skills is interesting for several reasons. First, Aron has based his evidence on observed experience. For example, he does not simply cite or copy Quintilian but imitates his style, which is full of specific anecdotes and descriptions of human behavior. This kind of argument, based on the writer's interpretation of observed behavior rather than on textual authority, will become more and more prevalent throughout the rest of the century.

Second, Aron is comparing the work of musicians to that of sculptors. He does not develop this analogy into any larger theory about the relationship between music and sculpture or the other arts, but he certainly perceives the two fields as similar. Further, he sees them as related not by the nature of the subject but by the nature of their practitioners; that is, his argument is based not on the resemblance between music and sculpture but on that between musicians and sculptors. While this line of argumentation will not become the

33. Ibid., fol. 15r: "la onde si puo credere che i buoni compositori nascono, et non si fanno per studio, ne per molto praticare, ma si bene per celeste influsso, et inclinatione, Gratie veramente, che a pochi il ciel largo destina."

34. Ibid.: "Et si come veggiamo, che per diversi scultori nel marmo, o in altra materia essendo introdotta la istessa figura, o forma, esse tra loro tuttavia haranno tanto piu di perfettione l'una dell'altra, quanto gli artefici di esse saranno piu eccellenti l'uno, chell'altro, Il simile dico avenire di questa nostra harmonica facolta, nella quale veggiamo ritrovarsi molti compositori, da ciascuno de quali la materia, overo distanze musiche essendo conosciute acconcie alla forma harmonica essa le è date in piu eccelenza dall'uno, che dall'altro, et con maggior soavità, et dolcezza prodotta secondo che l'uno ha piu cognitione, et gratia in tal facolta dell'altro, Et per tali argomenti, et dimostrationi si conchiude che l'arte del comporre l'harmonia consiste in altro che nella sola pratica."

dominant means of redefining the field, it is nonetheless original, interesting, and apparently influential for later writers. It offers a way to circumvent the discussions of the certainty of knowledge acquired by the exercise of the discipline, in favor of directing attention to the actions of the practitioners themselves.

Third, Aron remains committed to his Pythagorean approach. On the basis of the same observed evidence that had convinced Spataro simply that musicians need not study theory, Aron concludes instead that the ultimate source of this skill must be sought in larger celestial influences. This idea echoes the notion of "poetic furor" espoused by Brandolini and by Renaissance Platonists, implying that Aron's knowledge of the movement is greater than merely the standard acquaintance with music sources; such ideas had not been a part of the Boethian tradition. Thus Aron's emphasis on the practical tradition does not mean a rejection, or a relegation to the periphery, of the larger theoretical issues of musical science.

The Mathematicians

The mathematical scholars that followed Giorgio Valla shared his interest in addressing the subject of mathematics' place among fields of learning. Those who approached the discipline from Valla's syncretic Pythagorean perspective also continued to see their mathematical studies as closely related to the study of music. Thus, many mathematicians active during the first half of the sixteenth century felt the need to express in their writings the relationship between their own work and musical scholarship.

These expressions often lacked originality. Some, in fact, may reveal as much about the author's reliance on classical sources for his written opinions on the subject as they do about the role of musical scholarship in the author's own thought about mathematics. Had this been true of all mathematical writings from the early sixteenth century, the study of their passages on music might have revealed only the survival of a rhetorical formula lacking in substance. The extensive writings of a few figures such as Girolamo Cardano (see Chap. 4) are sufficient, however, to show that musical studies continued to fall very much within the range of the professional interests open to a sixteenth-century mathematician.

Even in the briefer treatments of the subject offered by Bartolomeo Zamberti, Niccolo Tartaglia, and Luca Pacioli, it is apparent that to them, music's place among the mathematical disciplines is not in doubt. In no case did they suggest any wish to reject Pythagorean assumptions or even simply to ignore them. The exact position of music among the mathematical disciplines did become a matter of some debate because of Luca Pacioli's desire to add the science of perspective to the quadrivium. Nonetheless, the fact that practicing mathematicians took the relationship seriously as an ongoing part of their own discipline is itself significant. It demonstrates that this classification of music was not confined to writers within the discipline of music itself but was also accepted by the scholars in these related fields.

Given the limited range of literary self-expression afforded the authors of mathematical treatises, it is not surprising that many mathematicians reserved their remarks on more general themes for use as introductions, dedications, and the like. One example is the group of introductions written by the early sixteenth-century translators of Euclid. An ongoing quarrel among these translators encouraged them to use their introductions not only to attack their rivals but also to display their own merits as translators, editors, and commentators. Their introductions thus became an arena for extended displays of learning. This tendency is even more marked owing to their confusion of Euclid of Alexandria (the mathematician) with Euclid of Megara (the fourth-century disciple of Socrates).[35] The consequent belief that the *Elements* had been written by a Neoplatonic philosopher encouraged the expression of similar ideas on the part of the translators.

Bartolomeo Zamberti's *Euclid* (1505, with several later editions) serves as an early example of such writings that include discussions of music. Relatively little is known about Zamberti's life and career.[36] A

35. Paul Lawrence Rose, *The Italian Renaissance of Mathematics: Studies on Humanists and Mathematicians from Petrarch to Galileo* (Geneva: Droz, 1975); Rose, "Bartolomeo Zamberti's Funeral Oration for the Humanist Encyclopaedist Giorgio Valla," in *Cultural Aspects of the Italian Renaissance: Essays in Honor of Paul Oskar Kristeller,* ed. Cecil H. Clough (Manchester: Manchester University Press, 1976), p. 301. Dominic J. O'Meara has noted that Proclus saw Euclid as a Platonist, the *Elements* as conforming to the *Republic's* description of mathematical discourse, and the work's goal as the construction of the *Timaeus's* geometric figures; such an opinion would have lent credence to similar Renaissance readings of Euclid. See O'Meara, *Pythagoras Revived: Mathematics and Philosophy in Late Antiquity* (Oxford: Clarendon, 1989), pp. 170–71. Allen Debus's edition of John Dee's preface to the *Elements* demonstrates that the use of these introductions as an arena for general discussions of the nature of mathematics and the classification of knowledge was not confined to Italian mathematicians and translators. See John Dee, *The Mathematicall Preface to the Elements of Geometrie of Euclid of Megara (1570)*, intro. Allen G. Debus (New York: Science History Publications, 1975).

36. Rose, *Italian Renaissance of Mathematics*, p. 50; Rose, "Zamberti's Funeral Oration," p. 301.

Venetian born about 1473, he was active as a lawyer and a humanist as well as a student of mathematics; among his other translations are works by Proclus, Nicomachus, and Alexander of Aphrodisias.[37] Zamberti's relationship with Giorgio Valla was sufficiently close that he composed Valla's funeral oration, though the details of that association are unclear. The 1546 Basel edition of his *Euclid* includes new introductory material of his authorship; Tartaglia also refers to Zamberti in his 1543 Italian translation of Euclid as if he were still alive (though this passage is retained in the 1565 edition, and it seems doubtful that he would still have been alive at that date).[38]

It is in his first edition of Euclid that Zamberti offers his most extended discussion of music and learning, in a manner reminiscent of Valla's treatment. Zamberti begins by describing various divisions made in the subject of philosophy as meditation upon death; the study of philosophy, he notes, is also similar to death in that it separates the soul from the body. He goes on to discuss the two parts of the soul, a higher, rational element and a lower, irrational one (fol. 3r), the higher element linked to the heavenly bodies and to contemplation of the divine. He cites the Neoplatonists Proclus and Plotinus in support of this part of his discussion. These remarks introduce, in turn, the subject of mathematics. Like Valla, Zamberti sees mathematics as occupying a middle ground in philosophy, connecting these two realms of the physical and the spiritual, so doing because it exists both in and outside of material reality. He distinguishes mathematics' two branches by the types of quantities studied, following Boethius in identifying arithmetic and music with discrete quantities, geometry and astronomy with continuous. At this point, Zamberti offers a survey of the development of each of the four mathematical disciplines, beginning with arithmetic.

The discussion of music follows the now-familiar outline. Zamberti begins with the invention of music by Mercury, continuing with a recitation of classical authorities who esteemed the subject highly (4r). He summarizes the usual general remarks about music: that the human body is composed of its ratios; that its pitch system consists of three harmonic genera, and its system of consonances is formed of the primary proportions; that various authorities named the subject's elements in various ways. Citing Boethius, he notes that music is more than simply a speculative science; because of its effects on the soul, it

37. Rose, *Italian Renaissance of Mathematics*, p. 50.

38. *Euclide Megarense . . . reassettato, et alla integrità ridotto . . .* (Venice, 1543, 1544, 1565, 1569, 1585), fol. 6v. Zamberti's introductions are found in his *Euclides Megarensis . . . Elementorum geometricorum Libri XV . . .* (Venice, 1505; Basel, 1546).

is also conjoined to morality. Thus it is a divine discipline, its use in worship having been commanded by the prophets. He concludes with a brief treatment of musicopoetic forms such as the heroic, epigrammatic, and so on. From music, Zamberti moves on to a similar passage on astronomy. The subsequent discussion of geometry's role in ancient learning leads him to the matter at hand, the work of Euclid.

This treatment of the subject is certainly not innovative; Zamberti uses no new sources, nor does he offer arguments not made before. Yet he does present a surprising amount of information and detail given that this is an introduction to a work on a different subject entirely. Further, he does not simply rely on older, standard sources but makes use of such works as Cleonides, which Valla had translated only very recently.

Nor does the organization of his sources simply mimic earlier writers. For example, in his discussion of those classsical genres that had arisen from music's spiritual functions, he employs several scriptural references to the prophets emphasizing music's role in divine service. This argumentative turn is modest but original; it indicates that Zamberti had sufficient interest in the subject to have organized this passage himself. That is, he did not simply summarize or copy a standard *laus musice* to insert mechanically into his text. Thus, though Zamberti's discussion does not represent a major change in musical thought, it does demonstrate the continued, active interest in the subject even among mathematical scholars whose main interests lay in different specialties.

Zamberti's introduction to the later Basel edition is a much more modest effort. In fact, it consists only of a dedication to the Venetian patrician Paolo Pisano, whose interest in astronomy is the real focus of the dedication. In it, Zamberti carefully recites the relevance of the other mathematical fields (including geometry) to astronomy, stressing mathematics' certainty of knowledge and its role in understanding the cosmos. In this dedication, Zamberti refers to music solely in terms of its ability to describe the motions of the heavenly bodies, citing Pythagoras and Nicomachus as authorities.

Taken together, Zamberti's two introductions serve as examples not of innovation but of the perceived classification and definition of the field of music in the minds of colleagues in related disciplines. Music is certainly not Zamberti's main concern. Yet his definition of the subject does not differ significantly from those offered by his contemporaries who were specialists. While he is not an active musical scholar himself, Zamberti is aware of and able to refer to the most recently available sources. He shows no evidence of reducing the field to a formulaic or purely rhetorical element among the mathematical disciplines, nor does he indicate that his colleagues might do so.

The introductions of Niccolo Tartaglia (1499–1557) resemble those of Zamberti in many ways.[39] Like Zamberti, Tartaglia addresses the subject of the quadrivium in general and therefore discusses music. He also treats the field of music solely in terms of mathematics. Further, Tartaglia makes use of a reasonable variety of recent sources and writings on music, revealing interest as well as serious thought about the topic itself. Yet the two sets of introductions are not merely copies of one another. Zamberti had stressed the role of philosophy in the service of the soul and the place of mathematical studies in that endeavor. Tartaglia writes a more general praise of geometry, similar in its Platonic or Pythagorean orientation but much less systematic. More significant is that Tartaglia chooses to treat a relatively new issue, the organization and classification of quadrivial fields themselves, thus bringing the relevant issues to the attention to a wide variety of readers.

Tartaglia's translation came out in two editions, 1543 (reprinted in 1544) and 1565 (reprinted in 1569 and 1585). The introduction to the second edition is a revised draft of the first, organized into two "lettioni" with numbered paragraphs. In both cases he begins with the reasons for studying geometry, relating it, as had Zamberti, to the other quadrivial fields. His statement on music leads into the one on astrology by way of the *occulta philosophia*:

> It is well known how much it [the study of mathematics] is nurse and mother of musicians (as Severinus Boethius affirms, and likewise Franchino Gaffurio in his *Music*). For without numbers and their properties, proportion, and proportionality, the consonances or dissonances of three or more voices cannot be known clearly. But with it one recognizes that a fifth or octave make the sweetest harmony and greatly delight the listeners' hearing. Likewise, with the above-mentioned science of numbers, we know that the fourth is a great dissonance and disturbs the hearing more than a little. With its rules, calculation, and the virtue of its numbers, it leads the way to the judicial art called astrology, and likewise to pyromancy, hydromancy, necromancy, geomancy, horoscopes, aurispices, auguries, auspices, and other reckonings. The above-

39. For recent scholarship on Tartaglia—important not only for his own works but also for his translations and editions, especially of Archimedes—see Arnaldo Masotti, *Studi su Niccolò Tartaglia* (Brescia: Ateneo di Brescia, 1962); *Quarto centenario della morte di Niccolo Tartaglia, Convegno di storia delle mathematiche* (Brescia: Ateneo di Brescia, 1959).

mentioned Isidore writes about this, and Cieco of Ascoli, and also Cornelius Agrippa in the second part of his *Occulta Philosophia*.[40]

This passage implies several lines of argument without discussing them in real detail. The first praise of number as a necessary part of music is fairly typical; the statement about the fourth is more interesting. Tartaglia assumes here that the fourth is a dissonance, and the reader is left to infer that this is consistent with the previously named authorities such as Boethius. Since Tartaglia offers no detail, there is no way to pursue this argument. Yet is does serve as evidence that the standard illustration of consonant and dissonant ratios is shifting away from acceptance of the fourth.

Tartaglia's brief flirtation here with *occulta philosophia* also illustrates one of the attractions to many writers of keeping musical proportion central to the mathematical disciplines. Pythagorean cosmology, with its musical consonance, forms the basis for understanding the "hidden" relationships between human fortunes and other aspects of the cosmos. Increased study of any aspect of this subject would involve an interest in musical proportion as well. Thus any sort of philosophical studies related to these divine secrets would tend to reinforce music's place in the quadrivium and the importance of the quadrivium itself. Tartaglia reminds the reader that according to Plato it is the ability to number that distinguishes humans from beasts; in this ability, human nature resembles the divine.

Tartaglia alters this passage somewhat in his later edition, giving more attention to problems of intonation. Of particular interest in this regard, he notes, is Euclid 7.8, devoted to the impossibility of dividing musical proportions into rational halves.[41] The slightly different organization of this introduction causes him to move his

---

40. Tartaglia, *Euclide* (1543), sig. Aiiii: "Certa cosa è qualmente quella è nutrice et matre delli Musici (come afferma Boetio Severino, et similmente Franchino Gaffuro nella sua musica), imperoche senza li numeri, et le sue proprieta, proportione, et proportionalita, non si puo cognoscere chiaramente la consonantia, et dissonantia di tre, over piu voci, ma con quella el si cognosce che una quinta, over ottava fanno soavissima armonia, et grandemente dilettano lo audito delli audienti, et similmente con la detta scientia de numeri sappiamo che una quarta grande dissonantia, et non puoco turba lo audito. Questa con le sue regole calculatorie, et virtu, de suoi numeri da la via all'arte giuditiaria detta Astrologia, et similmente alla Pyromantia, Hydromantia, Necromantia, Geomantia, Horospitio, Aruspitio, Augurio, Auspitio, et altri Sortilegii. E questo scrive il predetto Isidoro, et Cieco di Ascoli, et similmente Cornelio Agrippa nel secondo de occulta Philosophia."

41. Tartaglia, trans., *Euclide Megarense . . . reassettato, et alla integrità ridotto . . .* (Venice: Bariletto, 1569), fol. 3v.

discussion of *occulta philosophia* elsewhere and to tone it down somewhat; he does, however, remark that such figures as Nicholas of Cusa have demonstrated the usefulness of mathematics to the study of theology.[42]

Tartaglia begins the "seconda lettione" by addressing the identity of the various mathematical disciplines themselves.[43] He notes that there has been some disagreement about just which disciplines fall under the classification of "mathematics." Fields commonly so considered include arithmetic, geometry, music, astronomy, astrology, cosmography, chorography, perspective, reflection and refraction, the science of weights, and architecture.[44] Boethius and Giorgio Valla, whose works were based on Greek writings, had allowed only the first four; they considered the others to be subaltern subjects, dependent on the quadrivial disciplines. While Tartaglia finds this classification useful, he disagrees about the number of primary mathematical disciplines:

> But Fra Luca Pacioli of Borgo San Sepolcro claims that the mathematical disciplines are either five (adding Perspective to the above-mentioned four) or three, excluding Music from the preceding four. To support his opinion, he gives sufficient reasons and arguments, which we will leave aside as not being a matter of importance. Nonetheless, the Reverend Cardinal Pierre d'Ailly, in his first question on Giovanni di Sacrobosco, concludes that Music, Astronomy, and likewise Perspective are not pure Mathematics (as is the truth), but midpoints between Mathematics and Natural Science. Thus it follows that only Arithmetic and Geometry are pure Mathematics, and all others are medial, or dependent and mixed between the mathematical disciplines and Natural Science, excepting judicial astrology, which he concludes is purely natural in essence.[45]

42. Ibid., fol. 5r.
43. An equivalent passage is placed on the back of the title page of the 1543 edition; it differs in that several figures, such as Boethius, are discussed but not mentioned by name.
44. Tartaglia, *Euclide* (1569), fols. 5v–6r.
45. Ibid., fol. 6r: "Ma Fra Luca Parioli dal Borgo San Sepulchro, vuole che le dette discipline Mathematice siano overamente cinque (aggiongendo alle predette quattro la Perspettiva) overamente tre, iscludendo dalle predette quattro la Musica: et per sostentare tal suo opinione, aduce ragioni et argumenti assai, liquali per non esser cosa de importantia lasciaremo da banda. Nientedimeno il Reverend. Sig. Pietro de Aliasco Cardinale, nella prima questione sopra Giovanne di Sacrobusto, conchiude, la Musica et la Astronomia, et similmente la Perspettiva non esser pur Mathematice (come è il vero) ma medie fra le mathematice, et la scientia naturale: Per il che seguita solamente la Arithmetica, et la Geometrica esser le pure

Therefore, he concludes, the study of geometry treated here in speculative fashion by Euclid is one of the two pure mathematical disciplines.

This echo of Pacioli is especially noteworthy for keeping the latter's argument in the public eye. The Franciscan theologian and mathematician Luca Pacioli is perhaps better known for his lifelong association with the painter Piero della Francesca (also of Borgo S. Sepolcro) and their development and advocacy of the study of perspective. The work to which Tartaglia refers is Pacioli's *Divina proportione* (1505), of particular importance to the visual arts. Pacioli argues at the beginning of the treatise that the quadrivium should be changed: either perspective should be admitted as a fifth subject, or music should be removed to leave three. He argues that music, like perspective, involves natural senses, so perhaps neither should be classified as mathematics. If, however, music is to remain in the quadrivium, perspective has all the more reason to be included, because vision is "the first gate to the intellect" and hence superior to the sense of hearing.[46]

Since Pacioli was attempting to build acceptance for the new science of perspective, it is not surprising that he should make the strongest possible claims about its exalted place among the disciplines. Again, according to this argument music (and perspective) should be classified either among the mathematical disciplines or among the natural sciences. The distinguishing feature of the two subjects is their reliance on sense perception in addition to number. Tartaglia has borrowed this argument from Pacioli in order to elevate the position of geometry in turn. Both passages have the effect of establishing the essential basis of the field of music, though that is in fact not their main intent.

Tartaglia's argument also recalls Valla's claim that mathematics is partly in and partly out of the material, natural world. Tartaglia has shifted its meaning slightly, using the degree of participation in the material world as the criterion for determining whether a field is "pure" mathematics or somewhere between it and the natural sciences. Geometry qualifies as pure mathematics, since its principles are independent of physical references, while music and astronomy do not.

Mathematice, et tutte l'altre esser medie, over dependenti, et miste delle Mathematice discipline et della scientia naturale, eccettuando la Strologia giudiciaria, laqual egli conchiude esser pura naturale, in quanto alla sua essentia."

46. Luca Pacioli, *Divina proportione* (Milan: Paganinus, 1509), text fol. 3r (sig. Biii r).

Tartaglia does not claim to present any innovations in this discussion of mathematics; though he uses fairly recent sources, they are not new discoveries. Nor does he develop these arguments in greater systematic detail. Like Zamberti's writings, these passages are important not because they say things that are new but because of the kinds of thought they reveal about the field of music and those involved in its study.

First, it is clear that Tartaglia still, even in the 1560s, sees music as a mathematical discipline. It may not be "pure" mathematics, but he would still classify it with astronomy, considering both of them to fall somewhere in between mathematics and the natural sciences. Thus even in a brief discussion his attention is directed toward the field's traditional topics, intonation and the proportions between intervals.

Further, Tartaglia demonstrates the continuing importance of musical scholarship, as seen in the Pythagorean cosmology of harmonic proportion, to several aspects of Renaissance thought. The "occult philosophies" in particular depend on a harmonic cosmology, but Tartaglia relates the other mathematical subdisciplines to music as well, however sketchily.

Finally, the wide distribution of such a book made the subject both available and significant to a broad range of readers. Anyone who picked up an Italian *Euclid* could become acquainted with this argument about mathematics, and hence about the study of music, which Tartaglia clearly considers an issue of general interest and concern. Even though he may not have been a major scholar in music, Tartaglia's writings on the subject therefore mark a valuable contribution to Renaissance musical thought.

An End to Consensus

Spataro probably never read Brandolini's oration, nor Zamberti's *Euclid*; Tartaglia may never have studied the works of Spataro or Brandolini. This diversity is itself a sign of music's appeal to a wider range of thinkers and forms a distinctive feature of the writings on music through the midsixteenth century. Too many people wrote on music for them all to read one another's work or to have been scholars of major influence in the field. In some ways they seem to have been more engaged in dialogue with their predecessors than they were with each other. Yet while they did not form a single intellectual circle, neither were they entirely disconnected from one another.

Enough of them shared enough common traits and concerns that some generalizations are possible.

Perhaps the most important of these shared assumptions was the continuing Pythagorean orientation. For the mathematicians in particular, Pythagorean doctrine not only provided the connections between the quadrivial disciplines but also justified the importance of their study. So too it explained the "hidden" connections among great and small aspects of the cosmos, serving as an essential foundation for the group of sources and phenomena lumped under the heading *occulta philosophia*. Without this connection, there would have been no reason for Zamberti, Tartaglia, or Pacioli to discuss music at all in their writings. Though music was not the major subject of their scholarship, they felt the need to define their own work in relation to music and the other mathematical disciplines. Even Brandolini, who addressed a completely different aspect of the field, nonetheless justified music's effects ultimately in Pythagorean terms. Thus Brandolini and Tartaglia could see themselves, in the end, as participants in very different aspects of the same philosophical and cosmological system.

Further, both Brandolini and Aron revealed an interest in Platonic thought that extended beyond these Pythagorean, mathematical aspects of the discipline. Both of them addressed the problem of explaining a composer's creativity; they did so in the Platonic terms of "poetic furor," the poets' contact with the divine which they transmit to others through their art. This notion had not formed part of the standard discussions or praises of music during the fifteenth century. Rather, it is typical of the Renaissance Platonism expounded by Marsilio Ficino and his circle. Brandolini used the concept in his discussion of poets who write hymns; Aron introduced it to account for the differing levels of quality among composers, differences that might not correspond to the level of their training. For both writers, the notion of "poetic furor" played an important role in broadening the arguments extolling the power of music beyond the older, simpler Pythagorean explanations. It allowed them to account for the differing abilities of specific composers or compositions to move the listener, even when similar intervals were used in each case.

Even Spataro agreed that Pythagorean explanations were important parts of the musical thought of his day; he simply did not approve of that importance. Spataro's attacks on the relevance of studying the ancients to musical thought may at times seem defensive and even petty. They seem not to have attracted a large following; at least, no significant body of later writers identified themselves particularly with this aspect of Spataro's work. Yet his arguments against specific aspects of Pythagorean theory had a more noticeable impact. Later writers had to improve upon those points of Gaffurio's analyses that Spataro criticized, especially in their discussions of pitch.

Brandolini and Aron shared an interest in the relationship between music and language. Brandolini's oration marked the earliest example of this relationship treated as a topic for study in its own right. By making use of a different set of sources and approaching the subject from an entirely new viewpoint, Brandolini could develop the subject in ways that had not been open to Gaffurio. Since the technical aspects of the field did not color his reading of classical literary texts, he was able to make fuller use of essentially the same body of sources that had been available earlier. Aron stressed the importance of poetics as part of music's early historical development, and he also gave more attention to rhythmics than many of his predecessors. He also devoted considerable energy to defending the use of vernacular in writing and publishing. This transition from Latin to Italian marked an important widening of the audience for music treatises.

Aron's explanations of his own choice of language, his claims to emulate the Latin writers like Cicero who chose to enrich their native tongue rather than write in the more elevated Greek language, reveal a much greater concern with language-related issues. Humanistic interests have become more prominent, spreading beyond the choice of a gracious humanistic prose style to more explicit concerns about the text itself. Questions about a work's structure, audience, and appropriate modes of expression have all become issues not only for the author to consider but also to discuss as part of the treatise itself.

Spataro also alluded to this change, publishing exclusively in Italian. But he was more obvious about making a virtue of apparent necessity, arguing not so much in favor of the Italian language as against the usefulness of knowledge available only in Latin. He did resemble the others in the importance he accorded to metrics as well as pitch, though he relied mainly on medieval sources such as Marchetto and Franco. Despite his pronouncements against the value of ancient writers, Spataro willingly admitted their value in promoting his own work; he refers to a discussion of proportion from his own *Tractato* in a letter to Aron as "very learned, and founded in Mathematics."[47]

47. Letter from Spataro to Aron, no date, Vatican City, BAV, Vat. Lat. 5318, fol. 220v: "Io già feci uno tractato, dove se prova de la perfectione producta dà la sesqualtera ni le figure cantabile: molto docta, et in mathematica fondata."

Since Aron's concern with Platonism and the study of language so resembles that of Brandolini, and since it appeared in Aron's writings only after his stay in Rome, it appears likely that the two knew one another during those years. They both worked for Leo X, though Leo's group of clients was large and direct evidence is lacking. Nonetheless, the two seem to have moved in similar scholarly circles, as in their extended mutual acquaintance with the Flaminio family. Even at the stylistic level Aron's prose is reminiscent of Brandolini's.

The new interest in connecting music with rhetoric can also be seen in the surviving correspondence of Aron and other composers, several of whom wrote no treatises or other public writings and hence left no other record of their interests and concerns. A collection of letters in the Vatican library (Vat. Lat. 5318) which includes those of Spataro and Aron along with those of others such as Giovanni del Lago and Giovanni Molino offers a glimpse at topics of interest to working composers. Disputes with publishers were a constant source of irritation, as were problem students; they also addressed specific problems and solutions in music composition, focusing especially on such technical subjects as rhythmic notation and the tuning of scales. A few of these letters, however, reveal an interest in the parallels between textual composition and musical form. One example is a letter of Giovanni del Lago from 1541. Del Lago is enjoining composers to keep the text in mind when writing music for madrigals, barzelette, and the like:

Cadences are also necessary and not arbitrary, as some inconsiderately think, especially in song composed for words. This is to distinguish the parts of the oration; that is, to mark the distinction of the comma, the colon, and the period, so that it relates the perfect sense of the parts of the oration, whether in verse or in prose. Because the cadence in music is like a mark of punctuation. The cadence is a certain distinction, and repose in a song. Or rather, the cadence is a termination of that part of a song, as in the context of an oration, a medium distinction or a final.[48]

48. Giovanni del Lago, letter to Fra Seraphin, 26 August 1541, Vatican City, BAV, Vat. Lat. 5318, fol. 4r: "Le cadentie utramente sono necessarie, et non arbitrarie, come alcuni inconsideratamenti dicono, massimamente nel canto composto sopra le parole, et questo per distinguer le parti della oratione, cioè far la distintione del comma, et colo, et del periodo. acioche sia intesa la sententia delle parti della oratione perfetta, se nel verso, come nella prosa. Perche la cadentia in Musica è come il punto nella Grammatica. La cadentia è una certa distintione, et riposo nel canto. Overo la cadentia è una terminatione di essa parte del canto, come è nel contesto del'oratione, la media distintione, ut la finale."

This sort of attempt, to match musical accompaniment to a preexisting text that remains the center of attention, will become more and more common throughout the middle years of the sixteenth century.

Thus these early sixteenth-century writers devoted their attention to interesting, if often discrete, aspects of the study of music in ways that disclose significant similarities in addition to their more obvious differences.. Their work continued to follow the basic outlines traced by their immediate predecessors but was not itself without innovation. At the same time, it offers evidence that these outlines were not restricted to a small group of theorists or professionals but described the field as known to colleagues in related disciplines and as disseminated to a relatively broad vernacular public. The new issues raised during these years will continue to be addressed in the succeeding decades.

CHAPTER 4

Ancients and Moderns

No great divide of new discoveries or issues separates the writers of the early sixteenth century from those of the middle decades. Neither did a single scholar have a sufficiently powerful command of the field or of readers to impose his stamp on the discipline in the way Gaffurio had earlier, or several scholars would a few decades later. Perhaps the most obvious features of these midcentury sources are their number and diversity; a broad range of works aimed at an equally broad range of audiences had begun to circulate in print. Such a description could leave the impression of diversity without depth; nonetheless, these works shared several common themes and trends, many of long-term significance. Most often, the works of this period grew out of attempts at new readings of some part of the classical tradition to develop a basis for revising or reforming modern scholarship or practice.

The most tentative and least immediately productive of these efforts was the continued interest in connecting the study of music with poetry and language. Writers approached this subject in one of two ways. One was to take vocal music as the standard and to argue that the text of a piece and the poetic rules that governed its composition should have primacy in determining the style of music written for it; metrics provided the easiest focus, though writers such as Cardano and Vicentino both took on larger issues of pitch and musical style at the same time. The other took the form of a simile: music is like language; just as different peoples employ different languages, so too they have different types of music. Both language and music communicate ideas and, especially, emotions. This resemblance between

139

music and language was noted by numerous writers, especially after midcentury. Yet because the differences were so great between such an approach and the Pythagorean theory that still dominated professional discourse, these writers tended not to integrate these ideas well into the rest of their work, however appealing they might have found the subject.

Similar comparisons were drawn between music and the visual arts, likening, for example, musicians to painters, in that a musician selects pitches just as a painter chooses a color palate. Musical modes were also described as parallels to the classical architectural orders. As in the case of music and language, most writers did not follow through in developing such topics. They might find it interesting or significant that there is both a Doric mode and a Doric order but remain unable to articulate a specific connection between the two. Thus while many writers seemed to want, at least at times, to classify music with poetry or the visual arts, they did not address the issue on its own or maintain this classification throughout their work.

In the case of mathematical studies the results were more immediately substantial. Some scholars, such as Ludovico Fogliano, wanted to keep the mathematical analysis of pitch proportions yet reject the Pythagorean principles that underlay it; some other means had then to be found to connect these numbers in a system. This problem forced scholarly attention both to searching for the relationships between numbers and the behavior of sounding bodies, and to explaining why humans perceive musical intervals as consonant or dissonant. Girolamo Cardano tried to develop a system based both on Pythagorean music theory and Aristotelian-influenced notions of perception.

A better acquaintance with the ancient sources also led to broader concerns about the relations between ancient and modern music. Much of the basis for this comparison could be found in the *laus musice,* and perhaps the effort to compare is best seen as an attempt to bring the *laus musice* to life in modern practice. Of particular interest were the alleged miraculous effects of ancient music. These writers tried in several ways to resolve the discrepancies between the claims made for ancient music and the empirical evidence of the effect of modern music on the listener, but none involved impugning the credibility of the ancient sources. Instead, they addressed either the causes of ancient music's influence on the people of antiquity or the degree to which modern music resembled ancient music in this regard. They argued with one another about the historical causes of ancient music's effects, the nature of present observed effects, and the causes of those modern effects. Whatever solution a given writer might offer, the issue and the ensuing arguments threw into relief an acknowledgment of historical distance between ancients and moderns.

Within the Pythagorean tradition, the most logical solution to this problem was to attribute ancient music's effects to the ancient pitch systems. Writers who followed this path came to advocate a reform of composition styles, to increase the expressive power of modern music. Specifically, they proposed writing music that was not merely diatonic but also chromatic and enharmonic. These proposals launched an extended, heated debate over the use of the three ancient harmonic genera and, in the process, pushed the earlier debates about thirds and sixths far to the sidelines.

No consensus arose, and no transformation occurred during these years. This failure to resolve professional disagreements and questions was less a result of a lack of scholarly or professional ability than a symptom of the size and complexity of the issues.

Dialogues, Treatises, and Essays

Books on music, written in a variety of genres, seem to have become fairly standard fare for the publishers of the midsixteenth century. From the late 1520s through the 1550s, many books on music appeared in print, often by authors of lesser fame in the field than those of earlier years. The range of intellectual levels addressed also widened, from scholarly treatises like those of Ludovico Fogliano to books that, like the *Dialoghi* of Anton Francesco Doni, served mainly to frame sets of musical compositions intended for amateur purchase and performance.

The minor authors of these years resemble their earlier predecessors in that they are more recursive than actively discursive or dialogic; that is, they refer back to earlier writers more than they engage in dialogue with one another, or even mention one another. The more scholarly writers, such as Fogliano, will be read and cited by later authors; those who intended their works for a more popular audience certainly depended on earlier or contemporary scholarship but generally did not themselves contribute to the scholarly tradition with new insights or innovations. All these works tended to focus on a single, particular aspect of what was an increasingly large and intractable field.

Ludovico Fogliano (d. ca. 1539) probably had the widest influence. A singer at Modena's cathedral, he apparently remained there all his life, with the exception of a year's employment at Rome in the Capella Giulia.[1] The *Musica theorica* (1529) is Fogliano's sole surviving written work. He began translations of Aristotle and Averroes for publication but died before completing the project.[2] Thus his intellectual interests were broader than those of his older colleague Spataro; Fogliano was a professional singer who nonetheless emphasized Latin learning and the theoretical tradition in his written work.

In its scholarly intentions as well as its literary style, the *Musica theorica* is very conservative. Written in a technical and scholastic Latin, it focuses entirely on issues of pitch and mathematical proportion. His major influences appear to be Boethius and Ptolemy, except in chapters based on Guido's ecclesiastical tradition; Gaffurio's influence is clearly visible, though he is seldom named. Yet the work's importance to later writers lay not in its conservatism per se but rather in its innovative approach in addressing this traditional set of scholarly questions. Fogliano tries to take the classification of music seen in Valla's work and develop it to account for the non-Pythagorean consonances of thirds and sixths and to regularize the various approaches to tuning and tuning systems. The resulting accumulation of charts and technical illustrations makes very slow going for the modern reader; yet Fogliano's general theories, as well as his tuning diagrams, became a standad reference on this aspect of musical studies for the next several decades.

Fogliano divides his work into three sections: musical proportions, the application of those proportions in forming consonances, and the division of the monochord. He ignores the usual *laus musice*, noting in his brief preface to the reader, "Non enim oratione, sed ratione tantum: hic placere studeo."[3] Instead, he moves directly to a classic definition of music as "sonorous number." His careful qualification of the exact type of physical behavior to which those numbers apply reveals his concern for uniting mathematical theory with the observed behavior of sounding bodies:

1. For biographical information on Fogliano, see Henry W. Kaufmann, "Fogliano, Ludovico," *New Grove*. For a detailed examination of Fogliano's tuning system and further discussion of his argumentation, see Claude V. Palisca, *Humanism in Italian Renaissance Musical Thought* (New Haven: Yale University Press, 1985), pp. 235–44.

2. Paris, Bib. Nat., cod. XVI saec. 6757; see "Fogliano," *New Grove*.

3. *Musica theorica Ludovici Foliani Mutiensis . . . docte simul ac dilucide pertractata: in qua quamplures de harmonicis intervallis: non prius tentate: continentur speculationes* (Venice: de Sabio, 1529), unnumbered page: "It is not oratory but reason that I would like to examine here."

The subject of the faculty of music, which is called "sonorous number," is nothing other than the number of parts of a sonorous body, as for example, a string. Taking the ratio of distinct number, this expresses clearly to us the quantity of sound produced by it. Indeed, we judge a sound to be in quantity as much as the number given to the string; this is known by the quantity of the length of a string whose thickness and density are uniform and regular. Thus they can be compared to one another by us with certainty, according to sure and determinate proportions of grave and acute.[4]

Thus, he continues, by dividing a given string into five parts, we can strike one section of three parts and the other of two and recognize the sounding sesquialtera proportion. This leads him to a statement in support of the now-familiar classification of music as a field midway between mathematics and nature: "For this reason it happens that this science is called a mean between mathematics and the natural; without a doubt, sound, considered in that which is measured by ratio, cannot be divorced from motion. For sound without motion can neither exist nor be understood, since it is defined by motion (as will be made clearer to you in the section on sound). Wherefore music, being in part sound, is not called mathematics, but natural; however, being in part number considered in it (which, since music has proportional measure, is of course a mathematical term) it is called mathematical."[5] Further, says Fogliano, music is subaltern to arithmetic, through which its principles are demonstrated. It is by means of arithmetic and the mathematics of proportion that the musician's arguments are built. The rest of the first section continues a discussion of Boethian proportions and means in some detail.

Fogliano's book looks thus far like a typical Boethian theoretical treatise with some modern definitions thrown in. Only in Section 2 does his originality appear, and at first glance it seems modest at best.

4. Ibid., fol. 1r: "Musicae facultatis subiectum: Quod: Numerus sonorus: appellatur: nihil aliud est: nisi numerus partium sonori corporis: utputa: chordae: Quae numeri ac discreti accipiens rationem: nos certiores reddit de quantitate soni ab ea producti: Tantum enim esse iudicamus sonum: Quantus est: qui chordam metitur numerus: unde per numerum cognita secunda longitudinem quantitate chordae: cuius crassitudo ac densitas sit uniformis et regularis: statim possunt: a nobis soni secundum certas ac determinatas gravis et acuti proportiones ad invicem comparari."

5. Ibid.: "Ex cuius quidem positione contingit quod haec scientia dicatur media inter mathematicam et naturalem: nempe quantum ad sonum in illa sub ratione mensurati consideratum non abstrahit a motu: quia sonus absque motu necque esse necque intelligi potest: quum per motum definiatur: ut postea in materia de sono tibi constabit: Quamobrem Musica: ex parte soni: non dicitur: Mathematica: Sed Naturalis: ex parte vero numeri: in illa considerati: Qui proculdubio terminus est mathematicus: habens in musicis rationem mensurae: Dicitur: mathematica."

He begins (in Chap. 1) by noting that the Pythagoreans allowed only two types of intervals as consonant: the multiplex (as the octave) and the superparticular (fifths and fourths). This restriction, claims Fogliano, is manifestly false; for it contradicts the evidence of our sense of hearing. Citing the authority of Ptolemy on this point (and implying that Ptolemy approved of intervals such as the octave plus a sixth), Fogliano claims that intervals such as thirds and sixths, plus their equivalents at the octave, cannot be considered other than consonant. Performers on every type of instrument, all singers whether skilled or not, use these intervals and find them consonant. He concludes: "Let us say therefore that many more consonances have been discovered than those the ancients used and that more than two genera may be used in musical consonances; on the contrary, all genera of proportions are known to be capable of producing them."[6]

No single piece of Fogliano's argument here is new; Ramos and Spataro, and even Gaffurio, had all used various subterfuges based on Ptolemy to try to justify the use of thirds and sixths. The new direction in Fogliano's thought is his concern for uniting mathematical demonstration with sense experience. Fogliano's use of Ptolemy as the classical support for this argument is somewhat tenuous, but it allows him his desired result: mathematical description without the burden of Pythagorean theory.

To make this new line of reasoning work, Fogliano must make it very clear just what it is that his numbers measure, and why they are significant. Thus he continues this second section with a long discussion about the nature of sound. Sound is generated by a violent movement of the air, which can be caused in a number of ways. Yet sound is not, in itself, the same as the air, nor as the body which causes that air to move, nor as the motion of the air; sound is an accident, a type of quality: "I say that sound is an emotive quality, proceeding from the violent and rapid motions of air, having its being in equal measure with it."[7] Sound is an accident inherent to the subject of motion and is a natural phenomenon. For Fogliano, sound is not the same as number, as a more traditionally Pythagorean argument would have claimed; rather, its motion can be described through number.

6. Ibid., fol. 11v: "Dicamus igitur quod multo plures: quam antiqui posuerint: inveniuntur consonantiae: et quod plura quam duo genera ad musicas consonantias aptari possunt: immo omnia proportionum genera ad illas producendas valere comperiuntur."
7. Ibid., fol. 15v: "Dico quod sonus est passibilis qualitas proveniens ex motu aeris violento ac praecipiti habens esse in aequali mensura cum illo."

SECTIO

Figure 3 Dividing a monochord. From Ludovico Fogliano, *Musica theorica* (Venice, 1529), fol. 12v.

Fogliano does not develop this new approach in the numerous ways that might appear relevant: detailed observations of sounding bodies, say, or a broad attack on Pythagorean theories of perception. Instead, he devotes much of the rest of the treatise to describing and justifying his divisions of the monochord into useful scales (Fig. 3). Interestingly, he claims that part of the superiority of his monochord division based on sense perception is its superior rationality. Those who disagree with him on its division are bound rather by "authority and habit," he asserts, and ignore that which is more natural and reasonable.

In fact, Fogliano writes only briefly about another basis for justifying the rationality and naturalness of his monochord, one that may not at first seem entirely consistent with his earlier assertion that sense perception, since it comprehends forms in matter, is subject to material imperfections and hence is inferior to reason. Based on the Aristotelian dictum that "nature inclines to the good," he claims that the universal tendency of listeners to accept thirds and sixths as consonances proves that reason is inherent in these proportions:

> Nor should it be thought that we depart from nature in constructing the monochord; on the contrary, such an order of sounds distinguished by such intervals is so much according to nature that not only singers and practical musicians, but indeed the unlearned and the ignorant of every nation or custom sing this way. They cannot avoid it, but pass through such intervals, and come upon the distinct, clear sounds of our division. The reason for this is that nature, unless it be deficient, inclines toward the good, and toward those things which are well ordered. Therefore, since harmonic sounds are ordered toward consonance and harmony (which are good and desirable by nature), it seems plausibly to follow that men singing, even without art, nonetheless in their modulations incline toward accepting sounds which, according to their natural instinct, they feel to be appropriate for consonance and harmony. It happens that those very ones are those which ought to be found according to the distances ordered by our division [of the monochord].[8]

Fogliano, then, has described a new basis for the study of musical proportion. The orderliness for which nature strives, in this case seen in the musical practices of different peoples, can be expressed by means of number. This number expresses a specific characteristic about the body that produces the sound. Except that they are "or-

8. Ibid., fol. 40r–v: "Nec opinandum, quod nos in monochordi constitutione, a natura degrediamur immo talis sonorum ordo talibus distinctus intervallis, adeo secundum naturam est, quod non modo cantores et musici practici, sed etiam idiotae et ignorantes, cuiuscunque sint nationis, vel moris, dum cantant, non possunt evadere, quin per talia transeant intervalla, et incidant in sonos partitione nostra distinctos et signatos, cuius ratio est, Quia natura, nisi sit depravata, semper inclinat ad bonum, et ad ea quod in bonum ordinantur. Quare quum harmonici soni ad consonantiam et harmoniam: quae bonae sunt et secundum naturam appetibiles: ordinentur: probabiliter sequi videtur: quod homines etiam sine arte cantantes: in suis modulationibus: tantummodo inclinentur ad sonos accipiendos: quos naturali instinctu: sentiunt esse ad consonantiam et harmoniam aptos: et idoneos, quales in nostra partitione secundum debitas eorum distantias ordinatos invenire contingit."

derly," he makes no further claims about the nature of these numeric proportions, only that names (such as "octave") may be assigned to them. Supporting evidence for this position is the "natural" pleasurable response of all singers and listeners to such intervals.

Fogliano's line of argument is not equally strong at all points. For example, some specific proportions sound consonant while others are dissonant; yet both sorts could be described as "orderly," since they can be described by number, and Fogliano has developed no way to account for this difference. Nor does he develop his arguments to their apparent logical conclusion. His statements about quantity could be extended to other ways of measuring the objects that produce sound, but he does not do so. Yet later scholars will read Fogliano's work and begin to pursue these problems themselves. In this regard, then—the development of arguments if not always of results—Fogliano's treatise marks a turning point in the field that will become the science of sound.

Luigi Dentice, "gentilhuomo napolitano," treats a similar subject in a much more popular genre. His *Duo dialoghi della musica* (1553) promises one dialogue on theory, another on practice, all based on various Greek and Latin authors.[9] Its apparent interest in light, entertaining prose rather than detailed argumentation marks it as a work designed for a very general audience. The work's second dialogue, set at a concert at the house of Donna Giovanna d'Aragona, deals mainly with counterpoint and is of little interest here. The first, on "theory," which once again means largely pitch, follows the outlines of traditional Pythagorean musical thought more closely than had Fogliano. Yet Dentice is just as insistent as Fogliano about linking numbers, not to Pythagorean theory, but to specific aspects of the behavior of musical instruments.

Dentice reveals this concern from the work's beginning; in his discussion of *musica mundana, humana,* and *instrumentalis,* he denies that "music of the spheres" is in fact genuine music that can be heard. He acknowledges that the proportionate distances exist between the planets, as had Tinctoris before him. He simply denies that, just because there is proportion, there is music; the latter requires actual, audible sounds. After briefly covering this subject and the essentials

9. *Duo dialoghi della musica del Signor Luigi Dentice gentil'huomo napolitano, delli quali l'uno tratta della theorica, et l'altra della pratica: raccolti da diversi autori greci, et latini* (Rome: Lucrino, 1553); facsimile, intro. Patrizio Barbieri (Lucca: Libreria Musicale Italiana, 1988). See Barbieri for further discussion of Dentice and the music printed in the *Dialoghi;* see also Nino Pirrotta, "Commedia dell'arte and Opera," *Musical Quarterly* 41 (1955): 310.

of *musica humana,* Dentice's interlocutors dismiss the matter as "too high a subject" for their conversation.[10] So the dialogue is directed toward *musica instrumentalis* and moves directly into discussions of the process of sound production. Sound, he notes, is a motion of the air caused by percussive movement. This description, of course, is nothing new. Yet his interlocutors, Paolo Soardo and Giovanni Antonio Serone, develop this subject in more innovative ways.

Soardo notes, for example, that the pitch of a string may be raised not only by shortening it but by increasing its tension. Missing is the disclaimer typical of earlier treatises: that this change of tension results in merely a qualitative change. Soardo continues by linking this change in tension and pitch to frequency of vibration:

> The air will be disturbed as many times as it is hit by the vibrating string; but because of the velocities of sounds which so come together and unite, the ears cannot hear anything but a single sound, low or high, even though the one or the other consists of more—the low one slow and infrequent, the high one faster and more frequent.
>
> *Ser.:*   Thus if the high voices are caused by frequent and faster motion, and the low ones slower and less frequent, it is necessary to add some motion in going from the low to the high, and the contrary—a diminution of motion—from high to low.
>
> *Soar.:*   It is so because the high one comprises more movements than the low. In these the plurality makes the difference, and it is necessary that it consist in some number. Each of them, from small to great, is to each other, as number compared to number; and of those, all things which are compared according to number, some of them are equal, and others are distant by some inequality.[11]

For a treatise that is careful not to aim its subject "too high," this passage treats sound and quantity with surprising detail and sophistication. "Soardo" distingishes between the length of the string, used

10. Dentice, *Duo dialoghi* (1553), sig. Bv.
11. Ibid., sig. Bii r–v: "Mà tante volte sarà ferito l'aere, quante volte sarà percosso dalla corda tremante; mà perche le velocità de suoni si appressano et uniscono tanto, perciò l'orecchie non posson sentire altro, che un suono grave, overo acuto, benche e l'uno e l'altro consiste di più, il grave delle più tarde e rare, e l'acuto delle più preste e spesse. *Ser:* Dunque se le voci acuti per moti più spessi e più veloci, et le gravi per li più tardi et rari s'incitano, è di necessità per aggiuntion de moti, dalla gavità che vadi in acuto, et per lo contrario, per mancamento de moti dall'acuto in grave. *Soar:* Così è, perche di più consta l'acuto, che il grave; ne i quali la pluralità fà la differenza, et quella è necessario che consista in qualche numero. Ogni poco al più son così frà loro, come il numero comparato al numero, e di quegli, tutte le cose che conferiscono secondo il numero, parte à sè sono eguali, et parte sono distanti per inegualità."

to compare pitches with one another, and the actual cause of the difference in pitch, that is, the speed at which the string vibrates. In the absence of sophisticated scientific equipment, sixteenth-century scholars had no means of applying this distinction to the everyday use of musical instruments, whose construction was far more complicated than a simple monochord. They still had to be content with recourse to the secondary measure of string length under a monochord's controlled conditions. Nonetheless, this distinction is important for long-term changes in thinking about and studying the production of sound.

Although this analysis sounds anything but Pythagorean, Dentice claims to be a follower of Pythagoras's ideas when he restates the standard opinion that music depends on both sense and reason. Since Boethius and other authorities had always credited this opinion to Ptolemy and not Pythagoras, such a statement would not seem to constitute strong support for the latter. Dentice returns to more familiar Aristotelian arguments when he describes such factors as the string's dampness or dryness, or variations in its thickness, as random variations of quality (as opposed to quantity) that would also affect its pitch.

The rest of the dialogue is less original, an example of the usual topics of a music treatise presented in the form of a dialogue. Certainly Dentice would not have employed this genre had he intended to develop his ideas about musical quantity in a technical direction; simple expository prose, or at least a dialogue with a more serious tone, would have been his choice. The *Dialoghi* should be seen primarily as a popular work, not as a scholarly one; serious writers seem to have treated it accordingly and cited it far less often than that of Fogliano. Yet Dentice's discussion of sound is anything but frivolous. His concern for expressing the specific nature of musical quantity in terms of physical behavior shows, even in a work of this type, how widespread the interest in such matters had become by midcentury.

Some other minor treatises from these decades focus on particular aspects of or problems in music. Biagio Rossetti's *Libellus de rudimentis musices* (1529) is one of several such works published within a few years of one another. Rossetti, an organist, would naturally confront on a regular basis such issues of music performance as the relationships between vocal and instrumental composition and the role of music in divine service. Yet unlike Spataro, another church musician who had addressed issues of musical practice, Rossetti relies on the new humanistic approaches to the field in order to build a case for his suggested reforms of religious music.

Rossetti makes no claim to be writing a full music treatise, as his choice of title shows. He divides the work into a "Compendium musicae" and "De choro, et organo compendium." The former consists mainly of an introduction to the ecclesiastical tradition, discussing the church modes, Guidonian hand, and similar subjects. His "Choir and Organ" section is somewhat more original. Here, at one point, he produces a list of the authorities he has consulted: Boethius, Guido, Bernard [?], Marchetto of Padua, Burtius, and Augustine. He also refers frequently to Jerome.

Augustine's inclusion seems initially to be something of a surprise, since his writings had dealt with metrics and not musical practice. But metrics, especially the rhythms of chant texts, are an especial concern of Rossetti. He notes in the work's title that one of his goals is "removing some abuses in the temple of God." For Rossetti, a major abuse involved the use of chant rhythms that obscured the cadence of the words. He advocates altering these melodies so that the stresses and other types of musical emphasis help to project, rather than obscure, the words of the text.

Rossetti's other reform would consist of banning the use of musical instruments other than the organ in divine service. In building this argument he relies on Augustine and Jerome; he escapes Augustine's condemnation of the organ by claiming (with some justification) that the organ currently in use is far different from the Roman theater organs Augustine condemned. In this case, he notes especially the ability of other instruments to distract the minds of simple churchgoers away from devotional matters and toward sin.[12] The organ, properly used, should attract the listener's attention to the devotional text.

Even though Rossetti, as a practicing musician, has focused on the practical tradition, his major concerns grow out of the new interest in

12. Blasius Rossettus [Biagio Rossetti], *Libellus de rudimentis musices. De triplici musices specie. De modo debite solvendi divinum pensum. Et de auferendis nonnullis abusibus in Dei Templo*... (Verona: de Sabio, 1529), sig. n. ii r–v: "Idque non secus in pulsu organicu evenit, quippe sonus ipse intellectu captus nonnunquam ad lasciviam impellit non secus atque dicerentur ipsa verba lasciva. Et in huiuscemodi cantilenis pulsans ansam videtur dedisse transeundi in vagationem mentis abstrahendique mentem ab intentu devotionis. Unde plaerunque in his emergit peccatum etiam capitale, cuius et ipse pulsans proculdubio particeps censetur, quia iuxta iuris tritum dictum." (And it happens the same way with a musical sound; for sound itself, received by the intellect, sometimes incites wantonness the same way, and they may be called those wanton words themselves. And in this way the sound of a song seems to have given the opportunity to the mind's wandering and to drawing the mind away from attending to devotion. Whence arise many mortal sins, and the sound is without a doubt considered party to it, to use the legal commonplace.)

text and metrics. He does not attack the established arguments about the importance of pitch and proportion in accounting for music's emotional and spiritual effects. In fact, there is no reason to believe that he rejects them at all. Yet for Rossetti, the main impact of religious music is found not in its pitches or consonances but in its religious text; melodies should be organized in ways that draw the listener's attention toward that text. Anything that distracts the listener or obscures the listener's ability to hear and to understand the text is an error of composition to be avoided.

Rossetti urges reforms in the writing of church music, but not a totally new approach to composition. The effects of his treatise, either on composition or on theory, are thus hard to judge. Certainly his intended audience is the local church organist and chapelmaster, not the members of the intellectual community at large. That the new focus on music and poetics should spread so quickly to this level of treatise indicates the strength of its appeal. It also demonstrates the success of humanistic education in extending itself even to the education of local church musicians; the construction of such an argument requires not just a choirboy's Latin but a genuine study of Latin letters.

Similar reforms were suggested by the bishop of Loreto, Cirillo Franco, in a published letter of 1546.[13] Franco begins by noting the great emotional effects of ancient music, more powerful than modern music, rhetoric, or oratory. This power to move souls should be harnessed in the service of the divine; instead, he argues, modern composers have ignored the study of this theory in favor of slavish devotion to practice, claiming nonetheless that their art has reached a summit of perfection.

Based on his reading of ancient sources, he suggests, for example, that the Kyrie should be written in the Mixolydian mode, since the meaning of the text is a request for God's pardon, and the Mixolydian is the appropriate mode for such requests. Instead, "today they sing everything the same, in promiscuous and uncertain genera."[14] Franco, like Rossetti, wants the liturgical or other religious text to be taken as the guide for musical composition; the goal of the music should be to intensify the impact of that text through choice of mode

13. Cirillo Franco, bishop, letter to M. Ugolino Gualteruzzi, 16 February 1549, in *Lettere volgari di diversi nobilissimi huomini . . .* 3 (Venice: Manuzio, 1564), fols. 114r–18v.
14. Ibid., fol. 115r: "hoggi cantano tutte simil cose in genere promiscuo, et incerto."

and interval and by allowing the words of the text to be heard with maximum clarity and emphasis.

Franco compares this goal to that of religious art, in which not only the technical skill of the artist is important but also the appropriateness of the artistic composition to the intended devotional mood. Michelangelo's Sistine Chapel frescoes serve as a bad example, a case in which the artist's interest in displaying his talent conflicts with and overwhelms the religious sentiments to be conveyed.[15]

Franco does not favor the ongoing attempts to revive the enharmonic and chromatic harmonic genera, on the grounds that the ancients themselves had abandoned them. He specifically condemns the use of the melodies of popular songs in religious music as distracting and even damaging to the listener; likewise fugal counterpoint, in which different voices sing different words or phrases at the same time. Yet he also feels that the powers of musical consonances, based on their harmonic proportions, can have a powerful effect in inspiring the soul and should be harnessed accordingly: "In sum, I wish that when a mass is to be sung in church, that the music consist, according to the fundamental subject of the words, of certain concords and numbers apt to move our emotions to religion and piety."[16] Not a musician himself, Franco is nonetheless familiar with the theories and ongoing debates in the field, claims to have devoted considerable thought and attention to the subject, and finds these arguments to be important for understanding and promoting religious observance. Like Rossetti, he advocates a better understanding and application of Pythagorean theory to a humanistically inspired interest in religious texts in both devotional and literary terms.

Stefano Vanneo's Latin treatise, *Recanetum de musica aurea* (1533) came out only a few years after Rossetti's. Emphasizing the practical tradition, he divides his work into three parts: pitch, rhythm, and counterpoint. The *Recanetum* was originally written in the vernacular

15. Ibid., fol. 115v: "Io stimo il miracolo della natura su la pittura, e scultura Michelangelo Buonarroti. ma se quando volse rappresentare sul colmo della volta di Cappella vecchia quell'atto di Posteriora mea videbis, per mostrar l'arte del pingere, e tanti sbracati, e nudi, che ha fatti su ad ostentatione della sua virtù; gli havesse dipinti in una loggia di qualche giardino, havrebbe havuto piu del conveniente." [I esteem that miracle of nature in painting and sculpture Michelangelo Buonarroti. But when he wished to portray, at the summit of the vault of the Old Chapel, that act of "you may see my behind," to show off the art of painting, and all the trouserless and nude figures that he put up there to display his skill—it would have been more than appropriate if he had painted them in the loggia of some garden.]

16. Ibid., fol. 116r: "Io vorrei in somma, cha quando s'havesse a cantare una Messa in Chiesa, secondo la suggetta sostanza delle parole constasse la Musica di certi concenti, e numeri atti a muovere a religione, e pietà gli affetti nostri."

and translated for publication by Vicentio Rosseto; a third figure, Cornelio Buonamico Nursino, "artium et medicinae doctor," composed an introduction which consists largely of a listing of intellectual disciplines or other subjects (grammar, rhetoric, metals, animals, and so on, in a very loosely organized collection), each followed by a paragraph describing music's relevance to such study.

Some of these subjects, such as "scientific certainty," sound interesting but promise more than they deliver. In the case of this example, the writer notes that Aristotle had placed mathematics (which includes music) in the first degree of certainty, with physics following; likewise Plato valued it highly, as is seen in the inscription he placed at the door of the Academy ("nemo intret non Musicus").[17] Since this passage ignores some thirty years of published scholarship on the subject, it cannot be seen as the work of a serious scholar. Rather, like the remarks that form part of the more typical *laus musice,* it is meant merely to illustrate the ancients' high esteem for music. Specific content is less important.

Vanneo himself emphasizes the tale of Pythagoras and the hammers and follows Boethius, Burtius, Augustine, and Lefèvre d'Étaples[18] for definitions of music. Yet in his next chapter, a discussion of the divisions in the field of music, he shifts without notice to Isidore's division of music into harmonics, organics, and rhythmics.[19]

This division makes sense for a practical treatise but is inconsistent with his earlier Boethian orientation. Vanneo continues to cite Boethius, Martianus Capella, Isidore, and Burtius. The latter seems actually to be his principal source. Had Vanneo wished to make explicit these differences among his authorities, it would have been a simple enough task; in fact, he could simply have copied Gaffurio. It appears that Vanneo, like his translator, is simply not interested in doing so but believes that in putting together a Latin treatise on the ecclesiastical tradition, a certain amount of "things extracted from the works of famous authors," as Burtius had referred to them, must be included. He expresses no need to develop them into a single, comprehensive system of thought.

In many ways, then, the *Recanetum* seems to be a very conservative treatise. Published in Latin, covering a standard range of topics in the practical tradition, it relies on traditional theoretical sources such as

17. Stefano Vanneo, *Recanetum de musica aurea . . . nuper aeditum, et solerti studio enucleatum, Vincentio Rosseto interprete* (Rome: Dorcius Brixiensis, 1533), fol. 2v.

18. Jacopus Faber Stapulensis [Lefèvre d'Étaples], *Arithmetica et musica* (Paris: Higman et Hopyl, 1496), numerous reprints.

19. Vanneo, *Recanetum de musica aurea,* fol. 6r.

Boethius, Isidore, and Burtius. Further, it treats these sources in a very flat manner, paying little attention either to recent attempts to read them more fully or to current efforts to address literary and rhetorical issues. More than its contents, the work's mere presence as a published work of the 1530s is significant as an illustration of one end of the range of discourse on music.

Giovanni Maria Lanfranco published his *Scintille di musica* (1533) about the same time. An organist and chapelmaster like Rossetti, he worked in Brescia, Verona, Bergamo, and Parma over the course of his career.[20] The *Scintille* resembles other treatises by church musicians in several ways: it focuses on the practical, ecclesiastical tradition; its intended purpose is the training of choirboys; it does not contribute (nor does it so intend) to any larger scholarly questions. It differs in that it is truly an introductory treatise; it discusses not only rudimentary principles of practical subjects such as the Guidonian hand but also the ways and the order in which such subjects should be taught.

Lanfranco lists at the beginning the authors he has followed in putting together his work. They included Marchetto of Padua, Guido Aretinus, Burtius, Giorgio Valla, Gaffurio, Aron, and Spataro. He also names several others, mostly northerners, who had written in the practical tradition: Andreas Ornithoparchus, Heinrich Glarean, Bernard Bogentanz, and Andrea Vuollico.[21] As shown by the familiarity of much of this list, the core of sources cited includes a fairly standard group of writers.

The *Scintille*'s four parts cover notes and hexachords in learning measured chant, rhythmic notation, church modes, and counterpoint. Lanfranco's reliance on his sources as models has assured a better integration of theory into these practical matters than Vanneo achieved; and in numerous passages, Lanfranco follows Boethius more directly than does Vanneo, though in fact at second or third hand via Burtius or Gaffurio. Yet Lanfranco's treatise is recognizably similar to Vanneo's. Both try to present the theoretical tradition in ways that do not disturb the practical tradition, which is the major focus of their work. Both rely on the earlier generations of writers from

20. For biographical information on Lanfranco, see Peter Bergquist, "Lanfranco, Giovanni Maria," *New Grove;* see also B. Lee, "Giovanni Maria Lanfranco's *Scintille di musica* and Its Relation to Sixteenth-Century Music Theory" (Ph.D. diss., Cornell University, 1961).

21. Giovanni Maria Lanfranco, *Scintille di musica . . . che mostrano a leggere il canto fermo, et figurato, gli accidenti delle note misurate, le proportioni, i tuoni, il contrapunto, et la divisione del monochordo, con la accordatura de varii instrumenti . . .* (Brescia: Britannico, 1533), unpaged section.

Burtius through Aron. Both gloss over the issues that had caused such debate only a few years earlier. Writers such as Lanfranco or Vanneo do feel compelled to include basic discussions of the Boethian theoretical foundations, but they do so in a fairly uncritical way that marks them as recipients of, and not participants in, the major scholarly debates of their era.

Anton Francesco Doni's *Dialogo della musica* (1544) is an even more extreme example of a publication directed at a specific nonacademic audience. A peripatetic *letterato* and *poligrafo*, participant in several academies in Florence and Venice, and renegade cleric, Doni wrote and published widely throughout his lengthy career.[22] His *Dialogo* can hardly be considered a serious music treatise; rather, it is a collection of vocal pieces for purchase by amateur performers, held together with enough dialogue to compose a rough narrative. The second of the two dialogues, in fact, concerns women's beauty, apparently in order to frame a group of songs on the subject. Most of the conversation consists of light and playful comments about the texts of the pieces.

When Doni does turn the dialogue to the subject of musical theory, the interlocutors are brief but mention the basics: consonant intervals, rhythm, and counterpoint. The response to the suggestion of adding these subjects to their conversation is also brief. Octaves and fifths, they remark, are perfect consonances, while seconds and sevenths are imperfect; a series of successive fifths or octaves makes for bad counterpoint; and not all musicians are equally well trained, nor do they produce equally good results given their degree of training. Another interlocutor suggests they go argue out such matters at school, not here when they are all trying to enjoy themselves, and urges them on to sing the next piece.[23] Even in such an extremely nonscholarly publication, however, the one substantial mention of music as a discipline involves the traditional subjects of pitch and proportion.

Doni's published letters also contain a few references to music. These remarks reflect very different facets of his thought and writings: his anticlericalism, distrust and skepticism about the value of ancient learning, and criticism of contemporary society. In one letter he

22. For biographical information on Doni, see James Haar, "Doni, Anton Francesco," *New Grove;* see also Mario Emilio Cosenza, *Biographical and Bibliographical Dictionary of the Italian Humanists and of the World of Classical Scholarship in Italy, 1300–1800,* 2d ed. (Boston: G. K. Hall, 1962); Paul F. Grendler, *Critics of the Italian World, 1530–1560: Anton Francesco Doni, Nicolò Franco, and Ortensio Lando* (Madison: University of Wisconsin Press, 1969), pp. 49–65.

23. Anton Francesco Doni, *Dialogo della musica: Canto* (Venice: Scotto, 1544), fols. 14v–15r.

refers to the *Dialogo* and its composition, claiming that either he is unable to understand the standard descriptions of and theories about music's effects offered in ancient scources, or that he simply is disinclined to believe their inflated claims:

> But I want to tell you just one thing: do you believe the Theban [Pindar]—lame, halt, and shabby—that it was true that, by sounding the trumpet the Lacedemonians beat the Messenes? I know that many will be of my opinion, believing something less. Now you know I have not had the time to study and review it, but for four evenings I beat my head against it, for I lack the patience. I would rather be judged none too wise than quite mad. But since you should know my poets and musicians: Cicero claims that numbers, voices, and measure are all music. But this time in my *Dialogue* I have used neither compass nor square.[24]

In another letter, Doni derides religious music as a sort of ecclesiastical cosmetic, used to feed the pride of clergy and to fill their coffers.[25] The contrast between these positions and the light, positive tone of his *Dialogo* demonstrates the problems modern scholars have in assessing Doni's thought. Certainly he reveals no interest in developing a single systematic position. Nor is it easy to gauge the extent of Doni's technical knowledge; his professed ignorance of the subject does not correlate with his known skill as an amateur performer and acquaintance with professional musicians. The existence of a work such as the *Dialogo* does testify to the degree and speed with which publishing had expanded in a few decades.

Just how much, or whether, Doni had an impact on musical thought, even at the popular level, is also difficult to assess. Musical theory receives little serious attention from him, whether it is dismissed lightheartedly as in the *Dialogo* or skeptically as in the *Lettere*. But most contemporary music collections, among which the *Dialogo* should probably be classified, would not have mentioned the subject at all. Thus even this brief inclusion reveals some level of general interest. Later writers will neither refer to Doni's remarks nor copy the

---

24. *Tre libri di lettere del Doni* . . . (Venice: Marcolino, 1552), pp. 123–24: "Ma io vo dirvi una cosa sola: credete voi Dirceo sciancato, zoppo, et losco, che la fosse vera, che per sonar la tromba i Lacedemoni vincessero i Messentii? so che molti saranno della mia opinione di creder qualche cosa meno. Hora sappiate che io non sono stato i mesi à farlo, vederlo, et rividerlo: ma in quattro sere gli ho stiacciato il capo: perche io non ho tanta patientia. io voglio tosto esser giudicato poco savio, che molto pazzo. Ma perche sappiate Poeti, et Musici miei da dovero, Cicerone vuole che numeri, voci, et misure, tutto sia musica; ma questa volta nel mio Dialogo non ho usato ne compasso ne squadra."
25. Ibid., pp. 37–38.

mixed genre of his *Dialogo;* it would appear, then, that his writings can be seen as another set of endpoints in the range of opinions on music in public circulation.

If this loose collection of writers reveals any single trend, it would be a tendency away from strict adherence to the old tradition of the Boethian treatise as the sole model for content, genre, or even method. Several writers, for example, sought new ways of combining the theoretical tradition with the practical or ecclesiastical side of the field. Some focused on a single aspect of music in a given work, such as rhythmics and text, or pitch and mathematics. Others, like Doni, minimize the role of musical thought of any sort, relegating music performance to a private, pleasant pastime.

In part, the presence of so many minor treatises is due to the success of the publishing industry in Italy. Choirboy handbooks such as Lanfranco's manual would not have been published in such variety in the earlier days of printing; they probably would not even have received more than local circulation in manuscript and would have lacked not only the literary polish but also the theoretical discussion displayed by any of these works. These minor publications, then, attest not to a lowering in tone of theoretical treatises to the more practical level but, rather, to a rise in the publishing popularity and the intellectual tone of this older genre.

One effect of these new minor works is to raise the respectability, as well as the profile, of the practical treatise. Far less standardized as a genre, these works frequently make use of such stylistic innovations as vernacular language and dialogue form, innovations that will remain in use. These developments parallel a slowly growing attention to the nature of the reading audience, the form employed, and the kind of focus, not just in assembling the treatise but in thinking about the subject.

Nonetheless, in comparison with the works of such major scholars as Gaffurio or Valla, most individual treatises have little long-term impact. They represent derivative, not original, thought. When they do express new ideas, it is left for others to develop the implications. The opinions expressed by Fogliano and echoed by Dentice, for example, are potentially both interesting and important. Yet Fogliano by himself would have remained of minor interest, since he did not work his ideas out completely and present them clearly to others. The importance of Fogliano's arguments will be realized when later scholars such as Zarlino, thinking more systematically, read his work and incorporate his thinking into their own scholarship. Thus the placement of these works in the larger context of midsixteenth-century musical thought requires a balanced assessment. They played no major role in shaping the thoughts of contemporary scholars, but they had their own sort of impact, both on the nonscholarly audience and on the intellectual discourse of the era.

Girolamo Cardano

Girolamo Cardano (1501–76), physician and mathematician, enjoyed wide fame in both fields during his lifetime. He was also a prolific writer on many subjects, his *Opera omnia* filling ten large volumes.[26] Son of the famous mathematician Fazio Cardano (colleague of Gaffurio, Pacioli, and Leonardo da Vinci), Girolamo Cardano grew up in Milan and Pavia as his father's assistant and factotum as well as his student. Cardano's university training began there and continued in Padua.[27] His professional career involved both university teaching (at Pavia and Bologna) and a highly regarded private medical practice. As a mathematician, his fame rested on two accomplishments: he was one of the first discoverers of solutions to cubic equations, which involved him in extended polemics with Tartaglia;[28] and his treatise on algebra, the *Ars magna* (Nuremberg, 1545), came to dominate the field. He was also a talented amateur musician; his lessons in musical practice had been supported by his mother since his childhood.

26. Girolamo Cardano, *Opera omnia* (Lyons: Spon, 1663). Cardano's later treatise "De musica" (1574), Vatican City, BAV, Vat. Lat. 5850, is not included in the collection.

27. For biographical information on Cardano, see G. Gliozzi, "Cardano, Girolamo," *DBI;* see also *Cardanus, Hieronymus: Writings on Music,* ed., trans. Clement A. Miller (N.p.: American Institute of Musicology, 1973), pp. 15–21; Miller, "Cardan, Jerome," *New Grove;* Markus Fierz, *Girolamo Cardano, 1501–1576: Physician, Natural Philosopher, Mathematician, Astrologer, and Interpreter of Dreams,* trans. Helga Niman (Boston: Birkhäuser, 1983). Most biographical information on Cardano is based on his autobiography, *Liber de propria vita* (Rome, 1575; in *Opera omnia* 1). On some of Cardano's nonmusical writing, see George W. McClure, "The Renaissance Vision of Solace and Tranquillity: Consolation and Therapeutic Wisdom in Italian Humanist Thought" (Ph.D. diss., University of Michigan, 1981), pp. 490–501; see also Alfonso Ingegno, *Saggio sulla filosofia di Cardano* (Florence: Nuova Italia, 1980). McClure shows (pp. 330–31; 386–87; 446; 772–73) that Cardano (in *De tranquillitate*), the earlier Leon Battista Alberti (*Della tranquillità dell'anima*), and Marsilio Ficino mention the value of music in soothing the spirit. As he notes, their theories refer to the harmonic nature of the soul as described in the *Timaeus.* Given the importance of music to Cardano's theories of psychology and perception, music's role in these and similar fields deserves further study.

28. See Ettore Bartolotti, *I cartelli di matematica disfida e la personalità psichica di Girolamo Cardano* (Imola: Galeati, 1933).

Although Cardano wrote and published throughout his lifetime, many of his works were composed or revised during his last years, spent in Rome (1571–76). His most important music treatise dates from this period, completed in 1574. The extensive passages on music in other works were among those subject to late revision, though in these cases such revisions involved expansion rather than significant alteration. Works with substantial treatment of musical subjects include *De subtilitate* (1550);[29] *De proportionibus* (1570); and *De utilitate ex adversis capienda* (1561).

This profusion of writing on music contains much that is genuinely new. Cardano tries to combine the Pythagorean or Boethian tradition with Aristotelian-based notions of the senses and psychology, producing a music theory that proceeds from the study of proportion through music's social roles in a more or less logical fashion. His general approach is based less on close analysis of classical texts than on taking the ancient traditions and modern practice as points of departure for rational arguments to account for the phenomena known and described. In this he anticipates the approaches several scholars proposed in the decade or so after his death. His relative lack of interest in textual analysis also causes occasional inconsistencies in his writing, often owing to a lack of critical distance in synthesizing arguments in the works of others.

Cardano's writings and their influence are difficult to assess. He is often not only inconsistent but contradictory, even within the same work. A given passage may move without transition to an unrelated subject or may not itself relate closely to the chapters that precede and follow it. Later writers referring to Cardano will not always specify which treatise they are using; in any case, the extent of his influence seems relatively large but hard to measure precisely.[30] Since Cardano does not appear to have undergone any major changes in his thinking about music, it may be best to examine his writings topically rather than chronologically, thus minimizing the effects of his own organizational idiosyncrasies. Those matters he treats in contradictory ways or leaves unresolved, however, are in some ways as important a part of his work as those he addresses more successfully. They serve

29. The Nuremberg (1550) edition of *De subtilitate* is only partial; its complete, revised form is Paris, 1551; revised editions 1554, 1559, 1560. See Ian Maclean, "The Interpretation of Natural Signs: Cardano's *De subtilitate* versus Scaliger's *Exercitationes*," in *Occult and Scientific Mentalities in the Renaissance*, ed. Brian Vickers (Cambridge: Cambridge University Press, 1984), pp. 232, 246 n. 15.

30. For a fuller discussion of Cardano's idiosyncratic style, his works' reception among contemporaries, and his relationship to mainstream Aristotelianism, see Maclean, "Interpretation of Natural Signs."

to point out some serious limitations in his approach, limitations that will be examined by later writers.

Cardano's 1574 *De musica* addresses theoretical issues that received briefer mention in his 1546 *De musica*, which was mainly a practical treatise. The later work begins with a collection of axioms about proportion, thus grounding his thinking in the mathematical tradition, which for Cardano precedes both logically and metaphysically such physical phenomena as sounding bodies. He does not offer an extended discussion of cosmology at this point, though references in numerous other passages show that he subscribes to the standard notions of *musica mundana*.[31] After following these proportions through charts of consonant and dissonant intervals, tetrachords, and harmonic genera, Cardano moves to the topic of sound and its production. Based on both Ptolemy and the pseudo-Aristotelian *Problems*, this chapter begins with the usual statements about sound as a percussion of the air. Cardano then tries to relate this concept to the questions raised in the *Problems* about the pitch and the quality of sounds, especially a sound's strength or weakness in volume or timbre.

Cardano notes that the length of string or pipe is not the sole factor in determining the sound produced; this phenomenon can be observed most easily in pipes or flutes. For example, a pipe's apertures may be made so small in size (it is not clear whether Cardano is referring here to the pipe's bore, its lateral finger holes, its mouthpiece, or all of these) that no matter what the pipe's length, it can produce no sound at all.[32] Further, these physical factors affect the quality of the sound in several ways. A thin string makes a high sound, but only when stretched very taut; even then, the sound itself is weak and thin.

Given the extended attention offered to proportion in the preceding chapters, one might expect Cardano to associate these variations in quality and pitch with some sort of mathematical expression, as later writers will do. Yet Cardano does not use this approach, perhaps because he has based this passage so heavily on the *Problems*. Like other Aristotelian treatments of the subject, the *Problems* discusses these issues of pitch and sounding bodies in qualitative, descriptive terms, not in terms of mathematics. Cardano interprets the phenomena in terms of the sounding body's strength or fatigue. Just as the voice of a person who is exhausted sounds both high and weak, so a thin string sounds weak, and of course also sounds high. Cardano does not try to

31. See, for example, his *De proportionibus* (Basel, 1570), p. 175.
32. Cardano, "De musica," fol. 3v; also in *Cardanus, Hieronymus*, p. 86; subsequent citations are to the latter.

relate this highness of sound which is dependent on weakness to the more usual highness of sound produced by shortening the length of the sounding body.

In fact, Cardano simply brings this chapter to an abrupt conclusion; the next chapter discusses consonances based on his theories of perception. Whether this disjunction is intentional is unclear. The manuscript seems to be only a rough draft, not a final copy, and thus may not represent Cardano's full argument. Nonetheless, it is typical of Cardano's style in his published works as well. From the reader's point of view, this editorial sleight of hand might serve to cover over the inconsistencies in Cardano's argument. In this case, Cardano has moved from Boethian (or Ptolemaic) arguments about proportion to an Aristotelian discussion about the qualities of sounding bodies and back to theories about the consonances as perceived by the listener. The progression of subjects certainly appears logical, but close examination shows rather weak links between steps in the argument.

Cardano's theories of sound perception are, in contrast, not just interesting in themselves; they also provide a way to justify the long-established use of thirds and sixths. His general explanation of consonant proportions is traditionally Pythagorean. The originality lies in shifting the cause of music's effects on the emotions away from the proportions themselves, toward the ways those proportions are perceived. Cardano presents aspects of this argument in several works.

Perception itself is based on recognition of order. Because the human mind has been imprinted with divine reason and order, it can recognize those sounds composed out of similar order. Cardano takes this argument straight from Plato's *Republic* (Book 8), to which he refers in his *De subtilitate*.[33] It is this perceived orderliness that defines "beauty" and is equivalent in both hearing and vision:

> Truly, every sense especially enjoys things which are recognized; those recognized things are called consonance when heard, beauty when seen. Therefore, what is beauty? A thing perfectly recognized; for we cannot love things that are not recognized. Vision perceives those things that stand in simple proportions: duple, triple, quadruple, sesquialtera, sesquitertia. . . . Certainly there is delight in recognition, sadness in nonrecognition. Further, things are not recognized when they are imperfect and obscure; they are boundless, confused, and indeterminate. Those

33. Cardano, *Opera omnia* 2:116–17.

things that are boundless cannot be known; therefore the imperfect cannot delight, nor be beautiful. Thus, whatever is commensurate is beautiful, and wont to delight.[34]

Beauty, then, results both from the intrinsic orderliness of the object and the mind's ability to recognize that order. From these principles, Cardano builds the propositions about consonance which he relates as twelve axioms in his 1574 De musica. The more "perfect" consonances (octave and fifth) sound "better" because they are simpler proportions and hence more easily perceived as ordered sound. It follows that as the size of intervals increases beyond an octave, the interval's perceived consonance or dissonance decreases because of the increased difficulty in perceiving the exact proportion.

Similarly, by using rhythmic relationships too complex to be perceived themselves, one can decrease the sense of consonance or dissonance that the same pitches would normally possess. The mind also recognizes similarities in types of proportion; it will accept some intervals as more consonant than their actual proportions would suggest, if they closely resemble some other strong consonance. Thus listeners find a double octave more consonant than an octave plus a fifth, even though the former proportion (4:1) is farther from unity than the latter (3:1) and is therefore less consonant in the mathematical sense. Further, a consonant interval sounds even more obvious and more consonant if it is divided by a consonant (or nearly consonant) median tone; thus an octave divided into a fifth and fourth is easier to perceive as an octave.[35]

This analysis, combining the acknowledged effects of Pythagorean consonance with the mechanisms of human sense perception, allows Cardano to simplify his tuning system without abandoning standard definitions of consonance and dissonance. Thus he has no problem allowing a practical approximation of equal temperament for fretted instruments,[36] since it is the perception of the intervals that matters, not the intervals themselves. Whether Cardano would claim that the

34. Cardano, De subtilitate (1559), p. 494: "Verum omnis sensus cognitis maxime gaudet: cognita in auditu vocantur consonantia, in visu pulchra. Quid igitur est pulchritudo? Res visui perfecte cognita, incognita enim amare non possumus: eă autem agnoscit visus quae simplici constant proportione dupla, tripla, quadrupla, sesquialtera, sesquitertia. . . . Est enim delectatio in cognoscendo, ut non cognoscendo tristitia. Porrò obscura imperfectaque ob id non cognoscuntur, quod sint infinita, confusa, indeterminataque; talia igitur cum sint infinita, cognosci nequeunt, igitur imperfecta non possunt delectare, nec esset pulchra: pulchrum igitur quicquid commensuratum est, delectare etiam solet."

35. Cardano, De musica, pp. 73–75, 87.

36. Miller, "Introduction," Cardanus, Hieronymus, pp. 23–25.

deviations in tempered intervals from their true proportions are too small to be perceived at all, or that the human ear simply categorizes the interval as close enough to the truly consonant proportion to satisfy itself, is not certain from his writing; certainly either argument would support his position.

Most systematic music treatises would turn at this point from discussions of consonances and tuning systems to the modes and the harmonic genera and to their alleged emotional effects. Cardano treats the subject frequently, in various works and contexts, and not always consistently. Many treatments suffer from the same logical gaps as his discussion of sounding bodies. One of his least successful attempts appears in the 1574 *De musica,* where he parallels the development of Greek musical modes with that of the homonymous architectural orders: "In ancient times there were three modes, not only in music but also in other arts. The celebrated Dorian was sharp, unpolished, hard; Phrygian, on the other hand, was soft, elaborate, and given to pleasure. In architecture Corinthian was substituted to Phrygian, and between it and the Dorian the Ionian was interposed, just as the Lydian was in music, whence Philander."[37] Other modes, he continues, were added over the years.

This parallel between music and architecture, original though it may be, seems more picturesque than useful; just what it is about the Dorian mode (or order), for example, that makes it "sharp" or "unpolished" is never identified. Cardano's subsequent references to Plato and Aristotle are likewise ill defined. He notes that Aristotle preferred the Dorian mode because it encouraged moderation and withdrawal from passion, but he provides no details as to how the mode achieved these ends. Nor does he connect this statement to the preceding passage about the "unpolished" Dorian.

Cardano's discussion of the harmonic genera is also vague. Since he was not a composer of music, he does not use the subject simply as an attempt to justify his own use of chromaticism in musical composition, as would many of his contemporaries. He tries to treat the subject in context, yet he seems unsure of just what that context should be. At times his discussion is technical and focused on tuning.[38] At other times he discusses the modes as a historical development, created by the Greeks to solve certain specific problems of tuning and used for specific social purposes.[39]

37. Cardano, *De musica,* p. 97.
38. See, e.g., *De musica,* chaps. 11, 13.
39. Ibid., chaps. 1, 18.

It seems reasonable, of course, to argue that such a subject might properly belong to several contexts, depending on the aspect being examined; later scholars will make this distinction. For Cardano, however, it seems that in all these passages, the context is determined primarily by that of whichever ancient source or sources he happens to be following. At such times his approach to ancient sources is reminiscent of Gaffurio; he organizes texts simply by narrating parts of their contents one after the other, without always pausing to be sure that the result is entirely consistent. Cardano seems to want both his Pythagorean explanations and his historical or social ones but has not worked out a way to unite the two.

Cardano's general discussions of music's emotional effects are more successful. In his *De proportionibus,* he returns to the Pythagorean notions usually classified under *musica humana* in order to determine how music affects mood and which moods it can and cannot induce:

> It remains to be seen by what means sound affects mood. It is not due, however, to the soul, which is immortal and immaterial, but rather either to that part of the body which is the instrument of the soul (that is, the spirit), or to the principal conjunction by which the soul is joined to the body. So indeed it deserts the body; or if impeded in its relation with the body, the body dies away. The mind presages this; fear and sadness comprise the anticipation of death. So on the other hand, happiness is none other than communion between body and soul; and to the extent they are joined, it calls to mind only life. And therefore, as if immortal, he who is happy is oblivious to death. Thus the soul's ratio will be the one such that, as the soul perceives it perfectly, it is exhilarated by the voices' sweetness; this occurs in the diapason. So also the diapente, though less perfectly, and the diatessaron more imperfectly still. . . . Let us see, then, if anything is similar in the faculties of the soul; for there should be no doubt that understanding is formed from the exterior and interior senses. And the exterior senses consist in the sesquitertia; it is their imperfect perception. Greater by far is the faculty of memory of one thing and reasoning about the rest, from which intelligence arises. For indeed, we have an exact resemblance in the faculty of the human soul which perceives it.[40]

40. Cardano, *De proportionibus,* pp. 173–74: "Videndum est, quomodo sonus permutet affectus: hoc autem non quia animam, quae immortales est et immateria, sed quoniam aut corporis eam partem, quae est animae instrumentum, id est, spiritum, aut animae principalem coniunctionem qua corpori annexa est. Ut enim corpus deserit aut impeditur à corporis commercio corpus immoritur: hoc praesentiens animus, fiunt illa duo praevia ad mortem timor et tristitia. Ut contra, laetitia non est nisi communicatio animae corpori, et quatenus communicatur solum de vita cogitat, atque ob id quasi immortalis, qui laetatur obliviscitur mortis. Ergo

In this passage Cardano begins with a discussion of the perception of consonance reminiscent of arguments examined above. This time he moves beyond the beauty of consonant proportions in order to examine the mechanism of music's effect on the moods. He later rejects the idea that the genera of the tetrachords should be compared directly to the parts of the soul, as many scholars have done in an attempt to account for music's emotive power. The tetrachord divisions, he states, are not natural distinctions but voluntary or arbitrary ones. More specific connections must be found between the nature of emotional states and musical compositions.

After studying several affects of the soul to determine whether they can be induced by music, he allows three: happiness (*laetitia*), relaxation (*remissio*), and pity (*misericordia*). These he sees as proceeding from the same nature and essence as music and its consonances. Emotions he disqualifies are generally rejected on logical grounds, proceeding from their nature as he defines it. Love and hate, for example, exist only as directed toward some object; music, however, incites emotional states that are general and thus can incite neither love nor hate.

Cardano offers some general stylistic descriptions of the music that can cause the three emotions he admits to musical influence. *Laetitia* is induced by "a concord of voices and modulation from rough to smooth."[41] Thus, even though Cardano's theory of music's emotional effects is based ultimately on Pythagorean proportion, he does not simply base the former directly upon the latter. An emotion is not induced simply by the presence of certain consonant or dissonant intervals but by specific types of progression in musical passages between dissonance and consonance. Nonetheless, Cardano's analysis is far from thorough. Just what he means by such phrases as "from rough to smooth" is once again left vague.

In other treatises Cardano uses a similar approach in describing emotional responses to music: he proceeds from a Pythagorean analysis of consonance and perception to general prescriptions about the

---

animae ratio illa erit, quae ut cognoscit perfecte exhilaratur dulcedine vocum, et hoc fit in diapason. Ut vero imperfecte diapente, ut imperfectius diatessaron.... Videamus ergo an aliquid sit simile in animae facultatibus, nec dubium est quin ex sensibus exterioribus atque interioribus fiat intelligentia. Et sensus quidem exteriores sexquitertia constant: est enim illorum imperfecta cognitio: major longe memoriae unius et rationis reliquarumque facultatum, ex quibus intelligentia oritur. Iam vero habemus exactam similitudinem facultatum animae humane quam cognoscit."

41. Ibid., p. 175: "At laetitiae causae sunt, et concordia vocum, et mutatio ex aspera in suavem."

more complex aspects of musical style. A chapter in *De subtilitate* attempts to account for music's appeal in terms of its novelty, comparing it to the delight found naturally in learning:

> And in learning, too, there is pleasure, since that which we do not know, we learn. For truly, is there enjoyment in contemplating those things that we already know? Surely either none, or less than those things which we learn. We are not delighted by a continuous action, because there is no ignorance preceding it; there is a certain ignorance in any first action. Thus the poor seem to enjoy greater pleasure than the rich people and princes, because they have endured greater sadness. So it happens that a diapente placed above a diatessaron offends the ear, but the contrary order delights it. For the lower voice remains after the higher one and hurts the ear. When the low sound is the simpler, the high one will delight; if the contrary, it offends the ear. As we demonstrate above, the diapente is a simpler consonance than the diatessaron. A diatessaron above a ditone delights the ear and offends it if below, for the same reason. For the sesquiquarta is more easily perceived than the sesquitertia, since the sesquiquarta is dependent on the sesquialtera.[42]

Therefore, he continues, those things that offend the ear should be mixed with those that delight it, just as is true in painting. Composers must observe two rules to this end. First, those things that delight should be made to impress themselves more upon the sense than those that offend. Second, the composition must not be divided so minutely that the sense cannot perceive the consonant proportions.

Cardano brings these theories to their most profitable development when discussing the social uses of music and the personal benefits or harm to be derived from listening or performing. In his 1574 *De musica* he discusses three contexts in which music may be considered "useful": as a means of inciting the mind toward study and contemplation; as a purgative for the spirit; and as a useful pastime, to

---

42. Cardano, *De subtilitate* (1559), p. 495: "Et in discendo quoque voluptas est: quia quae non novimus, discimus. Utrum vero in contemplatione eorum quae iam novimus, delectatio sit? Certe aut nulla, aut minor quam quae sit dum discimus. Continuata vero actione non delectamur, quia ignorantia non praecessit. Est autem primus actus ignorantia quaedam. Videntur igitur pauperes divitibus et principibus maiore frui delectatione, quia maiore tristitia afficiuntur. Ea quoque ratione fit ut diapente in acutis, diatessaron in gravibus offendat aurem, contrario ordine delectet: nam gravis vox post acutam ferit aurem ac manet: igitur cum fuerit gravis simplicior acuta delectabit: si contrario modo, aurem offendat. At iam supra ostendimus, simpliciorem esse consonantiam diapente, quam diatessaron: eadem ratione diatessaron supra ditonum mulcet aurem, infra laedit; nam facilius percipitur sesquiquarta, quam sesquitertia, quod sesquiquarta à sesquialtera pendeat."

free the mind from more serious concerns.[43] The first he provides with little detail, perhaps because it would seem to be the aspect most closely related to the perception-based theories he has already discussed at length. Similarly, the Aristotelian notion of music as a favored way to fill hours of cultured leisure (*otium*) he had already incorporated as one of the three emotions induced by music, as relaxation (*remissio*). He expands his discussion of purgation, as based on the idea of catharsis, to include the cure of physical and mental ailments, including a brief reference to the survival in his own day of the tarantella dance for the cure of the spider's bite.

When Cardano turns to matters of musical style, the combination of his theories of perception with related subjects is also original and reasonably consistent. In discussing imitation, he distinguishes among that of sense, of sound, and of manner.[44] To imitate the chirping of birds, for example, does not involve imitation of sense, since the sounds they produce have no real meaning. Imitation of sense involves imitation of strong emotion. Cardano mentions the various ancient modes during the course of this discussion but also offers a specific example: "A mood of commiseration proceeds in music in slow and serious notes by dropping downward suddenly from a high range. This imitates the manner of those who weep; for at first they wail in a very high and clear voice, and then they end by dropping into a very low and rather muffled groan."[45] This explanation hints again at the idea that ancient modes derived their effects not just from the pitches of the component intervals but from the stylistic devices associated with them. Further, it implies that such devices are mimetic, imitating the physical manifestations of the emotions seen in an individual.

Cardano also notes the importance of the poetics of the texts in vocal music. Ancient compositions were of different types, he argues, because of the specific types of feet and meter as well as the convention of the dance styles that formed part of their performance.[46] At one point he makes it clear that he attributes the most extensive emotional force in music to vocal music or song and that it is the text that is responsible for this additional force: "A song is related to music just as it relates to sound. But since it pertains to poetry, it reaches the highest perfection in their combination. The ancients attributed great powers to this, as when Circe bewitched the companions of

43. Cardano, *De musica*, pp. 104–6.
44. Ibid., pp. 142–44.
45. Ibid., p. 143.
46. Ibid.

Ulysses with songs. Through the alluring charm of her songs, Circe corrupted the morals of the companions of Ulysses; for they were influenced by their sound, meter, and meaning."[47] Again, he significantly broadens the explanations of music's effects. As he sees it, these cultural or literary analyses could ultimately be traced back to their source, Pythagorean musical thought. Yet by including "meaning" as a distinct third branch of musical studies, he is free to treat it (for practical purposes, at least) as an independent subject in its own right.

Taken as a whole, Cardano's writings on music make an original and important, if not always systematic, contribution to the larger issues. His works are better at sketching out fruitful avenues for further study or new ways of organizing ideas than they are at charting each stage of an argument. Like those of his colleague Fogliano, the ideas Cardano generates will find their fullest and most useful expression, and also their greatest audience and influence, when amplified in the works of later scholars. Cardano's lifelong interest in music was always substantial, but at no point was it his major intellectual concern; he did not devote enough professional energy to the field to be capable by himself of recasting the entire subject. Nonetheless, his work contributes to a growing change in the way music was classified and studied. He raises the reader's attention from the minutiae of scale tunings or rhythmic notation to reconsider the larger issues, and he offers significant new ways to begin that reconsideration.

Music, Ancient and Modern: Vicentino, Lusitano, and Danckerts

Perhaps the written debate between the musicians Nicola Vicentino and Ghisilin Danckerts was not the longest-running or most acrimonious debate among sixteenth-century professionals in the field. Certainly it was not the most learned; several contemporaries, in fact, later lamented its low intellectual level. It may be the only one, however, to have originated in a public debate on which money was wagered: a debate between Vicentino and Vicente Lusitano in the papal chapel at Rome. Vicentino, the loser, published the documents from the debate along with a rebuttal in his major treatise, *L'antica musica ridotta alla moderna prattica* (1555, 1557). Danckerts, who had served

47. Ibid., p. 108.

as one of the judges, countered with his own version in his *Trattato sopra una differentia musicale* (ca. 1555–1560), which has remained in manuscript.[48]

Such publicly adjudicated disputes apparently took place fairly frequently among the papal musicians: Danckerts mentions another one in his manuscript, caused by a disagreement on the subject of accidentals and their notation.[49] Vicentino's and Lusitano's debate attracted widespread attention not simply because Vincentino published the results but also because its subject held a broad appeal, being an extension of the long-contested topic of tuning and scale types. Vincentino had quarreled with Lusitano, a papal musician, over the modern use of the three ancient harmonic genera. The latter had claimed that only the diatonic genus was in general use; Vicentino argued that in fact contemporary usage comprised a mixture of all three, and he further suggested that musical style would improve by using all three genera more deliberately and independently of one another.

Just why this issue should have become so significant to musicians and theorists at midcentury is perhaps not immediately obvious. The ancient harmonic genera had long formed a standard topic of Boethian music treatises, along with such other topics as the Greek string names, without generating much strong interest or emotion. Most writers before this generation had concluded their brief discussions of the subject with some general statement to the effect that, owing to the difficulty of the enharmonic and chromatic genera, both for singers trying to replicate the proper intervals and for instrumentalists trying to keep their instruments tuned, only the superior diatonic genus had continued to be used into modern times. The ancients had justifiably abandoned the other two. Lanfranco and Aron, for example, fell into this category;[50] Fogliano claimed that the

48. Ghisilin Danckerts, "Trattato sopra una differentia musicale . . . ," Rome, Bib. Vall. R 56, secs. 15, 33, fols. 348–92, 534–71; also Rome, Bib. Cas. 2880. The three manuscripts appear to be different revisions or drafts; Bib. Cas. 2880 is the most polished, but all lack numerous technical illustrations and other supporting material to varying degrees. For biographical information on Danckerts, see Lewis Lockwood, "Danckerts, Ghisilin," *New Grove*. For biographical information on Vicentino, see Henry William Kaufmann, *The Life and Works of Nicola Vicentino* (N.p.: American Institute of Musicology, 1966), pp. 15–48. The documents relevant to the debate are reprinted in Vicentino, *L'antica musica ridotta alla moderna prattica* . . . (Rome: Barre, 1555), fols. 95r–98v.

49. Danckerts, "Differentia musicale," Rome, Bib. Vall. R 56, fols. 56or–63r.

50. Lanfranco, p. 2; Pietro Aron, *Thoscanello de la musica* (Venice: Bernardino, 1523), 1.11–12.

other two genera are dependent upon the diatonic and cannot stand alone as pitch systems; and Spataro asserted simply that all modern music is diatonic, and therefore modern composers had no need to study the other two.[51] A given author might or might not have found the subject of much interest, but he would not have thought in either case that it warranted serious, detailed attention.

The increased use of chromatic accidentals in musical composition by the midsixteenth century seems to have been a major cause of the new interest in the chromatic and enharmonic tetrachords. Just as musicians of the late fifteenth century had turned to classical theory to justify their thirds and sixths, so musicians now turned to this long-known but little-invoked source for the notes whose use they wished to allow and to explain. This attempt also had more direct precedents in Ramos's work. Ramos had already tried to modify the old Guidonian hexachord system, which was too cumbersome to accommodate the ever more frequent departures from its standard range of notes; yet his work had remained controversial. A revival of the tetrachord system began to seem increasingly attractive as a way out of this dilemma. To begin with, its classical credentials were impeccable. It also offered composers some practical advantages. The system duplicated easily at the octave while the old hexachord system did not, making the tetrachord system a more useful way to organize pitches when composing sixteenth-century polyphony. It also used simple, four-note modules that could be easily interchanged and replaced by modules from another genus when a given altered note was needed, while the rest of the system remained intact.

Further, many aspects of ancient music theory and ancient musical sources had become better known since the early years of the century; several topics that had once seemed foreign and unusual had now grown more familiar. Fifty years of debates about tuning systems had reduced the mystery of these "other" two genera. In fact, the entire subject could look simple indeed when compared with the pages of tuning charts filled with Greek terms that had become the typical means of illustrating early sixteenth-century debates about pitch. Making sense of how the Greek harmonic genera functioned as a part of Greek musical theory thus became a subject in its own right, one with the added advantage of offering a solution to the technical problems of accidentals in music composition.

51. Fogliano, *Musica theorica*, fol. 39v; Giovanni Spataro, *Bartolomei Ramis honesta defensio in Nicolai Burtii Parmensis opusculum* (Bologna, 1491), fol. 12v.

The debate between Vicentino and Lusitano took place in the Vatican on or about 4 June 1551.[52] Vicentino had found himself in Rome as part of his extensive travels with his long-term patron, Cardinal Ippolito II d'Este. His quarrel with Lusitano apparently arose during a conversation about some vocal music they had just heard at a concert. Lusitano claimed that modern music was written solely in the diatonic genus; Vicentino argued that it was composed in a combination of the three genera. They wound up wagering two gold scudi and asking two of the papal singers, Ghisilin Danckerts and Bartholomeo Escobedo, to serve as judges. Danckerts apparently failed to appear at the debate itself and only read the written arguments submitted by the participants as additional support. After the judgment against Vicentino, he and his patron left Rome for Siena and Ferrara, returning to Rome some four years later; Vicentino had his treatise published during this return visit.

Vicentino's first written support of his argument, the one submitted to the judges, is only a brief paragraph,[53] in which he cites Boethius as his authority, basing his case solely on the melodic lines of modern compositions as compared with the Boethian descriptions of the harmonic genera. Since these melodic lines frequently move not by the intervals of tone and semitone (of which the diatonic genus is composed) but by thirds and other intervals found only in the other two genera, Vicentino concludes that the current system is a composite of the three.

Lusitano's response is also based entirely on Boethius's work as compared with modern musical pieces.[54] It offers more specific citations (2.11, 1.23, 4.5) and somewhat more detail. Lusitano claims that, in fact, one never sees an entire tetrachord of the enharmonic or chromatic genus in modern compositions. The "true progression" of melody through the combination of intervals that should characterize these genera simply does not exist in the music of their time. When Vicentino published this document collection, he inserted a response to this argument, citing Lusitano's own recently published composition manual (1553) as supposedly refuting Lusitano's position in favor of his own.[55] Vicentino repeats his claim that the mere melodic

52. See Kaufmann, *Vicentino*, pp. 22–33.
53. Vicentino, *L'antica musica*, fol. 95v.
54. Ibid., fol. 96r.
55. Vicente Lusitano, *Introduttione facillissima e novissima di canto fermo, figurato, contrapunto . . . generi s. diatonico, cromatico, enarmonico* (Rome: Blado, 1553; Venice: Marcolini, 1558).

presence of an interval contained in the other two genera proves the use (in mixed or composite form) of those genera in the piece.

As a single event, this argument appears petty and inconsequential. It does demonstrate that the issue of harmonic genera had become important enough to serve as the subject of public and bitter professional squabbles. It also reveals something about how those who were primarily performers (though Vicentino was also known as a composer at this point), not philosophers or scholars, understood issues of music theory. Their sole source of authority remained Boethius, though numerous other ancient and modern texts were available to them; yet they also displayed thorough familiarity and ease with that source, as well as a concern that its tenets be respected. One cannot conclude from this debate that all such musicians were ignorant of the ancient authors introduced by 1500, but Boethius certainly remained their sole standard authority in this case; each assumed the judges would be convinced by references to his treatise. To these musicians, the working out of disagreements between their two types of musical knowledge—the theoretical analysis of Boethius and their daily experience as performers and composers—was a matter of ongoing importance, not merely an arcane exercise relegated to some nonperforming scholar or pedant.

This particular debate dragged on throughout the decade. Though Lusitano's composition manual avoided the issue by remaining a practical treatise that need not address such subjects in detail, Vicentino not only published all the documentation in his 1555 treatise but directed the contents of the treatise itself to the subject of the harmonic genera. Danckerts, the former adjudicator, responded with his own short treatise, devoted almost entirely to a refutation of Vicentino and any others who may propound similar ideas. Vicentino moved north permanently in 1563, working first in Vicenza and then in Milan;[56] Danckerts lost his position during a reorganization of the papal chapel in 1565.[57] These factors, rather than some sort of truce, probably brought the argument to an end. The treatises they produced do manage to rise above dreary recitations of the debate to cover some very interesting issues and thus deserve attention independent of the narrative of the public dispute.

Vicentino's *L'antica musica* established his reputation as a composer not only of fame but of eccentricity. Divided into a short theory section and a longer practical manual, it is devoted to a revival of the

56. Kaufmann, "Vicentino," *New Grove.*
57. Lockwood, "Danckerts," *New Grove.*

three ancient harmonic genera as dominant features of composition and performance. The dedication (to Ippolito d'Este) states that Vicentino intends to bring to light "many secrets, which since the time of Pythagoras, inventor of music, until now have neither been put into practice nor seen in theory."[58] Further, he intends to show how this music can fit into religious observance as well as private entertainment. The enterprise is to be supported with references to the works of Boethius and also to all others who have discussed the subject.

In such a task, Vicentino was already aware that the main obstacle to success was the strangeness of such tunings to the ears of his contemporaries (a reaction shared by the average twentieth-century listener). Thus he takes the offensive immediately in a proem to the first book, which is devoted to music theory. He restates Boethius's passage about music's reliance on both sense and reason, rejecting Aristoxenus and Pythagoras in favor of Ptolemy's middle ground. In this case, however, the senses cannot always keep up with reason, because the failure to use all three genera for such a long time has deprived the modern ear of the experience necessary to form proper judgments.[59]

The body of Vicentino's short (seven-page) theory section is based very loosely on parts of Boethius, Book 1. His main point, not surprisingly, is the origin of the tetrachord system for organizing the ancient tunings. To this end, he narrates their development as an extension of Pythagoras's experiments with the hammers, completed with a little help from Ptolemy; he does not deal with the chronological gap between the two figures. Vicentino also includes the standard Boethian descriptions of the chromatic and enharmonic genera as, respectively, "sweeter than the diatonic" and "sweetest and smoothest

58. Vicentino, *L'antica musica*, unnumbered folio, sig. Aii: "L'Opera finalmente scoprirà molti segreti, li quali da Pittagora inventore delle proportioni Musicali insino à questo tempo non sono stati messi in prattica, ne vedute in Theorica." See Kaufmann, *Vicentino*, pp. 101–74; Kaufmann's discussion of Vicentino's treatise focuses primarily on musical composition itself.

59. He enjoins the reader (Vicentino, *L'antica musica*, fol. 3r.): "Ma per questa opera intenderete molte cose, ove la ragione non è amica al senso, ne il senso è capace della ragione; e per quanto il senso e la ragione si potranno insieme comporre, ve ne darò minutamente notitia, per ilche giudicarete quanto li tempi passati sieno stati privi di molti e dolci concenti Musicali." (In this work you will meet with many things where reason is not the friend of sense, nor is sense capable of reason; and insofar as sense and reason can be combined, I will give you careful notice; thus you may judge how far past times have been deprived of many sweet musical harmonies.)

of all,"[60] failing like so many other writers to offer any specific illustration or analysis to support such statements.

Oddly enough, Vicentino continues his theory section with a discussion—first, of the "species" of diatessaron, diapente, and diapason and then of the eight modes—which is based solely on the diatonic genus.[61] He offers no reason for this shift back to the more traditional pitch system, nor does he try to connect any of this information back to his discussion of tetrachords. This passage is followed by a brief section on ancient pitch notation, which suddenly brings the harmonic genera back again as part of musical analysis.

Although Vicentino gives no reason for ignoring these several steps of logical or narrative continuity, the rest of Book 1 consists of a long explanation of why he has omitted a considerable number of other topics that form standard parts of a discussion of theory. In fact, he offers an extensive list of items he has chosen not to discuss, including the Boethian species of inequality, the Greek string names, arithmetic and geometric means, and so on. Some of these subjects, claims Vicentino, are best dealt with in terms of musical practice; these he has not omitted but transferred to the appropriate part of the *musica practica* portion of the treatise. The others, however, he has simply abandoned because "they are no longer at all useful today in our musical practice."[62] At one point, he suggests that anyone who wants these details should simply consult Boethius, since he has no intention of introducing foreign or useless concepts into his treatise.[63]

This seems to be a curious position for a musician whose goal is to revive a portion of music theory no longer in modern practice, accessible only through the works of antiquity, and which sounds foreign to the modern listener. The apparent inconsistency may perhaps be resolved by returning to Vicentino's stubborn position throughout the Lusitano debate. He had claimed, and continues to claim in his

60. Ibid., fol. 4v.
61. Ibid., fol. 5r–v.
62. Ibid., fol. 6v: "Haviamo lasciato à dire tutte queste cose per non ci essere hoggi utile alcuno alla nostra prattica."
63. Ibid., fol. 4r: "Non hò posto li nomi Greci, acciò con la oscurezza di essi non offuschi l' intelletto dell'oditore, e chi vorrà saperli, legga Boetio; et mi pare anchora strano comporre un'opera in Lingua volgare, et parlare alcune volte con vocaboli Greci, ò altri strani, possendo però non farlo. S'alcuno adunque ne vorrà vedere piu à lungo vedrà Boetio." (I have not used the Greek names so that their obscurity might not cloud the mind of the listener, and whoever would like to know them may read Boethius; and it seems to me rather strange to write a work in *volgare* and sometimes use words from Greek or other foreign languages, being nonetheless unable to speak them. So anyone who wishes to see about this at greater length may consult Boethius.)

treatise, that modern music really does employ all three harmonic genera, but in a composite and confused form that results from a failure of understanding. Thus his task as a composer is to clarify this usage, maximizing the effective use of each genus. Analysis and use of the three harmonic genera is therefore not really the revival of a moribund practice to Vicentino, but rather the application of classical analytic principles to improve the understanding and composition of modern music as it already exists.

Vicentino considers modern music far superior to that of the ancients, so he has no interest in reviving the latter; he therefore dismisses the concerns of his contemporaries about the alleged emotional effects of ancient music. Like them, Vicentino believes that the occurrences reported in the ancient sources really did happen, but he attributes them to the relative lack of music of any sort in the ancient world, not to ancient music's superior powers:

> With respect to the [proportions] of antiquity, ours are more numerous and more sonorous. As to why one does not in our time see those effects caused by musicians which the authors state were caused in antiquity, I say it comes from the excessive abundance and frequency of music; though they seem good, nonetheless they do not cause such effects as they did in the beginning when first discovered. Because the novelty of a thing, even if small, causes much more admiration than when it is used often and then becomes greater. As in our times, in comparison with ancient compositions and performers, one sees that in singing or playing them, one is moved to laughter. Yet in their time they were considered excellent. Therefore we conclude that much more is known about music in our times than formerly; but because of its abundance it is less esteemed.[64]

One effect of this approach is to free Vicentino from the necessity of presenting musical laws as timeless, changeless truths. If the modern experience is so superior to the ancient, then ancient rules need not necessarily be taken as discoveries of universal principles, but rather

64. Ibid., fol. 6v: "Che respetto all'antiche le nostre [proportioni] sono più, et anchora molto sonore, ma perche ne nostri tempi non si vede fare da Musici quelli effetti che scrivono gli Authori anticamente farsi, dico che viene dalla tropp'abbondanza, e frequenza della Musica, che buone paiano, nientedimanco non muovano tanto come faccuano nel principio che furno ritrovate, perche la novità della cosa, benche sia poca dà molto piu admiratione, che la tanta dall'uso, poi accresciuta, come ne nostri tempi per la comparatione delle compositioni antiche, e anchor delli sonatori, si vede, che cantandole, ò sonandole muoveno à riso, et ne loro tempi erano tenute bonissime, per ilche si conclude molto piu sapersi di Musica ne i nostri tempi che innanzi, ma per la abbondanza di quella esserne fatta poca stime."

as preliminary descriptions of practices developed more fully in the present day. This position allows him to elevate some aspects of ancient theory and suppress others as he sees fit, his standard for judgment remaining that of superior, modern musical practice.

Vicentino's focus remains on modern music and not music's historical development, but brief discussions of ancient musical practices appear frequently throughout the treatise. In several ways, his approach to the subject resembles authors of the later sixteenth century much more than it does those immediately preceding him. For one thing, he constantly compares music to language. Each nation has its own language, unique to its people and used to communicate feelings; so, too, it has its own music:

> Reader, you should know that according to what I find written in ancient chronicles, music has always been practiced naturally by people and performed in various ways. So we see and hear that in all nations of the world, each nation has its accents and different grades of voice, and when they sing together, they find naturally some accord of consonances according to their countries, tongues, and nations, and if in singing well they discord from the proportions of practice approved by science, nonetheless such discordances seem to them consonances. And just as the practitioner, with reason and practice, develops a good habit, so the contrary with them, rules by nature (as are brute animals, without reason); it seems to them that all that which they sing is good, and the dissonances seem to them good.[65]

He seems not to approve completely of some of these dissonant habits (particularly in comparing some practitioners to wild beasts), and he distinguishes between peoples' approval of dissonance owing to habit and owing to defects of hearing. He also notes the superior capacities of some people who "with both nature and art" have studied and practiced music with care. Because of this variety among those who listen to music, however, Vicentino enjoins composers to write pieces that vary in style so that all listeners can find something attractive.

65. Ibid., fol. 7r: "Lettore hai da sapere, che secondo ch'io ritrovo scritto nella raccolta delle croniche antiche, la Musica è stata sempre naturalmente da gl'huomini pratticata, et per varii modi esercitata, come si vede, et ode, che in tutte le nationi del mondo, ogni natione ha gli suoi accenti, et gradi di voci differenti, e quando insieme cantano, ritrovano naturalmente qualche accordo di consonanze secondo loro paesi, linque, et nationi, et se bene cantando discordano dalle proportioni della prattica approvata della scientia, nondimeno tali discordanze à loro paiano consonanze, et come il prattico con la ragione et prattica, fa un'habito buono, così per il contrario è colui, che solamente dalla natura è retto, (come sono gl'animali bruti, senza ragione) alquale pare, che tutto quello che cantando prattica, sia buono, et li paiano buone le dissonanze."

Further, Vicentino likens the relationship between ancient musical customs and modern ones to that between modern regional or ethnic styles and professional music. In the above quotation, for example, he began with a reference to ancient music; later in this passage he notes that the same phenomenon is seen every day in common people, who sing dissonant songs but clearly enjoy hearing them. Such a comparison does more than just point out similarities between ancient and modern music or bring the experience of ancient music closer to the reader by analogy with something more familiar. The constant comparison of ancient music to modern "folk" music that is seen as more primitive than the music the reader can expect to produce tends to lower the image of ancient music from that of a superior tradition to one not only different but perhaps inferior.

By relying on the immediate reaction of the modern mixed audience as the aesthetic standard for judging the quality of a performance, Vicentino has also eliminated the musician's Pythagorean task of bringing the soul closer to contemplation of divine things. He avoids any injunctions to the composer to uplift the soul of the listener or to improve the listener's character through the choice of musical style. Otherwise, Vicentino's response to the variety of tastes and training he described might well have been to urge composers to write for the educated listener or to attract the uneducated ear and train it for the better. Instead he urges the composer to use stylistic variety simply to appeal to all tastes, educated or not.

Total reliance on variety for its own sake, however, is not Vicentino's goal in musical composition. He returns to the emphasis on language in his insistence on the importance of the chosen text as the center of vocal composition, with music as the vehicle for its communication. Many composers, he notes, still write without consideration of the nature of the words themselves: whether syllables are long or short, where in the word the accent falls, and so on. Each language is different in this regard, and the composer must have a good understanding of a language's rules before attempting to set its texts.

As he warms to his topic, Vicentino manages to reintroduce his pet subject, the harmonic genera. Linguistic accents often involve not just stress, he states, but also pitch; changes in pitch are important in the expression of meaning. His harmonic system and the instruments he has developed are best fitted for this task:

All people can set to music their own way of singing with the grades of division of our instrument. With the music now in use, one cannot write a single French song, nor German, nor Spanish, nor Turkish, nor

Hebrew, nor of other nations, because the steps and leaps of all nations of the world, according to their native pronunciation, do not proceed only in steps of tone, natural semitones, and accidentals, but by diesis and semitones, and tones, and by enharmonic leaps. Thus with this division of ours we have accommodated all the nations of the world, who can write their accents and write them in as many voices as they like. Because music for words is written for no other purpose than to explain their concepts, their passions, and their effects with harmony.[66]

Not all of Vicentino's arguments are this bold in their attempt to turn any subject into a promotion of his new tunings; in this case, he has also become (at least briefly) an advocate of a universal musical system. Yet this advocacy of his pitch system remained his major goal, not only in this treatise but throughout his career. Vicentino developed two musical instruments designed especially to play in all three harmonic genera; the one to whch he refers in the above passage is probably his archicembalo, which he discusses in Book 5. He promoted the other, the arciorgano, in a separate work, *Descrizione dell'arciorgano* (Venice, 1561). Copies of these instruments were built and purchased for several sixteenth-century instrument collectors; some of them still exist, though apparently they never sold widely. He wrote music to be performed on these instruments, as well as vocal music for all three harmonic genera; his written works allude to performances of these compositions at the Este court.

Vicentino also sent copies of his compositions to other courts and checked later to see whether they were performed and how well. Shortly after the publication of *L'antica musica*, he sent a copy to the duke of Mantua along with some of his vocal works in five parts. In a follow-up letter dated 15 December 1555, he complains that the music he sent has not been sung.[67] Yet he acknowledges that they differ considerably from more common fare: "I believe," he writes, "that to someone with little experience, such new practices will seem strange." To remedy the problem, he includes some pieces graded in difficulty,

66. Ibid., fols. 85v–86r: "Et tutti potranno porre in musica il suo modo di cantare con i gradi della divisione del nostro stromento, che con la musica che hora s'usa, non si può scrivere alcuna canzone Franzese, ne Tedesca, ne Spagnuola, ne Ungara, ne Turca, ne Hebrea, ne d'altre nationi, perche i gradi et salti di tutte le nationi del mondo, secondo la sua pronuntia materna, non procedeno solamente per gradi di tono, e di semitoni naturali, et accidentali, ma per Diesis, e semitoni, e toni, et per salti Enarmonici; si che con questa nostra divisione havremo accommodato tutte le nationi del mondo, che potranno scriver i loro accenti e comporli a quante voci a loro parerà; perche la musica fatta sopra parole, non è fatta per altro se non per esprimere il concetto, et le passioni et gli effetti di quelle con l'armonia."

67. Mantua, Archivio di Stato B 1252, unpaged.

to accustom the singers to his style: "They are easy to sing, and composed almost like common music. So that those who are inexperienced will not despair, and so that, little by little, by using them they will be able to sing every type of music, as we do."[68] This uphill struggle for the acceptance of his music may help to account for some of the logical inconsistencies and argumentativeness already noted in his treatise. Once Vicentino had committed himself to the three-genus tuning system, he became its advocate in any possible situation and was willing to adopt almost any argument that might convince others of its value.

It is apparent to a modern reader, as it probably was in the sixteenth century, that Vicentino's system is an example of the general interest not only in ancient music theory but in the revival of ancient music itself. Tetrachord genera had played no part in the medieval ecclesiastical musical tradition; the standard musical instruments were not designed to play them. Singers found them difficult to sing, and listeners thought they sounded strange. The only source of information about them, and justification of their use, was ancient music treatises.

Yet Vicentino finds himself caught in the contradictions of his own arguments. As a composer, he is convinced that the music of his day is far superior to that of earlier ages, though it should be noted that the "ancient" pieces he cites as laughable must be examples of earlier medieval or Renaissance music; no musical compositions from Greco-Roman antiquity were then known. But if he also wishes to reject large parts of ancient theory as irrelevant to the music of the present, then he cannot support his tuning systems by extolling the superiority of the ancient sources that are the sole genuine evidence for them. Thus he has no choice but to claim the genera exist, though in a confused way, in modern music, so that he is simply advocating a tool for analyzing forms found in practice.

If, however, he dismisses the source of his knowledge of the harmonic genera, Boethius, Vicentino has no authority for his arguments at all. In his foreward "alli lettori," for example, he alludes to this by noting the greatness of the task of "digging from the obscure darkness the practice of ancient music" and presents the dropping of Greek and Latin terms not as the elimination of useless minutiae but as a monumental effort of rendering ancient principles

68. Ibid.: "Che sono facili da cantare, et quasi fatti della commuma Musica; accio che, li non troppo pratici, non si disperino, et che cosi apoco, apoco, usandosi canteranno ogni sorte di Musica, come facciamo noi."

in the modern Tuscan language.[69] He also claims in numerous places that since the days of Pythagoras, the ancient invention of the harmonic genera has never been put into real practice except by himself.

The controversy that surrounded Vicentino is therefore easy to understand. He has one foot in the camp of those who claim that modern music is far superior to anything the ancients ever had, the other among those dedicated to the revival of ancient music. By seizing upon a single aspect of ancient musical theory, the harmonic genera, he nonetheless achieved more than the promotion of an idiosyncratic position; he was able to divert the previous generation's incessant preoccupation with pitch into a new and ultimately more productive set of issues. His new scales never became part of general musical practice, but his career does mark a major trend toward reviving specific aspects of ancient music.

Ghisilin Danckerts's response to Vicentino's treatise was in many ways a reaction and nothing more. He offered no new theories, no new types of analysis, and certainly neither new ancient sources nor new musical styles. The main focus of his wrath is Vicentino and his work, but he also uses Vicentino as an example in an attack on the new chromatic tendencies he sees in many composers. Yet Danckerts's treatise does more than do his contemporaries' negative reactions to Vicentino's work. It points as well to several weaknesses in Vicentino's approach to the subject; for Danckerts uses similar evidence and authority yet produces opposite conclusions.

Like Vicentino, Danckerts's main authority is Boethius. Further, Danckerts's sole interest, like that of Vicentino, is the advocacy of modern composition. Danckerts also assumes that the reactions of modern audiences form an authoritative evidentiary base for assessment of musical compositions or of any source on the subject of music. This approach is reminiscent of the Bolognese musicians such as Spataro from the earlier part of the century, though there is no record of professional contacts among the two troupes of musicians, and in fact when Danckerts mentions the writers of an earlier generation, his references are almost entirely to Gaffurio. The resemblances probably come from their similar interests and concerns as professional performers and composers; for both groups, the main attraction of ancient music or writings on music is applicability to the day-to-day tasks of the professional musician.

Danckerts's argument has two main facets. First, he argues against the presence of the "other" two harmonic genera in modern music

69. Vicentino, *L'antica musica*, unnumbered folio, sig. Aii. v.

and against their value even as judged by the ancients. Second, he advocates and praises the diatonic genus and the rules developed for its use. The first portion of his argument is probably the most convincing, though the least original. It is simply a more extensive exposition of Lusitano's argument, based on the comparison of a careful reading of the relevant portions of Boethius with modern compositional practice. Vicentino, he states, violates the nature of the harmonic genera when he claims that in a given melody, the mere presence of an interval found in the melodic intervals of the chromatic or enharmonic genera is sufficient evidence that the piece was written using that genus.[70] The proper use of a harmonic genus means using its notes as the sole structural notes of a composition, since that is the way Boethius describes them. Since no examples can be found of a modern piece in which all four notes of even a single enharmonic or chromatic tetrachord appear together, Danckerts claims that modern music does not make use of them.

This is indeed a weak point in Vicentino's argument, and nearly every later writer who comments on the debate, however briefly, will side with Lusitano and Danckerts on the matter. Less solid is Danckerts's subsequent claim that the ancients themselves rejected the other two genera. Since this argument had been the standard means employed by most earlier Renaissance writers on music when they wanted to dispense with the subject of harmonic genera, Danckerts may well have thought no proof was necessary. In any case, he offers none, although he does claim that the absence of the harmonic genera from the ecclesiastical tradition was due to their rejection by the saints Ambrose and Gregory. His assumptions about the use of these genera among the ancients actually resemble Vicentino's fairly closely. Both agree that the ancients did not make full use of all three genera; they simply disagree about why. Vicentino claims it was because the genera were not well understood; Danckerts claims that the ancients had understood the genera but disliked them as inferior types. Neither offers substantial evidence in support of his position, and in both cases the arguments about the past are secondary to the main concern, the composition and performance of modern music.

Danckerts cites Gaffurio (*Theorica* 5.2) to support his claim that all the harmonic consonances are present in the diatonic; the other two genera add nothing to the practice of "harmony," a term he assumes refers to polyphony when used by both ancients and moderns. Since harmony is the essence of music, this proves the superiority of the

70. Danckerts, "Differentia musicale," Rome, Bib. Vall. R 56, fols. 545r–46v.

diatonic: "This diatonic does not use any other consonances than those which the other two, unused, genera use; neither do they use other consonances than the very same ones which the diatonic uses in making said harmony. Harmony is the beginning, middle, end, and entire contents of music; music is nothing but harmony, which (according to the Philosopher) is none other than the concord of discords."[71] The diatonic genus, continues Danckerts, contains all these intervals in a system that is simple, delightful, and familiar. Nothing is gained in harmonic terms by forcing performers through the melodic difficulties of the other two. Then, by presenting a sort of modern *laus musice*, Danckerts further advances his claim that the other two genera have nothing substantial to offer modern music. Vicentino had argued that modern music, because of its abundance, no longer inspired the miraculous effects described in the ancient *laus musice;* Danckerts, not surprisingly, disagrees. Like Vicentino, Danckerts believes that the ancient accounts of music's miraculous effects are true. Yet Danckerts claims to see similar effects caused by the music of his own day. He recounts the major elements of a typical *laus musice:* music's ability to heal the sick, to inspire soldiers to fight, to cause listeners to abandon their tasks to dance and sing. In each case, he provides first-hand observations of these effects caused by the music of his own time. At one point he offers a specific individual's habits as proof:

Sig. Pierluigi Caraffa, gentleman of Naples, titled Grand Master Caraffa, took such delight in music, that he always kept salaried musicians at his house (of whom I was one) until his death. And it happened many times that when he was sick with a fever, he had music performed, singing or playing, and often after a few works were sung which greatly delighted him, he so enjoyed the music that the limit and time of the fever passed, without his having felt scarcely any pain or suffering. And likewise many times when he was tormented by gout, he had singing and playing; . . . he used to say that while he was listening to music, he felt much less the pains caused by the gout.[72]

71. Ibid., Rome Bib. Cas. 2880, fol. 34v: "Il qual diatonico non usa altre consonantie in fare l'harmonia, che usano li altri due generi inusitati: i quali neanche essi usano altre consonantie, che quelle medesime che usa il Diatonico in fare la detta Harmonia, essendo l'harmonia principio: mezzo: fine: et tutto il continente della Musica, ne essendo la Musica altro che harmonia, la quale (secondo il Philosopho) non è altro che discordia concors."

72. Ibid., fols. 35v–36r: "Ser Pierluigi Caraffa gentilhuomo Napolitano, intitolato il gran mastro Caraffa; il quale si dilettava di tal maniera della Musica, che sempre tenea musici salariati in casa sua, fin alla sua morte: delli quali ne sono stato uno io. Et è accaduto piu volte: che quando esso era amalato di febre, facea fare musica

He goes on at great length, describing other supporting scenarios in detail. And just as Vicentino had used every possible occasion to insert a line on the merits of his tuning system, so Danckerts continually reminds the reader that all these things were achieved with good old diatonic music.

Danckerts's relentless attacks on Vicentino and his music reveal more than stubborn disagreement with a single person. Danckerts occasionally broadens his remarks to indicate that Vicentino was perhaps not an entirely unique figure. At his most general, Danckerts criticizes the numerous composers who work in the "new manner"; that which they call "chromatic writing" he sees simply as ignorance or willful breaking of the rules of good composition. The taste for chromatic madrigals has infected all of Europe, complains Danckerts, and not just Italy;[73] thus, though Danckerts may limit his personal attacks to Vicentino, he sees similar tendencies becoming ever more widespread.

Further, Danckerts discusses a composition he has seen by a composer he refuses to name. In an attempt to notate each harmonic genus accurately, the composer has written the piece in three colors: black, red, and green. This is nonsense, claims Danckerts, "because colors properly pertain to the painter, and not to the musician. If this opinion were true, all the difference between the three genera would consist in writing their melodies with different colors, and not in singing or playing them. And this opinion is so absurd, founded on that name "chromatic," it would be as if someone professing to compose in the oratorical arts were to write his compositions in various colors and would therefore claim to use in his writings many rhetorical colors."[74]

Danckerts obviously is more angry than logical at this point; yet this passage nonetheless reveals some interesting information. It seems unlikely that Danckerts would have fabricated this anecdote himself,

cantando ò sonando: et cantandosi molte volte alcune opere, che alui sommamente dilettavano, gustava con tale intentione la musica, che passava il termine, et il tempo della febre, senza haverne sentito quasi dolore o passione alcuna; et similmente facea molte volte cantare et sonare quando era tormentato dalla podagra . . . et dicea che mentre stava attento alla Musica, sentiva assai meno li dolori che la podagra dà."

73. Ibid., fols. 37v–56r.

74. Danckerts, "Differentia musicale," Bib. Val. R 56, fol. 557v (= Cas. 2880, fol. 38r–v): "perche i colori propriamente s'appartengono al pittore, et non al musico. che se questa sua opinione fosse vera, tutta la differentia delli detti tre generi consisterebbe in scrivere le lor cantilene con diversi colori, et non in cantarle, ò sonarle. Et e così assorda questa sua opinione fondata sopra quel nome chromatico, come sarebbe, se uno facendo professione di comporre in arte oratoria, scrivesse le sue compositioni di varii colori: Et per questo esso si vantasse di usare nelli suoi scritti molti colori rhetorici."

since it seems to have upset him. It is also unlikely that the composer is Vicentino; for Danckerts has been anything but shy in naming him elsewhere. This implies that Vicentino was not the only composer trying to revive the "other two" harmonic genera at midcentury, simply the only one to write a treatise on the subject. This other composer (if he did exist) tried to develop his own notation system for the genera. He chose to keep the standard line-space staff notation and to distinguish the pitches found only in the other two genera through the use of colored notes. Thus, to some extent at least he worked independently of Vicentino, who used doubled accidental marks (b, bb; x, #) rather than color. It also appears that Danckerts is misreading this attempt, probably deliberately, in order to ridicule it.

However successful was the attempt by this unnamed composer, Danckerts's passage suggests the widespread nature of the efforts to revive at least this aspect of ancient music. It also shows, by Danckerts's hostile response, how controversial this effort was. Vicentino and Danckerts each perceived themselves as campaigning against ignorance; neither appears to have taken an empty rhetorical stance. Given their attitudes and Danckerts's anecdote, it would appear that all those involved in the revival of ancient music pursued their individual courses and became partisans of their own solutions, more or less independently of each other. All involved agree about the importance of their task but share little else, making for an environment at once confusing and exciting. Danckerts's own solution—a total rejection of the whole "nuova maniera" in favor of the traditional diatonic music supposedly favored by both the ancients and church—could not serve as a satisfactory resolution of all the issues involved. But his treatise does demonstrate the wide range of interest among practicing musicians of the midsixteenth century.

Daniele Barbaro and the Commentaries on Vitruvius

Daniele Barbaro's translation of and commentary on Vitruvius's *De architectura* was first published in 1556 and issued in Latin eleven years later. Certainly its greatest single contribution to scholarship lay in the field of architecture. Yet just as Vitruvius himself stressed the importance of harmony and proportion in architecture, so too did Barbaro in his commentary; the latter's remarks on music are extensive enough to form a small treatise on their own, and in fact they

were occasionally collected as an independent manuscript.[75] Thus the
audience for them would appear to be at least twofold: readers of Vitruvius's *De architectura* and readers with a particular interest in music.
Barbaro's commentary offers a general summary of the musical
scholarship accessible to many sixteenth-century readers of both Italian and Latin; in this sense, the work is similar to the remarks of the
mathematicians in their Euclids, but more substantial. Yet specialists
in music also took a particular interest in his scholarship. To this extent, he resembles Giorgio Valla, a scholar of Greek and Latin letters
rather than a specialist in music, who undertook the subject as part of
a larger project and whose work appealed both to generalists and specialists. Also like Valla, Barbaro defines the field in Pythagorean
terms and hence emphasizes mathematics rather than poetics.

Many of the differences between Valla and Barbaro are the result of
the intervening fifty years of humanistic scholarship, emphasized by
the different nature of their projects. Others relate directly to genre;
Valla had composed a general encyclopedia of learning, whereas Barbaro is commenting on a specific text, albeit one that stresses the importance of other fields to the study of architecture. Barbaro deals
not only with his subject itself but also with issues of textual criticism;
unlike Valla, he compares variant readings in different manuscripts,
refers the reader to specific locations and buildings as mentioned by
Vitruvius, and tries to place the author and his book as much as possible in a specific historical context.

This dual emphasis, on both the historical and the mathematical
contexts of the subject of music, will be characteristic of the study of
music in the later sixteenth century, by the writers who follow Barbaro. Barbaro himself, however, still advocates in the end not only
mathematics, but the traditional Pythagorean approach, as the most
fundamental and important aspect of the field. Thus he is very much
a transitional figure; he does not resolve all the potential conflicts in
his approach, but others who later address these issues will refer frequently to his work.

Barbaro was neither the only nor even the first sixteenth-century
editor of Vitruvius to include commentary in his publication. It
may be useful to survey these other works briefly in order to appre-
ciate the ways Barbaro is typical as well as original. Like the Euclid
editions, these Vitruvius commentaries are mostly important not for

75. See Bologna, Civ. Mus. B 26, fols. 1r–20r. For biographical information on
Barbaro, see G. Alberigo, "Barbaro, Daniele," *DBI.* For Barbaro's influence on
Venetian proportional architecture, see Manfredo Tafuri, *Venezia e il rinascimento:
religione, scienza, architettura* (Turin: Einaudi, 1985), pp. 185–212.

new information or innovative analysis but for their synthesis of the current state of musical knowledge and its dissemination to a broader audience. Barbaro's is more thorough than most and the product of more deliberate scholarly attention to the subject of music per se. Together, these commentaries provide a composite view of what the editors and commentators considered the necessary minimal knowledge of music required of architects and scholars of architecture.

Vitruvius's stress on the importance of harmonic proportion in buildings had arisen out of the Pythagorean tradition, so references to music are scattered throughout the work, though they are concentrated in a few major chapters. First in importance is Chapter 4 of Book 5, in which Vitruvius compares the desired proportions of buildings to those of the human body; this subject offers both him and his commentators the opportunity for a long passage on *musica humana.* The proem to the entire work (sometimes combined with 1.1) includes a general statement on the value of numerous fields to the architect, a passage some commentators use for general remarks about fields of knowledge and their interrelation.[76]

The translation and commentary on Vitruvius by Agostino Gallo and Alvisio da Pirovano (1521) offers a fairly typical example of such treatments of music. The later work by Gianbatista Caporali (1536) is essentially a pirate version of this work.[77] These commentators' remarks in 1.1 simply stress, in more detail than that offered by Vitruvius himself, the importance of musical proportion in architecture, citing Plato, Pythagoras, Euclid, and Gaffurio as authorities. In 3.1 their remarks are largely practical, noting the use of proportions in representations of the human form by modern painters and sculptors and giving the reader precise dimensions and proportions for parts of the body. They state that the subject is too complex for them to cover in adequate detail and refer the serious reader to various sources,

76. On the tradition of Vitruvian commentary in the Renaissance, see Pamela O. Long, "The Vitruvian Commentary Tradition and Rational Architecture in the Sixteenth Century: A Study in the History of Ideas" (Ph.D. diss., University of Maryland, 1979); Long, "The Contribution of Architectural Writers to a 'Scientific' Outlook in the Fifteenth and Sixteenth Centuries," *Journal of Medieval and Renaissance Studies* 15 (1985): 265–98.

77. *Di Lucio Vitruvio Pollione De architectura libri decem traducti de latino . . . commentati . . . Augustino Gallo e Alvisio da Pirovano* (Como: da Ponte, 1521); Pollio Vitruvius, *Architectura con il suo commento et figure in volgar lingua raportato per M. Gianbatista Caporali di Perugia* (Perugia: Bigazzini, 1536). Caporali's version is so much a pirate of the Como edition that even its illustrations are modeled on the earlier version. For the fortuna of Vitruvius through 1600, see Lucia A. Ciapponi, "Vitruvius," *Catalogus translationum et commentariorum: Medieval and Renaissance Latin Treatises and Commentaries* (Washington: Catholic University of America Press, 1976), 3:399–409.

Euclid, Boethius, Macrobius, and Martianus Capella among the ancients. Gaffurio is especially favored among modern sources.

Gallo and Pirovano (and of course Caporali) offer more extensive remarks in 5.4, beginning with a brief *laus musice*. They list once more the major ancient sources on music mentioned above and return to the subject later to include Aristoxenus (or Aristides Quintilianus), Bryennius, and Ptolemy. They also add several modern works: Giorgio and Lorenzo Valla (especially the former's work on Cleonides), Poliziano's *Panepistemon* (which in one edition was bound together with Vitruvius and Cleonides),[78] and once again Gaffurio. Gaffurio is their major source here; most of the discussion, in fact, seems to have been composed by condensing the relevant portions of Gaffurio's various treatises, placing them in the order in which the subjects are mentioned by Vitruvius, and connecting them with prose transitions. They even include a description and diagram of the Guidonian hand, certainly not part of the Vitruvius text but included in Gaffurio, "according to today's usage."[79] Gallo and Pirovano's list of ancient authorities suffers from some confusion; they conflate Aristides Quintilianus and Aristoxenus (whose treatise should have been available to them by this time) and insert a mysterious "Ardita," probably a misreading of "Archytas." They also appear to believe, as had earlier Renaissance scholars, that Bryennius dates from some point in antiquity.

It seems that these authors were not experts in music and relied on Gaffurio for most of their information, thus both demonstrating Gaffurio's intellectual influence and status and broadening that influence through their constant reference to him as the field's major modern authority. Like so many writers, then, these commentators were important as transmitters to a broad audience of a standard definition and content summary of music, with a standard list of canonical texts and set of relationships to other fields. Ignoring the professional controversies of their generation, they present the subject as one defined in Pythagorean terms and one that plays a major role in the understanding of related fields, in this case, architecture.

78. *Hoc in volumine haec opera continentur. Cleonidae harmonicum introductorium interprete Georgio Valla Placentino. L. Vitruvio Pollionis De architectura libri decem. Sextii Iulii Fronini De aquaeductibus liber unus. Angeli Policiani opusculum: quod Panepistemon inscribitur. Angeli Policiani in priora analytica praelectio, cui titulus est Lamia* (Venice: Papiensis [Bevilacqua], 1497).

79. Vitruvius, *Architectura . . . Caporali*, fol. 112r: "Et noi alla usanza d'hoggi habbiamo fatto la figura dalla Mano, come mediante laquale si perviene alla doctrina del canto fermo et affigurato."

A later Latin commentator, Gulielmo Philandro Castiglioni (1586), offers much briefer remarks.[80] His preferred texts are Martianus Capella and Boethius, though he refers to others for a short statement of their views on a given subject: Ptolemy, Porphyry, Bacchius, Aristides Quintilianus, Aristoxenus, Pappus, and Bryennius. For his modern sources, Castiglioni relies mainly on Gaffurio and Aron, but he also mentions many others, most of them northerners: Andreas Ornithoparchus, Joannes Froschius, Tinctoris, and Bishop Ortho Theogorus. Brief and schematic though this treatment is, it demonstrates the stability of the canonical list of sources, modified in this case for a northern audience only by the addition of some northern names to the ranks of noted modern writers.

In comparison with these other commentators and translators, the work of Daniele Barbaro stands out as a superior achievement. Barbaro's rendering of Vitruvius into the vernacular is better both in style and in its critical assessments of variant readings; his commentaries reveal careful interest and study in many fields. He introduces his historical approach, both to the subject and to his analysis of the text, at the outset. Here he offers a brief biography of Vitruvius gleaned from references in the text, including quotations from the relevant passages. Barbaro's emphasis on the treatise's historicity is at its most obvious when he compares Vitruvius's descriptions of specific buildings with their modern-day ruins, as he does when discussing the ruins of the forum at Giulia Aquileiana.[81] In this case, he combines the examination of alternate manuscript readings, linguistic changes in place names over time, and physical remains to clarify the meaning of the text in describing specific buildings at a specific time.

Barbaro also reveals his historical sense in more subtle ways. In discussing the famous passage in which Vitruvius compares the proportions of a building to the harmonic proportions of the human body (3.1), Barbaro acknowledges that there are distinct differences between ancient and modern preferences in these proportions. Ancients made heads smaller and fingers longer than do moderns, he notes.[82] He refers the reader to Albrecht Dürer's treatise on symmetry, stating that the subject was controversial in antiquity, that it remains so today, and that he has no plans to resolve the matter himself but will simply explicate Vitruvius's text. This sense of deliberate de-

80. M. Vitruvii Pollionis De architectura libri decem . . . , commentary Gulielmo Philandro Castiglioni (Lyons: Tornaesium, 1586), pp. 182–83.

81. I dieci libri dell'architettura di M. Vitruvio tradutti et commentati da Monsignor Barbaro eletto Patriarca d'Aquileggia (Venice: Marcolini, 1556), pp. 130–31.

82. Ibid., p. 63.

tachment, acknowledging a long-standing historical controversy without needing either to resolve it himself or to conflate it with a modern debate on a similar subject, marks a major change in how musical scholars approach the ancients texts so essential to their field.

At the same time, Barbaro views the Pythagorean reverence for mathematics not as a historical phenomenon but as the discovery of a universal truth. In his discussion of Vitruvius's passage on human proportion, he stresses two aspects of the importance of proportions. First is its demonstration of the human mind's capacity to reason: "Reason is the most excellent thing in the mind of man, and this is demonstrated excellently in proportion."[83] Second is the reality of these proportions in the natural world; God has created the world in an orderly manner, and thus people exercise their divine gift of reason in discovering that order: "Mistress nature teaches us how we should keep buildings consecrated to the gods in measure and proportion and wants us to learn the ratios of symmetry, which we should use in temples, just as the sacred temple is made in the image and likeness of God—that is, man—in whose composition all the other marvels of nature are contained. So with great foresight the ancients took every ratio of measure from the parts of the human body."[84]

In his proem, Vitruvius emphasized the importance of many fields for the architect; Barbaro's comments develop the interrelations between the theoretical and practical aspects of these fields. An architect must be able both to understand the principles of geometry and to draw geometric figures accurately in his building plans; both are necessary if a building is to be constructed on rational principles.[85] When he turns to the subject of music, Barbaro reiterates the importance of both theory, for establishing the harmonic proportions of the parts of buildings, and practice, as is necessary for the proper design and construction of buildings (such as theaters) intended for musical performance.[86] Not only are these matters related, but in fact all of

83. Ibid.: "Ottima cosa è nella mente dell'huomo la ragione, e questa eccellentemente si dimostra nelle proportioni."

84. Ibid.: "La natura maestra ce insegna, come havemo a reggersi nelle misure, e nelle proportioni delle fabriche à i Dei consecrate imperoche non da altro ella vuole che impariamo le ragioni delle Simmetrie, che ne i Tempi usar dovemo. che dal Sacro Tempio fatto ad imagine, e simiglianza di Dio, che è l'huomo, nella cui compositione tutte le altre meraviglie di natura contenute sono, e però con bello avvedimento tolsero gli antichi ogni ragione del misurare dalle parti del corpo humano."

85. Ibid., pp. 10–11.
86. Ibid., p. 14.

the sciences share a common source and are based on the same order of reason, though their manifestations differ. An architect must deal with both the rational source and its physical realization.

Barbaro carries this point through his main discussion of music (5.4). He emphasizes music's twofold basis in both mathematical ratio and physical sound. Reason, he states, cannot operate without the sense perception of sound. Since music affects both the mind and the emotions, music is relevant to both speculative thought and morality—a point made by many earlier writers on music, since it comes from Boethius. Yet it has greater significance in Barbaro's arguments; for it supports his claims about the value and use of proportions in architecture.

Vitruvius had intended the body of this chapter to be a brief summary of the musical knowledge needed by the architect. Barbaro follows suit with a commentary that is basically expository, offering a fuller discussion of what Vitruvius mentioned briefly. Initially he follows the familiar outlines of modern usage, explaining musical pitches strictly in terms of modern line-space notation. He continually notes where the Greek system differs, though he does not go so far as to discuss Greek notation.

Barbaro does mention some differences of opinion between himself and Vitruvius. He observes that Vitruvius claimed to follow Aristoxenus but in fact did not and had even skipped several topics that Aristoxenus had considered important. Vitruvius, indeed, seems to have referred to Aristoxenus simply to identify the tetrachord system, not to advocate Aristoxenus's more general ideas. To be able to make this distinction, Barbaro probably has had some acquantance with Aristoxenus beyond Boethius's brief and disparaging remarks, but he does not discuss the *Harmonics* itself in any detail. Yet perhaps because Aristoxenus's ideas differ so markedly from the Pythagorean tradition that influenced both Vitruvius and Barbaro, it seems unlikely that Barbaro was seriously affected by Aristoxenus's work. Barbaro also notes, "If I were to write on music, I would organize it differently, but now I intend to follow the manner proposed by Vitruvius."[87] Just how serious his objections are is impossible to tell, since Barbaro does indeed follow Vitruvius throughout the rest of the chapter. Barbaro apparently agrees with Vitruvius in matters of substance, differing only in how he organizes detail.

87. Ibid., p. 141: "Se io havessi à trattar della Musica io la ordinarei altrimenti, ma hora io intendo di sequitar ill modo proposto da Vitruvio."

The rest of Barbaro's discussion of music is free from the anachronisms that surfaced in other commentaries, and so it may appear to be only an unbiased, detailed exposition of ancient scale systems much like that of Valla. Barbaro does not discuss the Guidonian hand, the hexachords, or other topics from the medieval tradition. Instead, he remains true to the tetrachord system throughout the chapter, discussing pitches in terms of proportions, scale types, and harmonic genera. These are all terms used throughout by Vitruvius, and Barbaro does an admirable job of explaining them with both clarity and detail.

Yet Barbaro also uses this chapter to advocate the tetrachord system in its entirety as the principal means of organizing modern composition. Specifically, he wants to revive the other two harmonic genera, the enharmonic and chromatic. He does this first by way of his seeming objectivity; simply by integrating the distinctions of the three harmonic genera into all aspects of the subject (as if their presence aroused no controversy at all), he elevates the importance of the enharmonic and chromatic genera from their usual peripheral status.

Barbaro also addresses the issue more directly by attacking those who cling to the single-genus system. When tuning an instrument, he begins, one must know the genus in which the desired composition was written; for the genus helps express the emotion of the piece. This choice is similar to a painter's choice of colors for a given work, but the process has received too little attention from modern composers:

So among ourselves [the choice] is little regarded, and many think that with the diatonic genus they can satisfy every quality of things. And they remain obstinate, not wanting to listen to reason, either because it seems they might have to abandon all they have learned, or because it is impossible to observe these rules, or because they truly are ignorant and scorn things which they do not know. I wish this were the place to explain the ideas and colors suitable to every quality of thing according to their genera, because, with the living experience of their ears confirmed by invincible reasoning, I would make them confess their error. But it requires more time and a greater opportunity. So I will conclude that they tax themselves very much in vain, if they think that with the diatonic genus alone they can represent the human affections.[88]

88. Ibid.: "Cosi à di nostri è poco considerata, e molti pensano col genere Diatonico satisfare ad ogni qualità di cose, è stanno ostinati ne vogliono udire alcuna ragione, ò perche par loro dover perdere quanto hanno imparato, ò perche impossibil sia osservar queste regole, ò perche veramente sono ignoranti, e sprezzatori di quello, che non sanno. Io vorrei che qui fussi luogo di esponere le

Barbaro's contemporary Vicentino may have chosen an eccentric path for the assertion of similar ideas, but he was clearly not alone. Modern use of the harmonic genera is an issue tangential at best to the study of architecture; Barbaro cannot justify his tirade on the basis of the Vitruvian text. His advocacy of their revival, though it would seem to parallel his promotion of Vitruvian principles in modern architecture, also reveals the importance this subject has attained by the middle years of the sixteenth century.

Barbaro's distinction between historical context and modern application is therefore not entirely consistent. He stops short of admitting both an ancient and a modern standard for writing music, calling instead for a fuller understanding and use of ancient theory; despite his references to Aristoxenus, this ancient theory is very much in the Pythagorean tradition. Barbaro's careful textual criticism and avoidance of anachronism serve to clarify the precise nature of the classical fields he wishes to revive. Since he is not a composer, he is not burdened with the details of putting his musical standard into practice, as was Vicentino. But the revival of the harmonic genera seems to be no less a real goal than the revival of Roman architecture by way of Vitruvius.

The Vitruvian text offers Barbaro one chance to put these theories of consonance to a slightly different sort of practice, in the design of theaters. Vitruvius's theaters are harmoniously proportioned for the same general reasons that all other buildings should also be so designed. Since their purpose is the performance of drama and music, however, theaters have the additional task of ensuring that the audience hears the performance. To this end, Vitruvius does more than discuss the projection and echo of sound from the stage to the audience. He devotes the subsequent chapter (5.5) to a discussion of the placement of tuned vases along the walls of the theater, designed to amplify a given pitch.[89]

Barbaro's commentary on this passage does not go beyond a more detailed rendering of the text. Yet the presence of the subject raises some interesting issues for the reading audience, issues later writers will address in more depth. It links mathematical measurements of pitch with acoustic bodies that must be measured in three dimen-

idee, e i colori convenienti ad ogni qualita di cose secondo i loro generi, perche con viva esperienza delle orecchie, confermata da invincibili ragioni gli farei confessar l'error loro, ma troppo tempo, e maggior occasione si richiede, ben concludo che molto in vano s'affaticano, se pensano col genera Diatonico solo rappresentare gli affetti humani."

89. Ibid., pp. 148–51.

sions, not just in length, like strings. Further, it expands this mathematical measurement to discussions of the space in which music is performed. Both these phenomena had previously been classified, if addressed at all, as qualitative, not quantitative, matters. Finally, these subjects are raised not only in the forum of musical specialists but also that of architects and general scholars of antiquity. Barbaro presents them not as daring experiments but as standard components of ancient design which should form as much a part of the architectural lexicon as caryatids or Doric columns. Because of its nature as a commentary, Barbaro's work may not provide a fully consistent interpretive framework. But it does form part of a successful effort, undertaken by writers in the 1550s, to broaden the arena of study and debate on musical issues.

Reforms and Revivals

The midcentury quarrels over the harmonic genera seem far removed from the concerns of Rossetti or Fogliano, who had been writing only some twenty-five years earlier. Doni's interest in the field solely as a pleasant pastime contrasts with the scholarly concern of Cardano and Barbaro for the perception of music as a key to cognition. But despite both changes over time and serious disagreements among contemporaries, several new interests and interpretive frameworks, all arising from attempts to integrate the ancient traditions with the medieval heritage so as to understand or alter modern music, distinguish these writers from those that preceded and followed them.

The efforts to unite the study of music with that of language remained tentative but attracted many writers at some point in their work. The topic's admission to the ranks of standard subjects deserving at least brief mention in a treatise is more significant than any advances in the subject matter itself. For the professional musicians, this effort most often took the form of a heightened concern for vocal music, with the emphasis on clear expression of the text. Vicentino, for example, bases one of his arguments for his harmonic genera on the assumption that his fellow musicians will be swayed to his cause by the possibility of a more expressive rendering of texts.

Rossetti's treatise offers an early example of this approach. His main interest is religious music. Its purpose is to draw the listener closer to God, particularly by way of the divine word. Thus, for Rossetti, the music itself is the secondary feature of such a composition.

The music is valuable insofar as it helps to impress the textual meaning on the mind of the listener; but because of its own emotional power, it also has the potential to distract the simple churchgoer. Therefore Rossetti favors rhythmic and pitch accents that follow, rather than oppose, the meters and the meaning of the text. This emphasis on text implies not a break with the Pythagorean tradition but an interest in harnessing that tradition more effectively.

Writers such as Cardano work out a way of relating music and poetry by attributing the ancient powers of music to the combined effects of harmony and classical poetry. Although this position would seem to lead naturally to calls for the reform of modern music, most authors remained vague about just how music should express the text's meaning, beyond respecting metrics. Cardano offers some general suggestions in terms of melodic lines and the amounts of consonance or dissonance, but these passages may date from so late in his life (ca. 1574) that they do not participate in the debates of these early midcentury scholars but rather in those of the 1560s and onward.

This overriding concern with ancient music's alleged effects became the field's most characteristic feature by 1550. Since no one except Doni (who was a very minor figure at best) was willing to argue that the anecdotes retold as part of the ancient *laus musice* represented anything but the literal truth, most writers scrambled for some way to account for this apparent contrast between ancient and modern music. Only Danckerts argued that modern music produces similar effects; all others claimed only ancient music could do so. Where these others differ is in their attribution of cause, which, in turn, is directly related to their overall narrative of the history of music.

Vicentino assigns the cause to deficiencies in ancient culture: the ancients had so little music that its occasional presence caused awe and excitement. The modern age enjoys music that is both better and more abundant. This very abundance accounts for its less dramatic impact, though its quality is higher. Vicentino's argument assumes a historical narrative consisting of a more or less continuous improvement in an equally continuous tradition. Such a view of musical history is not new with Vicentino; it had appeared especially in works from the beginning of the century, notably those of Ramos, Tinctoris, and Spataro. Writers with this interpretation of history, all of them practicing musicians, had little or no interest in reviving ancient music as such; Vicentino is thus forced to claim that his system amounts to a reform and not a revival. These writers' interest in the past lies mianly in recovering its "best" aspects (which are seldom well defined) for the further improvement of present-day music.

More common, however, was the view that ancient music had virtues that modern music lacks. The historical narrative of those who
took this position is more typical of the general Renaissance interpretation: the classical world's brilliant achievements fell away during the
Middle Ages, to be revived through study and imitation in the modern era. These writers looked at modern music, found it lacking in
comparison with that of the ancients, and therefore proposed various
ways of meeting their goal, a restoration of music's power to cause
dramatic emotional effects. Their admonitions about the text of a
piece form a part of this restoration effort.

Yet most of the ancient tradition, and certainly the ancient sources
to which these writers had access, had discussed not metrics or poetics
but pitch. Issues of tuning and pitch were therefore the first natural
focus of this revival, owing both to the contents of the available
sources and to the tendencies of Pythagorean music theory itself. Further, the long debates on scale tunings from the early years of the century had ensured the topic's familiarity. Unlike the earlier writers,
however, the interests of these writers after Fogliano did not lie simply in finding a tuning system that allowed the use of thirds and
sixths. They wanted to revive the ancient Greater Perfect System (or
more accurately, that system as they understood it), since in fact only
its diatonic tunings, a mere third of those described in the ancient
sources, resembled modern usage. The revival of the "other" two harmonic genera, the alternative tunings of the two interior notes of the
tetrachords, also provided a way to account for several aspects of
modern practice that seemed otherwise not to coincide with theory,
not only the old familiar issues of thirds and sixths but also accidental
notes difficult to accommodate in the older hexachord system. The
restoration of these harmonic genera, and to some extent the ancient
modes as well, thus became the center of attention for many writers
and composers.

But while the ancient sources had offered tuning proportions in
abundant detail, they had not described with any precision the exact
role the harmonic genera had played in the composition of ancient
pieces. Further, not all sources seemed entirely consistent with one
another; thus they presented serious problems of interpretation. Because these midsixteenth-century writers still understood ancient music as a single, unified system rather than a field subject to debate and
change over the course of antiquity, they were not able to use historical approaches to the sources as a way of reconciling differences and
continuities. They could only identify a text as "ancient" or rank various texts on the single-value scale of the authors' relative mastery of

the (Pythagorean) field. They were therefore driven to other sources of evidence or ideas to shed light on the issue.

Some new evidence arose through the imitation of ancient authors and their sources. Danckerts, for example, paralleled ancient *laus musice* anecdotes about famous people affected by music, with anecdotes of his own that referred to specific modern persons. Other writers, inspired by references to various ancient peoples and their musical customs, turned to such sources as modern peasants from their own regions and elsewhere to point out particular, unique habits. Thus Cardano refers to the tarantella as a southern Italian custom that illustrates music's curative powers. Finally, a writer may attempt to generalize on the basis of observed behavior; Fogliano cites the fact that all people find certain intervals to be consonant as a proof of those intervals' consonant nature.

These new types of evidence began to raise new problems even as they solved others. Evidence drawn from everyday life may be contested by other observers; Danckerts can look around him and claim to see music work miraculous effects, while others observe the same society and yet deny that such effects occur. Fogliano thinks that all peoples find certain intervals consonant, yet Vicentino writes that many peoples enjoy singing dissonances. None of these writers address the problem of how to adjudicate such disputed evidence.

Further, when these writers use observed human responses as evidence, they seem unsure how to analyze the nature of cause and effect. At times they attribute these responses to natural tendencies, according to Pythagorean theory; at other times they allege them to be the result of culture and training, based mainly on Aristotelian notions of habituation. Fogliano's argument that people agree about consonances supposes this response to be natural, proving that "nature inclines toward the good." Vicentino assumes that the practice of singing in dissonance results from custom and perhaps lack of training and can therefore be changed. The only rule for the use of these contested types of evidence seems to be the author's assessment of the likelihood that the audience will agree with his assumptions. Later writers will have to resolve these issues of evidence and proof as they attempt to address the larger questions lurking behind them, about how far music participates in nature, how much in mathematics, and how much in culture.

Those writers interested in mathematical matters also raised general questions as they tried to answer specific ones. Fogliano and Dentice were both concerned with defining just what it is about the behavior of sounding bodies that musical proportions measure; Car-

dano flirted with these issues as well. Barbaro applied these principles of sound production to the building of theaters and argued that
mathematics applied to specific aspects of the physical world may be
as important for some purposes, certainly for the production of music, as the cosmological truths underlying the mathematics. The main
issues for these scholars were two: to try and specify what it is that
musical proportion represents when a sound is produced, or what it
is that these numbers quantify; and to learn to apply those mathematical proportions to other phenomena, such as the construction of
acoustically effective buildings.

Amid these issues, music's classification as a mathematical discipline grounded in Pythagorean thought seems stronger in some ways
and weaker in others. Barbaro's work was instrumental in extending
this classification as the theoretical foundation of other fields, specifically of architecture. Cardano takes its principles as a starting point
for developing new theories of perception and cognition. Most writers who focused on issues of music and poetry acknowledged the validity of Pythagorean proportions. Even Fogliano, who rejected
Pythagorean theory, nonetheless kept the definition of the field as
primarily mathematical. No mortal blow was struck against the system, and no serious alternative appeared.

But Fogliano's rejection and Doni's active disinterest formed only
part of the potential threat to the integrity of the discipline. The focus on music and text, or the analogies made between music and language, may not explicitly reject Pythagorean theory. Yet continued
attention to these subjects has the effect of pushing Pythagorean
mathematical analysis to the sidelines. If much of ancient music's effects can be attributed to the poetry of its songs, as many writers began to claim, this weakens the arguments about the powers of
consonant proportions to cause such effects on their own.

The field of music at midcentury has thus broadened in its range of
contested topics as well as of subjects that rely on its theory as part of
their own. The questions raised about the relation between ancient
and modern music, the most persistent theme of these years, affected
not only matters of composition but of overall approaches to studying
the past and to examining physical phenomena. These issues remained largely loose ends in the writings of this period, as partially
solved problems or as unnoticed inconsistencies. They will not be resolved as part of common discourse for several decades.

CHAPTER 5

The Science of Sound
and the Study
of Culture

During the last third of the sixteenth century the field of music underwent rapid change. Whereas the scholars of the 1530s through the 1550s had focused on discrete issues or details, those who succeeded them began to synthesize the mass of new information into a fuller and more coherent definition of music and the methods for its study. The task was complex and difficult and fostered many attempts and disagreements. The first such effort, not surprisingly, tried to accommodate the new complexities under the umbrella of a more sophisticated Pythagorean theory. Gioseffo Zarlino earned broad acclaim and many attacks for developing this position. Learned in Latin, Greek, and (it was claimed) Hebrew, he brought to the task great familiarity and sensitivity in the handling of ancient sources. Taking a syncretic approach, he tried to incorporate both Aristotelian natural philosophy and humanist textual criticism into the traditional study of music as numbered proportion.

Zarlino's contemporaries recognized him as the greatest musical scholar since Gaffurio and Giorgio Valla and saw his work as far surpassing that of his predecessors. His treatises, which he continued to produce and revise until his death in 1590, set the agenda for debate during this entire thirty-year period. Yet Zarlino's scholarship also exemplified the limitations of this analytic path; his work not only caused great debate about specific details but also inspired attempts to recast the field yet again to resolve the difficulties found in his work.

Zarlino eventually proposed dividing the field into two parts: history and method. This distinction, though not always made in

199

precisely these terms, quickly came to predominate in the study of music; later scholars might focus on just one half of the discipline or argue over what pertained to which half, but they maintained the new split. This division, having persisted, marks a major turning point in musical studies.

"Method" for Zarlino was the study of sounding bodies, whose physical behavior is measured and expressed by means of both mathematics and Aristotelian natural philosophy; it would later be known as acoustics, or the science of sound. "History" refers to the use of these principles in the writing, performance, or examination of musical pieces by individuals or peoples at specific times, studied by means of humanistic disciplines and the textual analysis of historical sources. Most scholars after Zarlino found these two categories distinct enough to stand on their own without the larger Pythagorean tradition to hold them together; in fact, the Pythagorean tradition itself withered under attack, eventually fading away because it was perceived as no longer necessary or useful to either half of the discipline. The transition to this new classification was itself as significant as it was sudden. Yet even this change did not immediately resolve all questions or problems in the field.

Several late sixteenth-century scholars elevated the importance of the historical or cultural study of music over that of sounding bodies. According to this approach, the distinction between sound and music is the same as that between sound and language: "music" or "language" lie in the meaning peoples or cultures give to sounds. Here the long but inconclusive attempts to link music and poetics finally began to bear fruit. Two major humanistic scholars, Girolamo Mei and Francesco Patrizi, devoted themselves to the study of music and poetics, both influenced by the relevant portions of Zarlino's scholarship. Mei continued to pursue this interest by producing a treatise on the historical development of the ancient musical modes.

Yet this approach to the study of music spawned disagreements of its own, caused by ongoing debates in the field it had chosen as its new mother discipline, poetics. Mei favored an Aristotelian poetics based on imitation. Patrizi countered with an analysis of poetry, its rules, and its power to move the listener founded on the Renaissance Platonic tradition of Ficino. Still, neither showed any interest in the Pythagorean tradition beyond the historical. Both saw music as a cultural product studied primarily in terms of the text with which it was connected, the social and cultural uses of the musical composition, and the historical period in which the work was composed. Nonetheless, the strenuous disagreements and debates on the nature of poetics kept this aspect of the field from crystallizing quickly into a single pattern of analysis.

Vincenzo Galilei, who incorporated many of Mei's historical findings and analyses into his own work, set himself the task of correcting Zarlino's arguments about the relationships between ancient music, modern music, and musical study. On the one hand, Galilei demolished the claims of Pythagorean theory that elevated the consonant proportions of 1:2:3:4 (and as Zarlino would add, 4:5:6) by proving that the musical consonances could be produced by other types of changes in sounding bodies which were equally measurable by mathematical proportions but would reveal completely different sets of proportional numbers. Thus, Galilei's own analysis of musical performance would tend to place more emphasis on the cultural side of musical studies.

Further, Galilei did not settle for the simple solution of advocating either Platonic or Aristotelian poetics, or Aristotelian natural philosophy (in the study of sounding bodies) as a single best key to the discipline. Instead, he took the further step of historicizing Aristotle and his works along with those of the other ancients, arguing that a true heir of the Aristotelian tradition would proceed according to the investigative methods Aristotle had advocated, rather than slavishly copying his results. Galilei thus left the field split even more, into separate pieces, each studied with a greater degree of relativism.

This new orientation of the discipline can be seen in the writings of scholars from the years around 1600. Ercole Bottrigari moved back and forth between the two parts of the field in his work, in combinations that varied according to the problem at hand. Thus, he could explain the use of different tuning systems by different types of musical instruments as caused both by the physical behavior of a given instrument and by the history and customs of its development. Similarly he could discuss the construction of ancient and modern theaters as a function of the acoustic properties sought by the ancients as well as the kinds of performance intended for each type of building. To Bottrigari, these distinctions between "science" and "art" were no longer contested; rather, they were givens from which his own analysis could proceed.

All the major writers of the later sixteenth century and some of the minor ones demonstrate a thorough familiarity with many ancient sources and several analytic tools for their study. Their works also show a knowledge of relevant developments in mathematics. The distinctions in professional education and career patterns that will come to characterize specialists in one or another of the new subfields (between historians of music and specialists in the behavior of sounding bodies, for example) have not yet come into being.

Many of the issues these writers address had been raised in the first half of the century; portions of their resolutions can also be found in earlier works. It is their synthesis that is new. A combination of accumulated scholarship, new information, more mature approaches to the reading of classical texts, and individual talent allowed these synthesizers to begin asking the larger questions that prompted rapid change.

Gioseffo Zarlino

Gioseffo Zarlino (1517–90) was the first sixteenth-century musician since Gaffurio to dominate his field so completely and set the terms of subsequent debate. Both the breadth of his written work and the depth of his scholarship earned him high esteem among his contemporaries as one of the great musical authorities of his day. His main music treatise, the *Istitutioni harmoniche*, went through at least four printings during his lifetime (Venice, 1558, 1562, 1573, 1589) and several after his death; his other two music treatises were reprinted as well. Zarlino also wrote on other subjects, such as the reform of the calendar, the history of the Capuchin order, the precise date of the Crucifixion, and the virtue of patience.[1]

Born and raised in Chioggia, Zarlino served Chioggia's cathedral as singer and organist and took minor Franciscan orders before moving across the lagoon to Venice in 1541.[2] Here he studied with S. Marco's

1. Zarlino's Italian works were collected, revised, and published together before his death, in *De tutte l'opere . . .* , 4 vols. (Venice: Senese, 1588–89). Volumes 1–3 consist, respectively, of *De institutioni harmoniche, Dimostrationi harmoniche*, and *Sopplimenti musicali*. Volume 4 contains nonmusical works: *Trattato della patientia; Discorso del vero anno, e giorno della morte di Christo;* and *Risolutioni d'alcune dimande fatte intorno alla correttione del calendario di Giulio Cesare.* Zarlino's musical treatises have been reissued in numerous facsimile versions. Parts 3 and 4 of the *Istitutioni* are available in English, as *The Art of Counterpoint*, trans. Guy A. Marco and Claude V. Palisca (New Haven: Yale University Press, 1968); and *On the Modes*, trans. Vered Cohen, ed., intro. Claude V. Palisca (New Haven: Yale University Press, 1981). Owing to variations in pagination and the inclusion of revisions (though some revisions are only stylistic), all citations refer to the editions of *Tutte l'opere*.

2. Most biographical information on Zarlino is based on the brief biography by Bernardino Baldi, whose information came largely from Zarlino himself; see Baldi, "Vite inedite di matematici italiani," ed. Enrico Narducci, *Bullettino di bibliografia e storia delle scienze matematiche e fisiche* 19 (1886): 633; see also Claude V. Palisca, "Zarlino, Gioseffo," *New Grove.* William A. Wallace has pointed out the inclusion of some of Zarlino's works in Giuseppe Biancani's *Dissertatio* (Bologna, 1615) as

famed maestro di cappella Adrian Willaert, in addition to his studies of Greek, philosophy, and Hebrew. Zarlino was named maestro di cappella at S. Marco in turn (after the departure of Cipriano Rore, another student of Willaert), a post he retained for the rest of his life. He was widely known not only for his learning but also for his vast library,[3] much of which was apparently dispersed after his death. He persuaded the physician Antonio Gogava to translate and publish the *Harmonic Elements* of Aristoxenus. Among his students, Zarlino could count not only several noted composers of the next generation but also the theorists and musicians Vincenzo Galilei (though the dates of his studies are unclear) and Giovanni Maria Artusi.

These students would go on to quarrel with Zarlino and with one another. Their arguments, particularly between Zarlino and Galilei, both fueled long-term professional rivalries and provided the proximate cause for the substantial reconsideration and restructuring of the field itself. Zarlino was the last major Italian theorist to attempt a synthesis of ancient and modern learning within the terms of Pythagorean discourse. This modern learning extended both to humanistic studies and to recent developments in Aristotelian natural philosophy.[4] Even as his work was being hailed as the epitome of such scholarship, other writers were pointing out the fundamental limitations and contradictions inherent in his Pythagorean orientation. The three decades of his career that followed the publication of the *Istitutioni* therefore encompassed not only the high point of Pythagorean musical theory but also its inevitable decline.

Zarlino's first publication, the *Istitutioni harmoniche,* serves both as an expository and an argumentative treatise; he sets several goals for the work. It is to be a reference work on musical theory in the old Pythagorean and Boethian tradition, incorporating the decades of study since the time of Gaffurio into a complete handbook of musical

recommended for the education of mathematicians. The persistence of music among the mathematical disciplines as classified by mathematicians during the seventeenth century deserves further study. See Wallace, *Galileo and His Sources: The Heritage of the Collegio Romano in Galileo's Science* (Princeton: Princeton University Press, 1984), pp. 146–47. D. P. Walker discusses the feud between Zarlino and Vincenzo Galilei with great sensitivity to the differing conceptions of harmony and consonance between them, as distinct from the tendentiousness and mutual hostility also evident in their writings; see Walker, "Vincenzo Galilei and Zarlino," in *Studies in Musical Science in the Late Renaissance* (London: Warburg Institute, 1978), pp. 14–27.

3. See Francesco Sansovino, *Delle cose notabili che sono in Venezia, libri due...* (Venice, 1602), fol. 258r; also in numerous eds. and reprs.

4. On Venice and Padua as centers of Aristotelian scholarship, see Charles B. Schmitt, "Aristotelianism in the Veneto and the Origins of Modern Science: Some Considerations on the Problem of Continuity," in *Aristotelismo veneto e scienza moderna,* ed. Luigi Olivieri (Padua: Antenore, 1983), 1:104–23.

science. It is also to be a history and analysis of music in the ancient world, making maximum use, through the methods of humanistic scholarship, of the major and minor references to music in classical writings of all types; the latter was especially important given the total lack of musical examples from antiquity at the time of the work's composition. The treatise is also to serve as a composition manual for the writing of counterpoint. Finally, based on the information about ancient music, it is to be a rebuttal of the claims of such composers as Vicentino, the "chromaticists" who argued that by reviving the harmonic genera as they conceived them, they might revive ancient music and its emotional power. These goals result in several shifts in focus, as Zarlino turns a given argument to one or more of these ends.

Perhaps the most noteworthy characteristic of Zarlino's *Istitutioni*, besides its abundance of scholarly references, is its attempt to elevate the rhetorical approach to musical studies to a role of central importance within the Pythagorean tradition. Zarlino uses several argumentative approaches toward this end, many of them visible in his opening chapters. His proem features an idealized history of music's origins, based on Cicero's *De inventione*, in which he links the historical development of musical skills to that of human language ability. Of all God's gifts, claims Zarlino, the articulated voice is the most important, since it lets people communicate their thoughts; this distinguishes them from the beasts and allows them to live in civil societies. Some of the more intelligent men of ancient times began to polish their rude speech and elevate it further. In their continued pursuit of perfection, they added harmony and meter and so were able to compose hymns, comedies, tragedies, and so on: "And so with Number, Speech, and Harmony, they were able to sing praises and render glory to God, and with them, according to what pleased them, they were able more easily and with greater force to restrain wayward souls and to move to greater pleasure the wills and appetites of people, returning them to a tranquil and orderly life."[5] Those who excelled in this pursuit, continues Zarlino, were called indiscriminately Poet, Musician, or Sage. Despite these impressive early achievements, this knowledge sank again into obscurity through the ravages of time, almost until the advent of his teacher, Willaert.

5. Zarlino, *Istitutioni* p. 2: "E cosi col Numero, col Parlare e con l'Harmonia potevano con quelli cantar le laudi e render gloria à Dio; e con questi, secondo che lor piaceva, più facilmente e con maggior forza ritener gli animi sfrenati, e con maggior dilettatione muovere i voleri e appetiti degli Huomini, riducendoli à tranquilla e costumata vita."

Zarlino parallels this narrative of the origins of music and language to the more familiar Boethian narrative of music and number, by returning in his Part 1, Chapter 1, to the early Greeks and retelling the story of music's invention by Jubal, Mercury, and Pythagoras. The process as Zarlino describes it was a gradual one of discovery, correction, and perfection of knowledge, based on logic and reason. Music's elevation to a mathematical science, a subject devoted not to the provision of life's necessities but the elevation of the soul, is the result. Number remains the aspect of the sciences with the greatest certainty, the highest truth in any given field:

So in our science of music, posterity pointed out past errors, and by adding their own authority, made it so clear and certain that they considered it, and made it part of, the mathematical sciences, and for no other reason than its certainty. For it with the others leads the other sciences in certainty, and holds the first degree of truth, as can be seen in its name. . . . These sciences make particular profession of this truth, since they consider things which by their nature have true being. In this they are different from some other sciences, which are founded upon the opinions of various men, having in themselves no stability at all. The former, having their positions in proof, come to have complete certainty. Thus mathematicians are all of the same opinion about essential matters, nor do they agree about anything except that which can be understood sensibly. And the certainty of these sciences is so great that by means of numbers one knows infallibly the revolution of the heavens, the various aspects of the planets, the eclipses of the moon and of the sun, and infinite other marvelous secrets, without there being any point of discord among them. Therefore it may be known that music is both noble and most certain, being part of the mathematical sciences.[6]

6. Ibid., pp. 6–7: "Cosi della nostra scienza della Musica i posteri mostrando gli errori de passati, e aggiungendovi la loro authorità, la fecero talmente chiara e certa, che la connumerarono, e fecero parte delle scienze Mathematiche; e questo non per altro, salvo che per la sua certezza; percioche questa con l'altre insieme avanza di certezza l'altre scienze e tiene il primo grado di verità; il che dal suo nome si conosce . . . della qual Verità queste Scienze fanno particolar professione; essendo che considerano le cose, che di lor natura hanno il vero essere. Et sono in tanto differenti d'alcune altre Scienze; che queste essendo fondate sopra le opinioni de diversi huomini, non hanno in se fermezza alcuna; e quelle havendo i Sentimenti per loro prova, vengono ad havere ogni certezza. Percioche i Mathematici nelle cose essentiali sono d'un istesso parere; ne ad altro consentono, che à quel, che si può sensatamente capire. Et è tanta la certezza di dette Scienze; che col mezo dè Numeri si sà infallibilmente il Rivolgimento de cieli, gli Aspetti varii de i pianeti, l'eclisse della Luna, e quello del Sole, e infiniti altri bellissimi secreti, senza esser tra loro punto di discordia. Il perche da questo si può conoscere, che la musica sia e nobile e certissimo; essendo parte delle Scienze mathematiche."

This very strong statement about music's status and the status of the "mathematical sciences" epitomizes Zarlino's overall approach.[7] Issues related to music and poetry must fit into this larger classificatory framework: for example, his earlier reference to metrics, speech, and harmony had taken care to use the term *number* in referring to meter. By defining poetry as the superior form of language and by examining poetics primarily via metrics (which is, of course, analyzed by means of number), Zarlino is able to account for poetry's power in terms of Pythagorean theory, avoiding a notion of poetics as a rival discipline to that theory. Such an approach allows him to discuss the importance of text and language at various levels throughout his treatises, while maintaining a consistent interpretive model.

If one possible threat to Pythagorean theory had lain in the study of rhetoric and poetics, another lay in the analysis of music's social or educational role, notably as discussed in Aristotle's *Politics*. Much cited by those who wished to minimize Pythagorean theories about music's effects on the soul, the passage (8.5) praises music as a pleasant pastime (generally rendered as *otium*), though its main purpose is simply to provide a wholesome diversion from the cares of the day. Zarlino, in his discussion of "to what end one should study music" (1.3), does not attack this position but once again tries to accommodate it to a Pythagorean reading. After rejecting the argument that music exists solely to provide delight to the ears as a claim fit only for "common people and mechanics,"[8] he gives qualified approval to the view that it should be studied as one of the liberal arts that dispose the soul to virtue. The study of music, he concludes, should do more than help

7. Although much work remains to be done on the role of the debates on the hierarchy and certainty of knowledge in the scientific thought of the later Renaissance, several valuable studies are worth noting: Giulio Cesare Giacobbe, "Il commentarium De certitudine mathematicarum disciplinarum di Alessandro Piccolomini," *Physis* 14 (1972): 162–93; his "Francesco Barozzi e la 'Quaestio de certitudine mathematicarum,'" *Physis* 14 (1972): 357–74; his "La reflessione metamatematica di Pietro Catena," *Physis* 15 (1973): 178–96; his "Epigoni nel seicento della 'Quaestio de certitudine mathematicarum': Giuseppe Biancani," *Physis* 18 (1976): 5–40; and his "Un Gesuito progressista nelle questioni 'De certitudine mathematicarum' rinascimentali: Benito Pereyra," *Physis* 19 (1977): 51–86; Charles B. Schmitt, "Aristotelianism in the Veneto"; Luigi Olivieri, *Certezza e gerarchia del sapere: crisi dell'idea di scientifica nell'Aristotelismo del secolo XVI* (Padua: Antenore, 1983); L. Laudan, "Theories of Scientific Method from Plato to Mach: A Bibliographic Review," *History of Science* 7 (1968): 1–63; Benjamin Nelson, "Probabilists, Anti-Probabilists, and the Quest for Certitude in the Sixteenth and Seventeenth Centuries," in *Proceedings of the Tenth International Congress of the History of Science* (Paris: Hermann, 1962), pp. 269–73; Walter Roy Laird, "The *Scientiae Mediae* in Medieval Commentaries on Aristotle's *Posterior Analytics*" (Ph.D. diss., University of Toronto, 1983).

8. Zarlino, *Istitutioni*, p. 11: "Imperoche è cosa da volgari e da mecanici."

an individual acquire "perfection of the intellect"; it should also re-
lieve people from the cares of the everyday world, leading them on to
better and higher concerns. He supports this statement with a reference to the *Politics,* arguing that its aim includes "passing time and
comporting oneself virtuously."[9]

Zarlino's argumentative goal is the association of this latter purpose with some of the Pythagorean ideas normally connected with
the goal of "disposing the soul to virtue." He does so by repeating that
music should not be studied because it is "necessary," that is, in providing the needs of daily life, nor because it is "useful" to some personal physical end like gymnastics, which strengthens the body. Music
should be studied as a discipline that is "liberal and upright," lightening the effort of learning the more "useful" or "necessary" sciences
and thus leading the individual to a more virtuous life. This solution
seems a bit forced, but it allows Zarlino the rhetorical space to discuss
a given topic in the terms of a more Aristotelian tradition when it
seems appropriate, without violating the larger outlines of the
Pythagorean approach that ultimately links all theory to number and
reason.

Zarlino does not limit his focus to the study of music and the individual; he also devotes considerable attention to issues of *musica mundana.* In the *Istitutioni* he offers an extended discussion of the cosmos
and its size, far past what the work's main subject would seem to require. Zarlino also wrote several other works based on his studies of
the calendar (in support of the reforms) and of astronomy (establishing the exact date and hour of Christ's death through the study of
heavenly configurations).[10] These treatises all rely on *musica mundana*
as a part of the subject's logical underpinnings. Thus, for Zarlino, this
analytic system itself formed a vital part of the classification and the
mastery of these other disciplines, in addition to its role in the study
of musical styles.

Most of the rest of the *Istitutioni* Part 1, some fifty pages, is devoted
to Pythagorean theories of number and its manifestations in the
world. As with most such sixteenth-century discussions, his approach
is encyclopedic; Zarlino intends not only to provide sufficient evidence to support his argument but also to compose a sort of reference
work that lists the appearances and applications of these notions since

9. Ibid., p. 12: "passare il tempo e trattenersi virtuosamente."
10. Two of these works, the *Discorso del vero anno, e giorno della morte di Christo*
(Venice, 1579) and the *Risolutioni . . . alla correttione del calendario di Giulio Cesare,*
were reissued in *Tutte l'opere* 4. The third, written in Latin, escaped this collection:
De vera anni forma (Venice, 1580).

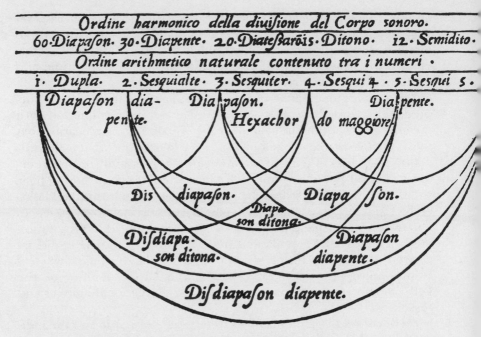

Ordine harmonico della diuisione del Corpo sonoro.

60·Diapason· 30·Diapente· 20·Diatessarōis·Ditono· 12·Semidito·

Ordine arithmetico naturale contenuto tra i numeri ·

1· Dupla· 2·Sesquialte· 3·Sesquiter· 4·Sesqui 4· 5·Sesqui 5·

Diapason dia-   Diapason.   Diapente.
        pente.   Hexachor do maggiore·

          Dis diapason.   Diapa son.
                            Diapa
                         son ditona·
              Disdiapa·   Diapason
               son ditona·   diapente.

                  Disdiapason diapente.

Figure 4 Harmonic proportion seen in the numbers 1–6. From Gioseffo Zarlino, *Sopplimenti musicali* (Venice, 1588), p. 98.

antiquity. Therefore his illustrations include not only the usual references to astronomy or the elements but also to attempts to apply these theories to other fields. He mentions especially secret interpretations of Scripture based on number, citing Augustine's *De doctrina christiana,* as part of God's gift of number to human rationality and for understanding things divine.

In this discussion of number, Zarlino's own originality lies mainly in his amplification of the primary numbers used in Pythagorean theory itself (originally 1:2:3:4, expanded to the series 1:2:3:4:5:6), an extension he proposes as a major analytic improvement (Fig. 4). While tradition had identified the first four integers as those expressing the fundamental order of the cosmos as well as the fundamental musical consonances, Zarlino wishes to take this number system as far as six, the first "perfect" number.

This extension itself is not entirely new; Ramos had used it in support of his tuning system some sixty years earlier. Yet Zarlino takes the argument much further by placing greater emphasis on Pythagorean principles and by carrying those principles throughout

his work. The number six, he argues, is "perfect" because its factors—
1, 2, 3—also produce six as their sum. Further, these factors of the
number six are themselves all extremely important in Pythagorean
symbolism as Unity (1), the first falling-away from Unity (2), and the
first true number (3). Zarlino goes into great detail in discussing not
only the properties of the number six but also its manifestations in
the natural world. Thus he proceeds with a long expository section
covering many topics, from the creation of the world in six days to the
six faces of a cube.

The main practical advantage Zarlino (like Ramos) gains from all
this effort is the admissibility of thirds as consonant intervals along
with fifths, fourths, and octaves. Just as the establishment of a harmonic mean in an octave produces the fifth and fourth, he argues, so
the mean of that fifth will produce a major and minor third.[11] Zarlino's commitment to Pythagorean theory as the foundation of musical
science can be seen once more in the high level of attention he devotes to this issue, which might otherwise seem to be so old as to have
faded away as a topic of major concern. Not surprisingly, Zarlino also
supports a tuning system, one of those propounded by Ptolemy,
which contains these thirds.

Zarlino, then, has devoted the first quarter of his treatise to establishing the Pythagorean grounding of the science of music. He demonstrates his mastery of the discipline in this first part through his
development of a detailed and consistent argument, of a creative and
syncretic synthesis of scholarship in that tradition, and through his
extensive and thoughtful references to sources in general. He offers
the most thorough and systematic discussion and analysis of
Pythagorean musical theory since Gaffurio and Giorgio Valla, clearly
benefiting by the fifty years of intervening scholarship.

The next subject to which Zarlino turns reveals a different approach to the ancient sources. He devotes Part 2 to ancient music, a
subject that had expanded considerably since the days of Gaffurio.
Through several chronological narratives and numerous expository
passages, Zarlino constructs a genuine history of music among the ancients. That is, he is concerned not only with narrative but also with
cause and effect; he assesses sources according to criteria such as bias
and anachronism; and he develops a portrait of the past that allows
for diversity as well as change over time.

11. Zarlino, *Istitutioni*, p. 30. Palisca discusses his use of the "senario" in some detail,
in *Humanism in Italian Renaissance Musical Thought* (New Haven: Yale University
Press, 1985), pp. 244–50, though he minimizes the importance to Zarlino of Platonic
and Pythagorean thought.

Zarlino establishes part of the pattern of his overall narrative at the outset, in discussing the development of instruments and consonances from the early Greeks through Pythagoras. Music among the very early ancients, he begins, was rough and primitive and improved gradually through the invention of more and more pitches and lyre strings to increase its range and variety. He follows the standard chronology of the invention of these various strings of the Greater Perfect System. When his narrative gets to Pythagoras, Zarlino notes that the range of acceptable consonances in that era was smaller than that of the modern age, and he feels compelled to account for this difference.

Pythagoras did know both the perfect and the imperfect consonances, argues Zarlino, just as the moderns do. Because the proportions that form the imperfect consonances can be so combined as to form dissonances, and because of his concern for simplicity and order, Pythagoras refused, however, to use them at all. Further, such proportions could produce intervals that were larger than the classical, two-octave Greater Perfect System, so Pythagoras also had practical reasons for barring their use. Therefore he had retained only the simpler proportions formed of the numbers one through four, which are capable of producing only consonances.

This preliminary narrative serves several purposes. It locates a primitive era of early antiquity, before Pythagoras, to which Zarlino can return when he wishes to hypothesize about music in early societies. Its sources are scanty, but he can pull references to the period from classical writers such as Apuleius, Horace, all of the ancient music theorists, Pliny, and of course early Greek sources such as Homer. Pythagoras's life marks the transition between this early music and musical science, which goes on to develop throughout later antiquity. Since Zarlino sees music as a science, he believes the essence of musical knowledge is cumulative; thus the modern world with its greater store of knowledge is free to move beyond the limits imposed by early scholars such as Pythagoras, without necessarily rejecting Pythagoreanism.

After presenting this introductory narrative of musical science, Zarlino turns to the compositions themselves, addressing general questions about the style of ancient music before developing arguments about the sources of its miraculous effects. He asserts that the major cause of modern misunderstandings about ancient music, and the reason why the ancients' use of consonances had seemed so primitive to modern scholars, is the false assumption that they had written music polyphonically in the style of modern composers. Zarlino is not the first scholar to have suggested this, but he is certainly the most thorough and definitive in his argumentation and analysis. He recognizes that this position will cause controversy and so devotes considerable space to the details of ancient practice as found in classical literary sources:

> It is indeed true that modern usage is so different, and far from the usage of antiquity, that it would be almost impossible to believe it when many worthy and honored writers who lived long before our era made no mention of such a thing. For the musicians of those days did not make music with so many varied sorts of instruments . . . nor were their songs composed of so many parts, nor did they use so many voices in their pieces, as we do. Rather, they performed them in such a manner that a musician accompanied his voice with the sound of a single instrument, that is, a pipe, or cythara, or lyre, and in that way brought great delight to himself and his listeners. . . . When there were two that sang, they did not sing together and at the same time, as we do, but one after the other.[12]

Zarlino supports this interpretation with an abundance of references from many sources, from Homer to Virgil, Plato, Livy, and numerous others. He discusses each quotation or group of quotations and references, to prove that the only consistent reading of them must assume monophonic, not polyphonic, styles. Further, he reports that the same basic style of Greek chorus singing, in which the dancers sing in unison, changing the direction of their dance with the change of verse, is still practiced in Cyprus and Crete.[13] He continues this examination of literary references to ascertain the general design and use of several types of ancient musical instruments.[14]

12. Zarlino, *Istitutioni*, p. 76: "È ben vero, che l'uso modern è tanto vario e lontano dall'uso antico; che sarebbe quasi impossibile crederlo; quando da molti degni e honorati scrittori, i quali sono stati per molto tempo avanti la nostra età, non ne fusse fatta mentione alcuna di tal cosa: percioche li Musici di quei tempi non usarono la Musica con tante variate sorti di Istrumenti . . . ne anco le loro cantilene erano composte di tante parti; ne con tante voci facevano i loro concenti; come hora facciamo: ma l'essercitavano di maniera, ch'al suono di un solo Istrumento: ò Piffero, ò di Cetera, ò di Lira, il Musico semplicemente accompagnava la sua voce, e porgeva in tal modo grato piacere à se e à gli ascoltanti. . . . Quando poi erano due, che cantavano; non cantavano insieme e ad un tempo, come si fa al di d'hoggi, ma l'uno dopo l'altro."

13. Ibid., p. 78.

14. This interest continued throughout his life. In one of his letters to G. V. Pinelli of Padua, he discusses the types of plectra Greek musicians used with various stringed instruments, based both on textual references and classical sculptures and reliefs. Zarlino, letter to Pinelli, 14 August 1586, Milan, Bib. Amb. R 118 sup., fols. 220r–22v.

Much of this discussion simply treats "ancient music" as a single unit covering anything falling between the chronological boundaries of Pythagoras and Boethius. In a few cases, however, Zarlino is able to identify a particular musical practice with a specific era. The practice of accompanying orators with music had, for example, been frequently cited by those Renaissance writers who sought to link music and rhetorical practice in antiquity. Zarlino dates the phenomenon to the time of Cicero, basing his arguments on classical writers and especially their remarks on the relevant passage of Cicero.[15] Zarlino frequently treats sources in this manner, comparing them with one another and assessing such features as genre, era, bias, and the writer's own expertise in the subject about which he is writing.

As part of this long exposition on ancient music, Zarlino addresses the issues of greatest general interest to his contemporaries: ancient music's emotional effects and the harmonic genera. He integrates the latter subject into the former and relates the whole back to his earlier arguments about music and language. He begins with a detailed discussion of the subjects on which the ancients wrote their songs; this apparent digression serves to emphasize once more the fact that ancient musical practice was defined primarily as vocal music. Ancient songs addressed subjects graver, more learned, and loftier than those of the present day, and each specific subject called for its own particular set of harmonies, rhythms, and meters. Music's elevated, often religious subject matter, the mathematical studies required in its mastery, and the literary expertise involved, all explain why the ancients considered the title "musician" synonymous with poet, sage, and prophet.[16]

It is this composite role, Zarlino argues, that modern writers have failed to understand when they try to revive the powers of ancient music. Modern music does not cause these effects, and ancient music should be greatly praised for this achievement. Careful examination of the ancient sources reveals a combination of four factors that worked together to this end: "There are four things which always occur together in these effects. If any one of them is lacking, little or nothing will be seen. The first is Harmony, born of sounds or voices. The second is the determinate number contained in the verse, which we call Meter. The third is the narration of something, which pertains to some moral; this is the Oration, or the Text. The fourth and last,

15. Zarlino, *Istitutioni*, p. 77.
16. Ibid., pp. 82–86.

without which little or nothing can be seen, is a well-disposed Subject, able to receive a given emotion."[17]

We can observe this cumulative effect, continues Zarlino, in the responses of listeners. Some person may hear a given harmony and feel a general "intrinsic" response, such as a disposition to happiness or sadness, but we do not see "extrinsic" responses such as laughter or tears. The addition of meter can cause a stronger effect, as is seen in dance, and the proper text brings the full effect. The result, however, is also dependent on the nature of the listening subject; thus a peaceable person may well not be moved dramatically by martial music, nor would a battle-ready soldier likely be induced to give up his arms by the influence of a single peaceable song. When all of these factors work together, however, music may work great marvels.

Zarlino attributes these "extrinsic" effects of visible emotional change to the power of music to affect the humors. These emotions, or "passions of the soul," are located in the "sensible, corporeal, and organic appetite"[18] and consist of a certain proportion among hot, cold, wet, and dry. Harmony and meter are thus the elements of music which have the strongest powers of this sort and can induce virtue by balancing the humors, or vice by causing an excess of one humor or another. Such properties are most effective when given specific direction by the proper text.

Once again, Zarlino uses several types of classical references to support his argument. Traditional music treatises such as Boethius offer the technical information about proportion. Various works of Aristotle, notably the *Ethics*, serve as a text for the development of virtues and vices. Numerous other sources, both prose and verse, are mined for specific examples or references to these concepts as put into practice by the ancients.

Zarlino's analysis of the ancient modes demonstrates his constant emphasis on the contexts of musical elements as the key to understanding their development as well as their nature and use. Zarlino first reminds the reader that past a certain level of detail, his remarks must be taken as provisional, since no specific examples of ancient

17. Ibid., pp. 86–87: "Quattro sono le cose, le quali sempre hanno concorso insieme in simili effetti: delle quali mancandone alcuna, nulla, ò poco si potrebbe vedere. Era la prima l'Harmonia, che nasceva dai suoni, ò dalle voci: la seconda il Numero determinato contenuto nel Verso; il qual nominiamo Metro: la terza la Narratione d'alcuna cosa, la quale conteneva alcuno costume; e questa era la Oratione, overo il Parlare: la quarta e ultima poi, senza la quale nulla, ò poco si potea vedere; è un Soggetto ben disposto, atto à ricevere alcuna passione."
18. Ibid., pp. 89–90.

musical compositions have ever been discovered. He must proceed on the basis of the information available, which is textual and literary. He begins by offering a very general definition of *mode* as the measure or form in which a given thing is made, relying on literary sources as examples of this meaning as commonly used by the ancients.

Zarlino then combines his previous arguments about the union of ancient music and poetry with an examination of ancient usage of the term *mode*. Ancient musicians referred to their compositions as "modes," and by this term they meant a piece's melody, text, and so on, all taken together as a whole. They might also use the term with a qualifier, referring to the piece's "melodic mode," such as dithyramb or tragic. "Mode" in musical terms referred to this whole system of customary associations, which formed part of a musician's repertoire of possible song types. Therefore, Zarlino argues, those moderns who try to understand ancient music solely in terms of pitch systems must of necessity fall far from their goal.

Since such conventions of naming "modes" would be so variable over time and place, it is hardly surprising that their names were not consistent among ancient writers. Zarlino considers any attempt to settle on a single, standard system of classical nomenclature to be extremely misleading. He has no quarrel with the ongoing efforts to rename modern modes, as long as any such naming system is based simply on a rational practicality and not on spurious claims to historical precedence.[19]

Zarlino supports this claim for the multiplicity of terms with his customary range of sources, particularly literary ones, but devotes special attention to the usage of words like *modus* or *harmonic* in the context of relevant passages of Plato, Pliny, Vitruvius, and Boethius. Zarlino's approach here is distinctly different from that of Gaffurio, who had assumed that a term like *mode* had a single, consistent definition among all the ancients and that ancient texts could be mined for information that would then be assembled to produce the most complete definition possible. Although Zarlino still believes that an absolute, mathematical truth lies somewhere behind this wide variety of customs and genres, he finds any approach that short circuits these humanistic methods of textual analysis to be simplistic and misguided.

19. Zarlino does, in fact, rename them in later editions of his work; see Palisca, in Zarlino, *Art of Counterpoint*, pp. 21–22, n. 1.

Zarlino also tries to extend his evidentiary base to the range of observable modern practice, including traditions that would now be considered ethnic or folk music. Thus, he had referred to modern-day dancers in Crete and Cyprus to support his claims about the monophonic nature of ancient Greek music and the practices of Greek choruses. But unlike Cardano, who had restricted his use of this type of evidence to unlettered peasants or common people, Zarlino adds references to identifiable national preferences in musical practice within the European written tradition. Differences in preferences among the ancients resembled the present differences among moderns; the various peoples shared many traits while differing in others:

> We see the same thing even today in various nations; for Italian uses number, that is, verse in feet or syllables, in common with French and Spanish, such as that of eleven syllables. Nonetheless, when we hear one or the other sung, we notice a different harmony, and another manner of proceeding. Thus an Italian sings differently from a Frenchman, and a Spaniard in a different manner than a German, leaving aside the barbarous nations of infidels, as is obvious. The Italians and Frenchmen use the lute often, and the Spaniard the citarone, though it differs but little from the lute, and other people use the pipe.[20]

In this case, Zarlino is not using the moderns as proof of the survival of a specific ancient musical practice. Rather, he argues that ancient music had been as complex and as stylistically variable as that of the modern era, and for similar reasons. Thus we can look to modern practice not for specific details about ancient music but to predict logical responses to particular problems. Zarlino does not claim that one can make assumptions about ancient behavior based on modern musical practice; in fact, he states consistently that this is the major flaw in the reasoning of many of his contemporaries. Rather, he believes that ancient music, proceeding from its own principles, developed into a variety of practices just as has modern music, and all scholarship on the subject must take this variety into account. This position

20. Zarlino, *Istitutioni*, p. 380: "Questo istesso vediamo etiando hoggidi in diverse nationi; imperoche l'Italiano usa'l Numero; ò'l Verso di piedi, ò sillabe commune col Francese e col Spagnolo; come è quello di Undici sillabe; nondimeno quando s'odono cantar l'uno e l'altro, si scorge un'Harmonia differente, e altra maniere nel procedere: conciosia che altramente canta l'Italiano, di quel che fà il Francese, e in altra maniera canta lo Spagnolo di quel che fà'l Tedesco; lasciando di dire delle nationi barbare e infideli; come'è manifesto. Usa lo Italiano e anco il Francese grandmente'l Leuto, e lo Spagnolo usa il Ceterone; ancora se questo varia poco da quello, e altri popoli usano il Piffero."

demands a much more complex view of antiquity and a more thorough and sophisticated reading of ancient sources.

Much of the rest of the *Istitutioni* is directed against the "chromaticists" and would-be revivers of various aspects of ancient music, particularly those like Vicentino who were attempting to resurrect ancient modes and harmonic genera. Zarlino has no quarrel with the interest in reviving ancient musical styles; on the contrary, he argues that only through imitating ancient music can modern musicians hope to induce similar emotional effects in the listener. He thinks, however, that their efforts to date have been seriously misguided by their ignorance about ancient music. Zarlino addresses this situation throughout the rest of the treatise both by rejecting their erroneous ideas and by presenting more accurate information.

Zarlino's attacks on the revivers of harmonic genera take several forms, and he attributes to the revivers positions often reminiscent of Vicentino. In one such case, Zarlino suggests they had introduced these new intervals the better to imitate human speech, an attempt he brands a failure. According to him, these experimenters have claimed that by imitating orators, they would be able to move the listener more effectively. Their attempts proceed from false premises, counters Zarlino, because they have confused the spoken word with singing, when the two are and always have been separate matters. The Greeks had kept the two traditions distinct, and so the attempts of these chromaticists are historically inaccurate.

Further, Zarlino argues that they have failed in their attempt to imitate speech, since speakers do not in fact use the "strange and rude intervals" these musicians employ in their compositions.[21] Finally, he condemns the style as "ridiculous" and an affront to the ears of anyone with reasonable judgment. In developing this attack, Zarlino has used two criteria for judging the acceptability of musical styles: historical accuracy and the appeal to the ears of the "reasonable" listener. To meet either one would have been sufficient; failure at both, however, merits condemnation.

This task of criticism forces Zarlino to distinguish constantly, between ancient and modern music and also among modern styles as practiced by earlier generations, modern music as currently composed, and proposals for the improvement of modern music.[22] As a result, he must balance the eternal verities and principles of Pythagorean theory with a historical analysis that acknowledges the

21. Ibid., p. 375.
22. Ibid., p. 365.

changes of musical style over time. Such a two-faceted approach necessarily produces some inconsistencies of its own. Yet the result, made
possible by Zarlino's thorough scholarship and the breadth of his inquiry, is a far more thoughtful and better-integrated examination of
these issues than those produced by his recent contemporaries, who
had generally focused on a single issue.

Zarlino's last chapters reveal not only this concern for balancing
Pythagorean and historical approaches but also his growing interest
in the relevance of Aristotelian natural philosophy. In a passage reminiscent of Vitruvius's or Quintilian's prescriptions for education,
Zarlino presents a list of the fields a good musician must, at a minimum, master. He begins, of course, with the mathematical disciplines
of arithmetic and geometry, followed by such practical skills as the
ability to use a monochord, the possession of perfect hearing, and the
knowledge of singing and composition. Both types of skills are required, Zarlino notes, because music has these two sides, the speculative and the practical, just "as does medicine."[23] To these subjects he
adds grammar, particularly metrics; history; dialectic, since musical
science is based on demonstrations; rhetoric, so that musicians may
express their thoughts clearly; and finally, natural science, because
music "is subject not only to mathematical science, but also to natural
philosophy."[24] For Zarlino, the mathematical sciences still hold pride
of place but are not the sole basis of analysis or understanding, even
with the addition of practical skills.

In his next work, the *Dimostrationi harmoniche* (1571), Zarlino pushes
even further the connections between music, mathematics, and natural science. The work is composed of a series of five dialogues, with
both Zarlino and his former teacher Willaert among the interlocutors. After an initial discussion of consonances, the group agrees that
one problem with the field is the lack of systematic study by the musicians of their day. They therefore decide that, since music is both a
mathematical field and a part of natural philosophy—and therefore
subject not only to mathematical order but to logical and physical
demonstration—they will proceed by those means, under Zarlino's
leadership, through the essential elements of the subject.

Zarlino returns to the scholastic distinction among three types
of science, based on their participation in material reality. Those
that have nothing to do with matter are classified as theology or

23. Ibid., p. 445.
24. Ibid.: "poi che la Musica non solamente è sottoposta alla Scienza matematica, ma
anco alla Filosofia naturale." Zarlino refers to this classification frequently
throughout his work. See, for example, *Resolutioni d'alcune dimande*, p. 124.

metaphysics. Those depending on matter for their existence and which cannot be defined except in terms of physical reality, are called physics or natural science. Mathematics, the final type, does not refer to a specific physical reality, but to principles expressed in physical reality. Music consists of mathematical quantities, but particularly those quantities as they act through given physical manifestations. That is, it studies not just the eternal, changeless consonant proportions that can be seen in physical representations, but consonant proportions in given combinations as observed in given sounding bodies. For this reason, it occupies a midpoint between pure mathematics and physics.[25] Zarlino uses this classification as he defines the field's various elements.

Zarlino's interlocutors go on to discuss the construction of syllogisms, types of definitions, the differences between indemonstrable premises or principles, general rules of logic, and other matters of dialectic such as suppositions, questions, and demonstrations. A geometric proof is presented as an example. From this point, they begin their definitions and demonstrations in earnest, starting with notions about sound.

These first few definitions are particularly significant in establishing Zarlino's emphasis on mathematical proportion as seen in specific physical behavior. Sound itself, he argues, is like the point in geometry, the principal quantity from which others proceed. Yet although music resembles this "pure" mathematical discipline, Zarlino repeats his argument that it also differs in significant ways. Thus, he disagrees specifically with Boethius: "The musician considers sound in a different manner from that which Boethius defines. He defines sound as something natural in universal terms, and the musician defines it in particular."[26] Zarlino expands on this notion that music studies not the eternal, stable proportions of Boethian theory but the very temporal action of producing physical sound by distinguishing between theory and act:

> If music in its speculative part is called Theory, nonetheless putting things into action and their end is called Action, or Practice. But things put into action in music do not remain forever, except as long as they are performed. Thus a dance lasts as long as the person performing it moves. One hears a cythara as long as the strings are sounded by the person who

25. Zarlino, *Dimostrationi*, p. 10.
26. Ibid., p. 20: "Imperoche il Musico considera'l Suono in un'altra maniera, di quel che lo definisce Boetio. Egli definisce il Suono, come cosa naturale in universale; e il Musico lo definisce in particolare."

strikes them. Likewise, a song is heard as long as the person singing it maintains his or her voice. And because all movements made by these actions are violent, they are not durable; once having passed, of necessity another must follow, if it be desired that the thing remain in practice. Or indeed, such movements having reached their end, they must start again from the beginning. Thus I have said that music is an active thing and that the things that it uses are not among those which remain, as those of the plastic arts, but among those that take place, one thing following another.[27]

By this means, Zarlino is able to focus the scientific study of music on the behavior of sounding bodies, while maintaining the larger metaphysical existence of the Boethian proportions. He also maintains the traditional definitions as to which aspects of a sounding body are studied as the manifestations of these proportional quantities. Only the length of vibrating strings of equal diameters and tensions are seen as measures of quantity; other features of sounding bodies he still classifies as "qualities," which may produce regular pitches but whose pitches can only be analyzed according to the quantitative standard of string length.

Zarlino himself sees this shift not as an abandonment of "theory" in favor of practice or performance but as a moving away from abstract mathematics toward a natural science studied in terms of mathematics. This process involves both progress in knowledge and advances in the discovery of musical principles. Thus for Zarlino, a disagreement with Boethius need not mean a break with the Boethian tradition; rather, it can be a participation in that tradition, because the tradition is cumulative and hence subject to discoveries and progress.

Zarlino makes heavy use of the monochord in describing the measurement of sound and the production of scales, as had all his predecessors. He also advocates the tools of geometry—both geometric proof and the tools of geometric measurement—as aids to the study of music and the proper understanding of pitch proportion. He

27. Ibid., pp. 22–23: "Et se bene la Musica dalla parte speculativa sia detta Theorica: tuttavia dal porre in atto e nel suo fine le cose, e detta Attiva, over Prattica. Ma le cose poste in atto nella Musica non sempre restano: se non tanto quanto elle sono essercitate: imperoche tanto dura il Ballo, quanto colui, che lo essercita si muove. E tanto si ode la Cetera, quanto sono mosse le chorde da colui, che le percuote. Simigliantemente, tanto si ode la cantilena, quanto colui, che canta, manda fuori la voce. Et perche tutti li movimenti, che sono fatti in questi atti, sono violenti: però non sono durabili. Onde passate l'uno, di necessità bisogna che l'altro succeda: se'l si vuole, ò che cosa la stia in atto, ò veramente essendo tali movimenti giunti al fine: e necessario che da capo si rinuovino. Però hò detto che la Musica e cosa attiva: e che le cose di che ella serve, non sono tra quelle, che rimangono: come quelle dell'arte fabrile: ma tra quelle, che l'una all'altra succedono, hanno luogo."

especially promotes a device new to music theorists, though not to geometers: the mesolabe. A simple template or gauge, the mesolabe determines harmonic means or establishes equivalent proportions for chords of varying lengths. Zarlino attributes its invention to Archytas or Eratosthenes and credits Giorgio Valla with introducing it into modern usage in the geometry section of *De expetendis*.[28] Zarlino repeatedly advocates its use as a tool that will better measure and regulate proportions in sounding bodies and facilitate the tuning of scale systems.[29] While the mesolabe represents no major conceptual innovation, it illustrates the extent to which Zarlino wishes to emphasize measured quantity (and especially geometry) as found in specific sounding bodies in the study of music.

Although Zarlino bases much of his argumentation directly on ancient sources, he does offer occasional critical assessments of modern scholarship and his place in it. In addition to his continual harangues against the chromaticists in the *Istitutioni,* Zarlino takes issue with composers more interested in technique or abstract mathematical constructions than with genuine composition, composers most of whom resemble the chromaticists in claiming erroneously to copy antiquity. Zarlino also criticizes his fellow theorists for sticking too closely to the letter of Boethius without building upon his work:

> As regards speculative music, there are few who have held to the right path. For besides that which Boethius wrote in Latin on the subject, which is found to be imperfect, no one can be found (leaving aside Franchino and Faber Stapulensis, who are, one might say, commentators on Boethius) who has proceeded further, speculating about things pertaining to music, discovering the true proportions of musical intervals. An exception is Ludovico Fogliano of Modena, who, after perhaps thinking about what Ptolemy had written about the syntonic diatonic, took the trouble to write a Latin volume on the subject, in order to demonstrate the true proportions of the intervals involved. The other music theorists, standing on that which Boethius wrote about similar matters, were either unwilling or unable to progress further; they devoted themselves to writing on things already demonstrated, which they called the quantitative genus. They comprise Modus, Tempus, and Prolation, as seen in the *Recanetum de musica,* in the *Toscanello,* in the *Scintille,* and in a thousand others like them. Further, one finds such varied opinions and lengthy disputations on these matters that there is no end to them. There are also many treatises, invectives, and apologies of some musicians written

28. Giorgio Valla, *De expetendis et fugiendis rebus opus* (Venice: Aldus Romanus, 1501), bk. 4, on geometry.

29. Zarlino, *Sopplimenti,* pp. 30, 88–97, 105, 179–89, 204–12.

against others, in which (even if they are read a thousand times), after having been read, reread, and examined, nothing is found but endless insults and slander about one another (they should be ashamed) without modesty, and in the end so little of value as to leave one amazed.[30]

Zarlino concludes his attack by referring to these writers and their work as "musical sophistry." He therefore sets himself apart from these shallow efforts and assumes the task of reestablishing the field on the solid bases of reason, experience, and scholarly studies of ancient texts.

In this he is largely successful. The issues that dominated the field after the publication of the *Istitutioni* took Zarlino as their starting point, reaching back to the "musical sophists" of the earlier generation only for the occasional reference. Zarlino devoted the rest of his scholarly career in music to responding to his own critics; yet their very criticisms would depend on the achievements of Zarlino's own scholarship.

Numerous later scholars followed Zarlino as their sole authority; some, like Giovanni Maria Artusi, devoted a significant amount of professional energy to defending his ideas, at least as they understood them.[31] Others attacked his work with great vehemence. Vincenzo

30. Zarlino, *Istitutioni*, pp. 361–62: "Quanti poi alle Ragioni, cioè, in quanto alla speculativa; pochi si vedono essere stati quelli, c'habbiano tenuto la buona strada; conciosiache, oltra quello che scrisse Boetio in lingua latina di tal scienza, che si trova anco esser'imperfetto; non si trova alcuno (lasciando Franchino e il Fabro Stapulense da un canto, i quali sono stati, si può dire, commentatori di Boetio) che habbia procedesto piu oltra speculando intorno le cose appartinenti alla Musica, ritrovando le vere Proportioni de gli intervalli Musicali; da Ludovico Fogliano da Modena in fuori; il quale havendo forse considerato quello, che Tolomeo lasciò scritto del Diatonico syntono, s'affaticò nel scrivere un volume latino in tal facultà; per mostrare com'ei puote, le vere Proportioni de i nominati Intervalli. Il resto poi de i Musici Theorici, stando à quel che scrisse Boetio intorno à simili materie, non volsero, ò non potero passar piu oltra; ma si didero à scrivere le cose mostrate, le queli chiamarono del genera Quantitativo; che sono contenute nel Modo, nel Tempo, e nella Prolatione; come nel Recaneto di Musica, nel Toscanello, nelle Scintille, e in mille altri libri simili si può vedere. Et di più si trovano anco sopra tali materie varie opinioni e disputationi lunghissime, da non venire mai al fine. Si trovano etiandio molti Trattati, Invettive e molte Apologie d'alcuni Musici, scritti contr'alcun'altri, ne i quali (se bene si legessero mille fiate) dopo letti, riletti, e essaminati, non si ritrova altro, che infinite villanie e maledicentie, che dicono l'uno dell'altro (ò che vergogna) senz'alcuna modestia; e finalmente poco di buono; di maniere ch'è un stupore."

31. Giovanni Maria Artusi (1540–1613) wrote several music treatises, most of which included defenses of Zarlino against detractors; one in particular, *L'arte del contraponto ridotta in tavole* (Venice, 1586) attempted to present many aspects of Zarlino's *Istitutioni* in the form of tables. At one point during his extended polemical exchange with Ercole Bottrigari, Artusi claimed that he had the manuscript of

Galilei's feud was probably the most widely published and is now the best known (see infra); he manages to have the last word simply by outliving Zarlino by a year.

The mathematician Giovanni Battista Benedetti also attacked Zarlino's tuning system in print, in one of his books of mathematical problems.[32] In response to a letter from Cipriano Rore questioning the accuracy of Zarlino's description of his favored scales as used by singers, Benedetti analyzes the proportions according to Zarlino's argument. Benedetti concludes that if a singer really sang a given series of intervals with the purity Zarlino describes, he or she would gradually become either sharper or flatter relative to the original key. Since this does not in fact happen with singers, Benedetti concludes justifiably that Zarlino's description is faulty. He goes on to suggest some ideas about the nature of sound that are very much reminiscent of modern notions of wave motion and pitch frequency (as noted by several modern scholars),[33] though he did not attempt to carry his assertions further into experiments or proofs.

Benedetti's own position on sounding bodies seems to be similar to that of Fogliano or Cardano, advocating quantification without Pythagorean theory. Zarlino was forced to concede in the *Sopplimenti* that Benedetti was right in criticizing the accuracy of his description. Yet he remained convinced of the truth of his original principle, that "nature always inclines toward the good." In the absence of modern electronic means for measuring very tiny pitch variations, it would have been impossible to determine exactly what sixteenth-century singers did do; and since past practice cannot be determined now on the basis of modern-trained singers, the answer can never be known. Thus Benedetti could attack Zarlino's description in this case but could not invalidate Zarlino's fundamental argument. For this prin-

Zarlino's Latin treatise *De re musica* in his possession and was preparing it for publication. See Artusi, *Seconda parte dell'Artusi, overo delle imperfettioni della moderna musica* (Venice: Vincenti, 1603), "A gl'amici lettori."

32. Giovanni Battista Benedetti, *Diversarum speculationum mathematicarum et physicarum liber* (Turin: Bevilacquae, 1585). For a discussion of Benedetti's argument, see Palisca, *Humanism*, pp. 186–87, 257–65. Benedetti adopted the increasingly popular position that sound did not exist in the mathematical proportions themselves but in sounding bodies that could be measured in mathematical proportions. D. P. Walker connects this work of Benedetti with that of Galileo Galilei through Vincenzo Galilei, as seen in Galileo's *Discorsi* of 1638; see Walker, "Galileo Galilei," in *Studies in Musical Science*, pp. 27–33. On Benedetti and Aristotelian physics, see Alexandre Koyré, "Giambattista Benedetti, Critic of Aristotle," in *Galileo: Man of Science*, ed. Ernan McMullin (New York: Basic Books, 1967), pp. 98–117; see also Carlo Maccagni, "Contra Aristotelem et omnes philosophos," in *Aristotelismo veneto e scienza moderna* 2:717–27.

33. See Palisca, *Humanism*, pp. 186–87, 257–65; Walker, "Galileo Galilei."

ciple—"nature inclines toward the good"—allowed Zarlino to account for deviations in behavior from the Boethian norm by attributing them to material limitations and inclinations. Insofar as possible, the instrument and the performer tend to produce perfect intervals; thus the voice, with fewer physical impediments to making small distinctions of pitch, will produce more perfect proportions than an artificial instrument performing the same melody. To refute Zarlino's theories would have required direct evidence of contrary behavior on the part of sounding bodies, such as that produced by Vincenzo Galilei.

To defend his theories against these and other detractors, Zarlino composed one last treatise, the *Sopplimenti musicali* (1588), published as part of the new collected edition of his other works.[34] It is composed in eight sections, each devoted to a subject Zarlino thought had been criticized or misunderstood since the publication of his earlier works. Zarlino does not depart substantially in this treatise from his earlier positions but offers some further thoughts on the nature of music and its study, as well as some arguments on matters of detail.

Although traditional musical Pythagoreanism predominates in the *Sopplimenti* as it had in his earlier treatises, several scholarly traditions once again hold positions of considerable importance. Both Aristotelian natural philosophy and poetics are especially prominent and dominate the relevant portions of his analysis. Zarlino continues to identify music primarily as one of the four mathematical subjects of the quadrivium. Yet he also uses several other classifications to make sense of the field and its study, in an attempt to reconcile the best of recent scholarship to his analytic framework; he reminds the reader of the proverb, "Amicus Socrates et amicus Plato, magis est amica Veritas."[35]

It is here that Zarlino acknowledges the two distinct halves to the field of music, based on the type of knowledge acquired and the means used to acquire and verify that knowledge, and labels them "history" and "method." When discussing the former, he will, he tells us, proceed by following the relevant authors; with the latter, he will rely on "reason and good method."[36] Although it might seem that this distinction could simply be another set of labels for theory and

34. Although Zarlino's responses to Galilei in the *Sopplimenti* are well known, Zarlino himself told Bernardino Baldi that the work was especially aimed against the attacks of his former student Francisco de Salinas; see Baldi, "Vite inedite."

35. Zarlino, *Sopplimenti*, p. 9: "Socrates is a friend and Plato too, but the greater friend is truth."

36. Ibid., p. 10.

practice, what he means by "Methodica" or "Prattica" is the study of sounding music in all its forms, from the "practice" of writing songs to the understanding of sounding bodies.

After a brief survey of the history of music (which recapitulates his earlier historical narratives), Zarlino returns to his more pressing arguments about method. The distinction between Nature and Art forms his first classification (originally used in *Istitutioni* 1.15). Things artificial can be considered natural in terms of the material of which they are composed, but in general they copy natural attributes by means of the artifice with which they are formed by their maker.[37] The consonant intervals and the human voice are natural; attempts to copy these phenomena with strings or pipes are artificial, hence to some degree less perfect than the natural.

From these principles of classification, combined with a reverence for the orderliness of simple number born of traditional musical Pythagoreanism, Zarlino develops the rest of his arguments about the study of musical science. His rejection of any attempt to divide intervals into equal halves, for example, does not derive simply from a rejection of irrational numbers per se as disorderly. "Irrational" numbers are so called because they are not commensurable with the other elements of the number system; that is, they are not reducible to integers using the same base unit as the other integral measures. Therefore, such "irrationals" may form part of a different commensurable system, but not the original system of proportion chosen for the analysis.

Despite this exception, Zarlino advocates the application of geometric principles to the study of music. He reiterates his support for the use of the mesolabe for measuring and duplicating musical proportions and proposes several similar tools for the analysis of intervals, such as the "geometric square."[38] To Zarlino, the use of these geometric tools and methods constitutes the strict adherence to reason and observation for which he strives. Even the sharpest criticisms by colleagues such as Galilei fail to shake this geometric approach; Zarlino interprets their attacks as failures to understand some detail of true musical thought, rather than recognizing them as fundamental conceptual differences. Zarlino never, however, offers a specific response to Galilei's finding about the nature of sounding bodies, which struck a major blow against the knowledge claims of

37. Zarlino is, of course, following Aristotle for this portion of his argument; ibid., pp. 18–19.
38. Ibid., pp. 88–93.

Pythagoreanism.[39] If he had planned one for inclusion in his Latin treatise, it died with him.

Zarlino's systematic approach to the discipline was the cause both of his great acclaim and of his eventual rejection. His thoroughgoing effort to combine mathematics with natural philosophy was instrumental in focusing scholarly attention on mathematically measured observation as a means of investigation. Further, by splitting the field into history and method, he cleared up numerous interpretive problems and defined a lasting division in the field. This division proved so successful, however, that later scholars came to find unnecessary his larger metaphysical categories and principles, whether they had originated in Pythagorean cosmology or Aristotelian physics and logic. Zarlino's younger contemporaries therefore frequently will express mixed feelings about his work, praising parts of it as they attack others, or offering a very selective reading of his scholarship. Not only does Zarlino recast the field anew in his writings; his own scholarship provides the impetus for further rapid changes by the end of the sixteenth century.

Girolamo Mei

Girolamo Mei's influence on musical thought was felt both directly, through his treatises and letters, and indirectly, because of his influence on the writings of Vincenzo Galilei. His work was fundamental in defining musical studies as a humanistic enterprise, based on the study of history and culture. Not only did Mei inspire a more historical approach to the study of ancient music as part of ancient culture, but he also added to current knowledge of the subject with an important discovery: he was responsible for bringing to public notice the first Greek musical manuscripts known to the modern era. Mei's work on the music of antiquity constituted only a portion of his scholarly writings, but because of its wide impact, it has formed the basis of his modern reputation.

The professional life of Girolamo Mei (1519–94) was typical of a sixteenth-century humanistic scholar. Born in Florence, he studied with Piero Vettori and joined several academies before beginning a peripatetic career as secretary for various lay and ecclesiastical

39. See discussion of Vincenzo Galilei, infra.

226   Musica Scientia

officials in Rome and France.[40] After a four-year stay in Padua
(1554–59), Mei spent the remainder of his life in Rome, again serving
mainly as a secretary.[41] In addition to his musical works, Mei helped
edit a number of Greek dramas and wrote on Tuscan verse and prose,
on the history of Florence, and several pieces relevant to a Florentine
academy (the Pianigiani) of which he was a member. These, along
with numerous surviving letters, remained for the most part in manuscript during his lifetime.[42]

Of the extended correspondence between Mei and Vincenzo Galilei, only Mei's letters are extant, and those only in part. They date
from the years 1572 through 1581, when Galilei's first music treatise
was published. During this period, Mei was also at work on his own
treatise, *De modis musicis antiquorum* (finished in 1573); he had only recently made his discovery of ancient musical manuscripts. The letters,
even in their partial state of preservation, are thus a valuable record
of the ways in which these scholars approached their study.

The correspondence was apparently initiated by Galilei, who had
sought help from Mei, an expert on ancient drama and by this time a
thorough scholar of ancient music, in order to clarify some issues
about music in antiquity. These questions were often technical, centering on the familiar subject of the proportions used in various tuning systems. Yet Mei frequently addresses even these detailed,
technical questions in ways that engage larger issues about ancient
music and its differences from that of the modern era.

40. For biographical information on Mei see Claude V. Palisca, "Mei, Girolamo,"
New Grove; Palisca, *Girolamo Mei: Letters on Ancient and Modern Music to Vincenzo
Galilei and Giovanni Bardi: A Study with Annotated Texts* (Neuhausen-Stuttgart:
American Institute of Musicology, 1977), pp. 15–34. For a discussion of his
nonmusical works, see Jacopo Rilli, *Notizie letterarie, et istoriche intorno agli uomini
illustri dell'Accademia Fiorentina* (Florence: Matini, 1700) 1:64–67.
41. Mei apparently attended the lectures of Giovanni Battista Benedetti in Rome on
De caelo and *De generatione animalium;* see Palisca, *Letters,* pp. 26–27.
42. For a complete list of Mei manuscripts, see Palisca, *Letters,* pp. 195–200. In
addition to "De modis musicis," Mei wrote two other musical works: "De' nomi delle
corde del monochordo," Milan, Bib. Amb. R100 sup., fols. 58r–97r; and "Trattato
di musica," Paris, Bib. Nat., lat. 7209² (partial copy in Vatican City, BAV, Reg. Lat.
2021, fols. 27r–31v). His one printed music treatise, *Discorso sopra la musica antica e
moderna* (Venice, 1602), is simply an edited version of his first letter to Galilei; see
Palisca, *Letters,* p. 90. Mei's other manuscript treatises are "Del verso toscano";
"Trattato sopra la prosa toscana, e della composizione delle parole"; "Istoria de
origine urbis Florentiae"; and the four Pianigiani pieces. Several of Mei's letters,
particularly those to Vincenzo Borghini about the origins of Florence, are reprinted
in *Prose fiorentine raccolte dallo smarrito academico della Crusca,* ed. Giovanni Gaetano,
Rosso Antonio Martini, and Tommaso Buonaventura (Florence: Tartini e Franchi,
1734), 4.2, pp. 64–173.

Mei's first surviving letter to Galilei (1 May 1572) centers on a matter already argued with great authority by Zarlino: that ancient music employed a single melodic line and not polyphony. Mei does not mention Zarlino by name in this letter, though he has certainly read the *Istitutioni*, since most of his arguments resemble those of Zarlino.[43] Mei notes that no ancient references to music make any mention of anything that could be interpreted as polyphony. Further, there is a logical objection to the use of polyphony in antiquity: a mixing together of various pitches, various types of melodic motion, and various rhythms would cause any emotional effects produced by any single voice to cancel one another out. Thus polyphony is inconsistent with these important aspects of ancient music theory. Clear evidence of polyphonic writing, he claims, dates back only some hundred and fifty years; we must therefore understand ancient music as fundamentally different from that of the modern age, and modern music as a very modern phenomenon.

This monophonic style explains why the ancients had not recognized the "imperfect" consonances that have so exercised modern theorists; since the ancients had used only a single melodic line and not chords or triads of any sort, they had no need of these intervals as such. Thus, argues Mei, the ancients kept these intervals out of consideration not so much because they were mathematically "imperfect" but simply because they were superfluous. This argument would seem to weaken Pythagorean theory by historicizing its principles. Yet Mei is vague about the ultimate cause of ancient music's effects. At some points, he seems to consider its imitation of emotion "natural"; at others, he assumes that it derives from social convention. Finally, Mei returns to Zarlino's argument that since musicians and poets were the same in antiquity, several factors were involved in music's emotional effects beyond that of pitch intervals.

Mei clarifies his opinions in addressing Galilei's next question, about the goal and object of composition. Galilei had suggested that "delighting the ear with harmony" was sufficient. As Mei reads the sources, this goal had received scant attention by the ancients. Rather, they had striven for an effective expression of text by means of imitation: "Thus I believe that the goal intended was to imitate the real nature of the instrument whose use they were employing, not the sweetness of consonances for delighting the ear (since one finds no witness or verification among the writers of their use in their singing).

43. Mei lists "Zerlino da Chioggia" among the writers in *volgare* in his summary, "nota di scrittori di musica che ancor oggi si trovano et che io ho veduti," Vatican City, BAV, Reg. Lat. 2021, fol. 24v; reprinted in Palisca, *Letters*, pp. 118–22.

Rather, it was the explanation, completely and effectively, of all that they intended to express in the text, by the means and assistance of the highness and lowness of the voice."[44] Imitation, he continues, was definitely the goal of ancient poetry, and so too of music. Even in this early letter, then, Mei has encapsulated many of the arguments that he will continue to develop in more detail.

In subsequent letters, Mei addresses numerous questions generated from his first response to Galilei. Many of these are technical matters about tuning systems. Galilei asked for information about the ancient names of various tunings of diatonic tetrachords; about the number of commas contained in a minor semitone (or lemma) and other small intervals; about Ptolemy's description of transposition between modes and genera within a piece; about Aristoxenus; diatonic tunings; about terminology used in the Aristotelian *Problems*. Mei offers detailed responses, complete with charts and equations, both on the solutions themselves and on the processes by which he arrived at them. He also responds to more general questions about the relative roles of musical theory and practice in antiquity. Despite the presence or absence of numbers, depending on the type of questions addressed, Mei's approach to the issues is quite similar throughout.

Mei reminds the reader constantly that the subject of his discussion is ancient music, particularly Greek music, which is a subject completely different from music in the modern era. Since Mei is not a practicing composer, he is free not only to study ancient musical texts entirely for their own sakes but also to turn an occasional critical eye toward modern music for what he sees as its recent development and advocacy of counterpoint. His preference for the musical styles and purposes of antiquity causes him to emphasize, even more strongly than Zarlino, the historical detachment of his own research. At one point he admits to his inclinations:

> Finally, regarding your desire to know whether I think the music and singing of the ancients was more beautiful or more ugly than ours, I do not know how to respond more clearly than to say that I enjoy pleasant things more when they lack artifice and are more natural, more according to the strengths of which they reasonably seem most capable, and to

44. Mei, letter to Galilei, 8 May 1572; in Palisca, *Letters*, p. 116: "Onde io pertanto mi credo che il fine propostosi fusse imitando la natura stessa de lo strumento del quale essi si valevano, non la soavità de le consonanze per contentar l'orecchio (conciosiache del uso di queste nel lor cantare non si truova ne testimonio ne riscontro alcuno appresso gli scrittori) ma lo esprimere interamente et con efficacia tutto quello che voleva fare intendere col suo significato il parlare per il mezzo et ajuto de la acutezza e gravità de la voce."

which they actually appertain. These are the accents and rhythms of the voice, and in the end, the ordered speech itself, because by this means the hearer understands that which the person using them wishes to signify. With these aids I believe that one better achieves this effect, which I prefer, and which gives me great delight.[45]

Elsewhere Mei claims that the rise of polyphony had corresponded to the triumph of lowly sense perception over reason. His focus on the music of Greek antiquity can thus be attributed not only to his related scholarly interests but also to these personal preferences. Therefore, unlike Zarlino, his efforts lie entirely with the attempt to understand ancient music as a historical phenomenon; with the exception of these occasional criticisms, Mei does not concern himself with modern music as such.

As a result, Mei's technical and mathematical definitions differ from those of earlier scholars. He seldom sees his task as an attempt to establish solutions to problems of physical phenomena or metaphysics, with independent truth value. Rather, he seeks to explicate a technical description that had formed part of the written corpus of an ancient writer. In one such case, Mei interprets and summarizes a specific portion of Ptolemy's treatise which had been sent to him by Giovanni Bardi for clarification. Mei's goal in this letter remains the accurate explanation of Ptolemy's text; he does not attempt to argue for or against some sort of absolute accuracy on the part of Ptolemy. At one point, for example, Mei explains that the reasons for his offering a summary of a certain passage of Ptolemy rather than a literal translation is the lack of clarity in Ptolemy's own writing style; a summary and paraphrase were the best way to present the information requested. Mei's own task thus remains the explication of Ptolemy's treatise, not the absolute analysis of the behavior of sounding bodies or musical compositions.[46]

45. Ibid., p. 117: "In ultimo intorno a che voi desiderate sapere se io tengo che la musica e'l cantar degli antichi fusse pju bello, ò piu brutto di quel de' nostri; non vi so rispondere altro pju distintamente, se non che à me dilettan vie più i piaceri quando essi sono con manco artifizio e pju naturali et pju secondo le potenze che ragionevolmente ne debbon essere pju capaci, e à chi perciò quelli realmente appartengono; onde essendo gli accenti de la voce et i suoi tempi, et in ultimo il parlare stesso ordinato perche per mezzo loro da chi ode s'intenda quello che chi l'usa vuol significare, quanto pjù efficacemente con questi ajuti si facesse questo effetto credo che sempre sarebbe approvato pju da me, e mi sarebbe di maggior diletto."

46. Mei, letter to Giovanni de' Bardi, 15 January 1578, in Palisca, *Letters*, p. 152. On Mei's approach to the study of history in general, see Eric Cochrane, "The Florentine Background of Galileo's Work," in McMullin, *Galileo: Man of Science*, pp. 125–26.

Mei uses various tools of textual analysis to reach these goals. He notes problems in understanding an author's meaning owing to manuscript errors,[47] and he discusses the usage of specific words and terms as keys for understanding the author's intent and the practices described.[48] A few times he warns us that a given subject he had been asked to explain was treated so inconsistently by various sources that not only is a consensus impossible to establish, but even to catalog and discuss separately every variation is useless and frustrating: "The particular name of the middle interval of the chromatic tetrachord is a lengthy matter to speak of sufficiently, because the diversity of its arrangement according to ancient musicians is so wide on this matter that it is a nuisance."[49]

Whatever the type of information in question, Mei's goal in these letters is the same: to transmit the most accurate reading possible of ancient sources, particularly Greek sources, and so to increase the reader's understanding about ancient music. To this end he also prepared abstracts and pages of brief notes of information culled from the entire repertory of classical writings on music, as an aid especially to Galilei when the latter was writing his treatise.[50] He also managed finally to date the writings of Bryennius to the proper period.[51]

In these nonpublic or semipublic writings, then, Mei consistently proceeds in the manner of a good sixteenth-century humanistic scholar of classical texts. He examines these texts at the several levels of language usage, quality of manuscript, literary context, intended audience, and intellectual circle. His goals are both to explicate a given text as fully as possible and to move from that text to an understanding of the subject to which it refers, that of ancient music and ancient scholarly thought about music. This effort is similar to and influenced by the research on ancient music undertaken by Zarlino; yet it is more specialized in that Mei focuses exclusively on this humanistic undertaking, while Zarlino extends his studies to issues of natural philosophy. Zarlino also favors Pythagorean interpretations of consonance and sound production; Mei does not attack Pythagorean theory, but clearly favors the view that consonances are

47. Mei, in Palisca, *Letters*, pp. 108–9, 147, 156.
48. Ibid., pp. 96, 110, 123, 130.
49. Mei, postscript of letter to Galilei, 22 November 1577, in ibid., p. 134: "Del particular nome del mezzano intervallo del tetracordo cromatico è cosa lunga à dirne à bastanza. perche la diversità de la distribuzione appresso i musici antichi è in questo affare tanto diversa che è un fastidio."
50. Vatican City, BAV, Reg. Lat. 2021, fols. 1r–12r.
51. Mei, letter to Giovan Vincenzo Pinelli, 19 May 1582, Milan, Bib. Amb. S 105 sup., fol. 74r–v; reprinted in Palisca, *Letters*, pp. 183–85.

merely rational ways to organize textual imitation, which is music's task and the source of its emotive power.

Nonetheless, when Mei wrote his major treatise on ancient music, it was just this Boethian topic, the modes and the pitch system in general, on which his attention was focused. *De modis musicis antiquorum* was the most thorough and specialized study of the subject available at the time of its appearance, copied and cited by the major scholars of his own generation as well as the next. Unlike earlier detailed discussions of the modes by Giorgio Valla or even Zarlino, Mei's treats the entire subject in historical terms. This approach has the effect of shifting attention away from presumed universals of physical behavior such as the vibration of sounding bodies, in favor of those elements that can clearly be seen, based on textual evidence, to have been subject to change over time.

Mei begins the work with only the briefest of introductions, addressed to his former teacher Vettori. He then moves immediately into the technical definitions, charts, and proportions involved in understanding the Greek pitch system. The usual topics—the development of the Greater Perfect System of named strings, the tetrachords and harmonic genera, the species of consonant intervals—are all here, discussed in a good hundred pages of detail. Mei's historical approach applies to both topic and texts. Not content simply to note the points at which various authorities disagree, he distinguishes among several major schools of thought and presents each in its entirety. Thus Aristoxenus, Ptolemy, Aristides Quintilianus, and Boethius are each discussed separately and independently of one another. Mei accounts for their disagreements both in terms of the historical distances and the philosophical differences among them.

Further, Mei's analysis is more thorough than that of his predecessors in the fuller understanding and sometimes substantially better explanations he offers of the Greek system. He notices, for example, that the Greek system used its modes as a means of transposing pitch to higher or lower ranges, unlike the church modes, in which a change in mode is marked by a change in the relative position of the semitones.[52] This discovery renders irrelevant, or at least significantly alters, many sixteenth-century arguments about the nature of modes and their genera.

52. "Hieronymi Maeii Florentini De modis musicis antiquorum ad Petrum Victorinum libri IIII," Vatican City, BAV, Vat. Lat. 5323 (autograph), pp. 80–82; see also "Mei," *New Grove;* and Palisca, *Humanism,* pp. 303–14, for discussions of Mei's statements about the nature of Greek musical modes.

His discussion of the modern (ecclesiastical) modes, the subject of
Book 3, consists in large part of a comparative analysis of the systems
discussed by Glarean and Gaffurio. Mei takes pains to point out
that the claims made by these writers for the resemblance of their system to that of the ancients have little foundation in fact. He also refuses to address their arguments about planetary motion, though his
own skepticism is apparent in his pretended objectivity: "Now that we
have explained these matters, it remains for us to say something about
their use. For we read in some sources about the influence of the
planets themselves as if by affinity, and their similarity of humors to
human bodies, many things devised about practitioners attracting
souls with their efforts. I think they should keep these things to themselves, and not waste more time explaining them any further."[53]

Many of the mundane arguments in *De modis musicis* were already
available in Zarlino's *Istitutioni* in one form or another. Yet Mei's lack
of commitment to contemporary musical practice, to the Pythagorean
tradition, or to the behavior of sounding bodies per se once again allows him to treat the analysis of the texts and the phenomena they
describe consistently as a set of problems in humanistic textual interpretation. Pythagorean theory, for Mei, is simply one important approach among several the Greeks used to understand and explain
their pitch system. As far as Mei is concerned, this system is conven-
tional and artificial; the greater claims to metaphysical or cosmological truth are unique to the Pythagorean school of Greek theory, and
many ancients knew this: "But it truly led them to believe that the
modes were not determined by the force of nature; rather they supposed they were determined completely according to the judgment
of the practitioners."[54] Mei's task becomes more complicated when he
turns, in Book 3, to the development of the church modes and the
theoretical tradition through the generation of Glarean. Not only
does he suffer the expected paucity of sources between late antiquity
and the age of Guido Aretinus, but he must address the claims made
by the ecclesiastical tradition that it was based on Greek theory, or
Greek theory as expounded by Boethius. Mei has already demolished,

53. Mei, "De modis musicis," p. 117: "His itaque explicatis, relinquitur ut nonnulla
de usu dicamus. nam quod de istorum cum planetarum influxu quasi cognatione
atque humorum cum humanis corporibus similitudine apud nonnullos legitur, atque
id genus permulta, ab artificum ingenio, quo suae industriae magis animos
concilient excogitata, illis, opinor, sibi habere prorsus iubendum est, neque in ijs
exponendis amplius tempus terendum."
54. Mei, "De modis musicis," p. 72: "Sed nimirum id eos induxit, quod non sua vi
modos naturam determinasse crederent, sed artificum arbitrio illud prorsus
factitatum suspicarentur."

in Book 2, the myth that the system described by Boethius was the same as that of Plato's day. The double task remains in Book 3 not only to explain the church modes themselves and their development but also to clarify how, despite the arguments of the medieval theorists, this tradition differed from that of Boethius and the rest of late antiquity.

This process takes yet another twist as his narrative approaches the Renaissance. These theorists of the past century, Mei notes, began to realize that differences exist between ancient and modern theory, but they did not understand those differences completely. Further, he writes, their attempts to revive aspects of ancient practice, based as they were on these incorrect understandings, have rendered Mei's task more difficult still. Much of Book 3 is therefore devoted to a line-by-line analysis and comparison of the technical arguments made by a given author, particularly Gaffurio and Glarean. The latter receives especial criticism for forcing a reading of ancient sources in order to make them conform to his own ideas about modes. Mei attributes this partly to Glarean's own obstinacy, partly to flawed manuscript sources. Ultimately he argues that such biased interpretations were due to the contemporary practice of counterpoint, which altered completely the approach musicians took to the modes and blinded them to alternative explanations.

To replace such ahistorical interpretations of ancient music and the cause of its alleged miraculous emotional effects, Mei offers an alternative to traditional Pythagorean theories: Aristotelian poetics of mimesis, or imitation. In so doing, of course, he must break from his usual stance of objectivity to favor one sort of classically based explanation over another. Mei therefore does not resort to some sort of argumentative comparison of one ancient author's thesis against another. Instead, he turns to the historical evidence about the nature and role of ancient musicians. They were the same as the ancient poets, he states, as many ancient authors have attested. The rules of ancient poetics therefore governed ancient music as well: Poetry "was usually recited in song by the ancient musicians, who were likewise poets, as we have already suggested. Wherefore, since we have proposed that the musician and poet necessarily imitate the same things, it follows necessarily that their power proceeded entirely with the same or similar nature."[55]

55. Mei, "De modis musicis," p. 172 (Book 4, p. 16): "Illa enim canendo in primis recitari solita esse à veteribus musicis, qui itidem et poetae fuere, iam admonuimus. Quamobrem cum eadem musico et poetae necessario imitanda essent proposita,

From Mei's point of view, he has resolved the problem of competing, time-specific explanations of music's power not by choosing a single "best" theory among them but by identifying music's historical sister discipline and thus its theoretical basis as the way best to understand ancient music. It is not Aristotelian musical thought per se but the field of poetics (best codified by Aristotle) that resolves the dilemma. Language and poetry were already accepted by Mei's contemporaries as fields subject to historical and cultural change, and Aristotelian poetics were also accepted as adequate to understanding the field in those terms.

Mei's argument thus runs: Music and poetry were performed in antiquity by the same people, at the same time, for the same goals or ends. Therefore the two fields should not be separated, but studied as different parts of the same endeavor. We already known that poetry is understood in terms of imitation. Therefore, music and its effects are to be understood as another aspect of that imitation.

Not all of Mei's colleagues followed him completely in this approach to music. Even Galilei, perhaps his closest intellectual associate on the subject, accepts this view only with some important qualifications. Yet Mei's analysis marks the most significant turning point in musical thought since Zarlino's recent recodification. Mei's analysis separates ancient from modern music by defining music as a cultural activity, by setting up a historical divide between ancient and modern music, and by offering a way to account for the differences among classical sources by subjecting them to historical analysis. He ignores the issues of the physical production of sound except as they impinge on his humanistic analysis, treating "music" as the cultural phenomenon of poet-musicians creating songs according to culturally defined rules, not as the physical laws governing the production of those sounds. Later scholars who will study musical sound will therefore not base their work on Mei's intellectual tradition; instead they will return to Zarlino. Yet Mei leaves the field of "music" substantially different than he found it, not simply by adding further emphasis to Zarlino's twofold division but by articulating new ground rules for the truly historical study of ancient music.

---

huius vim cum illius natura vel eandem omnino vel simillimam profecto extitisse necessario sequitur." Palisca discusses Mei's arguments on the general role of music in Greek drama in *Humanism*, pp. 418–26.

Francesco Patrizi da Cherso

Francesco Patrizi (1529–97) was one of many late Renaissance writers whose interest in music arose as part of his study of a related subject. In Patrizi's case, his main interest lay in poetics; his writings on music appear as part of his multivolume work *Della poetica*.[56] These passages got the attention of Ercole Bottrigari, who devoted an entire treatise, though a short one (*Il Patricio*, Bologna, 1593), to disputing Patrizi's discussion of the ancient harmonic genera. Because of this published dispute, Patrizi's writings on music should, like many others, be read not only as an example of the approaches taken to the study of music by and for writers with mainly humanistic interest but also as a work studied by specialists in the field.

The first section of Patrizi's *Della poetica* was published while he was professor of Platonic philosophy at the University of Ferrara.[57] Modern scholars have summarized his effort as an attempt to replace the dominance of Aristotle's *Poetics* with a new approach that is both Platonic and humanistic.[58] Essential to his analysis is an extended discussion of poetic furor, a point he returns to frequently throughout the work.[59] At the same time, Patrizi presents the reader with a considerable amount of information about the history of poetry in antiquity, as well as the history of poetics.

Although Patrizi raises the subject of music at points throughout the work, he treats it with the most detail in his "Deca istoriale," the section he published during his lifetime,[60] in books devoted to "the singing of ancient poetry" and to "harmony, companion of ancient poetry." Book 6 covers the subject of metrics and melody, while Book 7 presents the Greek harmonic system in reasonable detail. It is this latter discussion that receives most of Bottrigari's criticism.

56. Only one volume was published during Patrizi's lifetime: Francesco Patrizi, *Della poetica, la deca istoriale* . . . (Ferrara: Baldini, 1586). This volume was reissued with the unpublished volumes as *Della poetica, edizione critica*, ed. Danilo Aguzzi Barbagli (Florence: Istituto Nazionale di Studi sul Rinascimento, 1969). All page citations refer to this complete edition.

57. For biographical information on Patrizi as well as a general introduction to his thought, see Paul Oskar Kristeller, *Eight Philosophers of the Italian Renaissance* (Stanford: Stanford University Press, 1964), pp. 110–26.

58. See ibid., pp. 114–16; Patrizi, *Della poetica* 1:vi–xii; Bernard Weinberg, *A History of Literary Criticism in the Italian Renaissance* (Chicago: University of Chicago Press, 1961) 2:765–86, 1024–25. The work awaits more detailed study.

59. Patrizi, *Della poetica* 2, "La deca disputata," bk. 1; Patrizi's "Discorso della diversità de i Furori Poetici all'illustre signor Mariano Savello," 13 January 1552, is printed in *Della poetica* 3:447–62.

60. Patrizi, *Della poetica* 1, "La deca istoriale," bks. 6 and 7.

In his discussions of music, Patrizi uses all the sources, both technical and literary, that have by this time become the norm for scholarly works on the subject, focusing particularly on the Greek ones. References to his contemporaries are much fewer, though he uses brief musical examples from Galilei's *Dialogo* (which contained copies of Greek musical pieces Galilei had received from Mei, their apparent discoverer). Patrizi's work is reminiscent of Daniele Barbaro's in that it serves as a learned digression written for a work on a related subject.

Yet his analysis itself is unique. Perhaps the most striking feature, given its advocacy of a Renaissance Platonic tradition, is its almost total lack of Pythagorean theory, and even of mathematical proportions. Patrizi bases his theories of poetics on the notion of poetic furor and hence bypasses any interest in the mathematical and physical or cosmological concerns of the musical Pythagorean tradition.[61] Rather than analyze music in terms of the timeless consonances of mathematical proportions, Patrizi takes a historical approach, linking music's development to that of poetry, its stylistic conventions to those of literary practice.

Patrizi introduces his discussion of music in Book 6 by arguing at some length that not only was ancient poetry sung, but it was also often accompanied by instruments and dance. After a brief synopsis of the importance of rythmics as seen in the works of several Greek authors, he refers to the general subject as *"ritmopeia,"* divided into the three subsections of metrics, harmonics, and "orchestics," or rhythmics. The subsequent discussion of metrics and especially the poetic feet is taken from Aristides Quintilianus.[62] The rest of Book 6 is a discussion of "canto," taking each major type of ancient poetry and showing that it was sung. He ends the book with the construction and use of the odeum, a type of Greek theater used for the singing of poetry. Patrizi's goals, then, are two: to present information about the composition of Greek music, in this case especially the metric forms of song, and to impress on the reader the central importance of the musical tradition for an understanding of Greek poetry, since all types of Greek poetry were sung and not merely read or recited.

61. Patrizi did write about cosmology, although in other contexts. For a discussion of these writings (in particular on the nature of Ptolemaic spheres and epicycles), see Edward Rosen, "Francesco Patrizi and the Celestial Spheres," *Physis* 26 (1984): 305–24; see also Paolo Rossi, "Francesco Patrizi: Heavenly Spheres and Flocks of Cranes," in *Italian Studies in the Philosophy of Science*, ed. Maria Luisa Dalla Chiara (Boston: Reidel, 1981), pp. 363–88; John Henry, "Francesco Patrizi da Cherso's Concept of Space and Its Later Influence," *Annals of Science* 36 (1979):549–73.
62. See Patrizi, *Della poetica* 1:311, n. 2.

Book 7, on harmony, has a more complex argumentative path to tread. The role of metrics as a technical subfield of poetics (as seen in Bk. 6) is a straightforward matter, since it had routinely formed a part of earlier works on poetics. Patrizi could also reasonably expect to convince the late sixteenth-century reader that ancient poems involved melodies, since other writers on music or poetry had been making this point for several years. Yet just how or where to place the status of harmonics in relation to poetics was no simple matter. Further, there remained the potential problem of accommodating arguments about music's own ability to affect the emotions with the claims made by poetics. Patrizi's solution, to explain the emotional effects of harmony entirely in terms of the poetics of which the whole subject is now to form a part, will be increasingly favored by scholars at the end of the sixteenth century. Nonetheless, his explanation differs significantly from that of Mei, who had also advocated linking the same fields.

Patrizi begins his argument by noting that some very early Greek poetry had apparently not been sung. Yet after the career of Amphion, only a few poets failed to make use of harmony. This approach, focusing on the development of music and poetics, avoids the sort of emphasis on matters of metaphysics or cosmology found in a Pythagorean analysis; in its place is historical narrative. In framing this argument, Patrizi need only account for some reasons why Amphion and his followers embraced the use of harmony.

His first answer comes from Aristotle (*Politics*, 1340a): music has a certain natural pleasure, making it a friend to all ages and customs, and seems particularly related to rhythm. He adds an extensive quotation from the *Problems* (920b), which attributes music's natural attraction to rhythm and to custom: ordered motion is more natural than disordered motion and is the source of rhythm's "natural" appeal.[63] This argument sidesteps any emphasis on pitch proportions yet leads easily into his subsequent discussion of the order in the pitches that compose the modes.

Patrizi then offers a description of each of the five modes he has determined are the oldest (Dorian, Aeolian, Ionian, Lydian, and Phrygian), a description based not on a chart of specific pitches but

---

63. Ibid., 1:340–41. Patrizi modifies this approval of Aristotle considerably in his later discussions, "Se la poesia nacque per le ragioni da Aristotile assegnata," 2:2; "La deca disputata," 2:38–43. Here he emphasizes the point that instrumental music arose from verse, not the other way around.

rather on the types of emotion said to be expressed by each one. He attributes these emotions to the customs of the peoples after whom they take their names. Each of these modes, continues Patrizi, also varied by harmonic genus. He then proceeds to an illustrated discussion of the distinctions among the three genera.

This set of illustrations, only a few pages in length, inspired Bottrigari's *Il Patricio*. While Bottrigari takes issue with some details of Patrizi's classical references to the various modes, the bulk of his argument deals with the units of quantity Patrizi used for this demonstration. The details of this debate have only technical importance, but its general contours illustrate the new concerns of these authors about the nature of musical quantity and for that reason merit a brief digression.

Patrizi's analysis of the tetrachord divisions constituting the three Greek harmonic genera follows not the ancient theorists of the Pythagorean tradition but Aristoxenus. This path is consistent with the rest of Patrizi's approach to poetics, Platonic but in no way Pythagorean. Aristoxenus had divided the interval of a fourth (diatessaron) into thirty parts, not representing the lengths of the sounding strings but simply as reference points for differences of highness and lowness of sound. The two internal, variable notes of the tetrachord can thus be placed at various points along this unit scale: 6 and 18 for the diatonic; 6 and 12 for the chromatic; and 3 and 6 for the enharmonic.[64]

Patrizi's discussion of Aristoxenus's analysis is, however, rather confusing. His language is unclear, and he follows his initial description with diagrams that are equally hard to follow. His first statement about dividing the interval of a fourth into thirty parts is accurate enough. Yet he proceeds to apply those parts as a measure to the only quantifiable aspect of sound in general use, the length of a sounding string. Patrizi then illustrates the argument with a diagram of four strings (or perhaps the relevant portions of longer strings) stopped at the appropriate number of units. He admits, when he presents these diagrams, that the relationship between those tetrachords and the modes is not entirely easy to see: "But how the first five modes and harmonies were arranged among these spaces (the Dorian, Aeolian, Ionian, Lydian, and Phrygian), and the other six we have named above, has remained obscure; and if by chance we could clarify it with a long explanation, it might well be off the subject, which is to demonstrate in general how poetry was accompanied by harmony. It is sufficient to have traced these sources."[65]

Patrizi therefore abandons the topic and summarizes the use of various musical instruments and various types of verse. He returns to two of the most commonly used modes, Dorian and Lydian, for a more detailed discussion of their use for specific types of ancient poetry. The final section of Book 7 argues that harmony relied for its rhythms on metrics and poetic feet, thus providing a transition into the next book, on eurythmics or dance.

Ercole Bottrigari in his *Patricio* objects not to Patrizi's overall approach to the study of harmonics as part of poetics but to his interpretation of Aristoxenus. Whether the reading Bottrigari, in turn, offers of Patrizi is entirely his own or whether it is exaggerated for maximum rhetorical effect, Bottrigari presents Patrizi's discussion in the worst possible light in order to follow it with a clearer presentation of Aristoxenus's theories. He denounces Patrizi's description and illustrations as completely erroneous and misleading. Much of the *Patricio* is taken up with a ratio-by-ratio rebuttal of Patrizi's illustrations, showing that Patrizi has misunderstood the Euclidean description of Aristoxenus's scales upon which the chapter is based. Bottrigari also offers a commentary on and explication of the rest of Patrizi's discussion of modes and genera, sometimes in agreement with him, other times not.

Bottrigari also criticizes Patrizi's decision to include such a long and technical digression in a work on poetics. Yet he recognizes Patrizi's legitimate interest in making available a printed, vernacular digest of these topics, none of which had been issued before, except in Bottrigari's own translations of the works of Euclid.[66] He concludes the little work by expressing a hope for better understanding of the ancients. This little controversy is noteworthy not only because it hinges entirely on the interpretation of texts (without an axe to grind in contemporary practice), but also because neither side involves Pythagorean theories of any sort.

The rest of Patrizi's own treatment of the subject aroused less controversy. He tries to integrate his subsequent discussions of music

65. Ibid., 1:347: "Ma come tra questi spacii accomodassero i cinque primi tuoni e armonie (doria, eolia, ionia, lidia, e frigia), e l'altre sei sopranominate, in oscuro è rimasto, e quando in chiaro fosse lungo fora peraventura il divisarlo, e fuori del caso nostro forse, il quale è dimostrare solo in generale come l'armonie alle poesie s'accompagnassero. A che bene basta d'haverne questi fonti rintracciati."

66. Ercole Bottrigari, *Il Patricio, overo de' tetracordi armonici di Aristosseno, parere, et vera dimostratione* (Bologna: Benacci, 1593), p. 36.

more thoroughly into the rest of the work; his statements about the
origins of poetry explain this concern, rising from his conviction that
the origins of poetry are inseparable from those of music: "We de-
clare (and not without great reason, as will be made clear) that poetry
began when man began to sing. By "singing" I do not mean with the
voice alone, which many birds and many men do often, but singing
with words. . . . Whenever it was that the first measured song was
made, that was the first birth of poetry."[67] He traces the origins of
poetry to the Chaldeans (or "at least the Egyptians") after Noah, carried to Greece perhaps by Phoenicians. This historical narrative then
allows Patrizi to integrate the Greek musical sources that present the
origins of music into the similar histories of great poets, to provide
brief biographical sketches of the early poet-musicians.

Patrizi's narratives of the origins of melody are not always entirely
consistent, varying slightly according to the argumentative task at
hand or the particular source he may be following. Nonetheless, he
holds to this basic outline of Egyptian or Near Eastern origins, a
transfer to Greece after the time of Moses, and then a later flowering
of poetic styles. He offers a somewhat more specific historical chronology in his discussion of the development of the chorus.[68] Some
one hundred and forty-five years after the death of Moses, Cadmos
brought letters to Greece and built Thebes; twenty-three years later,
Phaemon began the oracles at Delphi, and Oleno began composing
hymns. Philamon began the use of the chorus shortly thereafter, and
Patrizi continues with more major events and dates in the development of song. He expands the narrative in a description of the rise of
singing to the accompaniment of instruments such as the cythara, the
lyre, and the aulos.

Patrizi returns once more to the subject of music, and to portions of
this historical narrative, as part of his attack on Aristotelian poetics.[69]
He rejects the Aristotelian claim that words, harmony, and rhythm
are all considered instruments that the poet uses in imitation; instead
he gives the text pride of place. Thus a song moves the soul of the
listener in a manner that copies the emotions of the poet, but these
effects are due primarily to the words of the poem: "And the song

67. Patrizi, *Della poetica* 1:9–10: "noi diciamo (e non senza molta ragione, che poi si
farà chiara) ch'allora cominciò la poesia quando huomo cominciò a cantare, canto
non dico di voce sola, quale molti uccelli e molti huomini spesso fanno, ma canto di
parole . . . quandunque è si fu che il primo canto a misura fatto fu, allora si fu il
primo nascimento di poesia."
68. Ibid., 1:399–425.
69. "Se l'antiche poesie imitarono con armonia e con ritmo," ibid., 2:168–77.

included the words, and in the words were the meanings and concepts. . . . These concepts made in the mind of the singing poet, together with the harmony of words and sound, pass through the ear
into the minds of the listeners, and move in them those same powers
which went out from the singer."[70] Music soothes the irrational portion of the soul, argues Patrizi, allowing the rational part to be affected by the meaning of the text.[71] Music without text or voice, called
musica nuda, had been considered primitive and little better than the
songs or cries of animals. Patrizi concludes that none of these musical
phenomena are themselves imitation; instead they are "signs and
symbols" of the movements of the soul.

The *Della poetica* offers one of the more significant approaches to
the study of music in the late sixteenth century. Patrizi takes the
subject of music seriously as a part of poetics; it permeates his treatise, and these frequent discussions reveal an attention both thoughtful and scholarly. Yet despite the Platonic influence seen in Patrizi's
overall approach to poetics, he has abandoned completely the
Pythagorean tradition. For him, music should be understood not as a
system of timeless, rational laws but as a cultural and historical phenomenon, undergoing development and change along with its related
cultural phenomena, literature and poetry. Its principal direct effect
on the soul is to appease its irrational elements and so, by removing
this distraction, to increase the impact of the real message, which is
contained in the text. Patrizi restricts his discussion to the music of the
ancients and especially to Greek music. Yet he has succeeded in out-
lining not only a program for further scholarly research but a new
aesthetic standard for the arts as they were understood at the end of
the sixteenth century.

Vincenzo Galilei

Many of Girolamo Mei's discoveries about ancient music, and the
implications of these findings for modern musical thought and practice, were made public by way of the published treatises of Vincenzo

70. Ibid., 2:168–69: "E comprese nel canto erano le parole, e nelle parole i
significati e i concetti. . . . I quali concetti fatti nell'animo del cantante poeta, insieme
con l'armonia delle parole e del suono, trapassano per l'orecchie ne gli animi de gli
ascoltatori, e muovono in loro quelle potenze dell'animo medesime, che dalle così
fatte del cantante sono uscite."
71. Ibid., 2:169.

Galilei.[72] Galilei's writings, despite the visible influence of Zarlino and Mei, are nonetheless far more than paraphrases of the works of other scholars. His works had a great impact on the scholarship of such younger contemporaries as Ercole Bottrigari, as well as on the better-known writings of his son Galileo, and changed the way later scholars thought about both musical science and musical history.

Galilei, a lutenist by profession, was born at S. Maria al Monte near Pisa sometime during the late 1520s.[73] Although details of his early life and career are sketchy, he seems to have studied in Florence, then lived in Pisa (ca. 1550–62), where he married. He apparently studied with Zarlino in Venice during the mid-1560s, under the patronage of Giovanni de' Bardi, whose support he retained throughout his career; his first treatise, the *Fronimo* (1568), on lute entablature, was written there. Galilei returned to Florence by 1572, remaining in that city (with the exception of brief employment in Munich, 1578–79, and Siena, 1587) until his death in 1591. He participated in the musical gatherings of Giovanni de' Bardi, whose melodramas served as prototypes of opera, and wrote several compositions in the group's new musical styles, though these have not survived.

In addition to his published works, Galilei left several volumes of manuscripts: an early, unfinished music treatise; translations and excerpts (including anonymous Italian versions of Plutarch and Aristoxenus); and numerous short pieces he was apparently revising for publication at the time of his death.[74] Perhaps because these working manuscripts passed into the hands of his son and remained in his possession, they were preserved while those of other scholars (such as

72. Scholarly opinion has undergone several major changes in assessing the relative contributions and originality of Galilei, Mei, and those of their circle. See, among others, Fabio Fano, *La camerata fiorentina: Vincenzo Galilei (1520?–1591); la sua opera d'artista e di teorico come espressione di nuove idealità musicali* (Milan: Ricordi, 1934); Henriette Martin, "La Camerata du Comte Bardi," *Revue de musicologie* 13 (1932): 63–74, 152–61, 227–34; 14 (1933):92–100, 141–51; Nino Pirrotta, "Temperaments and Tendencies in the Florentine Camerata," in *Music and Culture in Italy from the Middle Ages to the Baroque* (Cambridge: Harvard University Press, 1984), pp. 217–34—see also p. 419, n. 6 (a later addition to the original article), where he suggests that his earlier assessment of Galilei was perhaps too harsh; D. P. Walker, *Studies in Musical Science in the Late Renaissance* (London: Warburg Institute, 1978), pp. 14–26; Stillman Drake, "Vincenzo Galilei and Galileo," in *Galileo Studies: Personality, Tradition, and Revolution* (Ann Arbor: University of Michigan Press, 1970), pp. 43–62; and Palisca, *Letters*.

73. For biographical information on Galilei, see Claude Palisca, "Galilei, Vincenzo," *New Grove*.

74. These works, some in several drafts, are collected with the manuscripts of Galileo Galilei in Florence, BNC, Galileiani vols. 1–8. I follow the dating suggested by Palisca ("Galilei," *New Grove*), based on both internal and external evidence.

Zarlino) were lost. The development of Galilei's thought both before and after the composition of his published work can therefore be traced, at least in part.

Galilei's *Compendio della tehorica della musica,* his unfinished treatise, is probably his earliest surviving theoretical work, dating from the time between his study with Zarlino and his correspondence with Mei.[75] It shows Zarlino's influence very strongly; it also reveals some of the tendencies in Galilei's thought that later caused his combative break with Zarlino's theories and methods for studying music. Although Mei's letters may well have caused him to abandon the treatise, it is also clear that Galilei himself was already headed for a confrontation with significant aspects of traditional Pythagorean scholarship.

In this treatise he returns continually to the repertoire of anecdotes about music's emotional power and also offers traditional treatments of Pythagorean theories of number. He presents Zarlino's *senario* not as a new contrivance invented by his teacher, but as a revelation forming part of the Hermetic tradition, known to Moses and Mercury.[76] He also emphasizes the importance of these numbers both as abstract quantities and as manifested physically in sounding bodies, identified as act rather than merely potential.[77]

The *Compendio* deserves its name; for it is based at times so closely on Zarlino's *Istitutioni* that even many turns of phrase echo the original. Several subjects on which Galilei will later vent his strongest wrath against Zarlino's opinions he treats here in particular detail and still in Zarlino's terms: the mathematical principles grounding the modes, tuning systems, and the course of musical discoveries throughout history. Galilei repeats, for example, Zarlino's discussion of the tempering of intervals, one of the principal subjects of Galilei's later *Dialogo.* In that work, Galilei will be such an advocate of tempering intervals and so strenuously opposed to Zarlino's ideal scale tuning that the reader might well be misled into thinking Zarlino had never even discussed temperaments, let alone supported their use. Yet here in the *Compendio,* Galilei faithfully repeats Zarlino's arguments (*Istitutioni* 4) that most instruments deviate from the ideal tuning because of the physical restrictions of the instrument, though these variations are so slight that the listener usually does not

75. "Compendio di Vincentio Galilei: della tehorica della musica," ibid., vol. 4, fols. 3r–47v (ca. 1570).
76. Ibid., fol. 10r–v.
77. Ibid., fol. 11r.

notice.[78] The voice, however, being natural and not an artificial
instrument, can always be varied sufficiently to produce the true
interval; it does so in fact both because of this superior physical
capacity and also because "nature inclines toward the good." It is
this latter claim, that the human voice as a "natural" body is subject
to behavior different in kind from that of "artificial" instruments,
that Galilei will later reject.

Galilei also reiterates Zarlino's description of stylistic differences
among the musics of modern peoples when he turns to the subject of
modes. Yet he takes the implications of the argument much further,
by combining observations of both ancient and modern diversity. After reviewing the familiar descriptions by ancient authors of the emotional characters of the various modes, he notes that these authors
frequently contradicted one another. Galilei does not try to smooth
out these differences. He acknowledges that the diversity is mostly
genuine and reminiscent of modern variety. It shows that the effects
of the modes have arisen not from the nature of the sound but from
the customs of their use:

> These are the things they say about the nature of the modes. Thus we
> see a great variety among writers, some saying one thing, others
> something else. Therefore I think this variety may be born from the
> variety of customs in a region. They changed over a long time, and so
> the modes changed as well. So part of the writers spoke of those modes
> that maintained their original, pure simplicity, and others spoke of those
> that had already lost their early nature. For example, let us take the
> Dorian, being originally honest, grave, and severe; by changes of cus-
> toms, it was changed, too, and was then applied to matters of war. We
> should not marvel at this; for if from varieties of harmony are born va-
> rieties of custom, as we have said elsewhere, it is not inappropriate that
> from variation of custom one should find a variety of musical harmony
> and modes.[79]

78. Ibid., fols. 24r–28r.
79. Ibid., fol. 36 r–v: "Queste cose dicono intorno alla natura delli modi laonde si
scorge una gran varietà negli scrittori; volendo alcuni una cosa, et alcuni un altra: il
perche mi penso che tal varietà possa esser nata dalla varietà de costumi d'una
provincia, che sendo dopo molto tempo variati, variassero ancora li modi; et che una
parte degli scrittori parlasse di quelli modi che preserveravono d'essere nella loro
prima et pura semplicità; et l'altra parte parlassi di quelli che gia havevono persa la
lor prima natura, come per cagion d'essempio diremo del dorio, che essendo prima
honesto, grave, et severo; per la variatione de costumi, fusse variato anco lui; et
applicato poi alle cose della guerra: et per questo non ci dovemo maravigliare, per
cio che se dalla varietà dell'harmonie nasce la variatione de costumi come altrove si
è detto; non è inconveniente ancora che dalla variatione de costumi si venga alla
varietà dell'harmonie della musica, et delli modi."

The *Compendio* breaks off in the middle of a passage on the division of intervals. Galilei left it unfinished and later rejected many of its Pythagorean arguments. Nonetheless, his interest in separating several topics for independent analysis—the study of sounding bodies by means of number, the cultural and historical changes in the ways groups of people organize musical sounds, and the ways in which these factors combine to produce modern instrumental and vocal music—are already apparent in this relatively early treatise.

Galilei's more famous work, the *Dialogo della musica antica, et della moderna* (1581), sets out to answer one of those questions of apparently endless interest to sixteenth-century musical scholars: Which scale tuning, among the multitudes described by the ancients, is actually used in modern practice? Zarlino has claimed one (the incited syntone of Ptolemy); many other authors, another (diatonic ditone) favored by many Pythagorean followers. Galilei proceeds to show, through long and detailed sets of illustrations discussed by his interlocutors (Giovanni Bardi and Piero Strozzi), that neither of these scales produces a set of intervals that matches those our ears want to hear and that our reason tells us is correct; nor, in fact, does any other given ancient tuning produce them. From this rather dry and technical question, he proceeds to develop several innovative arguments and approaches to understanding the field as a whole.

Here, as elsewhere, Galilei breaks with Zarlino by following one of Zarlino's own arguments to its logical conclusion, beyond the position Zarlino had taken. Galilei takes Zarlino's subject of tuning as a description first and foremost of a physical phenomenon, not (as earlier writers had done) of an abstract idea. Rather than building his case on the basis of how instruments should ideally produce intervals given a certain mathematical division of the monochord, Galilei begins by examining the actual tunings used by the instruments of his day. He finds that while no instrument uses any of the ancient tunings in their exact form, different types of instruments vary in different ways from any given standard. Fretted stringed instruments (*viola d'arca*, lute, *lira con tasti*) use essentially the incited diatonic described by Aristoxenus, with a tone divided into two equal semitones. The organ, clavicembalo, and modern harp have unequal semitones. Wind instruments and the voice are able to vary their pitch to fit any system required.[80] In practice, only octaves in fact consist of the Pythagorean

80. Vincenzo Galilei, *Dialogo . . . della musica antica, et della moderna* (Florence: Marescotti, 1581), p. 30.

proportions in which they are normally described; all other intervals vary from these ratios to some degree.

This argument is certainly straightforward yet not necessarily as simple to support as it might first appear. All of these musical instruments are complicated devices, relying in their construction and use on complex combinations of materials and physical principles. A stringed instrument tends to use strings of different thicknesses and density and is tuned by varying the tension on these strings. None of these factors had been considered quantifiable; traditionally they had been seen as qualitative variables. To assess these tunings in measurable terms, he would need to compare them to the only accurate measuring device possible, a monochord; the monochord reduces these variables to one, the measurable length of the sounding string. And the only qualified tool to make that comparison between musical instrument and monochord (before the electronic pitch-measuring devices of the twentieth century) was the trained human ear. Galilei, then, must convince his audience that the ear can make accurate judgments, despite the antipathy of Pythagorean theory to reliance on sense perception:

> *Str.:* Cannot the sense of hearing be easily deceived?
> *Bar.:*   Very easily, as much as any other sense, and especially if untrained in such speculation. Nonetheless, the trained ear of someone well practiced, accompanied by natural judgment and good principles, is not so easily deceived. In fact, there are some so excellent that, given the proper circumstances, they recognize immediately the smallest difference.[81]

This assessment of the sense of hearing as a means of perception that can be both trained and acculturated, that can be subject to the expectations of habit even as it is capable of very accurate comparisons, will lead Galilei eventually into arguments still further afield from those of Zarlino.

One such argumentative development expands the role of these acquired listening habits in explaining an individual's or a society's response to a given sort of scale or interval, phenomena that Zarlino would still explain in Pythagorean terms. Galilei discusses the different tuning systems used by the lute and by keyboard instruments, fa-

---

81. Ibid., p. 32: "*Str.* Non può ingannarsi facilmente l'udito? *Bar.* Facilissimamente quanto altro senso, e maggiormente quello che in si fatte speculationi non è assuefatto. Nulla dimeno, il purgato udito di colui, che è bene esercitato, accompagnato appresso da naturale giuditio e da qualche buona regola, non s'inganna così di leggiero. Anzi ve ne sono de così perfetti, accompagnati dall'altre circunstanze, che ciascuna differenza minima in un subito capiscano."

voring the former for its greater versatility despite the presence of more tempered (hence imperfect) intervals. Yet he must address the issue of why, if this system is superior, it is not used in all instruments, especially those with keyboards. This, he explains, is simply because performers and listeners are accustomed to hearing keyboard instruments tuned differently and so expect these intervals that actually sound quite harsh in other contexts:

> *Str.:* How can it be that the same thing does not have the same nature in any place and at any time and that the tuning which is so delightful on the lute is so displeasing on keyboard instruments?
> *Bar.:* It can happen very easily, as I will demonstrate by experiment. And although the cause is difficult to understand well, I do not wish to omit any details that will assist me in satisfying you. It may perhaps arise from the sense having become habituated, from hearing on the lute always the intervals in the manner I have already showed you, and likewise our having used a different one in keyboard instruments. Wanting then to temper one according to the custom of the other, one cannot pass over the particular places in which the difference between the two is greatly manifest, without offense, having already grown old in the given temperament; and the particular places where the difference is heard are especially those between the major and minor semitone.[82]

Elsewhere, Galilei attributes to constant use and repeated hearings the common tendency to prefer the sound of a tempered fifth to the "true" 3:2 proportion, even if someone claims in principle to prefer the latter.[83] The practice of counterpoint requires these tempered intervals, and Galilei criticizes roundly those musicians who perpetuate this contradiction.

In fact, Galilei rejects the claim that Pythagorean tunings as such were ever the precise basis of the ecclesiastical pitch system. He also

82. Ibid., p. 47: "*Str.* Come può stare che la medesima cosa non sia in qual si voglia luogo e tempo, dell'istessa natura? E che dilettando nel Liuto questa si fatta Distributione, habbia à dispiacere nello Strumento di tasti? *Bar.* Puo molto bene stare, sendoci l'esperienza di mezzo che ce lo dimostra: e quantunque la cagione di ciò sia difficile à ben capirsi, non voglio per sodisfation vostra mancare di dirvi alcune poche cose che mi convengano in questo proposito. Può forse questo nascere dall'havere assuefatto il senso, d'udire sempre nel Liuto gli intervalli nella maniera che di già vi ho detto contenergli, e così parimente in altra diversa da questa siamo usati havergli dallo Strumento di tasti: e il volere hora, che questo si temperi secondo l'uso di quello, non può in alcuni luoghi particolari, dove la differenza che tra di loro è grandemente manifesta al senso, passare senz'offesa di esso; per essere di già invecchiato in quel si fatto temperamento: e i luoghi particolari son principalmente quelli, dove occorre udire la differenza del maggiore dal minore semituono."

83. Ibid., p. 55.

dismisses the contention that these scales were favored by such early authorities as Guido Aretinus, based on both practical and historical arguments. Since Guido's goal had been the singing of chant, claims Galilei, he did not use these intervals as chords and so had no other compelling reasons for the use of one tuning system over another. Guido simply chose the numbers of Plato and Pythagoras "to give some reputation to the matter,"[84] taking the scale that not only was believed to be the oldest but was also the one supposedly given by nature to mortals. Thus Galilei dispenses with Guido as an authority for supporting any larger metaphysical claims about these tuning systems.

By detaching the perception of consonances from these Pythagorean intervals and tunings, Galilei leaves an opening for the discussion and the advocacy of Aristoxenian ideas about pitch and number. Galilei sees in Aristoxenus's analysis of pitch an effective description of the type of tunings used by fretted instruments such as the lute. Aristoxenus has been falsely maligned, he claims, because of a failure to identify the unit that Aristoxenus divided into equal parts. Many critics have stated, either maliciously or through a misunderstanding, that he meant that the length of a monochord should be divided into equal segments. This would give such ridiculous results that no one could take it seriously, notes Galilei; even if one fails to understand Aristoxenus's meaning, it should be obvious that such a well-educated Greek would not make such absurd statements. Aristoxenus has resorted to these descriptions in order to find a way to measure the quality of the sound, not simply the quantity of string used to produce it: "Aristoxenus knew he had to distribute in equal parts the quality of the sound, and not the quantity of line, string, and space. Thus he worked as a musician in regard to sounding bodies, and not simply as a mathematician in regard to continuous quantity."[85] Even Daniele Barbaro, notes Galilei, has misinterpreted this important aspect of Aristoxenus's thought. The musician must consider here the quality of a sound, not the type of mathematical quantity, as would "a simple mathematician." While Galilei has not yet rejected the old terms *quality* and *quantity,* he is here beginning to develop new ways of expressing "quality" by means of number.

84. Ibid., p. 36: "per dare reputatione alla cosa."
85. Ibid., p. 53: "sapeva Aristosseno, d'havere à distribuire in parti uguali la qualità del suono, e non la quantità della linea, corda, e spatio: operando allhora come Musico intorno al corpo sonoro, e non come semplice Matematico intorno la continua quantità." For a discussion of Galilei's understanding of ancient pitch systems, see Palisca, *Humanism,* pp. 314–18.

The most significant development of these trends in Galilei's thought about pitch and number is his subsequent attempt to understand more precisely the relationships between mathematical expressions and sounding bodies. Interestingly, Galilei leads into this discussion not by way of physics or mathematics as such but as part of a problem in textual analysis. He has been discussing the descriptions of ancient musical instruments in various classical sources, and he has offered several drawings of probable reconstructions of these instruments and the plectra used to play them (Fig. 5).[86] A problem arises in his description of the four-stringed lyre supposedly invented by Mercury; the numbers offered in most sources for the tuning of its strings (12:9:8:6, the same ratios found in the stories of Pythagoras and the hammers) come nowhere near producing the pitches associated with the string names that also appear in the sources. Boethius had resolved the problem by dropping the string names in favor of new ones that seemed to match better with the numbers given and by associating the whole story with Pythagorean proportions and pitches.

Galilei finds a close reading of Plutarch's solution more convincing, allowing for an agreement between the ratios and string names present in the older sources. The numbers should not, he states, be understood as referring to string length, as divisions of a monochord. Rather, they refer to weights that place tension on similar strings. We see this effect in many types of instruments; the thickness of a bell or of a lute's strings affect pitch, and the sound's timbre as well.[87] These numbers from Plutarch can be seen in many types of instruments and experiments. Galilei describes several of these hypothetical situations.

First he describes the use of metal vases of equal size, partially filled with water in the above-mentioned proportions and struck to produce sound, producing pitches like the strings with weights; the more water, the lower the pitch. This resembles the pastime of boys who put water in a footed glass and run a finger around its wet rim, holding the foot steady with the other hand. The more water they add, the lower the sound in this case as well.[88] Then he describes organ pipes of equal thickness, but one twice as long as the other, producing an octave just as do strings of equal types and thickness.

86. Galilei was not alone in his attempts to reconstruct ancient musical instruments. The scholar Giovanni Vincenzo Pinelli solicited information from Zarlino on the nature of ancient plectra within a few years of the publication of the *Dialogo;* see n. 14 above.

87. Galilei, *Dialogo,* p. 133.

88. Ibid.

Forma della   antica Lira.

Alle quali openioni diuerse intorno all'inuentione della Lira , aggiugneremo quella di Filo-   Filostrato in
strato; il quale vuole che la prima si fac esse delle corna di capra insieme con l'osso di mezza la fró   materia della
tes & che il legno che vi si adoperaua intorno per qual si voglia bisogno, vuole che di bosso fus-   Lira di Mer-
se il meglio che adoperare vi si potesse; la quale Hyginio poi nel libro che egli fa dell'Imagini ce-   curio.
lesti, disegna in questa forma .   Nel libro 3.

Forma dell'antica Lira descritta da Hyginio nel libro 3. de segni celesti.

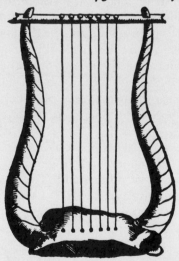

Figure 5 Attempted reconstructions of ancient lyres based on sculptural and textual evidence. From Vincenzo Galilei, *Dialogo . . . , della musica antica, et della moderna,* p.129.

Strings of varying types or thickness behave like pipes of various shapes, and gut taken from different parts of the same intestine and hence of different consistencies produces different results when strung.

Next Galilei turns to the question of pipes of different diameters but similar length. He notes that no one appears to have addressed the subject before:

> In regard, then, to the proportion of pipes of the same length and different width, I have found no record. But I firmly believe, in fact I am certain, that if one takes two pipes each two *braccia* long, and the opening of the one (through which the air passes in sounding it) has a circumference equal throughout of half a *braccio*, and the circumference of the other is three-quarters, if sounded together, one will hear between them the consonance diapente. The latter makes the lower sound, the former the high one. In the same way can be produced most musical intervals, from pipes of equal length and unequal capacity; but they will not all have the same excellence and sonority, as with proportions in length.[89]

He continues with some specific measurements and charts for producing several different intervals in several ways, that is, by varying pipe length, diameter, and volume. These examples have forced him to speak more specifically still about the distinctions between pitch production, by means of measurable attributes, and the timbre, to which the term *quality* increasingly refers.

After a few brief descriptions of similar phenomena, Galilei mentions plans to devote another treatise to the subject. Much of the rest of the *Dialogo* discusses the history of musical instruments, especially stringed instruments. He relates their different traditional uses and the types of music and moods associated with each to the physical construction of the instrument and its resulting sound quality. These associations are mainly imitative.[90] His descriptions of particular examples of ancient instruments, of modern performers, and of the development of the professional reputations of virtuosos provide

89. Ibid., p. 134: "Circa poi alla proporzione delle canne della medesima lunghezza e di diversa larghezza, non ne ho mai trovato alcuna memoria; ma tengo per fermo, anzi ne sono certissimo; che due canne ciascuna delle quali sia lunga due braccia e'l vano dell'una per il quale passa lo spirito nel sonarla habbia un mezzo braccio di circunferenza ugualmente per tutto, e che la circunferenza dell'altra sia tre quarti, sonante insieme si udirà tra di loro la consonanza Diapente; rendendo questa il suono grave, e quella l'acuto: e con i medesimi rispetti si potranno havere la piu parte degli intervalli musici da canne d'uguale lunghezza e disuguale capacità; ma non però si haveranno tutti di quella eccellenza e sonorità, dove la lunghezza ancora nella proporzion di esse per rata concorre."

90. Ibid., p. 139.

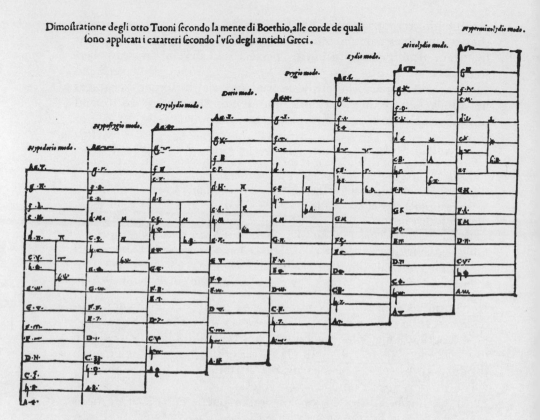

Dimoſtratione degli otto Tuoni ſecondo la mente di Boethio, alle corde de quali
ſono applicati i caratteri ſecondo l'vſo degli antichi Greci.

Figure 6 Discovery of Greek musical notation: the "Alypius Table" applied to
Boethius's pitch system, including modern (Roman letter) equivalents as ap-
plicable. From Vincenzo Galilei, *Dialogo . . . della musica antica, et della moderna*
(Florence, 1581), p. 95.

valuable and interesting commentary on the world of performers and
instruments during the 1570s and 1580s.

Because of this careful development of the study of pitch and number as a distinct subfield, Galilei is able to historicize the competing
schools of music theory to a much greater extent even than had
Zarlino. Some of this resulted from his correspondence with Mei, notably Galilei's extensive presentation of Greek musical notation (the
"Notation Tables of Alypius") and the ancient musical examples Mei
found and sent him (Fig. 6).[91]

91. Ibid., pp. 91–99.

Galilei insists throughout the treatise that vocal music of necessity uses the same tunings as the lute, unlike Zarlino's contention that the voice uses something more "perfect" because of its supposed status as the "natural" instrument. Nonetheless, though he sees the variations among individual voices as a physical phenomenon caused by differences similar to those underlying the variations found among examples of musical instruments of similar type, he is not consistent in the *Dialogo* in attributing the causes of such differences. When confronting the existence of distinctive vocal characteristics common to a single race or culture, he entertains a variety of possible causes, both natural and cultural; in his later manuscript works he will come to favor the cultural arguments. For example, in his discussion of the ancient modes, his analysis follows Mei; he states that the differences among ancient modes lay in pitch range, not (as had been earlier supposed and as was true of the church modes) in the placement of the semitone. These modes had taken the names of various ethnic groups, probably because of differences in the vocal pitch each group used. This likely explanation can be supported, claims Galilei, by examining the speech of modern Italians. Lombards speak with lower voices than Tuscans, and the Ligurians higher: "Whether this is caused by diet, by the water, by the air, or by climate, we will let the natural scientists dispute; it is sufficient that the same thing that occurs today in Italy, happened and must happen daily in Asia among the peoples of Lydia, Phrygia, and Doria."[92] This sort of explanation, however inconsistent or vague the ultimate attribution of responsibility for these ethnic differences, is of a substantially different nature than those of the usual Pythagorean tradition.

Galilei reveals mixed feelings about counterpoint and the ways in which musical pieces should express the chosen text. He does not go as far as Mei and condemn counterpoint completely. Yet he is not willing either to go as far as Zarlino, who simply claimed that ancient and modern music are two historically distinct styles with independent rules and standards. Galilei tries for a sort of middle ground, criticizing those practices that obscure the text and calling for a more direct imitation of the words. Though the compositions he wrote in

92. Ibid., p. 71: "Se questo poi avvenga da cibi, dalle acque, dall'aria, ò dal clima, lasceremo noi disputarlo à naturali; basta che l'istesso che occorre hoggi nell'Italia, occorse e deve occorrere giornalmente nell'Asia tra i popoli della Lydia, della Frygia, e della Doride."

this reformed style have apparently not survived, there is record of their having been sent to such cities as Mantua for performance.[93]

Galilei's manuscript works on consonance and dissonance treat in more detail the major arguments he raises in the *Dialogo*.[94] In the work on consonance, Galilei continues his attacks on Zarlino, not only for his misunderstanding of tuning systems, but also for his stubborn adherence to old-fashioned and ill-conceived styles of counterpoint. Galilei once again favors a simplified style, with more attention to the expression of the text than he sees in the works of Zarlino. The goal of ancient music, he notes, was to produce people of virtue through the presentation of uplifting tales of heroes and great deeds; that of moderns is simply to charm the senses, and hence it hardly deserves its name. Galilei combines historical and textual criticism in his call for the reform of modern practice.

More interesting in many ways is his treatise on dissonance. Galilei notes that writers in theoretical as well as practical traditions have thus far ignored the subject, perhaps because of old Pythagorean arguments that the soul is composed solely of consonances, while dissonance is an aberration. Although the old argument may have a slim foundation in some physical phenomena such as sympathetic vibration, in fact most things in life are a mixture of ugly and beautiful, of consonance and dissonance, full of contrary qualities. In this work, though he does criticize Zarlino, his real wrath is directed against those contrapuntal composers of his day who try to follow blindly a few practical books of rules, ignoring Zarlino's good example of making a thorough study of the liberal arts and philosophy.[95] It is no won-

93. On imitation, see ibid., pp. 80–90. Mantua, Archivio di Stato 1112 contains a letter from Galilei to the duke of Mantua dated 13 March 1582; Galilei mentions having already sent a copy of his *Dialogo* and now encloses a copy of his composition "Lamentations of Jeremiah"; he remarks, "Et satisfacendole, come io spero, chrederei essermi appressato all'uso vero di quelli antichi, e dotti musici; et d'havere nel medesimo tempo, vedendo accordate le mie speculationi del Dialogho sopranominato con l'alto prattico, conseguito il desiderato fine." [And having pleased you, as I hope, I might believe that I have approached the true practice of those ancient and learned musicians; and that at the same time, seeing my thoughts in the above-named *Dialogo* brought into tune with lofty practice, I have attained the desired goal.]

94. Both these treaties survive in multiple drafts: "[untitled] intorno all'uso delle Consonanze," Florence, BNC, Gal. 1, fols. 6r–53r, 55r–103v; and "Discorso di Vincentio Galilei intorno all'uso delle Dissonanze," Florence, BNC, Gal. 1, fols. 104r–47v, 148r–96v, and Gal. 2, fols. 55r–115v. Both treatises date from the years 1588–91.

95. Galilei, "Discorso . . . intorno alle Dissonanze," Florence, BNC, Gal. 1, fols. 121r, 168r.

der, he adds, that many writers had, like Jacopo Sadoleto, expressed
such mixed feelings about the role of music in educating the young.[96]

Galilei continues to attack these old Pythagorean arguments in favor of cultural explanations in his essay on the enharmonic genus.[97]
In this case, he relies on an assortment of textual and especially ob-
servational evidence, much of which relates less to the enharmonic in
particular than to the relativity of taste in general. Thus, he takes a
somewhat technical, if still popular, subject and turns it into a discussion of taste and its role in musical style.

The popularity of the enharmonic genus has come and gone
through the ages, Galilei notes, and he returns often to its particular
use among the ancients in religious service. The Greeks had used this
unique sort of tuning as one of their ways of showing the gods their
recognition of the gods' unique nature:

> And returning to the ancient Greeks and Latins, I would think it not far
> from the truth to believe that just as their gods did not speak, dress, walk,
> or feed themselves (according to what the ancient historians and poets
> tell us), nor do many other things according to the nature and customs of
> simple and ordinary people, so they would have used the enharmonic
> particularly to render thanks to them and to praise the heroes; thus with
> the diversity of intervals they distinguished sacred music from profane.[98]

To this argument based on historical and cultural context, Galilei
adds numerous examples of observable differences in musical preference among groups of people, and even among animals. He has
heard Turkish and Moorish string music in Venice, Messina, and
Marseille and disliked it, but he has also witnessed their musicians'
distaste for Western styles. Horses may be moved to battle by the
sound of trumpets, as the old *laudes musice* had demonstrated to prove

96. Jacopo Sadoleto, *Sadoleto on Education: A Translation of the De pueris recte
instituendis 1533)*, intro., notes E. T. Campagnac and K. Forbes (Oxford: Oxford
University Press, 1916).

97. Galilei, "Discorso di Vincentio Galilei, intorno all'uso dell'Enharmonico, et di
chi fusse Autore del Cromatico," Florence, BNC, Gal. 3, fols. 3r–34v (1590–91); see
also Galilei, "Dubii intorno a quanto io ho detto dall'uso dell'enharmonio, con la
solutione di essi," Florence, BNC, Gal. 3, fols. 62r–76r (ca. 1591).

98. Galilei, "Discorso . . . all'uso dell'Enharmonio," fol. 6v: "E tornando all'antica
Gentilità Greca, et latina, non terrei per cosa dal vero lontana il credere che si come
i Dei loro non parlavano, non vestivano, non caminavano, non si nutrivano (secondo
però che ci raccontano gl'antichi Historici, et gl'antichi Poeti) ne facevano molte
altre attioni secondo l'usanza et secondo la natura et costume degl'huomini semplici
et ordinarii, che ell' havesse usato l'enharmonio imparticolare per rendergli gratie et
per lodare gl'Heroi; affine di distinguere in quel mainiere con la diversità
degl'intervalli la musica sacra dalla profana."

music's natural power, but the noise is ignored by other types of animals. Similar diversity can be seen among peoples and animals in preferred foods, colors, and odors. Whole languages may perish as they are replaced with others more preferable, as his own region changed from Etruscan to Latin to Tuscan.[99]

Galilei continues with some detailed source criticism intended primarily to establish dates for sources and for individual historical figures, in order to rebut the claims of Zarlino and others that the ancients were united in criticism and rejection of the enharmonic genus. In this brief essay, then, Galilei has pushed the establishment and analysis of stylistic and other perceptual preferences entirely into the realm of historical and cultural research, far away from any claims about cosmology or the alleged mathematical nature of the soul.

This historical approach to understanding ancient music theory is continued in his *Discorso* on the three major schools of ancient music.[100] Aided particularly once again by Plutarch's treatise on music,[101] Galilei separates these "sects" into the usual three groups of Pythagoreans, Aristoxenians, and Ptolemaics not as earlier writers had done—by ranking them in order of "correctness"—but by distinguishing the goals and intentions of each group. Many of the rules propounded by each school (such as those regarding consonance and dissonance) should thus be understood as forming a part of one of these internally coherent systems of thought, he argues, and not as absolute dicta for all times and all circumstances.

Galilei's little *Discorso intorno all'opere di messer Gioseffo Zarlino* (1589) is his last published attack on Zarlino's arguments about these systems of intonation.[102] The first several pages of the work relate Galilei's troubles in getting his *Dialogo* published, allegedly because of Zarlino's hindrance. Yet most of the *Discorso* deals with more pressing and important issues. Galilei returns to one of his major intellectual concerns, the distinctions between nature and art, which he addresses by continuing his polemics against Zarlino's theories, demolishing Zarlino's claim that Ptolemy's scale is more "natural" than any other and that the human voice as a "natural" instrument will sing the purest

99. Ibid., fols. 7r–8v.
100. Galilei, "Discorso intorno a diversi pareri che hebbono le tre sette piu famose degli antichi Musici; intorno alla cosa de suoni, et degl'acchordi," Florence, BNC, Gal. 3, fols. 35r–43r.
101. Galilei used an anonymous Italian version of Valgulio's Latin Plutarch, "Traduzione d'un Discorso latino fatto da Carlo Valgulio Bresciano sopra la Musica di Plutarcho à Tito Pyrrhino," Florence, BNC, Gal. 7, fols. 3r–18v.
102. Galilei, *Discorso . . . intorno all'opere di messer Gioseffo Zarlino da Chioggia, et altri importanti particolari attenenti alla musica* (Florence: Marescotti, 1589).

intervals possible. First, says Galilei, the entire scale system, with its complex patterns of steps, half steps, and larger intervals, is obviously constructed by means of art and artifice. Consonances may arise as "natural" phenomena, but the system as a whole is the creation of people, even if that of people from antiquity.

Further, the intervals sung by the voice are no different in type than those played by an instrument and are subject to the same cultural rules that established scales for instruments:

> With wind and stringed instruments, one cannot pass outside of their order, because with that order of sounds found in them, the player achieves his goal; and no one with any judgment would say that some instrument does, or is capable of doing, that which it does not and cannot do. And with the ordering of voices made by nature, it is true that among them there are no boundaries or order naturally prescribed by the form and measure of these intervals or those, more or less taut or relaxed; they can form them as they please. But all these limitations come from art, every time they choose to sing one system or another, which (since it is true that these days they have chosen the Syntone of Ptolemy) reins in the voice, so to speak, assigning precise places to it of whatever intervals, just as do holes and keys on artificial instruments of wind or string in the fingers and hands of the player. And if they do otherwise, they are not sounding the Syntone of Ptolemy as it is designated. Further, voices learn from art to form and produce any musical interval, since in their greater excellence they contain their truer proportion and form. Likewise one learns the principles of painting from drawing, learning first to draw each part of a given body in supreme excellence and in their exact proportions and beauty. . . . Now the voice must do likewise; and although it may have the ability (not naturally as Zarlino claims, but after having learned through long practice the art of singing well) to form and to sing any notes in the given excellence of the intervals, when they then go to sing a particular system, they sing that which was established by the artifice of its author.[103]

103. Ibid., pp. 24–26: "Con gli strumenti di fiato e di corde non si puo passare fuor dell'ordine loro, perche con quell'ordine di suoni che tra essi si ritrova conseguisce il sonatore il suo fine: ne dice alcuno di giuditio, che quello strumento possa, or faccia quello ch'ei non fa e non puo. E gl'ordini delle voci fatti dalla natura, è vero che tra essi non è per l'ordinario e naturalmente termini prescritti delle forme e misure di questi che di quelli intervalli piu o meno tesi o rimessi gl'uni degl'altri, e gli possono formare come à loro piu aggrada; ma tutte queste limitationi prendono dall'arte ciascuna volta, ch'ei piglino a cantare questo o quel sistema; il quale (sendo vero che hoggi habbin preso a cantare il Sintono di Tomoleo) pone per modo di dire freno alle voci assegnando ad esse i termini precisi di qual si voglia suo intervallo, non altramente che si faccino i fori e i tasti de gli strumenti artifiziali e di fiato e di corde alle dità e mani del Sonatore. E se faranno altramente non soneranno il Sintono come ci è stato disegnato. più oltre. le voci imparano dall'arte a portare, e

If we continue to use Ptolemy's scales as an example, Galilei maintains, we see that he did not label some of its intervals natural and others artificial. Rather, he constructed the system as a whole, through his own artifice. It is wrong in any case to argue that art cannot improve on nature; for fields such as medicine, agriculture, and animal husbandry show that human arts may improve on many aspects of the natural world and even correct some of its defects.[104] Thus, for Galilei, any scale system must be understood as a human creation, a product of art and artifice, although one that necessarily uses physical phenomena that can themselves be studied in other ways. The voice, far from being superior in type, must actually learn to produce the specific intervals by following the example of other instruments.

In the end, by basing his arguments on "nature" and "the natural," Zarlino has founded his arguments on false principles, according to Galilei. It is true, he repeats, that birds, beasts, and even humans may utter cries; but to sing requires art.[105] The understanding of consonances and dissonances arises from understanding this art. The various schools of ancient musical thought all approached this understanding differently and accordingly composed slightly different scales.

Galilei returns to the issues of "nature" in two brief essays on sounding bodies, works that were probably intended to form part of the longer treatise on the subject to which he had referred in the *Dialogo*. The *Discorso particolare intorno alla diversita delle forme del diapason* is the more significant of the two; its title is perhaps somewhat misleading, since it refers not to the different species of diapason as described by ancient theorists but to different methods of producing an octave by sounding bodies.[106]

---

formare qual sia intervallo musico, in quell'eccellenza maggiore che gli contenghino le piu vere proportioni e di forme loro; non altramente che ci apprendino i principii della pittura dal disegno, che è d'imparar prima a disegnare ciascuna parte di qual si voglia corpo in suprema eccellenza, e nell'esatta proportione e bellezza loro . . . hora cosi parimente devono le voci; e quantunque l'habbino facultà (non naturalmente come vuole il Zarlino, ma dopo l'havere appreso con lunga prattica l'arte del ben cantare) di formare, e modulare per qual si voglino corde nell'eccellenza detta gl'intervalli, quando poi pigliono à cantare un particolar sistemo, l'hanno a cantare tale quale fu dall'artifizio del suo autore distribuito."

104. Ibid., pp. 70–71.
105. Ibid., pp. 98–99.
106. Galilei, "Discorso particolare intorno alla diversita delle forme del Diapason di V. G." Florence, BNC, Gal. 3, fols. 44r–54v; "Discorso particolare intorno all'unisono di V. G.," ibid., fols. 55r–61v. Several scholars have discussed the experiments described here and their impact on Zarlino's theory. Walker, in *Studies in Musical*

The octave, like any other interval, begins Galilei, can be produced in several ways, measurable by several different proportions. So too, the proportion 2:1 traditionally associated with the octave can describe several types of interval. The ratio 2:1 when connected with the octave describes the differences in length of two strings of equal thickness and composition, held under equal tension; this fact is well known. But if the length of the strings is kept equal while their tension is varied, the amount of weight added to one string in order to produce an octave with the other will have the proportion 4:1. Finally, by switching from strings as the producers of sound to concave bodies, the difference in interior volume needed to sound an octave is 8:1.

If in the sonorous bodies only one dimension is doubled, the result is a major third; if quadrupled, a major sixth. Further, if the proportion 2:1 is applied not to string length but to weights placing tension on the string, the result is the very dissonant tritone. Therefore, it is not correct to use terms such as *sonorous number* in discussing music; the numbers merely describe particular aspects of the sounding body:

> Thus they should not be considered simply as counted numbers but as numbers numerative of those portions of strings able to render sound when struck. Although Zarlino in the *Istitutioni* 1.15 says that number is sonorous, by no means can it be so, since it has no body in and of itself, and sound is not made without the percussion of some body which is able to produce sound when struck. Consequently, simple number cannot be sonorous; even if time and a line can be so divisible, they have no body either. But that which is able to produce sound can be sonorous, that body to which we apply a given number; and with the division of that body by means of number, we have a given musical interval.[107]

Science, pp. 23–26, and Palisca, in *Humanism*, pp. 273–79, both note that Zarlino's theory is partially vindicated as a description of the harmonic series, discussed in terms of the frequency of vibration (normally expressed in terms of cycles per second) of a sounding body; and Walker points out that Galilei's claims about the volumes of sounding pipes are too vague to be accurate or correct as they stand. Stillman Drake has emphasized the nearly certain participation of Galileo Galilei in these sound experiments and their impact on his later research; see *Galileo Studies*, pp. 43–62; and Drake, *Galileo at Work: His Scientific Biography* (Chicago: University of Chicago Press, 1978), pp. 15–17.

107. Galilei, "Discorso . . . intorno alla . . . diapason," fols. 45v–46r; in *The Florentine Camerata*, ed. Claude V. Palisca (New Haven: Yale University Press, 1989), pp. 180–83: "ma non per cio si considerino semplicemente come numeri numerati; ma come numeri numerativi di quelle tali portioni di corde atte dopo l'essere percosse a rendere il suono. Imperoche quello che nel capo. 15 del primo delle Istitutioni dice il Zarlino, volendo egli che il numero sia sonoro, non puo essere à patto alcuno,

Galilei has thus removed number from the center of the subject of music and positioned it as a means for measuring the phenomena observed by the senses. He has, at the same time, also vastly expanded the range of physical objects and characteristics subject to the measurement of number, characteristics earlier writers treated as "qualities." He clarifies his new definition of "qualities" in his essay on unisons, devoted to discussing measurable ways of producing the same pitch with different sounding bodies. These efforts affect the other qualities of the sound, or its timbre, which must be acknowledged if one wishes to label the resulting sounds as "unison." This is difficult for singers, since they must weigh all these factors constantly in singing with groups, whereas with lutes, one need worry only about tuning the strings properly before beginning to play. Galilei cannot resist a final argument in favor of the lute over the voice, but his attempt to keep pitch distinct from timbre, with a newer and more specific assessment of quantities and qualities, is a genuinely new development.

One last attack on Zarlino, this time on his *Sopplimenti,* might seem to promise yet another exercise in repudiating his former teacher's scale tunings.[108] Yet in this piece, which follows the *Sopplimenti* book by book in a concise format often more like an outline than a real piece of prose, Galilei offers remarks of varying length on several important subjects he had already begun to address in earlier works, remarks that serve both to clarify and to summarize his mature opinions on mathematics, physics, historical analysis, and the role of Aristotle in modern scholarship.

The least novel subject Galilei addresses here is, of course, the old matter of intonation; in the end, it is also the one that is least capable of resolution. In the absence of modern devices that can measure that precise pitches of singers in performance, this argument between Zarlino and Galilei involved intervals too small and too fleeting for either of them to verify exactly. The two of them might base their arguments in logic, philosophy, and experience combined in any proportions they chose, but the recourse to empirical evidence to

---

atteso che non havendo per se stesso corpo, et il suono non si da senza la percussione di alcun corpo atto dopo l'essere percosso a rendere suono; non puo consequentemente esser sonoro il numero semplice, quantunque egli com'il tempo et la linea sia divisibile che questi neanco hanno corpo: ma si bene puo essere sonoro cio è atto a rendere suono, quel corpo al quale noi applichiamo il numero detto; et con la divisione di esso corpo con il mezzo del numero, havere qual sia musico intervallo."

108. Galilei, untitled, incipit "Sopplimenti musicali," Florence, BNC, Gal. 5, fols. 3r–58r.

support one interpretation—which both scholars considered to be the ideal way to settle the issue—was impossible to achieve. In this treatise, Galilei once more cites Fogliano repeatedly as having resolved these issues a generation earlier.

Elsewhere, Galilei argues that the new and improved information contained in the *Sopplimenti,* as compared with Zarlino's earlier treatises, all comes straight from Galilei's own *Dialogo.* This includes material on Egyptian music, on imitation in setting texts, on the construction of organs, on ancient modes, and on a host of other minor subjects. Much of this claim is simple invective, serving little argumentative purpose beyond an attempt to establish himself as the superior scholar, especially since he also occasionally chides Zarlino for not having adopted Galilei's own opinions on other matters, despite conclusive and persuasive evidence.

More significant are Galilei's arguments about method. Specifically, he begins to define the extent of Aristotle's usefulness as a source for both general and specific knowledge about music and as a general authority on logic and method. He also discusses, as a result, the important relationship between textual sources and experimental verification. These issues first arise in his criticism of *Sopplimenti* 1.8–9, in which Zarlino has referred back to the Aristotelian *Problems* on the various qualities of sound. Galilei stands by his measurements, acknowledging that different qualities of sound are observable in organ pipes in different shapes, a subject he has written on before: "The large and low pipes take a lot of wind, and the small, high ones take little. . . . Highness and lowness are qualities; but those bodies which are their cause are quantities, in that they are large, small, thick, thin, and so on."[109]

Galilei continues (primarily in brief notes rather than full sentences) that, whereas Zarlino doubts (*Sopplimenti,* p. 62) that the thickness or thinness of a body is a quantity, the truth can be demonstrated by examining the sounds of bells, whose pitch does vary depending on the thickness of the bell's walls. The subject also shows Aristotle to be in error. In considering other dimensions of sounding bodies, however, he notes that perhaps Aristotle's error in simply assigning the octave a 2:1 proportion in all cases is understandable, insofar it could be said to lie "in saying that they are duple according to their nature," that is, depending on the body in question, duple in length, width,

109. Ibid., fol. 4r–v: "Le canne grandi et gravi vogliano molto spirito, et poco le pichole et acute. . . . L'acutezza et gravita sono qualitadi; ma quantitadi sono quei corpi che sono cagione di esse qualitadi, impero che sono grandi, piccoli, grossi, sottili, et altri."

and (according to just how the sound is produced) perhaps depth.[110]

Galilei compares the responsibility to verify these numbers as found in ancient sources against experience, with the writer's commonly expected responsibility to verify sources when the material in question is strictly textual. The nature of the material under study determines the type of verification required, whether it should come from consulting further texts or from further experience:

> When they find a writer who claims the authority of another more ancient one, they seek to look at the source of the matter. And one does the same when writing about things heard by an ancient writer. Besides, even when things are seen in a source, if the source treats of those matters subject to the senses, no matter who the writer is, one must examine whether or not they are true. And after having recited the author's opinion, if it is known that this cannot be, one should add one's own opinion with appropriate modesty.[111]

Galilei gives another example, naturally a bad example taken from Zarlino. Zarlino needed information on the trombone and asked a performer, receiving an answer that was partly true and partly false. Zarlino then published the material without either citing his source or verifying it. If he were in Zarlino's place, continues Galilei, he would have consulted not one trombonist but many and also witnessed the phenomenon himself. Zarlino also repeated erroneous information about the relationship between the dimensions of sounding bodies and their pitch, without ever verifying that the descriptions of sense experiences given by the ancient writers were actually correct. Just because one of these sources was occasionally Aristotle is no excuse; Aristotle himself was not an expert in this field and had to rely on the opinions of others, opinions that may later be found incorrect. Zarlino, on the other hand, has no excuse at all: "As a professor of music, he does not merit the excuse of Aristotle himself, and before he assented he should have experimented, which

110. Ibid., fols. 4v–5r: "et si puo scusare Aristotile, che considerate le canne come corpi, nel dire che havevono ad essere dupli istese seconda la natura loro ciò è con lunghezza et in altezza."

111. Ibid., fol. 42r: "Ma quando trovano uno scrittore che allega l'autorità d'un altro piu di lui antico, cerca di vedere in fonte quella tal cosa; et il medesimo si fa quando si scrivono cose udite degl'antici piu oltre quando anco sono vedute in fonte le cose di qual sia scrittore, che tratti però di quelle cose che sono sotto poste al senso; si examinano s'elle sono vere, o no; et dopo havere recitato le openioni loro et conosciuto realmente ch'elle non possano per quel verso gli si aggiugne il parere suo con quella modestia che conviene."

would have been even simpler than that regarding the trombone, about which he could, not being a professor of it, have excused himself by saying he did not know how to play it."[112]

Galilei has cut through several problems of method and the use of sources in a single passage, in the apparent simplicity of absolving poor Aristotle, and blaming Zarlino, for never having learned to play the trombone. By arguing that Aristotle wrote on more subjects than those in which he was a specialist and that as a consequence he relied on the information and expertise of others, Galilei has constructed a rhetorical position that allows the modern scholar to refute a vast amount of Aristotelian description in favor of modern findings; the modern scholar can claim not to be contradicting Aristotle so much as Aristotle's misinformed specialist advisors. Further, Galilei argues that in this subject, music, Zarlino has both greater expertise than Aristotle and a greater responsibility for accuracy as a result. Just as if he were verifying the accuracy of his text by means of humanistic criticism, when the subject involves sense perception, the writer must verify the source through experience, not just once but repeatedly, to ensure accuracy. The truest follower of Aristotle follows not his results but his method.[113]

Over the course of his writings, Galilei has come to recognize tacitly Zarlino's two major divisions in the field of music. One is this realm of physical behavior, studied by means of number. The other is the cultural artifact of musical composition, which organizes these sounds and gives them meaning based on social contexts and cultural expectations. He has attacked and abandoned any connection between the two based on the Pythagorean tradition. Yet Pythagorean musical thought does not immediately disappear. From this time, though, its claims become more and more limited. Galilei's work moves it decisively to the edges of the field.

The End of the Boethian Tradition: Minor Musical Writings of the Late Sixteenth Century

There appeared during the last decades of the sixteenth century some minor works on music that like those of earlier years, are

112. Ibid., fol. 43v: "Il quale [Zarlino] come professore di musica, non merita la scusa del medesimo Aristotile, et doveva prima che gli aconsentisse esperimenterle che essa cosa facilissima assai piu di quella del Trombone, di che potrebbe come non professore scusarsene con dire che lui non sa sonarlo."

113. Charles Schmitt, among others, has noticed this opinion expressed by Galilei's son Galileo; see his "Aristotelianism in the Veneto," 1:104–24.

derivative or idiosyncratic, citing major scholars but not cited by them in return. They are interesting for their diversity and what it indicates about the degree to which Zarlino, Galilei, and the others have transformed the field. Two examples of epideictic rhetoric have survived, noteworthy for assimilating a historical approach to the subject. The earlier one (that of Pietro Caetano) maintains Pythagorean arguments; the later (by Francesco Bocchi) explicitly rejects them in favor of a view of music as a leisure activity of marginal usefulness. A similar rejection of Pythagorean arguments—in fact the jettisoning of most of the Boethian tradition—is found in a little treatise by Orazio Tigrini, who claims, nonetheless, to be a follower of Zarlino. His colleague Pietro Ponzio, also a musician and treatise writer, clings to a sort of historicized Pythagoreanism much more obviously influenced by Zarlino.

The most significant survivals of Pythagorean musical thought can be seen in works least connected with the worlds of musical practice or scholarship. Two northern Italians, Fabio Paolini and Pietro Girolamo Gentile Riccio, composed works of religious speculation based on Pythagorean notions of music and harmony. The appeal of this model of universal harmony was sufficient to ensure its survival in such peripheral disciplines even after it had lost its explanatory power in music.

Pietro Caetano and Francesco Bocchi: In Praise and Blame of Music

The oration on the origin and dignity of music by Pietro Caetano (a singer at S. Marco in Venice) and offered to Guido Ubaldo, duke of Urbino, serves as an example of both continuity and change in the genre, especially when compared with that of Brandolini some fifty years earlier.[114] Caetano still uses many of the conventions of Pythagorean theory, but his analysis of instrumental music is primarily historical. A digression near the end of the oration takes a somewhat political turn, praising various contemporary rulers for their patronage and personal accomplishments in music. For the most

114. Petrus Caetanus Cantor Sancti Marci Venetiarum [Pietro Caetano], "Oratio de origine et dignitate musices," Venice, Bib. Correr, Cicogna 906, 33 fols. The oration is undated but is dedicated to Guidobaldo II (d. 1574) and refers to the emperor Maximilian II (ruled 1564–76); it also describes the musical era of Zarlino as having begun some twenty years earlier. These references point to a date for the oration between 1564 and 1574.

part, however, the oration constitutes a late version of the independent *laus musice*, one in which Pythagorean and non-Pythagorean arguments are used together in a manner that often seems derived from Zarlino.

Caetano's initial arguments are drawn from the tradition of *musica mundana* and *humana*. He emphasizes the divine source of the harmonic proportions of creation, the similar construction of the human soul, and the ability to perceive such order. This portion of the field he labels "animastic," as opposed to instrumental, music; its presentation occupies the first quarter of the oration.[115] But when he shifts to the subject of instrumental music, he takes a more historical approach. Although the claims about the identity of the first musician are too contested ever to be settled, he notes, music's invention certainly came very early in human history and was one of the moderating forces of human nature which had helped civilize people. Caetano traces the transfer of this knowledge and its civilizing power from the Greeks to the Romans, then to the rise of Christianity and its music of worship.

At this point, some of Caetano's modern argumentative agenda begins to assert itself in an extended claim for Italian supremacy in ecclesiastical music. The Greeks had lost their ancient musical learning and so adopted Gregorian chant. Further, when Charlemagne returned north after defeating the Lombards, he took Italian singers with him to form the core of northern European church music. Similarly important was Guido Aretinus (placed by Caetano in the same family line as St. Benedict), who developed the notation system and the hand for the teaching of chant, so that all singers ever since have been indebted to him.[116] Finally, Caetano turns, via Plato's *Republic*, to a praise of modern Habsburg leaders whose natural virtues have been brought to full flower through their dedication to harmony. He concludes the oration with another brief synopsis of his historical chronology.

Caetano's oration has maintained the Pythagorean basis of musical science, its role in the cosmos, and its effect on the individual. Yet his discussion of instrumental music is not only chronological but reasonably historical. He organizes his subject into historical periods and identifies important causal features in the transition from one to the next. He is careful to point out the latest thinking about Greek theory,

---

115. Ibid., fols. 6r–12v.
116. Ibid., fol. 18r–v.

labeling the followers of Pythagoras, Aristoxenus, and Ptolemy as rival interpretive schools throughout antiquity.[117]

Caetano has not, however, confronted the conflicts and potential contradictions between this historical thesis and his own advocacy of one of these positions. By turning his conclusion to a praise of contemporary political leaders who have profited by attention to music, Caetano deflects attention away from such matters of substance in the subject at hand. Thus, while his oration does not serve as a serious forum for investigation of these issues, it does offer an example of the relatively sophisticated understanding of issues undergoing debate among major figures such as Zarlino and Galilei.

If Caetano's oration constituted a later example of the *laus musice* as an independent genre, the *Discorso sopra la musica* (1580) of the Florentine Francesco Bocchi offers just the opposite. Bocchi was a humanist by education and profession; except for a brief stint with the Roman curia in 1572, he spent his whole life in Florence, where he worked as a teacher for several prominent families and as a writer of numerous orations and occasional pieces.[118] The *Discorso* arose out of Bocchi's ongoing interest, fueled by the works of Machiavelli, in understanding and explaining the rise and fall of states, especially the decline in Italian political independence. Bocchi focuses his attention in the *Discorso* on music as a cause not of moral good but of decay and decline. He blames excessive devotion to music for contributing to political decadence.

Bocchi begins by reciting the standard praises of music; he then asks the reader to consider this praise in the light of the purposes for which the arts were created. This purpose is human happiness, and the good political state must decide which of the arts are to be advocated or avoided depending on the needs of its citizens. Yet the rulers of the state cannot themselves spend much time on music without ignoring politics, to the state's detriment. In fact, few rulers have themselves known much about music, so involvement with it has caused no such problems.

Now that his rhetorical stage is set, Bocchi returns to many of the specific marvelous effects of music first described in his *laus*, in order to rebut them. These arguments take any of several approaches. In some cases, Bocchi shows that music's observed effects can be attributed to simpler and more mundane causes. In others, he refers the

117. Ibid., fol. 14r–v.
118. For biographical information on Bocchi, see S. Monchi, "Bocchi, Francesco," *DBI*.

reader to similar modern situations in which the miraculous effect does not exist. Thus he accounts for the alleged use of music to rouse soldiers to battle by noting that martial music accompanies the sounds of war, which are far louder and more horrible than any sort of music; these noises of battle are the real cause of any stirring of the blood that the warrior experiences.[119] Bocchi also offers the examples of numerous famous ancients (for example, Cicero), who though noted for their great learning, apparently never studied music. Finally, he simply dismisses some arguments about music's power; he finds the claim that celestial motion could be a guide and help in life to be absurd, since the heavenly bodies move continuously and have nothing to do with human actions.

To Bocchi, music's goal is the Aristotelian notion (from the *Politics*) of providing a cultured pastime. It is far inferior to the study of letters, and its overuse can be genuinely hazardous. Since music's specific task is to soothe the soul from the labors of the day, it cannot serve as a substitute for those labors, and if used too often it will soften the soul so as to render it unfit for virtue. This excessive concern with music had brought ruin to the Greeks. Both Scipio Africanus and Cato the Elder wanted to avoid its ruining the Romans in turn, but to no avail: "The luxurious and too-exquisite delights were the cause of the ruin of its cities and its peoples, because these things dulled their valorous nerve and pulled up the roots of virtue."[120] He concludes that music, while inferior to letters, does an adequate job of soothing the spirit if its use is limited. Any expansion of this minor role may lead to ruin, both for the individual and for society.

Bocchi's opinions may be seen as idiosyncratic. Nonetheless, several of the arguments he makes are similar in thinking to those of other writers who view music in a more positive light. He has defined the subject and its goals in Aristotelian terms (that is, after the *Politics*): "music" is the playing of musical pieces, a pleasant and educated pastime with only minor importance either for the individual or for the state. Further, he has rejected Pythagorean theory for several reasons. He sees no evidence to connect celestial motion with human activities. He also believes that the ancient anecdotes about music's emotional powers that prove and illustrate Pythagorean theory must

119. Francesco Bocchi, *Discorso . . . sopra la musica, non secondo l'arte di quella, ma secondo la ragione alla politica pertinente* (Florence: Marescotti, 1580), pp. 15–16.
120. Ibid., p. 34: "Le delizie, e i diletti troppo isquisiti sono cagione della rovina delle città, e delle genti: perche mozzano queste cose i nervi del valore, e diradicano le radici della virtù."

be subject to the empirical verification of contemporary experience. They fail this test, and simpler explanations can be found, either in modern experience or in the ancient texts themselves. The examples of the lives of great ancient men, as seen in classical literature, further support the analysis of music's role given in the *Politics* and not that of the *Republic,* and these examples are corroborated by the lives of modern political leaders.

Bocchi would probably fail to share the conviction of many of his colleagues that ancient poetry cannot be understood fully outside its musical context. Despite this major disagreement, he shares many of their arguments against Pythagorean theory itself. This animosity toward the subject prevents his developing a detailed theory of his own, beyond following Aristotle and limiting music's role. His *Discorso* serves as a reminder that not all humanists eagerly embraced the new musical scholarship, even if they had never been fond of the old.

Orazio Tigrini

The little counterpoint treatise published by the canon Orazio Tigrini of Arezzo, *Il compendio della musica* (1588), is typical of many such minor treatises that appeared during or immediately after the major scholarly controversies of Zarlino, Galilei, and Mei.[121] Tigrini makes a point of taking Zarlino as his main authority, dedicates the treatise to him, and prints a brief note of thanks from him, along with a collection of laudatory verse, at the beginning of the work. These poems, full of references to the music of the spheres, Pythagoras, and Orpheus, are the most Pythagorean section of the whole work. Despite the general conservatism of Tigrini's treatise and his reiteration of the importance of reason over sense perception, he shows little real interest in the substance of the Boethian or Pythagorean tradition. He expresses admiration for Zarlino above all for his scale tunings and secondarily for his reliance on experience as the basis of musical thought.

In a brief proem, Tigrini gives his reason for composing the work: he has decided to present a brief compendium for those who wish to learn the art of counterpoint but are lacking in time, background, and knowledge of Latin. He also offers a short argument, more or less condensed from Zarlino, that supports the rule of reason over sense

121. For biographical information on Tigrini, see Imogene Horsely, "Tigrini, Orazio," *New Grove.*

perception, "like master and servant,"[122] and that (also like Zarlino) incorrectly identifies the Pythagoreans as the middle ground between exclusive reliance on one over the other. Tigrini includes a list of references in the margins here and throughout the treatise, as much to encourage further study as to identify his own sources.

Tigrini's intended audience and goals for the work place it at the general level of popular treatises such as those written earlier by Lanfranco or Dentice. A lack of interest in theoretical issues, particularly when those issues have become the source of controversy, is therefore not surprising. Tigrini has included no *laus musice*, no introductory sections on proportion or the cosmos, and no general statements about music's ultimate goal. His brief praise of reason in the proem seems to refer not to mathematics but simply to rules for composition.

This total lack of interest in any of the issues that so engaged Zarlino seems odd for a work that claims to follow in his footsteps. Tigrini's longest argument in support of reason over mere performance does not even mention Zarlino and relies on Burtius, Marchetto of Padua, Aron, and Guido.[123] Tigrini reverts back to the threefold distinction from Boethius and Guido that separates performer, composer, and *musicus* in ascending levels of esteem, and as an Aretine, he is particularly proud of Guido's distinction between *musicus* and cantor. None of this argument follows the outlines of Zarlino's thought; the reader must seek elsewhere for Tigrini's debt to the *Istitutioni*.

Such influence, and it is modest enough, is to be found in Tigrini's discussion of consonances. There, he mentions why he has chosen to follow Zarlino exclusively: Boethius, Gaffurio, and others have all erred in their division of the octave. This mistake was born of too little attention to good practice, in favor of theory alone. Overreliance on theory, states Tigrini, had been evident as long ago as Guido. Zarlino finally found the proper balance and, so, discovered the best intonation. Through his research, Zarlino has even surpassed the ancients, a feat not accomplished by earlier writers:

Nor should it seem impossible if among so many writers over such a long stretch of time, that no one else discovered these proportions. This is due not only to lack of practice, as he already states, but also because they did not compare the proportions of such consonances, nor carefully

122. Orazio Tigrini, *Il compendio della musica, nel quale brevemente si tratta dell'arte del contrapunto, diviso in quattro libri* (Venice: Amadino, 1588), 1:1.
123. Ibid., 3:153–54.

investigate the truth with such study and diligence, as Zarlino has done, because they were content with the wisdom of the great authors. Zarlino, collecting various things from the good ancients, has not only simplified some things but also discovered others.[124]

For the practical purposes of Tigrini's treatise, Zarlino's main accomplishment was his advocacy of a good tuning system. Tigrini praises Zarlino's skill as a practicing musician and as an investigator of physical experience, in addition to his study of theory or philosophy. To content oneself with ancient authority inhibits advancement of knowledge in music and musical studies. This very partial reading of Zarlino has allowed Tigrini to draw up a practical treatise with an invocation of one of the field's major thinkers. It also illustrates the wide impact of Zarlino's emphasis on direct observation and experience in establishing musical laws. Tigrini's little treatise exemplifies the ease with which these minor writers could use the name of a major scholar to dignify an approach they might have taken anyway, but also shows the importance of Zarlino's thought in elevating the role of experience.

Some Late Pythagoreans

During the same years in which Galilei and Zarlino exchanged polemics and Bottrigari was beginning his study of acoustics, several minor authors published works that make use of the Pythagorean tradition but take only the most cursory notice of the larger, ongoing scholarly controversies. These treatises appear not to have generated a strong following, or even a debate, in the field. Among the last of their kind, they show that the tradition still had its adherents into the beginning of the seventeenth century.

One of these writers was the Parman musician Pietro Ponzio (1532–96).[125] Ponzio served as maestro di cappella at several churches in Bergamo, Milan, and Parma. His two treatises were published late in

124. Ibid., p. 22: Nè anco dee parere impossibile, se fra tanti Scrittori, in così lungo spatio di tempo, da nessuno altro non siano state conosciute tali Proportioni: perche questo, come si è detto, non solo è nato per la poca prattica, ma ancora, perche acquietandosi alla sentenza di così gravi Authori, non hanno fatto altro paragone delle proportioni di tali Consonanze, nè cosi sottilmente investigatone la verità con quello studio, e diligenza, c'hà fatto esso Signor Zarlinò; ilquale raccogliendo diverse cose da i buoni Antichi, le ha non solo facilitate, ma anco n'ha ritrovate dell'altre di nuovo."

125. For biographical information on Ponzio, see Roland Jackson, "Pontio, Pietro," *New Grove*.

his career, after his return to Parma. The *Ragionamento di musica* (1588) is a series of four dialogues, three of which are devoted to practical music in general and counterpoint in particular. It begins, like many treatises of an earlier generation, with music theory. Ponzio's initial definitions are cast in terms of "ordered sound" and come from a host of earlier writers, many of them at the popular or practical level, in particular Lanfranco, Gaffurio, Biagio Pelacani, and Aron. These writers and a few others are his authorities.

Ponzio combines several organizational schemes to arrive at his divisions in the subject of music. The field is composed of two major categories, he states, natural and artificial. The Boethian *musica mundana* and *humana* constitute "natural" music; "artificial" music is practical music, composed of plainchant, figured vocal music, and instrumental music. He does note that the first two "artificial" forms use a "natural" instrument, the voice, but refuses to magnify this ancient distinction and leaves them all in the same category. His discussions of *musica mundana* and *humana* consist in large part of quotations from other writers, given in Italian or Latin: a Frate Angelo (who wrote a Latin treatise on musical practice called the *Fior angelico*), Poliziano, Lefèvre d'Étaples, Plutarch, Plato, Boethius, Dentice, and Celio Rodigino.

Ponzio's general treatment of the subject is displayed in a brief exchange of dialogue in which one of his interlocutors asks why, if people are composed of music, they need to study it. The main interlocutor (Il Rev. Sig. Don Paolo) responds that the nature of the soul is a difficult matter to study, and there has been wide disagreement as to where the soul is located in the body. The relation between the body and soul thus consists in a certain "hidden harmony,"[126] which cannot be heard but is manifest in a similarity of proportion. Yet just because we are formed out of music, it does not necessarily follow that we know the subject automatically, "because nature in this case cannot work by itself without the help of practice. Thus it happens that the person who wishes to know music must practice it."[127] Although Ponzio does not pursue this argument into a longer discussion of musical perception, the passage explains his continued

126. Pietro Ponzio, *Ragionamento di musica* . . . (Parma: Viotti, 1588), p. 5: "E cioè aveniva per non sapere il luogo suo certo; cosi voglio dire, che trà il corpo, e l'anima è un'occulta harmonia, nè si può sentire" (That is, it happened by not knowing its precise place; thus I wish to say that between body and soul there is a certain hidden harmony that cannot be heard).

127. Ibid.: "perche la natura in questo non può da se operare. se non con l'aiuto dell'essercitio: quindi nasce, che fa bisogno essercitarsi volendo saper Musica."

willingness to accept arguments based on Boethian or Pythagorean tradition, though that tradition has broadened sufficiently for him to have included this Socratic-sounding statement about musical education. Most of the rest of the treatise discusses practical matters, such as the composition of pieces in specific musical forms.

Ponzio's *Dialogo* (1595), his second treatise, resembles the *Ragionamento* in its combination of a Boethian introduction with an essentially practical treatise on composition, but it resolves the inconsistency in a much more satisfying way. In this work, Ponzio turns from an extended *laus musice* to an equally long discussion of Boethian proportion types and harmonic, arithmetic, and geometric means. Only in these proportions themselves, he notes, only in the discussion of number, do writers on music still agree; in their compositions they may differ radically from one another. Ponzio attributes these differences to some nine factors, all relating to the skill of the composer in exercising various elements of composition, such as observation of mode, variety or style, appropriateness of variation, and so on.[128]

He returns to this issue of disagreement among authors and rectifies his own abrupt narrative break between issues of theory and those of practice, when he discusses consonant and dissonant intervals in the writing of counterpoint. The interlocutors (Girolamo Sarego, Marco Verità, and Alessandro Bevilacqua) raise the familiar old question of whether the fourth is a consonance or a dissonance, citing numerous authorities, and frequently the same authorities, on both sides of the issue. Alessandro resolves the problem with a series of responses. First, he claims that when the philosophers called the fourth a consonance, they spoke according to theory and not practice; the ancients accepted only multiple and superparticular ratios as consonant (since they were "pure and simple") and believed that all consonant intervals were contained in the *senario*, or number six. Since the fourth met both criteria, they labeled it consonant.

This argument may avoid the question of why the ancients set up such criteria, but it has nonetheless the effect of historicizing the categories. Alessandro continues to explain the ancients' choices in terms of their historical context, by looking at their musical practice: "So in conclusion I will say that the above-mentioned philosophers called the fourth a consonance for the reasons already mentioned. Further, in their songs one did not see (as one sees in our time) three

128. Ponzio, *Dialogo, ove si tratta della theorica, e prattica di musica* . . . (Parma: Viotti, 1595), p. 45.

or four parts sounding together; but rather, there was one single musician with an instrument, with which he accompanied his voice, explicating his idea, and singing the poetry with diversity, and since he was alone, one could not discern any consonance or dissonance."[129] After people began singing with many parts together, they learned from experience that the fourth was not consonant like the other intervals in some similar categories. This experience came solely "from the judgment of the purified ear."[130] Alessandro turns for support to Zarlino (*Istitutioni* 1.1), who states that music reached its perfection through being heard, in the ability of its listeners to judge the good from the bad.

Ponzio's thought is thus not entirely a simple matter. Given that the bulk of each of his treatises is devoted to counterpoint and the practical tradition, it could be argued that the ability to historicize Pythagorean theory away to the sidelines is merely a more satisfactory means of marginalizing it than earlier writers had been able to muster. Yet the rest of the treatise is substantially improved in clarity in comparison with many earlier practical treatises, simply because such distracting issues as the harmonic genera have been relegated out of the discussions of modern practice and are classified as artifacts of antiquity. Like Tigrini, Ponzio invokes the authority of Zarlino in ways that serve the practical orientation of the subject at hand; he does not follow Zarlino in all his genuine complexity. "Zarlino" has come to mean, for many of these writers, a shorthand justification for relying on trained experience as the basis of musical judgment.

Among the writings of Fabio Paolini of Udine is a work devoted to the study of universal harmony, *Hebdomades, sive septem de septenario libri* (1589). Paolini, professor of Greek and philosophy in Venice, published several other works on the classics and on religion.[131] The *Hebdomades* is best understood in this context, a tradition especially

---

129. Ibid., pp. 80–81: "Si che per conchiusione diro', che i Filosofi già nominati per le ragioni predette chiamarono la Quarta, consonanza, stando ancora, che nelle loro cantilene non si vedevano (come à tempi nostri si vede) trè, e quattro parti insieme modulando, ma vi era un solo Musico con un'istromento, co'l quale accompagnava la sua voce, explicando il suo concetto, e cantando con diversità di Poesia, e per esser solo non si poteva discernere alcuna consonanza, nè dissonanza."

130. Ibid., p. 81: "Co'l guiditio della purgata orecchia."

131. The work's title describes him as "Fabii Paulini Utinensis Philosophi, et Graecas literas Venetiis profitentis." Fabio Paolini, *Hebdomades, sive septem de septenario libri* . . . (Venice: Senesi, 1589). Some of Paolini's other published works are *De Christi cruciabilis* (Venice, 1600); *De doctore humanitatis oratio* (Venice, 1588); and *Praelectiones Marciae seu commentaria in Thucydides* (Venice, 1603).

well-established in Venice of combining encyclopedic classical learning and Pythagorean number mysticism in a work whose main goal is the expression of a unity of knowledge crowned by theology.

As its title implies, the *Hebdomades* is a collection of seven books, each with seven chapters; unlike the similarly organized work by Giorgio Valla, the symbolism of the number seven is made explicitly manifest throughout the work. Paolini takes the reader through a set of topics, beginning with poetics and followed by music in general, *musica mundana* and *humana*, astrology, arithmetic, natural mysteries, and concluding with theology. Most of the actual information presented is argumentative rather than simply expository, selected to support his arguments about the unity of knowledge.

Paolini mines sources such as Zarlino, Vicentino, and Vanneo for information about Greek music; equally important to him are the usual works of Aristotle, Plato with Ficino's commentary, and Proclus. Orpheus is an especially prominent figure, exemplifying the unity of learning in poetry, music, and things divine. Music as a field is of secondary importance to Paolini; his main concern lies with the Pythagorean cosmology and metaphysics of harmony, and his intended audience seems to be mainly scholars of philosophy and theology. For Paolini, then, the Pythagorean harmonic tradition is very much alive but independent of music per se.

Pietro Girolamo Gentile Riccio's treatise, *Dell'armonia del mondo* (1605) is one of the last of these little works seriously devoted to Pythagorean musical thought. Gentile Riccio, "nobile savonese," wrote numerous minor literary works.[132] The *Armonia*, like the *Hebdomades*, illustrates one avenue that remained open to the Pythagorean tradition at and after the end of the century, that of encyclopedic religious speculation. Gentile Riccio's main interest throughout the *Armonia* is the contemplation of things divine; he wishes to advocate contemplation of the harmonic order of creation through his treatise.

Not surprisingly, Gentile Riccio takes little notice in his work of the philosophical and scientific controversies of the generation of musical scholars that immediately preceded him. His models seem rather to come from other encyclopedic Pythagorean works with a religious bent, such as that of Paolini. The first portion of the treatise offers a

132. Some of them are *Delle fisiche . . . intorno alla scienza dell'anima* (Venice, 1618); *I sospetti, favola boschereccia* (Venice, 1608); and various collections of his own poetry, as well as editions of other poets.

standard Pythagorean discussion of *musica mundana, humana,* and *instru-mentalis.* Gentile Riccio explicitly rejects any related pagan arguments about the nature of the soul as seen in classical authors in favor of Christian doctrine,[133] but otherwise he offers little that is new.

The second half of the treatise discusses the importance of the effect of contemplation and enjoyment of music on the human soul. The closer the soul gets to the divine, he argues, the more delight it can take in music itself. This was even true of ancient musicians like Arion and Orpheus. He concludes that the Scriptures mention music in the service of God as well as the constant singing of the heavenly hosts: "The claim is very evident that music has its immediate origin in heaven and that the language of that angelic citizens of that blessed land is also harmonic."[134]

Gentile Riccio's goal, then, is to further the religious devotion of the reader, not the study of music for its own ends. A task of this sort need have little to do with the professional debates of his generation, as long as it does not seek its adherents among those who are participating in such debates. This lack of ongoing contact with the field's active scholarship tends, however, to limit the creativity of further writing or scholarship in this direction. Thus this Pythagorean-influenced religious prose, while it does not disappear immediately, gradually loses its intellectual impetus.

Ercole Bottrigari

In the musical writings of the Bolognese aristocrat Ercole Bottrigari (1531–1612), the new definitions and methods in the field have begun to settle into place. Bottrigari's writings on music date from the later years of his life, when he had retired to a family home in S. Alberto.[135] In addition to several works on music (both published and in manuscript), Bottrigari published Italian translations of

133. Piergirolamo [Pietro Girolamo] Gentile Riccio, *Dell'armonia del mondo . . .* (Venice: Combi, 1605), p. 28.
134. Ibid., p. 161: "Evidentissimo argomento, che la Musica ha immediata origine in Cielo, poi che la favella de gli Angioli Cittadini di quella beata patria altresi è tutta armonica."
135. For biographical information on Bottrigari, see O. Mischiati (with A. Cioni), "Bottrigari, Ercole," *DBI;* Carol McClintock, "Bottrigari, Ercole," *New Grove;* also Giovanni Fantuzzi, "Bottrigari, Ercole," in *Notizie degli scrittori bolognesi* (Bologna, 1792), pp. 320–31; Ugo Sesini, "L'Umanesimo musicale di Ercole Bottrigari," in *Momenti di teoria musicale tra medioevo e rinascimento,* ed. Guiseppe Vecchi (Bologna: Tamari, 1966), pp. 43–76. The small booklet by Enrico Bottrigari, *Notizie biografiche intorno agli studi e alla vita del Cavaliere Ercole Bottrigari* (Bologna, 1842), is less than reliable.

Latin treatises (both ancient and modern) and some collections of poetry. Eleven years at the court of Alfonso II in Ferrara brought him
into contact with numerous men of letters, not only Patrizi but also
Tasso, whose side Bottrigari took in the ongoing literary debates. He
also corresponded with Zarlino.[136]

Bottrigari wrote no single, comprehensive music treatise. Many of
his works are dialogues; most of them take issue with the arguments
of at least one contemporary. Bottrigari maintains in his writings
Zarlino's distinction between "history" and "method," though he does
not accept Zarlino's Pythagorean approach to number or his claims
for the superiority of "natural" musical instruments over artificial
ones. He has read of Galilei's sound experiments and, apparently, duplicated some of them himself. Yet he does not turn his back on the
scholarly traditions of earlier generations; he does not reject or abandon classical authority, be it Aristotle or Boethius. Rather, his attitudes toward their authority and the kinds of uses to which he puts
them show the effects of the steady and cumulative change since the
days of Burtius and Valla.

In his dialogue *Il Desiderio* (1594), Bottrigari takes up the familiar
topic of intonation and tuning. Although this subject had been addressed by scholars for the past hundred years, his concerns are far
different from those of the early years of the century, as are the tools
of his argument. To set the context of the dialogue, Bottrigari opens
the work as one of the interlocutors (Sr. Gratioso Desiderio, who also
appeared in Zarlino's *Dimostrationi*) returns from a concert in which
different types of instruments (winds, strings, and keyboard) were
played together. The result had been unpleasantly discordant, despite
the skill of the performers. The other interlocutor, Sr. Benelli, proceeds to explain this discord in terms of the physical nature of the instruments, the ways in which each type produces sounds of distinct
pitches.

Bottrigari (in the person of his interlocutor Benelli) identifies
some instruments, the "alterable" ones, as possessing more or less
infinitely variable pitch within the limits of their range; such instruments include the trombone and the lira (using unfretted strings,
like a modern violin). Others are totally stable in pitch; that is, once
they are tuned, their pitches are produced by exciting individual
parts of the instrument, each one of which produces a single, stable
pitch. Keyboard instruments such as the organ or harpsichord fall

136. See Bologna, Civ. Mus. B 46, fol. 163v.

into this category. He defines a third, intermediary class of instruments whose established pitches can be altered easily. Lutes, whose frets can be moved, are classified in this group; so are flutes, whose fixed fingerholes can be altered through half-holing or changes in embouchure.[137]

Because of these characteristics, continues Bottrigari, each type of instrument is tuned differently. Those of fixed pitch such as harpsichords are traditionally tuned to Ptolemy's diatonic, the scale "closest to sense and reason" (though of course it limits the number of available keynotes in a given tuning). Lutes, owing to their frets, are tuned according to Aristoxenus's scale, with equal semitones. Flutes fall somewhere in between, approximating the Ptolemaic scale but in fact usually constructed more by trial and experiment than by method.

Therefore, instruments may play together without discord only if the fixed-pitch and partly alterable instruments do not play together in the same group, because they play different types of scales. Bottrigari then goes on to discuss tempered intervals and scales, the development of the chromatic genus in antiquity as an adjunct to the diatonic, and other details of tuning, concluding with extensive descriptions of performing musical groups that combine instruments in various ways. In addition to the usual range of classical authorities, Bottrigari mentions several moderns who have written on the subject of temperaments: Fogliano (whom Bottrigari favors), Aron, Lanfranco, Galilei, Zarlino, and Salinas.[138]

Throughout the treatise, Bottrigari examines musical pitch and proportion either in terms of the specific behavior of types of physical objects or in terms of a system of pitches designed by historical persons for the purposes of pleasing the ear. Although he observes that consonances can be measured in orderly proportions, there is no reverence for the Pythagorean tradition; Bottrigari does not invoke cosmology to account for why a given scale is preferred, though neither does he offer a detailed alternative. Lest there be any doubts about locating music's effects in the level of culture rather than cosmic mathematics, he recounts a fictitious narrative about the earliest origins of tempered scales. Here he argues that the temperaments have

137. Ercole Bottrigari, *Il Desiderio, overo de' concerti di varii strumenti musicali: dialogo di Allemanno Benelli* (Venice: Ricciardo Amadino, 1594), p. 5; for an English translation, see that of Carol MacClintock, *Il Desiderio, or Concerning the Playing Together of Various Musical Instruments* (N.p.: American Institute of Musicology, 1962). Citations are to the former.

138. Bottrigari, *Desiderio*, pp. 36–37.

no theoretical basis and that this lack is in fact in accordance with music's true task, that of delighting the ear:

> Now, my opinion about the origin and discovery of temperament is this: these early masters, practical builders of clavicembali or organs, proposed building them within the bounds of the most perfect Diatonic Ditone. . . . When they came to giving each string or pipe its particular sound, perhaps even with the help of the Harmonic Rule or, as we say, monochord, . . . they found some of its consonances still lacking, or to put it better, very far from their forms. They knew that such a system could not contain more than a certain number of voices or strings, or keys, so they tried to see if by leaving reason aside and those things known only by their true proportion, whether they could satisfy and please the sense of hearing, which is the principal object of harmony.[139]

Bottrigari further deflates the Pythagorean tradition in his treatise *Il Melone* (1602).[140] In the final pages of this short work, which singles out Zarlino for special criticism, Bottrigari attacks the common portrayal of the music of the spheres. By analyzing several classical passages on the subject (particularly Psellus and Pliny), he concludes that the celestial harmony they claimed to find in the distances between the planets was that of the chromatic genus, not the diatonic as has been assumed by modern writers (as well as by the writers of late antiquity).[141] Further, Bottrigari has removed himself so far from the Pythagorean analytic tradition that he uses this discovery only to impugn the critical abilities of his colleagues in their textual analysis and historical understanding. To Bottrigari, this new evidence does not demolish the Pythagorean tradition simply because, to him, it is no longer standing.

139. Ibid., pp. 37–38: "Hora l'opinione mia d'intorno alla origine, e ritrovamento di essa participatione è questa, che essendosi quei primi Mastri pratici fabricatori de'Clavacembali, ò Organi proposti la fabrica di quelli dentro à'termini del Systema Diatonico Diatono incitato perfettissimo. . . . Venuti essi à dare il suono particolare à ciascuna corda, ò canna, forse bene anchora, con l'aiuto della Regola Armonica, ò diciamo Monacordo, . . . trovando . . . di esse consonantie anchora mancarne alcune, ò per dir meglio, molto lontane dalle forme loro: e sappendo essi insieme, che tal sistema in se non contiene, se non essa certa quantità di voci, ò corde, ò tasti dimostrativi, si posero à far prova, se col lasciar da banda la ragione, e le non conosciute piu che tanto da loro proportioni vere di esse consonantie potessero sodisfare, e compiacere al senso dell'udito, ilche è proprio principale oggetto dell'Armonia."
140. Bottrigari, *Il Melone, discorso armonico* . . . (Ferrara: Baldini, 1602; facsimile with intro. Giuseppe Vecchi, Bologna: Forni, 1969). Vecchi dates the composition of the *Melone* to about 1592.
141. Bottrigari, *Melone*, pp. 34–37.

Bottrigari returns to a textual and historical approach to Pythagoreanism in his unpublished essay, *Lo enimma di Pitagora* (1609).[142]
This brief essay is based on Galilei's experiments as described in his
Dialogo. Bottrigari illustrates and explains the construction of a device to demonstrate the changes in pitch caused by increased tension:
a monochord with a pulley serving as one of the bridges, to permit
the easy fixing of various weights to the end of the string.[143] His results duplicate those of Galilei, yet he still finds fault with Galilei's interpretation. Galilei should have realized, claims Bottrigari, that since
so many other ancient sources repeated the incorrect stories of
Pythagoras and the hammers, even though these anecdotes contradicted observable fact, there must be another way to interpret these
texts than simply the (factually incorrect) literal one. Bottrigari offers
some brief suggestions for alternate interpretations: perhaps the ratios might refer to dimensions of the relevant weights, or to weights
attached to the string in various other ways. Perhaps the whole passage should be understood as some sort of allegory.

The manuscript breaks off without coming to a conclusion. Nonetheless, the completed portion is sufficient to display Bottrigari's analytic process. He is convinced by the demonstrable evidence about
sounding bodies and their behavior. This behavior seems so obvious,
in fact, that he cannot conceive of the ancients' having been ignorant
of it. Thus the discrepancy must lie in the proper—in this case, probably allegorical—reading of ancient texts.

Bottrigari also applies his knowledge to sounding bodies to new use
in his studies of theaters and acoustics. His unpublished treatise *La
mascara* (1598), based heavily on Barbaro's Vitruvius, deals with the
construction of theaters using geometric principles. These geometric
symmetries and proportions serve not simply for aesthetic effect but
also to maximize the transmission of sound. Also from Vitruvius
comes the basis for his discussion of acoustic dishes around the edges
of the theater, designed to assist in amplifying sounds of particular
pitches.[144] Bottrigari applies his knowledge of resonant spheres and
hemispheres in discussing their size and placement.

Bottrigari's approach to the study of music, whether it be history,
acoustics, or performance, is one that modern readers would find relatively familiar. Although they might disagree with him on details,
they would find his use of observed phenomena described by means

142. Bottrigari, "Lo enimma di Pitagora delle proportioni delle consonantie
musicali ritrovate da lui per li favolosi suoni de' Martelli . . . ," Bologna, Civ. Mus. B
44, fols. 21r–26r.
143. Ibid., fol. 24r.
144. Bottrigari, "La mascara, overo della fabrica de' teatri, e dello apparato delle
scene tragisatiricomiche, dialogo . . . " Bologna, Civ. Mus. B 45, pp. 168–87.

of mathematics, his textual analysis of historical sources, and his stylistic criticism of modern musical performance all to be well-established and perhaps even obvious methods of musical scholarship. Comparison with the writers of even a half-century earlier, however, reveals the speed and degree of change, not just in degree of knowledge but in method and classification of the discipline. By the early years of the seventeenth century, the definitions of music and its study that Bottrigari employs have become the typical approach for Italian scholars and musicians.

Toward a New Synthesis

The changes in the field of music between about 1560 and 1590 were more sweeping and fundamental than those of the entire preceding century. Yet many, perhaps most, of the individual arguments that constituted these later changes had been posed originally by the scholars of the late fifteenth and early sixteenth centuries. The achievements of these late sixteenth-century writers, from Zarlino to Bottrigari, lay in their ability to distance themselves from particular issues and battles and widen their vision to an analysis of the field of music as a whole. This ability, in turn, required mature readings of ancient texts as understood in a variety of contexts, as well as a critical distance in appraising the efforts of earlier generations of modern scholars.

This newer, more complex approach to ancient and modern textual authority arose from several causes, foremost among them the appearance of the last important new sources for understanding Greek music and music theory. The discovery of Greek musical examples by Mei confirmed the claims Zarlino had put forward on the basis of textual analysis. This new evidence laid to rest the claims of persons such as Vicentino (or his rival Danckerts) that ancient music, like modern, was polyphonic. As a result, musical scholars could no longer assume that ancient practice resembled that of the modern age and that therefore ancient theory could speak directly to modern custom. However simple or complex might be a given writer's response to this historical discontinuity, its existence had to be admitted once Galilei's *Dialogo* had brought the evidence into public view.

Another cause was access to the treatise of Aristoxenus (awkwardly translated though it was), direct knowledge of which brought to an end the use of Aristoxenus as a straw man for the promotion of Ptolemy's moderate Pythagorean theory as advocated by Boethius. When read by Galilei, Mei, and Bottrigari, Aristoxenus's theories began to emerge as a thoughtful and reasoned alternative to Pythagorean theory. These scholars ceased to speak of ancient theory as a monolith, favoring instead the notion that there existed three rival schools of thought about music in antiquity. This reassessment of the past caused, in turn, a rethinking of the ways in which ancient thought could speak to modern experience.

Musical scholarship was also able to reap the benefits of the accumulating generations of general humanistic scholarship and textual criticism. In some cases, this meant a more complete reading of a given ancient author; the interpretation of Plato by Patrizi as compared with that by Gaffurio serves as a useful example. Zarlino's careful assessments of passing references and brief remarks about music and musical practices in classical literary sources, employing notions such as anachronism, audience, intent, and word usage as aids to interpretation and understanding, mark the beginning of this new era of textual analysis as the research tool of a second discipline.

Of equal importance is Zarlino's attempt to link systematically the mathematical study of proportion as seen in sounding bodies, with Aristotelian natural philosophy. This connection goes back to Giorgio Valla, who had promoted the status of music as a midpoint between mathematics and nature. Scholars such as Fogliano and Cardano had begun to explore elements of that connection. As a result of their work, scholars began to move away from definitions of "music" as pure proportion and toward the study of proportion as seen in specific sounding bodies.

Zarlino's efforts to unite these Pythagorean and Aristotelian systems, with their different claims about causality and the rationality of nature itself, were perhaps doomed to cause controversy and dispute. Yet they forced the articulation of new arguments by others as they tried to establish the exact nature of their disagreement. Vincenzo Galilei's long quarrel with Zarlino illustrates this process at work. To attack Zarlino's descriptions of the intonation of modern singers, he had to defend the role of the trained human ear as an objective measuring device. Without this argument, the testing of observed phenomena against known, controlled measurements (normally the monochord) could not proceed. This process in turn allowed for the expression of Aristotelian "qualities" (such as the changes in pitch caused by a body's thickness or thinness) by mathematical means. Finally, by historicizing Aristotle as humanistic interpretations had historicized other types of musical analysis, Galilei shifted scholarly attention from the results of ancient authors to their methods, distinguishing the notion of progress in the understanding of nature from that of historical understanding.

Pythagorean theory suffered at the hands of both humanistic and scientific analysis. No longer could musical scholars claim that antiquity spoke with the single voice of the Pythagorean musical tradition. Further, they had to be more specific in defending the relationship between ancient theory and the modern world. The new evidence about the importance of ancient poetics (of whatever sort) to ancient music could not be ignored; Zarlino's attempt to subsume poetics under Pythagorean theory via metrics simply did not bear up under the argumentative strain, and it faded away from scholarly discourse without serious attack or defense.

Further, Galilei's findings about the production of musical consonances by means of non-Pythagorean ratios dealt the claims of Pythagorean theory to universality a blow from which it never fully recovered. Perhaps if the articulation of theories about sound as wave motion and the discovery of the harmonic series had occurred during the sixteenth century, Zarlino would have been partly vindicated, as some modern scholars have suggested. Yet the claims about the ontological status of pure number as prior to nature and the source of its order would in any case have been subject to serious revision when not only different proportions, but irrational ones, were found to produce the same audible consonances as those on which Pythagorean theory was based.

These new approaches to the study of music left some serious issues for later resolution. How far the differences in musical practice among different peoples should be attributed primarily to culture or how much to natural factors was never directly addressed. The musician's own task in light of these differences in musical preference is likewise unresolved; whether the musician should "delight the ears" or "elevate the mind" had been a matter of debate since Gaffurio's day and before. Elimination of the old Pythagorean theories of musical consonance and their effects on the listener altered the terms of this problem but could not resolve it.

Once this Pythagorean standard for judging the value, effectiveness, and purposes of music had been removed, a new way of assessing the quality of musical composition and performance needed to be established. If vocal music is to be connected closely with poetics, some provision must be made for the place of purely instrumental music. If musical styles are understood as subject to change, the causes of those changes must be understood and evaluated. These issues survived to confront the musical scholars of the seventeenth century.

Conclusions

The distance between Burtius and Bottrigari seems greater than the years that separate them. Their argumentation, use of sources, mathematical analysis, and even their prose styles stand in sharp contrast to each other. Despite these differences, they can still be seen not simply as opposites but as participants at either end of a single scholarly program; many of the questions answered by Bottrigari and his contemporaries—the interpretation of the tale of Pythagoras and the hammers, the nature of music among the ancient Greeks and Romans, the kinds of tuning systems used when different sorts of instruments play together—had first been raised a century earlier. The route to satisfactory answers had been far longer and more twisted than the earlier scholars had anticipated; for such questions had gone to the heart of the discipline itself.

The main cause of the beginning of the transformation was the volume of Greek sources translated at the end of the fifteenth century. Yet, as in any field, access to sources could not be equated with their mastery. Progress in the depth of understanding and sophistication with which these texts could be used was slow and uneven over the next fifty years or so, as they were gradually incorporated into the field's canon. Such lengthy periods of assimilation of ancient sources are hardly unique to music; for they were common to Renaissance scholarship in many disciplines.

The particular configurations of this development, however, are different in each case. In music, a strong scholarly tradition had already existed, a tradition based on a few classical sources. Its principal ancient text, Boethius's *De musica,* not only advocated a particular

283

interpretive tradition but offered a synthesis and summary of ancient scholarship in a manner that presented that tradition as the culmination, and ultimately the consensus, of ancient learning on the subject. It therefore made sense for Renaissance writers to assume initially that these "new" ancient sources could be accommodated to this tradition as they knew it, according to the standards and criticisms of Boethius. In fact, many of these courses did come from the Pythagorean tradition that Boethius promoted. Moreover, an error of dating led them to accept initially the works of the late Byzantine encyclopedist Bryennius, also based on the Pythagorean tradition, as texts from late antiquity. These factors reinforced the initial sense that ancient tradition, in the end at least, was unified in its agreement on analytic terms and methods.

The earliest uses of these sources by Renaissance scholars in their written works followed a similar pattern. Gaffurio, among the first to employ them, tended to use them as collateral or anecdotal evidence for arguments based on Boethius or another traditional source; the new sources appeared simply as a brief reference. Giorgio Valla, in contrast, paraphrased long sections interspersed by organizational materials of his own authorship; nonetheless, he revealed his own philosophical orientation in the choices he made regarding that organization and the selection of the summaries or paraphrases.

Yet despite their evident usefulness, these ancient sources also served almost immediately as the occasion for dispute and debate. In particular, they lay behind the apparently incessant squabbles over the minutiae of tuning systems throughout the first half of the sixteenth century. Not only had the Boethian tradition focused on pitch, but the new sources offered new sets of numbers and names for pitch systems. Scholars began to see almost immediately that these descriptions did not quite agree with one another, but the location of the causes eluded them. Proceeding on the assumption that the ancient tradition was essentially uniform, they attempted to account for these discrepancies in various ways. The scholarly expertise of a dissident author might be impugned, allowing the Renaissance scholar to dispense with that source. Terminology and definitions could be adjusted among various authors to reveal a basic agreement hidden beneath apparent conflicts; yet the precise details of this supposed agreement could not be fixed to the satisfaction of all, or even most, Renaissance scholars at any given time. These conflicts could not be resolved until the analysis of both ancient musical practice and ancient musical scholarship was historicized. In the meantime, scholars might continue to wage war over the nature of Ptolemy's "syntonic" scale or the size of the minor semitone without any possibility of settlement.

The solution to these problems of sources had to lie, at least in part, in the development of better principles for interpreting the sources, and those principles were to come from the realm of humanist textual criticism. At first, however, the humanists themselves only offered more complications. Their initial contribution to the technical field may have been the new translations, but their own interest in music arose particularly from their studies of poetry and drama and the social roles music played in antiquity. The sources employed for these tasks, primarily the standard literary texts read by humanists, appeared not to correlate at all with the technical discourse on music, either in antiquity or in the Renaissance, and to contribute most to the rhetorical *laus musice*. It is only reasonable, then, that the development of a comprehensive approach to these very diverse source materials took some time.

Yet musical scholarship did not consist solely, or for many scholars even primarily, of the analysis of ancient writings on the subject. Because it was a quadrivial field, the study of music had proceeded not by historical investigation but by means of logical and mathematical proofs; many of the newly translated sources themselves emphasized a definition of music as a midpoint between pure mathematics and natural philosophy. The scholarly issues in such a subject could hardly be reduced to matters of textual criticism, especially since the important questions began increasingly to deal with the relationship between mathematical analysis and physical experience.

This basis in the quadrivium also contributed to the general framework and narrative for understanding changes in the informational content of the field. Since musical consonances were understood as the fundamental order of the universe, statements about them could be true or false to varying degrees in any given case, but the standard for evaluating those statements was seen as objective and unchanging. Ancient sources might be correct or incorrect in their description of this order, and knowledge about this order might accumulate or be dispersed through the passage of time. Ancient sources could also be superseded by new knowledge; but in every case, the acquisition of that knowledge was understood as the discovery of universal laws. When this approach was used as a method of textual criticism for interpreting the newly available ancient sources, it was impossible to impose a consistent reading, or one that found agreement among working scholars; yet it did not itself display flaws sufficient to single it out as a cause of the interpretive problems.

It is not surprising, given the complexity of these issues and the effect any major changes in music would have on other disciplines, that, after this first wave of scholarly interest, an extended period of lively but uneven experimentation accompanied by often-acrimonious dissent and debate would precede any new attempts at synthesis. The variety in musical studies by 1550 testifies to the subject's broad interest and appeal. In the later debates can be seen not only the importance of music as a discipline in relation to other disciplines but also the parallels and distinctions between the changes in musical studies and those underway in the related fields. The importance of the changes in musical thought should be viewed, therefore, in terms of their impact on related disciplines as well as on the music itself.

Zarlino's division of the field into a humanistic art of music and a science of sounding bodies served, even as it inaugurated a new classification of musical studies, to distinguish the dual influences on the subject since the late fifteenth century. The most significant advances came as a product not of mathematical or humanistic means alone but of the application of a combination of these analytic tools by numerous scholars. The field, then, should be seen in the context of the debates and changes taking place concurrently in both humanistic studies and those of mathematics and natural philosophy.

Music's position as a quadrivial discipline yet related to natural philosophy and closely linked to practice and experience would suggest an important role for it in the scientific debates on the use of mathematics and experimentation in the sciences in general. Historians have already examined this change in scholarly method in the fields of astronomy and mechanics. The case of musical studies resembles these other disciplines in some ways and is unique in others. Certainly Renaissance musical scholarship did not have the same relationship to its scholastic past as did many other scientific fields, for which change was marked by the rejection of a medieval Aristotelian tradition. Despite Boethius's professed desire to reconcile Platonic and Aristotelian thought, his *De musica* had placed the discipline firmly in the very non-Aristotelian camp of late Pythagorean analysis, though admittedly with greater or lesser Aristotelian influence of various types at any given time. Since music's position as a subdiscipline of mathematics was not initially contested, any debates about the suitability of mathematical analysis did not question its role in some absolute sense, as was the case in some other fields. Rather, they questioned the nature of the relationship between mathematics and physical phenomena. The most common arena for such discussion lay in the behavior of sounding bodies, especially though not exclusively musical instruments.

Fogliano's work was an important early step in these changes. He took the mathematical proportions of the Pythagorean tradition as true, verifiable descriptions of the phenomena of sounding strings. Yet he shifted his definition of sound slightly, from the "sonorous number" of Boethius to the disturbances of the air which can be measured by the number attached to a sounding body or string; similarly, he altered the definition of a consonant interval to include only mathematical regularity and the listening ear's pleasurable response. These changes allowed him to pursue the measurement of sounding strings with more detail because he had thereby discarded the normative requirements of the Pythagorean tradition. They also allowed an expansion of mathematical measurement beyond those narrowly defined aspects of sounding bodies which had been labeled "quantities," to those previously classified as nonquantifiable "qualities."

These changes seem, nonetheless, not to have been widely perceived as threats to the Pythagorean tradition. One reason was Fogliano's own disinclination to pursue many of his most original ideas to their logical conclusions. In addition, his work conformed in many other ways to the expectations of contemporary music treatises. It focused on the use of the monochord to demonstrate the value of one or more tuning systems over others, a very standard subject. Also, unlike later writers, his work maintained the traditional view of the discipline's progress and development: as the progressive accumulation of knowledge about natural or universal laws of behavior.

Cardano expanded on some of the issues raised by Fogliano, especially in his attention to the human perception of consonance. He too did not break out of the basic arguments considered acceptable within the Pythagorean tradition; his statements about the nature of consonance are based on the mathematical orderliness of sounds, recognizable by the soul because of its similar nature. Yet by developing an explanation of consonance based primarily on theories of sense perception, Cardano expanded the range of subjects normally studied in terms of number. Moreover, his work continues the trend away from immediate recourse to Pythagorean explanation, in favor of analysis based on physical objects, their perception, and their measurement. It also demonstrates an eclectic combination of approaches to not only music but numerous disciplines, mixing traditional musical mathematics with a variety of Aristotelian and other analytic principles, in addition to such fields as judicial astrology.

The development of a genuinely independent study of sounding bodies, which followed Zarlino's division of the field into history and method, began to bear fruit with the work of Galilei and Bottrigari. At this point, the study of sound as vibratory motion comes most nearly to resemble mechanics, which had previously undergone a very different historical development. Bottrigari's writings also recall the importance of the Vitruvian architectural tradition, both for raising anew questions about harmonic proportion and aesthetics and, especially, for encouraging the application of physical measurement and analysis not only to small sounding bodies such as musical instruments but to large constructions such as theaters.

Yet the role of mathematics in the analysis of these physical phenomena should not be understood simply as an expansion of the measurement and mastery of physical objects and experience. Musical mathematics also lost some very important ground during this transition; most obvious was the demise of its ability to explain music's beauty and its emotional effects on the listener. The effects of this change in turn were, however, much greater. From this point, there began the slow retreat from scholarly belief in Pythagorean proportion as providing a unified set of principles for explanations of cosmic order at any other level. The retreat was very gradual and extended well beyond the bounds of this discussion. Many astronomers, for example, still tended to find notions of cosmic harmony appealing (as did, for example, Kepler, though Vincenzo Galilei's son Galileo certainly did not); but they no longer shared this discourse with musical scholars. While this explanatory system disappeared at different rates in different fields, it lost any infusion of new energy or research from its former core discipline, musical scholarship.

This loss, however, could also be seen as a gain for humanistic studies. These fields were equally contributors to the changes in music and beneficiaries of the results. A great difference can nonetheless be seen in how modern scholars have tended to shape their historical studies of the sciences and humanities in the sixteenth century. To the sciences have gone the search for origins, the essential early stages of the rapid development of the sciences in the seventeenth century. To the history of humanism, on the other hand, has fallen the question of endings, of when to mark the conclusion of the Renaissance as a humanistic project. In the case of musical thought, that project looks sufficiently lively not only to maintain itself but to undertake some significant intellectual conquests. From this perspective, music—a field never considered a humanistic discipline—was, during the middle and later sixteenth century, taken over and assimilated by humanistic studies. Even the name itself, "music," no longer referred to the study of sounding bodies but to the cultural product that made use of them, which was studied by the increasingly well-honed humanistic tools of historical analysis and social appropriateness. The dominant sense is one of change and development, not decline.

The antagonism toward scientific thought that had frequently been the rhetorical stance of early humanists is certainly no longer present. One reason for its absence is the evident success of the humanists in establishing themselves in general Italian curricula, so that by 1500 even mathematicians received some humanistic training. By 1600 the lines have become very blurry indeed; while Mei could certainly be identified as a humanist, the cases of Galilei or Bottrigari are not nearly so clear. The latter two wrote especially on subjects that had little to do with humanistic studies as such, and they often relied on experiment or experience to support an argument. Yet all three could move with ease from mathematics to textual analysis as the argument demanded. This ability bespeaks an increasing familiarity with the acceptance of humanistic studies even in nonhumanistic disciplines.

Most striking in the involvement of late Renaissance humanism with musical thought is the degree to which humanism had come to denote not simply subject fields but methods of study. The importance of later humanist thought in the development of historical writing, analysis, and sensibility has in recent years come to be more greatly appreciated. In the case of musical thought, these principles of historical analysis are applied to a field in which they had previously been of only minor analytic importance. The central role of specifically historical analysis is seen in Zarlino's terminology; he referred to the humanistic portion of the field, that which later kept the name "music," as "history." He and his successors claimed that these studies did more than offer better ways of reading ancient texts or of writing the poetry they might wish to set to music; they spoke to the general principles by which the field was defined and studied. Historical explanations had to compete directly with the Pythagorean interpretive tradition in offering solutions to the field's major questions, and usually the historical explanations won.

Further, these principles of cultural analysis could be extended, in smaller but significant ways, from changes over time to changes over space. The differences between ancient Greek or Roman customs and those of sixteenth-century Italian cities and courts began to be compared with differences between Italians and Germans, Moslems, or modern Greeks, or between Tuscans and Lombards. These issues remained peripheral for most musical scholars, but they reveal a continued level of creativity and change in the use of humanistic methods and interpretative strategies.

The frequent combination of humanistic and mathematical training in the same persons weighs against an attempt to account for the changes in musical thought by explanations based on professional, institutional, or even geographic rivalries between camps of scholars; yet it is difficult, given the relatively few persons involved, to speak of significant trends in this regard. The changing roles of such scholars as professionals in the sixteenth century, and the effects of these changes on their work, have received increasing attention of late. Musical thought might appear to contribute little definitive evidence to this issue except its variability. Nonetheless, a few features merit brief discussion.

First, the career paths of these writers were fairly diverse. Some held posts as professors or lecturers; others lived mainly from private patronage. Many worked as cathedral musicians. Others held various humanistic appointments. No particular trend stands out, though the number of university mathematicians writing on music did decline by the end of the sixteenth century. Those employed as professional musicians tended to place a greater emphasis on their work on the practical tradition than did those who apparently did not perform at all, though this seems only to be expected. The latter, conversely, tended to be freer from modern conventions in their approach to ancient sources in particular. But of course the example of Zarlino serves as a reminder that such descriptions are tendencies and not dichotomies.

Diversity also marks the geographic location and geographic mobility of these scholars. Some, such as Zarlino, remained in one place at a single position for most of their careers. Others, for example, Gaffurio, moved fairly frequently. No city stands out as a particular center; while Florence and Venice produced or employed quite a few of these scholars, many also worked at Bologna, Rome, and Milan. This diffusion of scholarship among urban centers would tend to limit the effects of any one political regime, or change of regimes, on the field. The political upheavals of sixteenth-century Italy have left no measurable impact on the writings or argumentation of individual scholars or on the field itself. In this regard, the case of musical thought contributes to an interpretation of sixteenth-century Italian cultural and intellectual life that is only partially related to the political narrative of the period. It also supports the notion that this era saw the increasing development of a common cultural and intellectual community across the peninsula, in which particular urban centers might or might not play a significant role.

Also notable in its absence is the Tridentine church. While the council issued some general statements about musical style and some individual reformers took an interest in religious music, these efforts seem not to have affected scholarship. Research and writing offer no evidence of having been steered one way or another because of ecclesiastical interests or restrictions; nor do scholars appear to have been driven either into or out of the discipline as a result of ideological conflict, religious or otherwise. It is quite possible that related fields such as Pythagorean cosmological speculation, especially prominent in sixteenth-century Venice, would show more evidence of such concerns, especially owing to the subject's links both with theology and with Cabalistic thought. Musical scholarship as such, however, was apparently neither seriously promoted nor discouraged by religious interests or institutions. It can be added to the large list of examples illustrating the limitations of another common assumption, that the Counter-Reformation exemplified and monopolized Italian thought in the later sixteenth century.

The case of musical thought thus appears not to support many of the standard historiographic conventions demarcating the end of the Renaissance with a narrative of decline. It does, however, offer some points of departure for an alternative discussion of the epoch's later stages; certainly it would tend to push the chronological limits, given that most significant changes took place after 1550. This fact, if standing alone, might help to support a claim that these changes in musical thought should be thought of as belonging to some later period. Yet, as has been seen, the questions and issues that drove the field had been set by 1500, in ways that seemed consistent with other contemporary developments. Insofar as such labels are useful, there seems to be no reason to regard musical thought as belonging to anything but the "Renaissance." By 1600, conversely, the field was recognizably different; writings on music began to treat different problems and address different questions, and to do so in methods and terms based on the field's redefinition in the late sixteenth century. Some other label would appear to be appropriate for writings after this point.

But larger issues can be seen as well, especially since the debates about the nature of music involved debates about the nature and even the identity of related disciplines. The boundaries, however loosely circumscribed, between groups of scholarly, literary, and intellectual interest in the fifteenth century—circles identifiable as humanists, scholastics, Platonists, and so on—have helped to identify and predict such matters as interest in classical sources, career paths, issues and methods of concern, and the relationships between disciplines as studied and practiced. During the course of the debates on music, many of these labels were being stretched and altered. None of the traditions in musical scholarship appear to have been sterile or moribund; in fact, it is the very liveliness and creativity with which so many tools and methods were combined that changed them. Yet the degree of change is difficult to overlook.

Humanists and their influence in musical thought may serve here as a useful example, since they are so often considered exemplary of the Renaissance in general, though other traditions can be seen to undergo similar changes. By the late sixteenth century, humanistic influence has so permeated the field at every level as to be no longer clearly distinguishable as a separate element. It did not serve as a predictor of which ancient sources a scholar used or how they were read, nor of more general professional, intellectual, and political interests. Scholastic classifications such as the "quadrivium" had essentially ceased to exist, and the histories of disciplines could be discussed as distinct from the disciplines themselves. By 1600, the Renaissance questions and debates about music had been successfully resolved. Their resolution set a new agenda for scholarship in the arts and sciences.

Glossary

For a fuller discussion of these terms, see Boethius, *Fundamentals of Music,* trans. Calvin M. Bower (New Haven: Yale University Press, 1989).

Diapason: The octave, composed of the ratio 2:1, or duple; a consonant interval. Some sources treat these three types of terminology (diapason, octave, duple) as synonyms; others prefer one or the other depending on whether they wish to focus attention on the interval as constituted by stepwise motion through a scale (octave or diapason), or by the ratio of string length used to produce the sounds (duple).

Diapente: The perfect fifth, composed of the ratio 3:2, or sesquialtera; a consonant interval.

Diatessaron: The perfect fourth, composed of the ratio 4:3, or sesquitertia; traditionally a consonant interval, but gradually perceived as dissonant.

Genera of harmony: Three possible ways of dividing the tetrachord in establishing a particular pitch system; the highest and lowest strings maintain their fixed proportion and pitch, while the middle two are moved to achieve a series of intervals in some version of the listed fractions of the tone (ratio 9:8): *diatonic,* ½–1–1; *chromatic,* ½–½–1 ½; or *enharmonic,* ¼–¼–2.

Greater Perfect System: The fifteen-note system of strings and pitches described by ancient (Greek) theorists; its approximate pitch ranged from a' to A. The system was based on tetrachords and could employ any of the three harmonic genera.

Guidonian hand: The singing system attributed to Guido Aretinus that allows a choirmaster or other instructor to teach or lead chant without a notated text. One pitch of the hexachord pitch system is assigned to each joint of the left hand, to which the choirmaster can point with the right hand.

Hexachord: The first six notes of an ascending diatonic scale, used as part of the solfege system produced by Guido Aretinus; composed of whole tones except the interval between the third and fourth notes, which is a semitone.

Mean: The establishment of three terms in a series, or proportion. Three types are used: *arithmetic,* where the mean falls at the arithmetic midpoint between the two extremes: m = (a + b)/2, where m = mean and a, b, = extremes (Ex: 1:2:3); *geometric,* where the mean falls at the "geometric" midpoint, that is, so that each extreme, when compared to the mean, produces a similar ratio: a/m = m/b (Ex: 1:2:4); and *harmonic,* where the mean falls so as to cause the most consonant proportion: m = 2ab/(a + b) (Ex: 3:4:6).

Mode: An apparently simple term with several, often confusing meanings, most commonly, the organizational scheme of pitches used in a composition. In "ordinary" usage this refers to some version of a diatonic scale (s.v. *genera of harmony*), named according to the placement of semitones (and in this usage may be synonymous with *tone* or *tonos*); names may follow conventions of Greek (Dorian, Phrygian, etc.) or ecclesiastical (numeric) nomenclature. The term may also refer to a rhythmic pattern (similar to the poet's selection of metric feet). *Mode* is also used, following some ancient writers, to refer to the entire composite of a composer's selection for a piece: scale type, range, style.

Monochord: A single-stringed instrument used from antiquity for establishing proportional relationships between pitches and the construction of pitch systems or scales. Measurements could be made along its neck from a bridge to the point where the string was stopped to produce a given pitch, thus assuring a single standard in assigning pitches and ratios. Hence scales may be referred to as "divisions of the monochord."

Musica humana: The proportions that order the human form at every level: the physical substances of the body; their relationship to the soul; the parts of the soul itself.

Musica instrumentalis: Music as commonly understood, that is, the ordered sounds produced by artificial musical instruments or by the natural instrument of the human voice.

Musica mundana: The proportions found in the distances among the heavenly bodies, not normally considered audible; the "music of the spheres"; also the Timaean World Soul. Within the terrestrial orb, the proportions governing the combinations of elements to form composite substances.

Phthongus: A sound of unvarying fixed pitch (that is, a musical note), used especially when such simpler terms as *tone* or *note* would be ambiguous.

Proportion, multiplex: A ratio of the form x:1; a consonant proportion, that is, all pitch intervals of this type are considered consonances.

Proportion, superparticular: A ratio of the form *x* + 1:*x;* a consonant proportion.

Proportion, superpartiens: A ratio of the forms *x* + 2:*x,* x + 3:*x,* and so on; not a consonant proportion type, though there is disagreement over the ratio

8:3 (producing an octave plus a fourth) as to whether it can be considered an exception and hence consonant. Ptolemy was cited in support of this position.

Semitone: The smallest interval normally used in a diatonic scale, constituting a ratio close to half a tone. In most pitch systems, a tone cannot be evenly divided, so that the ratio is either slightly larger than half a tone (a major semitone) or slightly smaller (a minor semitone). The precise ratios were a matter of some dispute.

Sesquialtera: The proportion 3:2, producing the interval commonly called a perfect fifth; a consonant interval.

Sesquiquarta: The proportion 5:4, producing an interval within the range of those commonly called a major third or ditone.

Sesquitertia: The proportion 4:3, producing the interval commonly called a perfect fourth; traditionally a consonant interval.

Tetrachord: A four-note unit of pitches, used in antiquity as modules for assembling larger pitch systems that form the basis for a given melodic construction. Composed of two outside pitches constituting a perfect fourth (4:3) and two internal strings whose pitch may vary according to the type of tetrachord desired (see *genera of harmony*). In assembling a larger scale, tetrachords may be linked conjunctly (so that the highest note of one is the same as the lowest note of the next) or disjunctly (so that the lower is separated from the higher by the interval of a tone).

Tone: The whole step, composed of the ratio 9:8, or sesquioctava. The term may also be used (1) to denote a single note of fixed pitch (*phthongus* may be substituted to avoid confusion) and (2) as a synonym for *mode* (ancient pitch systems may use the Greek term *tonos*).

Select Bibliography

Manuscript Sources

Bologna. Civico Museo Bibliografico Musicale (cited as Civ. Mus.).
  B 26. Mss. varii, Ercole Bottrigari (autograph). Including copy of Daniele Barbaro, commentary on Book 5 of Vitruvius *De architectura* (Venice, 1556), fols. 1r–20r.
  B 43. Mss. varii, Ercole Bottrigari (autograph).
  B 44. Mss. varii, Ercole Bottrigari (autograph).
  B 45. Ercole Bottrigari, "La mascara, overo della fabrica de' teatri, e dello apparato delle scene tragisatiricomiche, dialogo . . . " (autograph). 1598.
  B 46. Mss. varii, Ercole Bottrigari (autograph).
  B 120. G. Mei. "De modis musicis veterum." Copied by Lorenzo Mehus from ms. Florence, Ricc. 815, ca. 1761.
——. Biblioteca Universitaria (cited as Bib. Univ.).
  326. Mss. varii, Ercole Bottrigari (autograph).
  1998. Joh. Ant. Flaminius, Letters, including to Raphael Lippus Brandolinus, Franchino Gaffurio; Gaffurio to Flaminius.
Florence. Biblioteca Nazionale Centrale (cited as BNC). Galileiani vols. 1–8.
  Mss. varii, Vincenzo Galilei (autograph).
——. Biblioteca Laurenziana (cited as Bib. Laur.).
  Fondo Ashb. 978. Domenico L'Ongarno, Abate. "Trattato della musica scripero sulla Musica Gio. Spataro Bolognese e Niccolo Burzi di Parma."
——. Biblioteca Riccardiana (cited as Bib. Ricc.).
  815. Girolamo Mei. "De modis musicis."
Mantua. Archivio di Stato.
  B 1252. Nicola Vicentino. Letter to Duke of Mantua.
  1112. Vicenzo Galilei. Letter to Duke of Mantua, 13 March 1582.
Milan. Biblioteca Ambrosiana (cited as Bib. Amb.).
  D 332 inf. [Mei]. Questio de modis musicis ad Victorino, fols. 174r–81v.

H 165 inf. Jan de Muris. "Theorica musice"; "Libellus." With glosses by Franchino Gaffurio.

R 100 sup. Letters, including Girolamo Mei, fols. 58r–97r.

R 118 sup. Letters, including Gioseffo Zarlino, fols. 220r–23r.

R 119 sup. Letters, including Girolamo Mei.

S 105 sup. Letters, including Girolamo Mei, fols. 74r–75v, 190r; Gioseffo Zarlino, 14r–17v.

S 107 sup. Letters, including Ercole Bottrigari.

Rome. Biblioteca Casanatense (cited as Bib. Cas.).

805. Raffaele Brandolini. "De musica et poetica opusculum."

2880. Ghisilin Danckerts. "Trattato sopra una differentia musicale . . . " (autograph).

——. Biblioteca Vallicelliana (cites as Bib. Vall.).

R 56, secs. 15, 33 (fols. 348–92, 534–71). Ghisilin Danckerts. "Trattato sopra una differentia musicale . . . " (autograph).

Vatican City. Biblioteca Apostolica Vaticana (cited as BAV).

Reg. Lat. 2021. Girolamo Mei. Notes and translations on Greek music; letters to Vincenzo Galilei and Giovanni Bardi.

Vat. Lat. 3537. Giorgio Valla. Miscellaneous writings and letters.

Vat. Lat. 5318. Letters of Giovanni Spataro, Pietro Aron, Giovanni del Lago, et al.

Vat. Lat. 1543. Copies of letters in Vat. Lat. 5318.

Vat. Lat 5323. "Hieronymi Maeii Florentini De modis musicis antiquorum ad Petrum Victorium libri IIII" (autograph).

Vat. Lat. 6287. Copy of Vat. Lat. 5323.

Vat. Lat. 5850. Girolamo Cardano. "De musica." 1574.

Venice. Biblioteca Nazionale Marciana (cited as BNM).

Latini XIV, 246 (4683), fol. 8. Letter, "Franchinus Gaffurius Philippino Bononio Laudensis. . . . "

——. Biblioteca Correr.

Cicogna 906. "Petrus Caetanus Cantor Sancti Marci Venetiarum, Oratio de origine et dignitate musices."

Printed Sources

Anselmi, Giorgio. *De musica* (1434). Introduction, text, and commentary Giuseppe Massera. Historiae Musicae Cultores 14. Florence: Olschki, 1961.

Aristides Quintilianus. *On Music, in Three Books.* Trans. Thomas J. Mathiesen. New Haven: Yale University Press, 1983.

Aristotle [pseudo]. *Problems.* Trans. W. S. Hett. 2 vols. Cambridge: Harvard University Press, 1936.

Aristoxenus. *Harmonicorum elementorum libri tres, et alia.* Trans. (Latin) Antonio Gogavino. Venice, 1562.

——. *The Harmonics of Aristoxenus.* Ed. and trans. with notes Henry S. Macran. Oxford: Clarendon, 1902.

Aron, Pietro. *Compendiolo di molti dubbi segreti et sentenze intorno al canto fermo, et figurato, da molti eccellenti & consumati musici dichiarate. Raccolte dallo eccellente & scienzato autore frate Pietro Aron del Ordine de Crosachieri.* . . . Milan: G. A. Castellione, ca. 1550. Facsimile. Bibliotheca Musica Bononiensis 2.11. Bologna: Forni, 1970.

———. *Libri tres de institutione harmonica editi a Petro Aaron Florentino interprete Io. Antonio Flam. Forocornelite.* Bologna: Hecter, 1516. Monuments of Music and Music Literature in Facsimile 2.67. New York: Broude, 1976.

———. *Lucidario in musica di alcune oppenioni antiche, et moderne con le loro oppositioni, & resolutioni, con molti altri secreti appresso & questioni da altrui anchora non dichiarati, composto dall'eccellente, & consomato musico Pietro Aron.* . . . Venice: Girolamo Scotto, 1545.

———. *Thoscanello de la musica di Messer Pietro Aaron Fiorentino canonico da Rimini.* Venice: Bernardino, 1523. Facsimile. Ann Arbor, Mich.: University Microfilms, 1965.

———. *Toscanello in musica.* Venice, 1539. Facsimile. Kassell: Bärenreiter, 1970.

———. *Trattato della natura et cognitione di tutti gli tuoni di canto figurato non da altrui piu scritti, composti per Messer Pier Aaron Musico Fiorentino canonico in Rimini.* . . . Venice: Bernardo di Vitali, 1525. Repr. with addenda, 1531. Facsimile. Ann Arbor, Mich.: University Microfilms, 1965.

Artusi, Giovanni Maria. "All'Illustrissimo Senato di Bologna," "Alli Cortesi Lettori" (prefaces). In *Desiderio di Annibale Meloni [Bottrigari].* Milan: Stampatori Archiepiscop., 1601.

———. *L'arte del contraponto ridotta in tavole.* Venice, 1586.

———. *Impresa del molto Rev. M. Gioseffo Zarlino da Chioggia . . . dichiarata.* Bologna, 1604.

Augustine, St. *Della musica libri VI.* Trans. (Italian) and annotation Rafaello Cardamone. Florence, 1878.

———. *On Music: De Musica.* Ed. and trans. R. C. Taliaferro. The Fathers of the Church, a New Translation: Writings of St. Augustine 2. Annapolis: St. John's Bookstore, 1939.

———. *St. Augustine's De musica: A Synopsis.* Ed. and abr. trans. W. F. Jackson Knight. London: Orthological Institute, 1949.

Baldi, Bernardino. "Vite inedite di matematici italiani." Ed. Enrico Narducci. *Bullettino di bibliografia e storia delle scienze matematiche e fisiche* 19 (1886): 633.

Bardi, Giovanni de'. "Discorso mandato da Giovanni de' Bardi a Giulio Caccini detto Romano sopra la musica antica, e l'cantar bene." In G. B. Doni, *Lyra Barberina Amphicordos,* 2 vols., ed. Antonio Francesco Gori. Florence: Caesareis, 1763.

Benedetti, Giovanni Battista. *Diversarum speculationum mathematicarum et physicarum liber.* Turin: Haeredes N. Bevilaquae, 1585. Venice, 1586, 1599.

Bocchi, Francesco. *Discorso . . . sopra la musica, non secondo l'arte di quella, ma secondo la ragione alla politica pertinente.* Florence: Giorgio Marescotti, 1580.

Boethius, Anicius Manlius Torquatus Severinus. *Boethian Number Theory: A Translation of the "De institutione arithmetica."* Trans. with intro. Michael Masi. Studies in Classical Antiquity 6. Amsterdam: Rodopi, 1983.

————. *De institutione arithmetica libri duo; De institutione musica libri quinque.* Ed. Gottfried Friedlein. 1867. Frankfurt a.M.: Minerva, 1966.

————. *Fundamentals of Music.* Trans. with intro. and notes Calvin M. Bower, ed. Claude V. Palisca. Music Theory in Translation Series. New Haven: Yale University Press, 1989.

Bottrigari, Ercole. *Il Desiderio, or Concerning the Playing Together of Various Musical Instruments.* Trans. Carol MacClintock. Musicological Studies and Documents 9. N.p.: American Institute of Musicology, 1962.

————. *Il Desiderio, overo de' concerti di varii strumenti musicali: dialogo di Allemanno Benelli.* Venice: Ricciardo Amadino, 1594. Facsimile. Veröffentlichungen der Musikbibliothek, ed. Paul Hirsch, vol. 5. Berlin: Breslauer, 1924. Facsimile. Bibliotheca Musica Bononiensis 2.28. Bologna: Forni, 1969.

————. *Il Melone: discorso armonico . . . et Il Melone secondo: Considerazioni musicali del medesimo sopra un discorso di M. Gandolfo Sigonio intorno ai madrigali, et ai libri dell'antica musica ridotta alla moderna pratica di D. Nicola Vicentino.* Ferrara: Vittorio Baldini, 1602. Facsimile. Intro. Giuseppe Vecchi, Bibliotheca Musica Bononiensis 2.29. Bologna: Forni, 1969.

————. *Il Patricio, overo de' tetracordi armonici di Aristosseno, parere, e vera dimostratione.* Bologna: Vittorio Benacci, 1593. Facsimile. Bibliotheca Musica Bononiensis 2.27. Bologna: Forni, 1969.

Burtius, Nicolaus. *Musices opusculum.* Trans. with intro. Clement A. Miller. Musicological Studies and Documents 37. N.p.: American Institute of Musicology, 1983.

————. *Musices opusculum . . . cum defensione Guidonis Aretini: Adversus quendam hyspanum veritatis prevaricatorem.* Bologna, 1487. Facsimile. *Nicolai Burtii Parmensis: Florum libellus,* ed., intro. Giuseppe Massera. Florence: Olschki, 1975.

————. *Nicolaus Burtius: Musices opusculum.* Ed., trans. Clement A. Miller. Musicological Studies and Documents 37. N.p.: American Institute of Musicology, 1983.

Cardano, Girolamo. *Cardanus, Hieronymus: Writings on Music.* Trans. and ed. with intro. Clement A. Miller. Musicological Studies and Documents 32. N.p.: American Institute of Musicology, 1973.

————. *De proportionibus.* Basel, 1570.

————. *De subtilitate libri XXI.* Pacis: Gulielmus Rovillius, 1559.

————. *Opera omnia.* 10 vols. Lyons: Charles Spon, 1663.

Cassiodorus; Isidore of Seville. *Questiones de musicis scriptoribus romanis.* Ed. Carl Schmidt. Darmstadt: G. Otto, 1899.

Caza, Francesco. *Tractato vulgare de canto figurato.* Milan, 1492. Facsimile. Ed. and trans. (German) Johannes Wolf. Berlin: Martin Breslauer, 1922.

Cicero, Marcus Tullius. *On the Commonwealth.* Trans. with intro. G. H. Sabine and S. B. Smith. Columbus: Ohio State University Press, 1929.

Coussemaker, Edmond de. *Scriptorum de musica medii aevii.* 4 vols. Paris: Durand, 1864–76.

Dentice, Luigi. *Duo dialoghi della musica . . . delli quali l'uno tratta della theorica, et l'altro della pratica: raccolti da diversi autori greci, et latini.* Rome: Vincenzo Lucrino, 1553. Facsimile. Intro. Patrizio Barbieri. Lucca: Libreria Musicale Italiana, 1988.

Doni, Anton Francesco. *Dialogo della musica: Canto.* Venice: Girolamo Scotto, 1544.

———. *Tre libri di lettere del Doni; e i termini della lingua toscana.* Venice: Francesco Marcolino, 1552.

Doni, Giovanni Battista. Letters. In *Prose fiorentine* 4.3, pp. 277–97. Florence, 1734.

Drake, Stillman, and I. E. Drabkin, eds. *Mechanics in Sixteenth-Century Italy: Selections from Tartaglia, Benedetti, Guido Ubaldo, and Galileo.* Madison: University of Wisconsin Press, 1969.

Fineo, Orontio, d. Delfinato. *Opere, divise in cinque parti: aritmetica, geometria, cosmografia, & oriuoli,* tr. Cosimo Bartoli, *et Gli Specchi,* tr. Ercole Bottrigaro. Venice: F. Senese, 1587.

Fogliano, Ludovico. *Musica theorica . . . docte simul ac dilucide pertractata: in qua quamplures de harmonicis intervallis: non prius tentatae: continentur speculationes.* Venice: de Sabio, 1529. Monuments of Music and Music Literature in Facsimile 2.43. New York: Broude, 1969. Facsimile. Bibliotheca Musica Bononiensis 2.13. Bologna: Forni, 1970.

Franco, Cirillo, di Loreto. "Lettera a M. Ugolino Gualteruzzi." In *Lettere volgari di diversi nobilissimi huomini . . .* 3, fols. 114r–18v. Venice: Aldo Manuzio, 1564.

Gaffurio, Franchino. *Angelicum ac divinum opus musice.* Milan: Gotardus, 1508.

———. *Apologia adversus Ioannem Spatarium & complices musicos Bononienses.* Turin: Augustinus de Vicomercato, 1520.

———. *De harmonia musicorum instrumentorum opus.* Milan: Gotard Pontano, 1518. Facsimile. Bibliotheca Musica Bononiensis 2.7. Bologna: Forni, 1972.

———. *Franchini Gaffurii De harmonia musicorum instrumentorum opus.* Trans. with intro. Clement A. Miller. Musicological Studies and Documents 33. N.p.: American Institute of Musicology, 1977.

———. *Franchini Gaffurii Extractus parvus musice.* Ed. F. Alberto Gallo. Antiquae Musicae Italicae Scriptores 4. Bologna: Forni, 1969.

———. *Practica musicae.* Milan, 1496. Monuments of Music and Music Literature in Facsimile 2.99. New York: Broude, 1979.

———. *Practica musicae.* Trans. with transcriptions Clement A. Miller. Musicological Studies and Documents 20. N.p.: American Institute of Musicology, 1968.

———. *The Practica Musicae of Franchinus Gafurius.* Trans. and ed. with transcriptions Irwin Young. Madison: University of Wisconsin Press, 1969.

———. *Theorica musice.* Milan: Philippus Mantegatius dictum Castanum, 1492. Facsimile. Bibliotheca Musica Bononiensis 2.5. Bologna: Forni, 1969. Monuments of Music and Music Literature in Facsimile 2.21. New York: Broude, 1967.

——. *Theorica musicae*. Ed. Gaetano Cesari. Rome: Reale Accademia d'Italia, 1934.

Galilei, Vincenzo. *Dialogo . . . della musica antica, et della moderna*. Florence: Giorgio Marescotti, 1581. Facsimile. Rome: Reale Accademia d'Italia, 1934. Monuments of Music and Music Literature in Facsimile 2.20. New York: Broude, 1967.

——. "Dialogo della musica antica, et della moderna: Translation and Commentary." Robert H. Herman. Ph.D. diss., North Texas State University, 1973.

——. *Discorso . . . intorno all'opere di messer Gioseffo Zarlino da Chioggia, et altri importanti particolari attenenti alla musica*. Florence: Giorgio Marescotti, 1589. Facsimile. Milan: Bollettino Bibliografico Musicale, 1934.

——. Letters to Vincenzo Borghini, Messer Pier Vettori. In *Prose fiorentine raccolte dallo smarrito academico della Crusca*, ed. Giovanni Gaetano, Rosso Antonio Martini, and Tommaso Buonaventura 4.2, pp. 64–173. Florence: Tartini e Franchi, 1734.

Gentile Riccio, Piergirolamo [Pietro Girolamo]. *Dell'armonia del mondo, lettione due. Havute nell'Accademia de' Sig.ri Arditi d'Albenga . . . nelle quali si danno a veder molte belle cose pertenenti alla simmetria dell'universo; et vi s'insegnano a fuggire gl'errori dell'armonia viziata.* Venice: Sebastiano Combi, 1605.

Guido Aretinus. *Micrologus*. In *Hucbald, Guido, and John on Music: Three Medieval Treatises*. Trans. Warren Babb, ed. with intro. Claude V. Palisca. Music Theory in Translation Series. New Haven: Yale University Press, 1978.

Hothby, John. *Johannis Octobi: Tres tractatuli contra Bartholomeum Ramum: Three Treatises against Bartholomeo Ramos*. Ed. Albert Seay. Corpus Scriptorum Musicorum 10. Rome: American Institute of Musicology, 1964.

Hucbald. *De harmonica institutione*. In *Hucbald, Guido, and John on Music: Three Medieval Treatises*. Trans. Warren Babb, ed. with intro. Claude V. Palisca. Music Theory in Translation Series. New Haven: Yale University Press, 1978.

Iamblichus of Chalcis. *Iamblichus' Life of Pythagoras*. Trans. Thomas Taylor. 1818. Reprint. London: Watkins, 1965.

Isidore, St. *Etymologiarum sive originum libri XX*. Ed. W. M. Lindsey. 2 vol. Oxford: Oxford University Press, 1911.

Lanfranco, Giovanni Maria. *Scintille di musica . . . che mostrano a leggere il canto fermo, et figurato, gli accidenti delle note misurate, le proportioni, i tuoni, il contrapunto, et la divisione del monochordo, con la accordatura de varii instrumenti, dalla quale nasce un modo, onde ciascun per se stesso imparare potra le voci . . .* Brescia: M. Lodovico Britannico, 1533. Facsimile. Intro. Giuseppe Massera. Bibliotheca Musica Bononiensis 2.15. Bologna: Forni, 1970.

Leoniceno, Niccolo. Letters. In "Nuove notizie sulla famiglia e sull'opera di Nicolo Leoniceno," *Archivio Veneto*, ser. 5, 72 (1963): 5–22.

———. Letter to Giorgio Valla. Bologna, Bib. Univ., miscellanea Tioli, 19:83–84. In Domenico Vitaliani, *Della vita e delle opere di Niccolo Leoniceno Vicentino*. Verona: Sordomuti, 1892.

Macrobius, Ambrosius Aurelius Theodosius. *Commentary on the Dream of Scipio*. Trans. with intro. and notes Will Harris Stahl. New York: Columbia University Press, 1952.

Marinati, Aurelio. *La prima parte della somma di tutte le scienze*. Rome: Bartolomeo Bonfadino, 1587.

Martianus Capella. *Martianus Capella and the Seven Liberal Arts*. Trans. Will Harris Stahl and R. Johnson, with E. L. Burge. 2 vols. New York: Columbia University Press, 1977.

Mei, Girolamo. *Letters on Ancient and Modern Music to Vincenzo Galilei and Giovanni Bardi: A Study with Annotated Texts*. 1960. 2d ed. with addenda Claude V. Palisca. Musicological Studies and Documents 3. Neuhausen-Stuttgart: American Institute of Musicology, 1977.

Pacioli, Luca. *Divina proportione*. Milan, 1505. Venice: A. Paganius Paganinus, 1509. Facsimile. Fontes Ambrosiani Series 31. Milan, 1956. Facsimile. Como: Dominioni, 1967.

———. *Divina proportione*. Ed. and trans. (German, Italian) Constantin Winterberg. Vienna: Graeser, 1889.

Paolini, Fabio. *Hebdomades, sive septem de septenario libri, habiti in Uranicorum Academia in unius Vergilii versus explicatione*. Venice: F. F. Senesi, 1589.

Patrizi, Francesco, da Cherso. *Della poetica, edizione critica*. Ed. Danilo Aguzzi Barbagli. 3 vols. Florence: Istituto Nazionale di Studi sul Rinascimento, 1969.

———. *Della poetica, la deca istoriale*. . . . Ferrara: Vittorio Baldini, 1586.

Plato. *The Collected Dialogues*. Ed. Edith Hamilton and Huntington Cairns. Bollingen Series 71. New York: Pantheon, 1961.

———. *Plato's Cosmology: The Timaeus of Plato Translated with a Running Commentary*. F. M. Cornford. 1937. Reprint. Indianapolis: Bobbs-Merill, 1957.

Pontano, Giovanni. *De fortitudine*. Naples, 1490.

Ponzio, Pietro. *Dialogo, ove si tratta della theorica, e prattica di musica*. . . . Parma: Erasmo Viotti, 1595.

———. *Ragionamento di musica. Ove si tratta de'passaggi delle consonantie, & dissonantie, buoni, & non buoni, del modo di far motetti, messe, salmi, & altre compositioni et d'alcuni avertimenti per il contrapuntista, et compositore, & altre cose pertinente alla musica*. Parma: Erasmo Viotti, 1588.

Prosdocimo de Beldomandi. *Contrapunctus: A New Critical Text and Translation*. Jan Herlinger. Lincoln: University of Nebraska Press, 1984.

Ptolemaeus, Claudius. *Ptolemaios und Porphyrios über die Musik*. Ed. and trans. Ingemar Düring. 1934. Reprint. New York: Garland, 1980.

Quintilian, Marcus Fabius. *Institutio Oratoria*. Trans. H. E. Butler. London: Heinemann, 1921.

———. *Quintilian's Institutes of Oratory*. Trans. with notes J. S. Watson. 2 vols. London: Bell, 1903.

Ramos de Pareja, Bartolomeo. *Musica practica.* Bologna: Baltasar de Hiriberia, 1482.

——. *Musica Practica Bartolomei Rami de Pareia Bononiae.* Ed. Johannes Wolf. Leipzig: Breitkopf und Härtel, 1901. Facsimile. Bibliotheca Musica Bononiensis 2.3. Bologna: Forni, 1969.

Rilli, Jacopo. *Notizie leterarie, et istoriche intorno agli uomini illustri dell'Accademia Fiorentina.* Florence: Pietro Matino, 1700.

Rossettus, Balsius [Biagio Rossetti]. *Libellus de rudimentis musices. De triplici musices specie. De modo debite solvendi divinum pensum. Et de auferendis nonnullis abusibus in dei templo. Quae omnia sub compendio candidus lector inveniet.* Verona: de Sabio, 1529.

——. *Libellus de rudimentis musices.* Ed. Albert Seay. Colorado Springs: Colorado College Music Press, 1981.

Sadoleto, Jacopo. *Sadoleto on Education: A Translation of the De pueris recte instituendis (1533).* Notes and intro. E. T. Campagnac and K. Forbes. London: Oxford University Press, 1916.

Spataro, Giovanni. *Bartolomei Ramis honesta defensio in Nicolai Burtii Parmensis opusculum.* Bologna, 1491. Facsimile. Antiquae musicae italicae. Monumenta Bononiensia. Opera omnia 1. Bologna: Forni, 1967.

——. *Dilucide et probatissime demonstratione . . . contra . . . Franchino Gafurio.* Bologna: Hieronymus de Benedictis, 1521. Facsimile with trans. (German) J. Wolf. Berlin: Martin Breslauer, 1925.

——. *Errori di Franchino Gafurio da Lodi. . . .* Bologna: Benedetto di E. Faelli, 1521.

——. *Tractato di musica.* Venice, 1531. Facsimile. Bibliotheca Musica Bononiensis 2.14. Bologna: Forni, 1970. Monuments of Music and Music Literature in Facsimile 2.88. New York: Broude, 1979.

——. *Utile e breve regole di canto.* 1510. Ed. G. Vecchi. Bologna: Università degli studi, 1962.

Tartaglia, Niccolo, ed. and trans. *Euclide Megarense reassettato, et alla integrità ridotto . . .* Venice: Venturino Rossinelli, 1543; Giovanni Bariletto, 1544. 2d ed. Venice: Curtio Troiano, 1565; Bariletto, 1569, 1585.

Tigrini, Orazio. *Il compendio della musica, nel quale brevemente si tratta dell'arte del contrapunto, diviso in quattro libri.* Venice: Ricciardo Amadino, 1588.

Tinctoris, Johannes. *The Art of Counterpoint.* Ed. and trans. Albert Seay. N.p.: American Institute of Musicology, 1961.

——. *Complexus effectum musice: Sulla estetica di Johannes Tinctoris.* Ed. and trans. (Italian) with commentary Luisa Zanoncelli. Bologna: Forni, 1979.

——. *Concerning the Nature and Propriety of Tones.* Ed. and trans. Albert Seay. 2d ed. Colorado College Music Press Translations 2. Colorado Springs: Colorado College Music Press, 1976.

——. *De inventione et usu musicae.* Naples, 1485.

——. *Johannes Tinctoris und sein unbekannter Traktat de inventione et usu musicae.* Ed. Karl Weinmann. Regensburg: F. Pustet, 1917. Reprint. Tutzing: Hans Schneider, 1961.

——— . *Opera theoretica.* Ed. Albert Seay. 2 vols. in 3. N.p.: American Institute of Musicology, 1975.

Valla, Giorgio. *De expetendis et fugiendis rebus opus.* Venice: Aldus Romanus, 1501.

Vanneo, Stephano. *Recanetum de musica aurea . . . nuper aeditum, et solerti studio enucleatum, Vincentio Rosseto interprete.* Rome: Valerius Dorcius Brixiensis, 1533. Facsimile. Documenta Musicologica 1.28. Kassel: Bärenreiter, 1969. Facsimile. Bibliotheca Musica Bononiensis 2.16. Bologna: Forni, 1969.

Vicentino, Nicola. *L'antica musica ridotta alla moderna prattica, con la dichiaratione, et con gli essempi di i tre generi, con le loro spetie, et con l'inventione di uno nuovo stromento, nel quale si contiene tutta la perfetta musica, con molti secreti musicali.* Rome: Antonio Barre, 1555, 1557. Facsimile. Documenta Musicologica 1.17. Kassel: Bärenreiter, 1959.

——— . "Vicentino's *Arciorgano:* An Annotated Translation." Henry W. Kaufmann. *Journal of Music Theory* 5 (1961): 32–53.

Vitruvius Pollio. *Architectura con il suo commento et figure in volgar lingua raportato per M. Gianbatista Caporali di Perugia.* Perugia: Bigazzini, 1536.

——— . *Di Lucio Vitruvio Pollione De architectura libri decem traducti de latino . . . commentati . . . Agostino Gallo e Alvisio da Pirovano.* Como: Gotardo da Ponte, 1521.

——— . *I dieci libri dell' architettura di M. Vitruvio tradutti et commentati da Monsignor Barbaro eletto Patriarca d'Aquileggia.* Venice: Francesco Marcolini, 1556. 2d ed. Venice: Francesco de' Franceschi Senese, 1567. Facsimile. With Essays by Manfredo Tafuri and Manuela Morresi. Milan: Polifilo, 1987.

——— . *M. Vitruvii Pollionis De architectura libri decem. . . . ,* Commentary Gulielmo Philandro Castiglioni. Lyons: Ioan. Tornaesium, 1586.

Zamberti, Bartolomeo, trans. and ed. *Euclides Megarensis philosophi platonici mathematicarum disciplinarum janitoris. . . .* Venice: Ioannes Tacuinus, 1505. Basel, 1546.

Zarlino, Gioseffo. *De tutte l'opere del r. m. G. Zarlino.* 4 vols. Venice: Francesco de' Franceschi Senese, 1588–89.

——— . *Dimostrationi harmoniche.* Venice: Francesco de' Franceschi Senese, 1571. Monuments of Music and Music Literature in Facsimile 2.2. New York: Broude, 1965. Facsimile. Ridgewood, N.J.: Gregg, 1966.

——— . *Istitutioni harmoniche.* Venice, 1558, 1573. Facsimile, 1558 ed. Monuments of Music and Music Literature in Facsimile, 2.2. New York: Broude, 1965. Facsimile, 1573 ed. Ridgewood, N.J.: Gregg, 1966.

——— . *Istitutioni harmoniche, Part 3, The Art of Counterpoint.* Trans. Guy A. Marco and Claude V. Palisca. Music Theory in Translation Series. New Haven: Yale University Press, 1968.

——— . *Istitutioni harmoniche, Part 4, On the Modes.* Trans. Vered Cohen. Ed. with intro. Claude V. Palisca. Music Theory in Translation Series. New Haven: Yale University Press, 1981.

———. *Sopplimenti musicali.* Venice: Francesco de' Franceschi Senese, 1588. Monuments of Music Literature in Facsimile 2.15. New York: Broude, 1965. Facsimile. Ridgewood, N.J.: Gregg, 1966.

Secondary Works

Albert, Hans. "Musik und Dichtkunst im 16. Jahrhundert." *Musikforschung* 8 (1955): 335–45.

Alexanderson, Bengt. *Textual Remarks on Ptolemy's Harmonics and Porphyry's Commentary.* Gothenburg: Universitet, 1969.

Allaire, Gaston G. *The Theory of Hexachords, Solmization, and the Modal System: A Practical Application.* Musicological Studies and Documents 24. N.p.: American Institute of Musicology, 1972.

Arts libéraux et philosophie au moyen âge. Actes du Quatrième Congrès International de Philosophie Médiévale. University of Montreal, 1967. Montreal: Institut d'Études Médiévales, 1969.

Barbour, J. Murray. *Tuning and Temperament: A Historical Survey.* 1951. Reprint. East Lansing: Michigan State University Press, 1972.

Barker, Andrew D. "Music and Perception: A Study in Aristoxenus." *Journal of Hellenic Studies* 98 (1978): 9–16.

Bartolotti, Ettore. *I cartelli di matematica disfida e la personalità psichica di Girolamo Cardano.* Imola: Galeati, 1933.

———. *La storia della matematica nella Università di Bologna.* Bologna, 1947.

Beaujouan, Guy. "L'enseignement du 'quadrivium.'" *La scuola nell'occidente latino dell'alto medioevo.* Settimane di Studio, Centro italiano di studi sull'alto medioevo 19.2:639–67. Spoleto: Centro, 1972.

Beck, Hermann. *Die venezianische Musikerschule im 16. Jahrhundert.* Wilhelmshaven: Heinrichshofen, 1968.

Becker, Oskar. "Frühgriechische Mathematik und Musiklehre." *Archiv für Musikwissenschaft* 14 (1957): 156–64.

Benade, Arthur H. *Horns, Strings, and Harmony.* Garden City, N.Y.: Doubleday, Anchor, 1960.

Berger, Karol. *Theories of Chromatic and Enharmonic Music in Late Sixteenth-Century Italy.* Studies in Musicology 10. 1976. Ann Arbor, Mich.: University Microfilms International, UMI Research Press, 1980.

Boncella, P. A. L. "Denying Ancient Music's Power: Ghisilin Danckerts' Essays in the 'Generi inusitati.'" *Tijdschrift van de vereniging voor Nederlandse muziek geschiednis* 38 (1988): 59–80.

Bottrigari, Enrico. *Notizie biografiche intorno agli studi e alla vita del Cavaliere Ercole Bottrigari.* Bologna, 1842.

Bowen, Alan C. "The Foundations of Early Pythagorean Harmonic Science: Archytas, Fragment I." *Ancient Philosophy* 2 (1982): 79–104.

Bowen, William Roy. "Music and Number: An Introduction to Renaissance Harmonic Science." Ph.D. diss., University of Toronto, 1984.

Bower, Calvin M. "Boethius and Nicomachus: An Essay Concerning the Sources of the *De institutione musica*." *Vivarium* 16 (1978): 1–45.

Bragard, Roger, "L'harmonie de spheres selon Boethius." *Speculum* 4 (1928): 206–13.

Brink, Paul Robert. "The Archicembalo of Nicola Vicentino." Ph.D. diss., Ohio State University, 1966.

Brown, Howard M. "How Opera Began: An Introduction to Jacopo Peri's *Euridice* (1600)." In *The Late Italian Renaissance, 1525–1630*, ed. Eric Cochrane, pp. 401–43. London: Macmillan, 1970.

Browne, Alice. "Girolamo Cardano's *Somniorum synesiorum libri IIII*." *Bibliothèque d'humanisme et de la Renaissance* 41 (1979): 123–35.

Bukofzer, Manfred F. "Changing Aspects of Medieval and Renaissance Music." *Musical Quarterly* 44 (1958): 1–18.

Burkert, Walter. *Lore and Science in Ancient Pythagoreanism*. Trans. Edwin L. Minar, Jr. Cambridge: Harvard University Press, 1972.

Burkhalter, A. Louis. *Music of the Renaissance*. Trans. Doris C. Dunning. New York: Doubleday, 1968.

Cardenal, Gianna. "Cronologia della vita e delle opere di Giorgio Valla." In *Giorgio Valla: Tra scienza e sapienza: Studi di Gianna Cardenal, Patrizia Landucci Ruffo, Cesare Vasoli*, ed. Vittore Branca, pp. 93–97. Florence: Olschki, 1981.

Caretta, Alessandro, Luigi Cremascoli, and Luigi Salamina. *Franchino Gaffurio*. Lodi: Archivio Storico Lodigiano, 1951.

Carugo, Adriano. "Giuseppe Moleto: Mathematics and the Aristotelian Theory of Science at Padua in the Second Half of the Sixteenth Century." In *Aristotelismo veneto e scienza moderna*, ed. Luigi Olivieri, pp. 509–17. Padua: Antenore, 1983.

Casimiri, R. "Il Codice Vaticano 5318, carteggio musicale autografo tra theorici e musici del sec. XVI, dall'anno 1517 al 1543." *Note d'archivio* 16 (1939): 109.

Catalogo dei codici Pinelliani [latini] dell'Ambrosiana. Milan: S. Giuseppe, 1933.

Cattin, G. "Nel quarto centenario di Nicola Vicentino teorico e compositore." *Studi musicali* 5 (1976): 3–28.

Cazden, Norman. "The Definition of Consonance and Dissonance." *International Review of the Aesthetics and Sociology of Music* 11 (1980): 123–68.

——. "Pythagoras and Aristoxenus Reconciled." *Journal of the American Musicological Society* 11 (1958): 97–105.

Chadwick, Henry. *Boethius: The Consolations of Music, Logic, Theology, and Philosophy*. Oxford: Clarendon, 1981.

Chamberlain, David S. "Philosophy of Music in the *Consolatio* of Boethius." *Speculum* 45 (1970): 80–97.

Cochrane, Eric. *Florence in the Forgotten Centuries, 1527–1800*. Chicago: University of Chicago Press, 1973.

——. "Science and Humanism in the Italian Renaissance." *American Historical Review* 81 (1976): 1039–57.

——— . *Tradition and Enlightenment in the Tuscan Academies, 1690–1800.* Rome: Storia e Letteratura, 1961.

Cohen, H. Floris. *Quantifying Music: The Science of Music at the First Stage of the Scientific Revolution, 1580–1650.* Dordrecht: Reidel, 1984.

Coleman-Norton, P. R. "Cicero Musicus." *Journal of the American Musicological Society* 1 (1948): 3–22.

Comotti, Giovanni. *Music in Greek and Roman Culture.* Trans. Rosaria V. Munson. Baltimore: Johns Hopkins University Press, 1989.

Corbin, Solange. "Musica spéculative et cantus pratique: Le rôle de Saint Augustin dans la transmission de sciences musicales." *Cahiers de civilisation médiévale Xe–XIIe siècle* 5 (1962): 1–12.

Cosenza, Mario Emilio. *Biographical and Bibliographical Dictionary of the Italian Humanists and of the World of Classical Scholarship in Italy, 1300–1800.* 2d ed. 5 vols. Boston: G. K. Hall, 1962.

Crocker, Richard L. "Aristoxenus and Greek Mathematics." In *Aspects of Medieval and Renaissance Music: A Birthday Offering to Gustave Reese,* ed. Jan La Rue, 2d. ed., pp. 96–100. New York: Pendragon, 1978.

——— . "Musica Rhythmica and Musica Metrica in Antique and Medieval Theory." *Journal of Music Theory* 2 (1958): 2–23.

——— . "Pythagorean Mathematics and Music." *Journal of Aesthetics and Art Criticism* 22 (1963–64): 189–98, 325–35.

Crombie, A. C. "Mathematics and Platonism in the Sixteenth-Century Italian Universities and in Jesuit Educational Policy." In *Prismata: Naturwissenschaftsgeschichtliche Studien* (Festschrift for Willy Hartner), ed. Y. Maeyama and W. G. Saltzer, pp. 63–94. Wiesbaden: Steiner, 1977.

——— . "Mathematics, Music, and Medical Science." *Organon* 6 (1969): 21–36.

——— . "Science and the Arts in the Renaissance: The Search for Truth and Certainty, Old and New." *History of Science* 18 (1980): 233–46.

Dahlhaus, Carl. "Relationes harmonicae." *Archiv für Musikwissenschaft* 32 (1975): 202–27.

——— . "War Zarlino Dualist?" *Musikforschung* 10 (1957): 286–90.

D'Amico, John F. *Renaissance Humanism in Papal Rome: Humanists and Churchmen on the Eve of the Reformation.* Baltimore: Johns Hopkins University Press, 1983.

Davari, Stefano. *La musica a Mantova.* Ed. Gherardo Ghirdini. Mantua: Buffaldi, 1975.

De Bruyn, J. "Ghisilino Danckerts, Kapelaanzanger van de Pauselijke kapel van 1538 to 1565." *Tijdschrift der vereenigung voor Nederlandsche muziekgeschiedenis* 16 (1946): 217–52; 17 (1949): 128–57.

De Gaetano, A. "The Florentine Academy." *Bibliothèque d'humanisme et Renaissance* 30 (1968): 19–52.

Drake, Stillman. *Galileo at Work: His Scientific Biography.* Chicago: University of Chicago Press, 1978.

——— . "Renaissance Music and Experimental Science." *Journal of the History of Ideas* 31 (1970): 483–500.

———. "The Role of Music in Galileo's Experiments." *Scientific American* 232 (1975): 98–104.

———. "Vincenzio Galilei and Galileo." In *Galileo Studies: Personality, Tradition, and Revolution,* pp. 43–62. Ann Arbor: University of Michigan Press, 1970.

Eco, Umberto. *Art and Beauty in the Middle Ages.* Trans. Hugh Bredin. 1959 (Italian). New Haven: Yale University Press, 1986.

Ellefson, Roy Martin. "Music and Humanism in the Early Renaissance: Their Relationship and Its Roots in the Rhetorical and Philosophical Traditions." Ph.D. diss., Florida State University, 1981.

Fano, Fabio. *La camerata fiorentina: Vincenzo Galilei (1520?–1591); la sua opera d'artista e di teorico come espressione di nuove idealità musicali.* 2 vols. Istituzioni e monumenti dell'arte musicale italiana 4. Milan: Ricordi, 1934.

———. "Vita e attività del museo teorico e pratico Franchino Gaffurio da Lodi." *Arte lombarda* 15 (1970): 19–62.

Fantuzzi, Giovanni. *Notizie degli scrittori bolognesi.* Bologna, 1792. Facsimile. Bologna: Forni, 1965.

Favaro, A. "I lettori di matematiche nella Università di Padova dal principio del secolo XIV alla fine del XVI." *Memorie e documenti per la storia della Università di Padova* 1 (1922): 1–70.

Fellerer, Karl Gustav. "Church Music and the Council of Trent." *Musical Quarterly* 39 (1953): 576–94.

Fenlon, D. *Heresy and Obedience in Tridentine Italy: Cardinal Pole and the Counter-Reformation.* Cambridge: Cambridge University Press, 1972.

Fenlon, Iain. *Music and Patronage in Sixteenth-Century Mantua.* 2 vols. Cambridge: Cambridge University Press, 1980.

———. ed. *Music in Medieval and Early Modern Europe: Patronage, Sources, and Texts.* New York: Cambridge University Press, 1981.

Fierz, Markus. *Girolamo Cardano, 1501–1576: Physician, Natural Philosopher, Mathematician, Astrologer, and Interpreter of Dreams.* Trans. Helga Niman. Boston: Birkhäuser, 1983.

Florimo, Francesco. *La Scuola musicale di Napoli.* . . . Naples: Morano, 1881.

Fowler, D. H. *The Mathematics of Plato's Academy: A New Reconstruction.* Oxford: Clarendon, 1987.

Gallo, F. Alberto. "Musici scriptores graeci." In *Catalogus translationum et commentariorum: Medieval and Renaissance Translations and Commentaries,* ed. F. Edward Cranz and Paul Oskar Kristeller, 3:63–73. Washington: Catholic University of America Press, 1976.

———. "Le traduzioni dei trattati musicali di Prosdocimo de' Beldomandi." *Quadrivium* 6 (1964): 57–84.

———. "Le traduzioni dal greco per Franchino Gaffurio." *Acta Musicologica* 35 (1963): 172–74.

———. "La trattatistica musicale." In *Storia della cultura veneta: Il trecento,* pp. 469–76. Vicenza: Pozza, 1976.

Gaspari, Gaetano. *Musica e musicisti a Bologna: Ricerche, documenti, e memorie risguardanti la storia dell'arte musicale in Bologna.* Bologna, 1867. Facsimile. Bibliotheca Musica Bononiensis 3.1. Bologna: Forni, 1969.

Giacobbe, Giulio Cesare. "Il Commentarium de certitudine mathematicarum disciplinarum di Alessandro Piccolomini." *Physis* 4 (1972): 162–93.

——. "Epigoni nel seicento della 'Questio de certitudine mathematicarum': Giuseppe Biancani." *Physis* 18 (1976): 5–40.

——. "Francesco Barozzi e la 'Quaestio de certitudine mathematicarum.' " *Physis* 14 (1972): 357–74.

——. "La reflessione metamatematica di Pietro Catena." *Physis* 15 (1973): 178–96.

——. "Un Gesuito progressista nelle questioni 'De certitudine mathematicarum' rinascimentali: Benito Pereyra." *Physis* 19 (1977): 51–86.

Gibson, Margaret, ed. *Boethius: His Life, Thought and Influence*. Oxford: Blackwell, 1981.

Grendler, Marcella. "A Greek Collection in Padua: The Library of Gian Vincenzo Pinelli (1535–1600)." *Renaissance Quarterly* 33 (1980): 386–416.

Grendler, Paul F. *Critics of the Italian World, 1530–1560: Anton Francesco Doni, Nicolò Franco, and Ortensio Lando*. Madison: University of Wisconsin Press, 1969.

Gundersheimer, L. "Toward a Reinterpretation of the Renaissance in Ferrara." *Bibliothèque d'humanisme et Renaissance* 30 (1968): 267–82.

Gysin, Hans Peter. *Studien zum Vokabular der Musiktheorie im Mittelalter: Eine linguistische Analyse*. Amsterdam: Knuf, 1958.

Haar, James. "Zarlino's Definition of Fugue and Imitation." *Journal of the American Musicological Society* 24 (1971): 226–54.

Hall, Marie Boas. "Renaissance Science and Professionalisation." *Annali dell'Istituto e museo di storia della scienza di Firenze* 7 (1982): 53–64.

Handschin, Jacques. "Anselmi's Treatise on Music Annotated by Gafori." *Musica Disciplina* 2 (1948): 123–41.

——. "The *Timaeus* Scale." *Musica Disciplina* 4 (1950): 3–42.

Hanning, Barbara. "Apologia pro Ottavio Rinuccini." *Journal of the American Musicological Society* 26 (1973): 240–62.

——. *Of Poetry and Music's Power: Humanism and the Creation of Opera*. Ann Arbor, Mich.: University Microfilms International, UMI Research Press, 1980.

Harrán, Don. "Sulla genesi della famosa disputa fra Gioseffo Zarlino e Vincenzo Galilei, un nuovo profilo." *Nuova rivista musicale italiana* 21 (1987): 467–75.

——. *Word-Tone Relations in Musical Thought from Antiquity to the Seventeenth Century*. Musicological Studies and Documents 40. Neuhausen-Stuttgart: Hänssler/American Institute of Musicology, 1986.

Hayburn, Robert F. *Papal Legislation of Sacred Music, 95 A.D. to 1977 A.D.* Collegeville, Minn.: Liturgical Press, 1979.

Heiberg, J. L. "Beiträge zur Geschichte Georg Vallas und seiner Bibliothek." In *Beiheft zum Centralblatt für Bibliothekwesen* 16:3–44. Leipzig, 1896.

Hellman, C. Doris. "The Gradual Abandonment of the Aristotelian Universe: A Preliminary Note on Some Sidelights." In *Mélanges Alexandre Koyré*, intro. I. Bernard Cohen and René Taton, 1:283–93. Paris: Hermann, 1964.

Heninger, S. K., Jr. *The Cosmographical Glass: Renaissance Diagrams of the Universe*. San Marino, Calif.: Huntington Library, 1977.

Henry, John. "Francesco Patrizi da Cherso's Concept of Space and Its Later Influence." *Annals of Science* 36 (1979): 549–73.

Hertz, David Larry. "The Classical Premise: The Relationship between Mathematics and Philosophy in Greek Thought." Ph.D. diss., Columbia University Teachers College, 1985.

Hine, William L. "Marin Mersenne: Renaissance Naturalism and Renaissance Magic." In *Occult and Scientific Mentalities in the Renaissance*, ed. Brian Vickers, pp. 165–76. Cambridge: Cambridge University Press, 1984.

Hintikka, Jaakko, David Gruender, and Evandro Agazzi, eds. *Pisa Conference on the History and Philosophy of Science, 1978: Proceedings, vol. 1, Theory, Change, Ancient Axiomatics, and Galileo's Methodology*. Boston: Reidel, 1981.

Hoegler, Fritz. "Bemerkungen zu Zarlinos Theorie." *Zeitschrift für Musikwissenschaft* 9 (1927): 518–27.

Hollander, John. *The Untuning of the Sky: Ideas of Music in English Poetry, 1500–1700*. Princeton: Princeton University Press, 1961.

Howell, Standley. "Ramos de Pareja's 'Brief Discussion of Various Instruments.'" *Journal of the American Musical Instrument Society* 11 (1985): 14–37.

Hunt, Frederick Vinton. *Origins in Acoustics: From Antiquity to the Age of Newton*. Foreword R. E. Apfel. New Haven: Yale University Press, 1978.

Hutton, James. "Some English Poems in Praise of Music." In *Essays on Renaissance Poetry*, ed. Rita Guerlac, pp. 17–73. Ithaca, N.Y.: Cornell University Press, 1980.

Ingegno, Alfonso. *Saggio sulla filosofia di Cardano*. Pubblicazioni del Centro di studi del pensiero del cinquecento e del seicento in relazione ai problemi della scienza . . . Univ. degli Studi di Milano 1.17. Florence: Nuova Italia, 1980.

Jeppeson, Knud. "Eine musiktheoretische Korrespondenz des früheren Cinquecento." *Acta Musicologica* 13 (1941): 3–39.

Jones, Robert C. "Ramos and Some Polemic Theorists of the Renaissance." *Missouri Journal of Research in Music Education* 2 (1968): 40–48.

Kassler, Jamie Croy. "Music as a Model in Early Science." *History of Science* 20 (1982): 103–39.

Kaufmann, Henry William. *The Life and Works of Nicola Vicentino*. Musicological Studies and Documents 11. N.p.: American Institute of Musicology, 1966.

———. "More on the Tuning of the Archicembalo." *Journal of the American Musicological Society* 23 (1970): 84–94.

———. "The Motets of Nicola Vicentino." *Musica Disciplina* 15 (1961): 169–85.

———. "Vicentino and the Greek Genera." *Journal of the American Musicological Society* 16 (1963): 325–46.

Kinkeldey, Otto. "Franchino Gafori and Marsilio Ficino." *Harvard Library Bulletin* 1 (1947): 379–82.

Kirkendale, Warren. "Ciceronians versus Aristotelians on the Ricercar as Exordium." *Journal of the American Musicological Society* 32 (1979): 1–44.

Koenigsberger, Dorothy. *Renaissance Man and Creative Thinking: A History of Concepts of Harmony, 1400–1700.* Brighton, U.K.: Harvester, 1979.

Koenigsberger, H. G. "Republics and Courts in Italian and European Culture in the Sixteenth and Seventeenth Centuries." *Past and Present* 83 (1979): 32–56.

Koyré, Alexandre. "Giambattista Benedetti, Critic of Aristotle." In *Galileo: Man of Science,* ed. Ernan McMullin, pp. 98–117. New York: Basic Books, 1967.

Kristeller, Paul Oskar. *Eight Philosophers of the Italian Renaissance.* Stanford: Stanford University Press, 1964.

———. "Music and Learning in the Early Italian Renaissance." *Journal of Renaissance and Baroque Music* 1 (1946/47): 255–74.

———. *Studies in Renaissance Thought and Letters.* 1956. Rome: Storia e Letteratura, 1969.

La Croix, Richard R., ed. *Augustine on Music: An Interdisciplinary Collection of Essays.* Studies in the History and Interpretation of Music 6. Lewiston, N.Y.: Mellen, 1988.

Laird, Walter Roy. "The *Scientiae Mediae* in Medieval Commentaries on Aristotle's *Posterior Analytics.*" Ph.D. diss., University of Toronto, 1983.

———. "The Scope of Renaissance Mechanics." *Osiris,* 2d. ser., 2 (1986): 43–68.

Laudan, L. "Theories of Scientific Method from Plato to Mach: A Bibliographic Review." *History of Science* 7 (1968): 1–63.

Laven, P. J. "Daniele Barbaro: Patriarch Elect of Aquileia with Special Reference to His Circle of Scholars and to His Literary Achievement." Ph.D. diss., University of London, 1957.

Lee, B. "Giovanni Maria Lanfranco's *Scintille di musica* and Its Relation to Sixteenth-Century Music Theory." Ph.D. diss., Cornell University, 1961.

Levin, Flora R. *The Harmonics of Nicomachus and the Pythagorean Tradition.* American Classical Studies 1. University Park, Pa.: American Philological Association, 1975.

Lewis, C. *The Merton Tradition and Kinematics in Late Sixteenth and Early Seventeenth Century Italy.* Centro per la storia della tradizione aristotelico nel veneto, saggi e testi 15. Padua: Antenore, 1980.

Lippman, Edward A. *Musical Thought in Ancient Greece.* 1964. Reprint. New York: Da Capo, 1975.

———. "The Sources and Development of the Ethical View of Music in Ancient Greece." *Musical Quarterly* 49 (1963): 188–209.

Lockwood, Lewis. *The Counter-Reformation and the Masses of Vincenzo Ruffo.* Studi di musica veneta 2. Venice: Fondazione Giorgio Cini, Universal Edition, 1967.

———. "Vincenzo Ruffo and Musical Reform after the Council of Trent." *Musical Quarterly* 43 (1937): 342–71.

Lohmann, Johannes. "Die griechische Musik als mathematische Form." *Archiv für Musikwissenschaft* 14 (1957): 147–56.

Long, Pamela O. "The Contribution of Architectural Writers to a 'Scientific' Outlook in the Fifteenth and Sixteenth Centuries." *Journal of Medieval and Renaissance Studies* 15 (1985): 265–98.

——. "The Vitruvian Commentary Tradition and Rational Architecture in the Sixteenth Century: A Study in the History of Ideas." Ph.D. diss., University of Maryland, 1979.

Lowinsky, Edward. "The Musical Avante-Garde of the Renaissance, or: The Peril and Profit of Foresight." In *Art, Science, and History in the Renaissance*, ed. by Charles Singleton, pp. 111–62. Baltimore: Johns Hopkins University Press, 1967.

——. "Music in the Culture of the Renaissance." *Journal of the History of Ideas* 15 (1954): 509–33.

——. "Music of the Renaissance as Viewed by Renaissance Musicians." In *The Renaissance Image of Man and the World*, ed. Bernard O'Kelly, pp. 129–77. Columbus: Ohio State University Press, 1966.

——. *Tonality and Atonality in Sixteenth-Century Music*. Berkeley and Los Angeles: University of California Press, 1961.

Maas, Martha, and Jane McIntosh Snyder. *Stringed Instruments of Ancient Greece*. New Haven: Yale University Press, 1989.

Maccagni, Carlo. "Contra Aristotelem et omnes philosophos." In *Aristotelismo veneto e scienza moderna*, ed. Luigi Olivieri, 2:717–27. Padua: Antenore, 1983.

McClain, Ernest G. " 'Musical Marriages' in Plato's *Republic*." *Journal of Music Theory* 18 (1974): 242–73.

——. *The Pythagorean Plato: Prelude to the Song Itself*. Stony Brook, N.Y.: Hayes, 1978.

McClure, George W. "The Renaissance Vision of Solace and Tranquillity: Consolation and Therapeutic Wisdom in Italian Humanist Thought." Ph.D. diss., University of Michigan, 1981.

Mace, Dean T. "Marin Mersenne on Language and Music." *Journal of Music Theory* 4 (1970): 2–35.

McKeon, Richard. "The Organization of Sciences and the Relations of Culture in the Twelfth and Thirteenth Centuries." In *The Cultural Context of Medieval Learning: Proceedings of the First International Colloquium on Philosophy, Science, and Theology in the Middle Ages,* ed. John E. Murdoch and Edith D. Sylla, pp. 151–86. Boston: Reidel, 1975.

——. "Renaissance and Method in Philosophy." *Studies in the History of Ideas* 3 (1952): 37–114.

——. "The Transformation of the Liberal Arts in the Renaissance." In *Developments in the Early Renaissance*, ed. Bernard S. Levy, pp. 158–223. Albany: State University of New York Press, 1972.

Maclean, Ian. "The Interpretation of Natural Signs: Cardano's *De subtilitate* versus Scaliger's *Exercitationes*." In *Occult and Scientific Mentalities in the Renaissance*, ed. Brian Vickers, pp. 231–52. Cambridge: Cambridge University Press, 1984.

McMenomy, Christe Ann. "The Discipline of Astronomy in the Middle Ages." Ph.D. diss., University of California at Los Angeles, 1984.

McMullin, Ernan. "Medieval or Modern Science: Continuity or Discontinuity?" *International Philosophical Quarterly* 5 (1965): 103–29.

Maier, Ida. "Un inédit de Politien: La classification des arts." *Bibliothèque d'humanisme et Renaissance* 22 (1960): 338–55.

Maniates, Maria Rika. *Mannerism in Italian Music and Culture, 1530–1630*. Chapel Hill: University of North Carolina Press, 1979.

——. "Vicentino's 'Incerta et occulta scientia' Reexamined." *Journal of the American Musicological Society* 28 (1975): 335–51.

Martin, Henriette. "La Camerata du Comte Bardi." *Revue de musicologie* 13 (1932): 63–74, 152–61, 227–34; 14 (1933): 92–100, 141–51.

Masotti, Arnaldo. *Studi su Niccolò Tartaglia*. Brescia: Ateneo di Brescia, 1962.

Massera, Giuseppe. *Severino Boezio e la scienza armonica tra l'antichità e il medio evo*. Parma: Studium Parmense, 1976.

Mathiesen, Thomas J. "An Annotated Translation of Euclid's *Division of the Monochord*." *Journal of Music Theory* 19 (1975): 236–58.

——. "New Fragments of Ancient Greek Music." *Acta Musicologica* 53 (1981): 14–32.

Matthews, John, ed. *Boethius: His Life, Thought, and Influence*. Oxford: Blackwell, 1981.

Maylender, Michele. *Storia delle Accademie Italiane*. 5 vols. Bologna: Cappelli, 1930.

Meier, B. "Reservata-Probleme, ein Bericht." *Acta Musicologica* 30 (1958): 77–89.

Memorie e contributi alla musica del medioevo all'età moderna (festschrift for F. Ghisi). 2 vols. Bologna: A.M.I.S., 1971.

Mendel, Arthur. *Pitch in Western Music since 1500: A Reexamination*. 1978. Kassel: Bärenreiter, 1979.

Michaelides, Solon. *The Music of Ancient Greece: An Encyclopaedia*. London: Faber and Faber, 1978.

Mignucci, M. "Teoria della scienza e matematica in Aristotle." *Rivista critica di storia della filosofia* 32 (1977): 204–33.

Monterossa, Raffaelo. "L'estetica di Gioseffo Zarlino." *Chigiana*, new ser., 4 (1967): 13–28.

Monterossa Vacchelli, Anna Maria. *L'opera musicale di Anton Francesco Doni*. Cremona: Athenaeum Cremonense, 1969.

Motta, Emilio. *Musici alla corte degli Sforza: Ricerche e documenti milanesi*. 1887. Geneva: Minkoff, 1977.

Münxelhaus, Barbara. *Pythagoras Musicus: Zum Rezeption der pythagorischen Musiktheorie als quadrivialer Wissenschaft im lateinischen Mittelalter*. Orpheus: Schriftenreihe zu Grundfragen der Musik 19. Bonn: Verlag für systematische Musikwissenschaft, 1976.

Murdoch, John E. "From Social into Intellectual Factors: An Aspect of the Unitary Character of Late Medieval Learning." In *The Cultural Context of Medieval Learning: Proceedings of the First International Colloquium on Philos-*

ophy, Science, and Theology in the Middle Ages, ed. John E. Murdoch and Edith Sylla, pp. 272–348. Boston: Reidel, 1975.

——— . "Music and Natural Philosophy: Hitherto Unnoticed *Questiones* by Blasius of Parma (?)." *Manuscripta* 20 (1976): 119–36.

Nardi, Bruno. "La scuola di Rialto e l'umanesimo veneziano." In *Umanesimo europeo e umanesimo veneziano,* ed. Vittore Branca, Civiltà europea e civiltà veneziana: Aspetti e problemi, 2: 93–139. Florence: Sansoni, 1963.

Nelson, Benjamin. "Probabilists and Anti-Probabilists, and the Quest for Certitude in the Sixteenth and Seventeenth Centuries." In *Proceedings of the Tenth International Congress of the History of Science,* pp. 269–73. Paris: Hermann, 1962.

Nowak, Adolf. "Die 'numeri judiciales' des Augustinus und ihre musiktheoretische Bedeutung." *Archiv für Musikwissenschaft* 32 (1975): 196–207.

Oldrini, Gaspare. *Storia musicale di Lodi.* Lodi, 1883.

Olivieri, Luigi. *Certezza e gerarchia del sapere: Crisi dell'idea di scientifica nell'Aristotelismo del secolo XVI.* Padua: Antenore, 1983.

——— , ed. *Aristotelismo veneto e scienza moderna.* 2 vols. Padua: Antenore, 1983.

O'Malley, John. *Praise and Blame in Renaissance Rome: Rhetoric, Doctrine, and Reform in the Sacred Orators of the Papal Court, ca. 1450–1521.* Duke Monographs in Medieval and Renaissance Studies 3. Durham, N.C.: Duke University Press, 1979.

O'Meara, Dominic J. *Pythagoras Revived: Mathematics and Philosophy in Late Antiquity.* Oxford: Clarendon, 1989.

Palisca, Claude V. *The Florentine Camerata.* Documentary Studies and Translations. New Haven: Yale University Press, 1989.

——— . "Girolamo Mei: Mentor to the Florentine Camerata." *Musical Quarterly* 40 (1954): 1–20.

——— . *Humanism in Italian Renaissance Musical Thought.* New Haven: Yale University Press, 1985.

——— . "The Impact of the Revival of Ancient Learning on Music Theory." In *International Musicological Society: Report of the Twelfth Congress, Berkeley 1977,* ed. Daniel Heartz and Bonnie Wade, pp. 871–73. Kassell: Bärenreiter, 1981.

——— . "Musica Reservata and Osservata: A Critical Review." *Journal of the American Musicological Society* 7 (1954): 168–69.

——— . "The Science of Sound and Musical Practice." In *Science and the Arts in the Renaissance,* ed. John W. Shirley and R. David Hoeniger, pp. 59–73. London: Associated University Presses, 1985.

——— . "Scientific Empiricism in Musical Thought." In *Seventeenth Century Science and the Arts,* ed. Hedley Rhys, pp. 91–137. Princeton: Princeton University Press, 1961.

——— . "Ut Oratoria Musica: The Rhetorical Basis of Musical Mannerism." In *The Meaning of Mannerism,* ed. Franklin W. Robinson and Stephen G. Nichols, Jr., pp. 37–65. Hanover, N.H.: University Press of New England, 1972.

——. "Vincenzo Galilei's Counterpoint Treatise." *Journal of the American Musicological Society* 9 (1956): 81–96.

Pastorelli, Ester. *Epistolario Manuziano, inventario cronologico-analitico 1483–1597.* Biblioteca di Bibliografia Italiana 30. Florence: Olschki, 1957.

Patch, Howard Rollin. *The Tradition of Boethius: A Study of His Importance in Medieval Culture.* New York: Oxford University Press, 1935.

Philip, J. A. *Pythagoras and Early Pythagoreanism.* Toronto: University of Toronto Press, 1966.

Pietzsch, Gerhard. *Die Musik im Erziehungs- und Bildungsideal des ausgehenden Altertums und frühen Mittelalters.* Halle: Niemeyer, 1932.

——. *Zur Pflege der Musik an den deutschen Universitäten bis zur Mitte des 16. Jahrhunderts.* 1936. Hildesheim: Olms, 1971.

Pirrotta, Nino. *Music and Culture in Italy from the Middle Ages to the Baroque.* Cambridge: Harvard University Press, 1984.

Pirrotta, Nino, Willem Elders, Ludwig Finscher, Don Harrán, Dietrich Kämper, Dean T. Mace, Thomas Mathiesen, and Claude V. Palisca. "Humanism and Music" (discussion panel). In *International Musicological Society: Report of the Twelfth Congress, Berkeley 1977,* ed. Daniel Heartz and Bonnie Wade, pp. 870–93. Kassel: Bärenreiter, 1981.

Pirrotta, Nino, and Elena Povoledo. *Music and the Theatre from Poliziano to Monteverdi.* Trans. Karen Eales. 1969 (Italian). Cambridge: Cambridge University Press, 1982.

Potiron, Henri. *Boece: Theoricien de la musique grecque.* Travaux de l'Institut Catholique de Paris 9. Paris: Bloud et Gay, 1961.

Rashdall, Hastings. *Universities of Europe.* Ed. F. M. Powicke and A. B. Emden. 3 vols. Oxford: Oxford University Press, 1936.

Rilli, Jacopo. *Notizie letterarie, et istoriche intorno agli uomini illustri dell'Accademia Fiorentina.* Florence: Pietro Matini, 1700.

Roncaglia, Gino. *La cappella musicale del duomo di Modena.* Florence, 1957.

Rosand, Ellen. "Music in the Myth of Venice." *Renaissance Quarterly* 30 (1977): 511–37.

Rose, Paul Lawrence. "Bartolomeo Zamberti's Funeral Oration for the Humanist Encyclopaedist Giorgio Valla." In *Cultural Aspects of the Italian Renaissance: Essays in Honor of Paul Oskar Kristeller,* ed. Cecil H. Clough, pp. 299–310. Manchester: Manchester University Press, 1976.

——. "Humanist Culture and Renaissance Mathematics: The Italian Libraries of the Quattrocento." *Studies in the Renaissance* 20 (1973): 46–105.

——. *The Italian Renaissance of Mathematics: Studies on Humanists and Mathematicians from Petrarch to Galileo.* Geneva: Droz, 1975.

——. "Professors of Mathematics at Padua University, 1521–1588." *Physis* 17 (1975): 300–304.

Rose, Paul Lawrence, and Stillman Drake. "The Pseudo-Aristotelian *Questions of Mechanics* in Renaissance Culture." *Studies in the Renaissance* 18 (1971): 65–104.

Rosen, Edward. "Francesco Patrizi and the Celestial Spheres." *Physis* 26 (1984): 305–24.

Ross, James Bruce. "Venetian Schools and Teachers, Fourteenth to Early Sixteenth Century: A Survey and a Study of Giovanni Battista Egnazio." *Renaissance Quarterly* 29 (1976): 521–66.

Rossi, Paolo. "Francesco Patrizi: Heavenly Spheres and Flocks of Cranes." In *Italian Studies in the Philosophy of Science*, ed. Maria Luisa Dalla Chiara, pp. 363–88. Boston Studies in the Philosophy of Science 47. Boston: Reidel, 1981.

Sarton, George. *The Appreciation of Ancient and Medieval Science during the Renaissance, 1450–1600*. Philadelphia: University of Pennsylvania Press, 1955.

Schmitt, Charles B. "Aristotelianism in the Veneto and the Origins of Modern Science: Some Considerations on the Problem of Continuity." In *Aristotelismo veneto e scienza moderna*, ed. Luigi Olivieri, 1:104–23. Padua: Antenore, 1983.

——. *The Aristotelian Tradition and Renaissance Universities*. London: Variorum, 1984.

——. *A Critical Survey and Bibliography of Studies on Renaissance Aristotelianism, 1958–1969*. Padua: Antenore, 1971.

——. "Experience and Experiment: A Comparison of Zabarella's View with Galileo's in *De motu*." *Studies in the Renaissance* 16 (1969): 80–138.

——. "The Faculty of Arts at Pisa at the Time of Galileo." *Physis* 14 (1972): 243–72.

——. "Filosofia e scienza nelle università italiane del XVI secolo." In *Il Rinascimento: Interpretazioni e problemi*, ed. M. B. Hall, pp. 355–98. Rome: Laterza, 1979.

——. "L'introduction de la philosophie platonicienne dans l'enseignement des universités à la Renaissance." In *Platon et Aristote à la Renaissance*, XVIe Colloque International de Tours, pp. 93–104. Paris: Vrin, 1976.

——. "Philosophy and Science in Sixteenth-Century Universities: Some Preliminary Comments." In *The Cultural Context of Medieval Learning: Proceedings of the First International Colloquium on Philosophy, Science, and Theology in the Middle Ages*, ed. John E. Murdoch and Edith D. Sylla, pp. 485–530. Boston: Reidel, 1975.

——. "Towards a Reassessment of Renaissance Aristotelianism." *History of Science* 11 (1975): 159–93.

Schrade, Leo. "Music in the Philosophy of Boethius." *Musical Quarterly* 33 (1947): 188–200.

Schueller, Herbert M. *The Idea of Music: An Introduction to Musical Aesthetics in Antiquity and the Middle Ages*. Early Drama, Art, and Music Monograph Series 9. Kalamazoo, Mich.: Medieval Institute Publications, 1988.

Seay, Albert. "The Dialogues of Johannes Ottobi Anglici in Arte Musici." *Journal of the American Musicological Society* 8 (1955): 86–100.

——. "The Fourteenth-Century Cappella at Santa Maria del Fiore in Florence." *Journal of the American Musicological Society* 11 (1958): 45–55.

Seigel, J. E. *Rhetoric and Philosophy in Renaissance Humanism: The Union of Eloquence and Wisdom, Petrarch to Valla*. Princeton: Princeton University Press, 1968.

Sesini, Ugo. "Studi sull'umanesimo musicale: Ercole Bottrigari." *Convivium* 13 (1941): 1–25.

Smiley, Marilynn. "Eleventh Century Music Theorists." In *The Eleventh Century*, ed. Stanley Ferber and Sandro Sticca, Acta 1:61–90. Binghamton, N.Y.: Center for Medieval and Early Renaissance Studies, 1974.

Smits van Waesberghe. Joseph. *Musikerziehung: Lehre und Theorie der Musik im Mittelalter*. Leipzig: Deutscher Verlag für Musik, 1969.

Solerti, Angelo. *Le origini del melodrama*. Turin: Bocca, 1903.

Soppelsa, M. L. *Genesi del metodo galileiano e tramonto dell'aristotelismo nella scuola filosofica di Padova*. Centro per la storia della tradizione aristotelica nel veneto, saggi e testi 13. Padua: Antenore, 1974.

Sternfeld, Frederick W. "Music in the Schools of the Reformation." *Musica Disciplina* 3 (1948): 99–122.

Stevenson, Robert. "Vincente Lusitano: New Light on His Career." *Journal of the American Musicological Society* 15 (1962): 72–77.

Storia della musica: vol. 1, *Il Medioevo I*, ed. Giulio Cattin; vol. 2, *Il Medioevo II*, ed. F. Alberto Gallo; vol. 3, *Il Rinascimento*, ed. Claudio Gallico. Società italiana di musicologia. Turin: EDT, 1977.

Strunk, William Oliver, "A Cypriote in Venice." In *Natalica musicologica Knud Jeppeson*, eds. Bjørn Hielmborg and Søren Sørensen, pp. 101–14. Copenhagen: Hansen, 1962.

——. "Vergil in Music." *Musical Quarterly* 16 (1930): 482–97.

Tafuri, Manfredo. *Venezia e il rinascimento: Religione, scienza, e architettura*. Turin: Einaudi, 1985.

Taylor, Alfred E. *A Commentary on Plato's Timaeus*. Oxford: Clarendon, 1928.

Terni, Clemente. "Galileo Galilei e la musica." *Chigiana*, new ser., 1 (1964): 249–60.

Testi, Flavio. *La musica italiana nel medioevo e nel rinascimento*. 2 vols. Milan: Bramante, 1969.

Turrini, Giuseppe. *L'Accademia filarmonica di Verona dalla fondazione (maggio 1543) al 1600 e il suo patrimonio musicale antico*. Verona: Tipografica Veronese, 1941.

Ullman, B. L., and P. A. Stadter. *The Public Library of Renaissance Florence*. Padua: Antenore, 1972.

Ullman, Ernest. *Die Lehre von den Proportionen*. Dresden, 1958.

Van Helden, Albert. *Measuring the Universe: Cosmic Dimensions from Aristarchus to Halley*. Chicago: University of Chicago Press, 1985.

Vasoli, Cesare. "The Contribution of Humanism to the Birth of Modern Science." *Renaissance and Reformation*, new ser. 3 (1979): 1–15.

——. *Profezia e ragione: Studi sulla cultura del cinquecento e del seicento*. Naples: Morano, 1974.

Vescovini, Graziella Federici. "L'importanza della matematica tra aristotelismo e scienze moderne in alcuni filosofi padovani della fine del secolo XIV." In *Aristotelismo veneto e scienza moderna*, ed. Luigi Olivieri, 2:661–84. Padua: Antenore, 1983.

Vickers, Brian, ed. *Occult and Scientific Mentalities in the Renaissance.* Cambridge: Cambridge University Press, 1984.

Vogel, Martin. *Die Enharmonik der Griechen*: vol. 1, *Tonsystem und Notation;* vol. 2, *Der Ursprung der Enharmonik.* Orpheus: Schriftenreihe zu Grundfragen der Musik 3 and 4. Düsseldorf: Verlag für systematische Musikwissenschaft, 1963.

Wagner, David, ed. *The Seven Liberal Arts in the Middle Ages.* Bloomington: Indiana University Press, 1983.

Walker, D. P. *Music, Spirit and Language in the Renaissance.* Ed. Penelope Gouk. London: Variorum, 1985.

——. *Studies in Musical Science in the Late Renaissance.* Studies of the Warburg Institute 37. London: Warburg Institute, 1978.

Wallace, William A. "The *Calculatores* in Early Sixteenth-Century Physics." *British Journal for the History of Science* 4 (1969): 221–32.

——. *Galileo and His Sources: The Heritage of the Collegio Romano in Galileo's Science.* Princeton: Princeton University Press, 1984.

Warren, Charles. "Brunelleschi's Dome and Dufay's Motet." *Musical Quarterly* 59 (1973): 92–105.

Weinberg, Bernard. *A History of Literary Criticism in the Italian Renaissance.* 2 vols. Chicago: University of Chicago Press, 1961.

Weisheipl, James. "Classification of the Sciences in Medieval Thought." *Medieval Studies* 27 (1965): 54–90.

Wells, Robin Headlam. "The Orpharion: Symbol of a Humanist Ideal." *Early Music* 10 (1982): 427–40.

Werner, Eric. "The Last Pythagorean Musician: Johannes Kepler." *Aspects of Medieval and Renaissance Music: A Birthday Offering to Gustave Reese,* ed. Jan La Rue, 2d. ed., pp. 867–82. New York: Pendragon, 1978.

Westman, Robert S. "The Astronomer's Role in the Sixteenth Century: A Preliminary Study." *History of Science* 18 (1980): 105–47.

——. "Humanism and Scientific Roles in the Sixteenth Century." In *Humanismus und Naturwissenschaft,* ed. R. Schmitz and E. Krafft, pp. 83–99. Boppard a.R.: Boldt, 1980.

Wienpahl, R. "Zarlino, the Senario, and Tonality." *Journal of the American Musicological Society* 12 (1959): 27–41.

Wille, Günther. *Musica Romana: Die Bedeutung der Musik im Leben der Römer.* Amsterdam: P. Schippers, 1967.

Wind, Edgar. *Pagan Mysteries in the Renaissance.* New York: Barnes and Noble, 1968.

Winn, James. *Unsuspected Eloquence: A History of the Relations between Poetry and Music.* New Haven: Yale University Press, 1981.

Wittkower, Rudolf. *Architectural Principles in the Age of Humanism.* 3d. ed. New York: Norton, 1962.

Wood, Alexander. *The Physical Basis of Music.* Cambridge: Cambridge University Press, 1913.

Young, Irwin. "Franchinus Gafurius, Renaissance Theorist and Composer (1451–1522)." Ph.D. diss., University of Southern California, 1954.

Zeigler, K. "Plutarchea, I: Zu *De Musica*." In *Studi in onore di L. Castiglioni,* 2:1107–35. Florence: Sansoni, 1960.

Zenck, Hermann. "Zarlinos 'Istitutioni harmoniche' als Quelle zur Musikanschauung der italienischen Renaissance." *Zeitschrift für Musikwissenschaft* 12 (1930): 540–78.

Index